BIAS

BIAS
Epistemological Bias in the Physical and Social Sciences

Edited by
ABDELWAHAB M. ELMESSIRI

THE INTERNATIONAL INSTITUTE OF ISLAMIC THOUGHT
LONDON • WASHINGTON

© The International Institute of Islamic Thought, 1427AH/2006CE

THE INTERNATIONAL INSTITUTE OF ISLAMIC THOUGHT
P.O. BOX 669, HERNDON, VA 20172, USA
WWW.IIIT.ORG

LONDON OFFICE
P.O. BOX 126, RICHMOND, SURREY TW9 2UD, UK
WWW.IIITUK.COM

*This book is in copyright. Subject to statutory exception
and to the provisions of relevant collective licensing agreements,
no reproduction of any part may take place without
the written permission of the publishers.*

ISBN 1–56564–416–6 paperback
ISBN 1–56564–417–4 hardback

*The views and opinions expressed in this book are the author's
and not necessarily those of the publishers.*

Translated by

AHMED EL-EZABI
SHOKRY MEGAHED
AHMED SEDDIK AL-WAHY

Design and typesetting by Sohail Nakhooda, Cover design by Saddiq Ali
Printed in the United Kingdom by Biddles Limited, King's Lynn

CONTENTS

	page
LIST OF CONTRIBUTORS	vii
Foreword	x
INTRODUCTION	xi
1 *The Gate of Ijtihad: An Introduction to the Study of Epistemological Bias* ABDELWAHAB ELMESSIRI	1
2 *Bias in Western Schools of Social Thought: Our Heritage as the Starting Point for Development* ADEL HUSSEIN	77
3 *Theories of Political Development: A Case of Biased Discourse in the Political Sciences* NASR M. ARIF	105
4 *Modernizing vs. Westernizing the Social Sciences: The Case of Psychology* RAFIK HABIB	126
5 *Bias in Curricula and Course Contents* HODA HEGAZY	145
6 *An Exploration of the Nature of Human Artificial Intelligence and the Qur'anic Perspective* MAHMOUD DHAOUADI	158
7 *Confronting Bias in Third World Culture* FERIAL J. GHAZOUL	174

CONTENTS

8   *Beyond Methodology: Forms of Bias in Western Literary Criticism*   192
    SAAD ABDULRAHMAN AL-BAZIʿI

9   *Theories and Principles of Design in the Architecture of Islamic Societies: A Ceremonial Approach to Community Building*   218
    A. I. ABDELHALIM

10   *Reflections on Technology and Development: A Cultural Perspective*   227
    HAMED IBRAHIM EL-MOUSLY

11   *Philosophical Beliefs Underlying the Formulation of Physical Laws*   271
    MAHJOOB TAHA

NOTES   287

LIST OF CONTRIBUTORS

ABDELWAHAB M. ELMESSIRI is professor Emeritus of English literature and critical theory at Ain Shams University, Cairo. He has published many articles and books on various subjects (Zionism, modernism, post modernism, secularism, materialist philosophy, etc). He has also published two collections of poetry and a number of stories for children. One of his most important works is *Epistemological Bias* published by IIIT in Arabic. The present book is an anthology of the articles published therein.

ADEL HUSSEIN (d. 2001) was a leading Egyptian intellectual and economic theoretician of world renown. He was the secretary general of the Labour Party, the most important opposition party in Egypt, and the editor in chief of its weekly newspaper *Al-Shaab* (The people). His book *Egyptian Economy from Independence to Dependence*, is considered a major contribution to dependency theory and had a deep impact on general economic theory, especially in Latin America.

NASR MOHAMED ARIF got his Ph. D. from the Faculty of Economics and Political Science, Cairo University, in 1995, and is currently teaching there. He has published many articles in several scholarly journals. IIIT published his latest book titled *Theories of Comparative Politics and the Methodology of Studying Arab Political Systems: An Epistemological Approach*.

RAFIK HABIB is a senior researcher at the National Center for Social Research. He got both his M. A. and Ph. D. from Ain Shams University, Cairo. His research interests and studies are quite diverse (psychology of religion – class struggle – westernization – Christian Zionism). Among his most important works are *The Sacred and Freedom* and *The Nation and the State*.

HODA HEGAZY got her Ph.D. from the School of Education at Rutgers University and is currently a professor Emeritus at Ain Shams University, Cairo. She has lectured on the philosophy and sociology of education at various Arab universities. She has also contributed to several scholarly journals and encyclopedias.

MAHMOUD DHAOUADI obtained his Ph.D. from the university of Montreal, Canada and is currently a professor of Sociology at the University of Tunisia. He has published several articles in Arabic, English and French. Among his latest books (in English) are *Toward Islamic Sociology of Cultural Symbols* and *Globalization of the Other Under development*.

FERIAL J. GHAZOUL is an Iraqi critic, translator, and professor of English and Comparative Literature at the American University in Cairo. She has published extensively on medieval literature, postcolonial studies, and literary theory. She is the editor of *ALIF Journal of Comparative Poetics*, and the author of an important study (in English) of *Thousand and One Nights*.

SAAD A. AL-BAZI'I is a professor of English and American Literature at the Department of English, College of Arts, King Saud University, Riyadh, KSA. He has published extensively in areas such as: contemporary literary theory, modern Arabic poetry, and the literature of the Arabian Peninsula. He has also acted as editor-in-chief of the *Global Arabic Encyclopedia* (30 vols), and is currently a member of the Advisory Board to the Ministry of Culture in Saudi Arabia.

ABDELHALIM I. ABDELHALIM got his Ph.D. in Architecture from the U. C. Berkeley in 1978. Since 1980 he has been in Cairo University, holding a position of Professor of Architectural Design and Theory. Abdelhalim has designed and developed many projects in several places in Egypt and the Arab world, including the "Cultural Park for Children," designed and built in Egypt between 1983 and 1991, and received the Agha Khan Award for Architecture in 1992.

HAMED IBRAHIM EL-MOUSLY is Professor at the Faculty of Engineering, Ain Shams University, and former Director of the Centre for

Development of Small-Scale Industries and Local Technologies and Chairman of the Egyptian Society for Endogenous Development of Local Communities (an NGO). He has also worked in the area of Renewable Material Resources(RMR). He has participated in many international conferences, and contributed to many scholarly journals.

MAHJOOB TAHA (d. 2000) was a leading Sudanese specialist in theoretical psychics. He lectured at various Arab universities and published various papers in scholarly journals. He was also interested in Islamic studies and made some very important contributions in that field.

FOREWORD

THE INTERNATIONAL INSTITUTE OF ISLAMIC THOUGHT is pleased to present this important work on *Epistemological Bias in the Physical and Social Sciences*. These collection of papers explore in detail an academic issue seldom given attention and largely taken for granted in Muslim academic circles; a near total adoption as well as unqestioned acceptance of paradigms, terminologies, and research models that are alien to the socio-economic-religio realities of the Muslim world. Written in a clear and lucid style, the book will benefit both general and specialist readers alike increasing their awareness of the existence of bias and the deep-seated cultural-specific values inherent in alien paradigms.

The IIIT, established in 1981, has served as a major center to facilitate sincere and serious scholarly efforts based on Islamic vision, values and principles. Its programs of research, seminars and conferences during the last twenty-five years have resulted in the publication of more than two hundred and fifty titles in English and Arabic, many of which have been translated into several languages.

We would like to express our thanks and gratitude to the editor, Professor Abdelwahab M. Elmessiri as well as the translators of the work. We would also like to thank the editorial and production team at the IIIT London Office and all those who were directly or indirectly involved in the completion of this book including, Nancy Roberts, Dr. Maryam Mahmood, Maida Malik, and Shiraz Khan. May God reward them, the editor and the translators for all their efforts.

ANAS S. AL-SHAIKH-ALI
ACADEMIC ADVISOR, IIIT LONDON OFFICE, UK
9 Shawwal 1427 AH / November 2006 AC

INTRODUCTION

THE QUESTION OF BIAS in methodology and terminology is a problem that faces researchers east, west, north and south; however, it faces Third World intellectuals with special keenness. For although they write in a cultural environment that has its own specific conceptual and cultural paradigms, they nevertheless encounter an alien (foreign) paradigm which attempts to impose itself upon their society and upon their very imagination and thoughts.

From the end of the 18th Century and the gradual diffusion of Western culture throughout the world by means of Western colonialism and the internationalization of Western cultural and epistemological paradigms, there began what has been loosely called "cultural invasion," which is an attempt by the West, conscious and unconscious, intentional and unintentional, to force its cultural paradigms onto the people of the world. These paradigms, the advantages of which have been established in the Western world mostly in the economic and political domains, do not necessarily have any strong connection to the reality of the non-Western peoples of the world (i.e., the majority of the peoples of the Earth). For this reason, these paradigms cannot contribute to the process of interpreting or changing this reality; on the contrary, they tend to distort it. Nevertheless, many people have begun to abandon the indigenous paradigms and biases that arise from their own particular existential and historical situations. In the process, they have begun to adopt Western paradigms and to view themselves from a Western point of view even when it is biased against them. It is a well-known fact that the identity of any community, be it ethnic or religious, is threatened as a result of its adopting imported alien paradigms and points of view, sometimes without any profound knowledge of the epistemological implications of such paradigms.

The idea of bias has been raised and disputed by many. With the rise of

Arab nationalist thought, talk about identity, cultural specificity and the necessity of preserving the two has intensified. However, no one has tried to study the matter in a comprehensive and methodical manner. Modern Arabs (and Muslims in general) have not laid the foundations for any of the modern sciences. When the term "developmental psychology" is used in the West, Arab scholars also say "developmental psychology"; when "applied psychology" is mentioned, they repeat right along, "applied psychology"; when the term "deconstructive psychology" gains currency in the West, they hurry to use the very same term. That is to say, they parrot the latest fashion, be it in dress or thought. The establishment of a new set of sciences that might contribute to the interpretation and possible solution of our own problems has not yet taken shape in modern Arab history.

For this reason we need to ask: Why not establish a new science with its own mechanisms, methodologies and points of ultimate reference to deal with epistemological biases and open up the gate of ijtihad with respect to them? In my paper entitled, "The Gate of Ijtihad: Introduction to the Study of Epistemological Bias," I advocate doing this very thing, i.e., opening anew the gate of ijtihad, or interpretation.

There is a pervasive feeling amongst Arab intellectuals that the methodologies used currently in the Arab social sciences are not entirely neutral. Instead they are seen as expressing a system of values that define the field of investigation and the direction of research, and which very often determine their results in advance. This is what we call "bias," i.e., the totality of latent values underlying the paradigm, and the procedures and methodologies which guide researchers without their being necessarily aware of them. If they do become aware of them, they discover that such values are inextricably tied up with their research methodologies, and that it is extremely difficult to separate the one from the other.

These values sometimes take the form of models or latent conceptual metaphors. If we speak of "progress," we have adopted a metaphor which compares the movement of history to a straight line leading to a definite point, which in turn implies that we have abandoned the concept of cyclicality. At the same time, we have taken on the notion of cumulative effect and made an *a priori* judgment about the value of the old and the new, such that the former is viewed unfavorably and the latter favorably. Finally, we have accepted the view that change and flux in all fields are the ultimate and perhaps absolute truth. The same is true of the term "growth" (*tanmiyah*, from *namā*, "to grow"). If we were to use such a term, we would have taken an organic or semi-organic metaphor which presupposes the inter-relatedness of all elements as if they were concatenated like the members of a single body; the development of one member necessitates a change in all or most others. The adoption of a metaphor does not necessarily imply the adoption of the totality of the paradigm latent in it, with all its ideological and philosophical implications; it only creates an "elective affinity" between the researcher and such an ideology, or fertile ground in which said ideology grows and thrives. Researchers, therefore, find themselves biased toward some phenomena and data while disregarding or avoiding entirely others that fall outside the scope of the underlying metaphor or models. Many of these implicit epistemological metaphors come ready-made from the West. Neither neutral nor innocent, they deprive researchers of much of their freedom and limit their movement and range of vision. This is because such metaphors, as indicated above, are presented as neutral, whereas they really are biased to the core.

It is now high time to give open, clear expression to these private sentiments regarding bias and to put together these individual efforts aimed at detecting epistemological bias in the hope that some knowledge of the problem of bias in methodology might be gained and some of its features and mechanisms identified. In this manner, we may arrive at solutions which will lead ultimately to the appearance of an alternative paradigm.

Therefore, we invited researchers to present studies addressing this issue. Each study was to include the following:

1. An introduction to the issue of bias in the researcher's particular field.
2. Citation of specific examples of latent biases in said field.
3. An explanation of how the mechanisms of these biases work, and how they orient the researcher (and the research) toward certain findings, while precluding others.
4. Citation of examples of elements and features which have been overlooked owing to the bias of the prevalent model, and which can only be observed by means of a new methodology expressing a new paradigm.

Contributions were to be case studies which concentrate on a few points or on a single point, thereby defining the core of the problem and identifying some of the mechanisms of bias. It was hoped that the papers presented would manifest the core of every researcher's experience in his respective discipline. Proposed alternatives were not to be considered final conclusions but rather, as attempts to open the gate of ijtihad concerning Western culture and its epistemological paradigms. Such studies would inevitably reflect Arab/Muslim biases. However, this would be offset by the fact that:

1. Every researcher would attempt to state his/her own biases so that the reader might be aware of them and thereby transcend them, if necessary.
2. The alternative epistemological paradigms might not necessarily replace prevalent paradigms but, rather, function as more complex means for studying Arab-Muslim societies and phenomena particular to the patterns of the Arab-Islamic regions, particularly given that their biases would not be imported but be intimately tied to the region.
3. It was also hoped that the new paradigms would enrich prevalent ones and widen their parameters, thereby transforming them from closed paradigms based upon modern Western assumptions into open-ended universal human paradigms based on knowledge of all cultural formations in all of their specificities and manifestations and attempt to arrive at a higher level of abstraction and, therefore, universality.
4. It was assumed that the presence of an independent Arab/Muslim voice and paradigm – which might or might not agree with the prevailing paradigms – would not imply a denial of the value of Western culture.

There can be no denying the importance of the many discoveries of the various schools of Western thought, many of which are indeed universal in character, and there is nothing wrong with utilizing them in the theoretical structure specific to us. These discoveries, however, are included in comprehensive systems or theories (or particular versions of them) which have been exported ready-made to us as "universal science" immediately operable in our societies. This is hard to accept, inasmuch as it contradicts the true spirit of science, based, as it is, on individual efforts.

It was suggested (but not required) that the studies follow the following pattern:

1. A general theoretical introduction to the problem of bias in general and how it applies to a given field of specialization.
2. Demonstration of how the employment of the biased paradigm has limited explanatory power because of its emphasis on some theoretical elements at the expense of others, or its exclusion of important elements which are considered unimportant from its viewpoint.
3. The definition of the new paradigm, its application to the case being studied, and the rationale for choosing it.
4. General conclusions together with a comparison of the explanatory and predictive capacities of the two paradigms. A hypothetical example of this might be put forward using the concept of "progress":

The concept of progress, a pivotal concept of Western thought has been defined (principally in a materialist utilitarian way) as maximization of interest and pleasure for the largest number.

When the aforementioned paradigm of progress is employed in measuring what has taken place in Arab cities over the past twenty years, researchers investigate such things as the rate of protein consumption, the number of roads built and their rate of use, average production, varieties of health services available, and so on. But they may not investigate the extent of family cohesion (disintegration of the family is classified as one of the "inevitable by-products" of progress, and a reasonable price to be paid). Similarly, they may make no indication of the decline of folk art or address the role of religion in civilizing and humanizing society.

The new paradigm might either widen the parameters of the concept of progress or dispense with it altogether. Even the Arabic term is simply a loan translation of the Western concept; that is, it springs from Western soil and is a product of a particular phase of Western history which has no applicability or legitimacy beyond its own time and place. By means of the new paradigm and the new concept, a more complex method of observation can be developed; it is even possible to suppose that the new paradigm will be more objective because it does not pass judgment on the

(Arab) situation from the extraneous (Western) viewpoint, but only attempts to observe and describe it in all of its complexity and specificity. Its explanatory powers are undoubtedly much greater than those of the discredited paradigm.

The study would conclude with some generalizations about its author's particular field of specialization and suggestions for new applications in light of the new paradigm.

By 1987 we had collected a number of studies, at which point it was decided to hold a conference on the subject of bias under the sponsorship of the International Institute of Islamic Thought and the Egyptian Engineering Association. It was held between 19–21 February 1992 AC (15–17 Shaʿbān 1412 AH). The conference triggered a great deal of interest and enthusiasm and many more specialists decided to write papers on the subject of epistemological bias. The outcome was a book comprising not only the proceedings of the conference, but some new studies as well.

After all the papers were submitted, they were classified by subject and read with close scrutiny so as to extract their basic premises and recurrent patterns and paradigms. They were then arranged so as to come up with a new discipline called *fiqh al-taḥayyūz*, or "The Scholarship of Bias," which would focus on the issue. We employed the Arabic word fiqh in place of ʿilm because, although both words imply "understanding," "knowledge" or "application of knowledge," the former restores the probabilistic dimension of knowledge and emphasizes the generative power of the human mind, whereas the latter emphasizes only the aspects of precision, certitude, neutrality and definitiveness. The net result was some seven volumes comprising over eighty studies. To translate them all into English would take years. Therefore, it was decided that a number of representative studies from different fields of knowledge might give the reader an idea of the central argument of the original as well as its range.

The goal of this book is to discover some of the biases (principally Western) latent in our terminology, methodologies, research tools, and conceptual principles, and to propose alternative ones marked by a greater degree of independence and neutrality. The concept of economic progress, defined as "catching up with the West," turns the West into an ultimate point of reference and its concept of progress into an absolute principle which we must adopt. Current methodologies, operating within the framework of this concept, attempt to define progress and backwardness from this standpoint: the more we approach the West, the more advanced we are, and the more distant we get from it, the more backward. As a measure of advancement and backwardness, one Arab researcher used the number of hours people listen to symphonic music. By this measure, however, we all are backward, since many of us, not to mention many Third World peasants and intellectuals, are not exactly connoisseurs of this kind of music!

Political thinker Adel Hussein rejects this concept, defining progress as the ability to define appropriate patterns of consumption by independent standards; that is, he removes the West as the absolute, final, authoritative point of reference. Progress, accordingly, is the ability to redefine 'progress' in terms of one's needs as defined by one's culture and society, thereby giving it a specific content, and the development of technological innovations needed for the production of that content; that is, he opens the door for ijtihad, innovation, and creativity with respect to what may be and what ought to be.

Although this book addresses the problem of bias in general, we nevertheless think it good to concentrate on the Western biases latent in the methodologies and research tools used by Arab researchers. Such biases are the most pervasive, bearing in mind that most Arab researchers consciously or unconsciously see Western values as universal, and adopt them without realizing their Western specificity, thereby denying their own Arab/Muslim particularities.

This book does not aim to present the net result of intellectual endeavors. Rather, it seeks to emphasize the creative, revolutionary character of rebutting bias and to acquaint readers with the means by which bias can be recognized and surmounted. This cannot be accomplished unless readers see for themselves the avenue by which the shift can be made from a discredited (biased) paradigm to a new (independent) one. Thus, for example, if Adel Hussein directly presented his attempt at subverting the concept of "economic progress" by showing its latent materialistic biases, his readers would simply adopt his thought as a new idea to be added to the arsenal of extant ideas, without realizing the radical nature of moving from a biased concept to an independent one, and without understanding the way in which biases are discovered and rejected and new concepts are developed. Hence the importance of starting with the discredited paradigm and moving on from there. Through observing the process of rejecting the old paradigm and moving on to the new one rather than merely adopting the product of the process, we may be able to enrich modern Arab thought not only with a new vision, but with a new methodology as well, since readers will be able to deduce for themselves the rules by means of which to discover biases inherent in methodologies, and principles not directly addressed in this book.

In sum, it should be pointed out that we are by no means belittling the human value of the West's creative contributions, which are well known to all. The reason they have not been emphasized in this study is that while the number of educated Arab and Third World intellectuals who know the history of the West and appreciate its contributions is quite large, there are far fewer who know the history and contributions of Arab-Muslim civilization, being limited to the very few specialists in the field.

Neither do we claim that the West is responsible for the present decline of Arab and Islamic societies. It is my conviction that the question regarding who is to blame is irrelevant and unimportant. It is far more fruitful to dwell on the causes of the decline and the means of reformation and renewal. Instead of talking about imperialism, we rather need to speak about "the willingness (or amenability) to be colonized" (to use Malik Bennabi's celebrated phrase). The Qur'an states that, "Verily never will Allah change the condition of a people until they change it themselves (with their own souls)" (13:11). After all, Western civilization is not unique in claiming centrality – this is a natural human tendency (though it should be pointed out that the Western claim of centrality is an extreme case, supported as it is by huge colonial armies, enormous research institutions as well as an unprecedented network of communications).

It is hoped that the aim of this new science (*fiqh*) of bias will not be merely deconstructive. Having deconstructed the Western epistemological paradigm, identified its basic traits, relativized it, and turned it from an absolute center and ultimate point of reference into one cultural formation among others, it is hoped that we can then discover the generative potentialities within ourselves and look at the West without apprehension. We no longer have to accept it wholesale with all its positive and negative aspects (as advocated by some Westernizers), nor do we have to reject it wholesale (as some rigid fundamentalists would have us do); rather, we can study Western civilization as having its share of positive and negative points. We can then open up to it in a way which is at once creative and critical just as we would open up to other cultural formations. We can then benefit from the fruits of human knowledge, Western knowledge included, separate the elements imported from the paradigm that underlies it, then assimilate it into our own system after adapting it to our values and world outlook. This is what the various studies of the present work seek to accomplish.

Despite its Islamist and Third World orientation, the science (*fiqh*) of bias is addressed to all, especially members of our Islamic nation (Ummah), irrespective of their religious beliefs or political orientation. For Muslims, Islam is a faith they believe in, whereas for non-Muslim members of the Ummah, it is the basis of the civilization they belong to and which they have helped to build. For members of other nations, Islam is the source of an alternative paradigm that challenges the dominant Western materialist paradigm that has contributed to plunging the world into its present crisis.

Unless Muslims and other Third World people become aware of the danger of cultural invasion that threatens to erode us from within and without and to subvert our identity as well as our specific cultural forms and epistemological, ethical and aesthetic systems, we will continue to survive not as a cultural formation with a specific identity worth maintaining, but rather as an external shell with no core or content. It is hoped that the science (*fiqh*) of bias will contribute to the defense of the specific, the particular and the human against the deconstructive, the abstract, the general, and the non-human. *And God knows best.*

THE EDITOR

I

The Gate of Ijtihad: An Introduction to the Study of Epistemological Bias

ABDELWAHAB ELMESSIRI

WHAT IS BIAS?

HUMAN BEINGS' lives consist of gestures, deeds, behaviors, incidents as well as thousands of other taken-for-granted acts. Apart from such basic physiological functions as breathing, for example, everything else done has its own significance and is the outcome of a (conscious or unconscious) selection representing the adoption of some and the rejection of others. A few examples will illustrate the foregoing.

Examples
• In some cultures, only two or three colors are distinguished, and therefore the natives can see only these colors. Some other cultures are not familiar with the concept of the Self and when a person is asked about his life story, he usually relates his grandfather's. Cultures also identify different levels of causality (material, mystical). To utter such a sentence as "Look at the snow," an Inuit child has fifty different words for "snow," each describing a different form or case of snow. That is why such a child would actually "see" in the snow more than what a "snow specialist" from a different culture, using a different language, would.

A hurricane hit an Inuit tribe and a family was dispersed for a few hours. One woman was missing for a year and when ultimately found, she was sewing herself a dress. Despite the hard life she had to live and despite the fact she was living all alone, she did not forget to embroider her dress as is the tradition in her culture. This means that such a 'primitive' woman discovered intuitively that the aesthetic component is necessary for the welfare of human beings. Otherwise, why would she have done such a thing when all she needed was physical warmth and survival? A utilitarian pragmatist would describe her behavior as backward and a mere waste of time.

• A friend of mine lived in an African country for some years. One day he was visited by four friends who, rather than chatting with him, just sat silently without uttering a word. After a while, he started to worry and wondered what they wanted. "Nothing," one of them said. "We've just come to be in your presence." In that part of the world, it seems, silence is considered more eloquent than words. So, my friend learned a lesson about the function of silence and, since then, has become wiser.

• With other tourists, I stood before the barbed wire wall separating the two halves of the Egyptian and Palestinian town of Rafah. The occupied part of the sad town was under curfew, which turned it into a ghost town. The only visible sign of life was three Israeli armored cars moving together. A fourth luxury car would be speeding by every now and then. Impressed by the scene, a smart journalist from Cairo remarked, "Look at the Israeli armored cars! They're moving in perfect discipline; and the military governor's car never stops checking on them. The Israelis' efficiency is really admirable." An Egyptian soldier guarding the border gate overheard the conversation and burst out laughing. "The Israeli armored cars move together out of fear," he corrected. "Despite the curfew, everybody is still scared to death of the Palestinians," the soldier added. "And the military governor is in more panic than they are, which explains why his car runs at this mad speed."

Then the Egyptian soldier went on relating stories about the heroic behavior of the oppressed people of Rafah, who resist the occupation and support each other through acts of mercy and collaboration. During the curfew, one household runs out of flour, so they throw their neighbors a paper ball message which is received by another family, which in turn throws it to another till it lands in a house that has a surplus of flour. Immediately then, a sack of flour flies from their house to another till it lands in the house of the family that needs it. Pointing to the gate we stood by, the guard said, "As for this gate, it is Saladdin's Gate through which he passed to liberate Jerusalem centuries ago." What a difference between inner defeat transforming everything into a sign of downfall, and inner victory transforming the very same objects into signs of triumph. What a difference between bias in favor of disgrace and humiliation, and bias in favor of honor and dignity!

• During my tenure in the Department of English Language and Literature, King Saud University, a faculty member presented research he had done for promotion to the rank of professor. A number of his writings dealt with the image of the Arab in Jewish American novels with explicit Zionist attitudes. In its pursuit of objectivity, the University decided to send the papers to Arab and non-Arab scholars for evaluation. An American stated that Zionism is only a "buzzword," and declined to evaluate the papers. This was his way of saying that there is no such thing as Zionism, which would be a viewpoint worthy of consideration had the children of the intifada (who lost eyes, limbs, and family members) not found it difficult to accept. Their wounds are not mere buzz wounds.

• When I obtained my Ph.D. from Rutgers University in the USA, my academic supervisor David Weimer was especially enthusiastic about my dissertation. It dealt with a subject considered then quite novel, namely the end of history and of man. In my research, I contended that the problematic of the "death of history" (as I called it then) is implicit in the materialist Western outlook. Then I compared William Wordsworth, with his historical imagination, to Walt Whitman, with his anti-historical imagination, concluding that while in the USA Whitman is called "the poet of American democracy," he is in fact the poet of dictatorship and fascism and an advocate of the death of history and of man.

With high recommendations, my supervisor sent my dissertation to a number of publishers. They all refused to publish the work, sometimes for comical reasons and sometimes for no reason at all. In his response, the representative of one particular university press said that the research was a unique academic work, pioneering in the field as an integrated comparative work on romantic criticism in England and the USA. However, he concluded by saying that his press would not publish it because the author of the dissertation had criticized one of the American sacred cows (meaning Walt Whitman), which was "naturally" unacceptable behavior.

• On its front page, an Arab newspaper published an eye-catching headline about an accident involving a train and a car in India, which caused the death of more than 50 people and the injury of 100. On the society page of the same issue, statistics were presented to the effect that one-third of all children in England are born out of wedlock. And one is tempted to ask: How could a news item about a car accident be more important than a news item concerning one-third of British babies who were deprived of the right to caring parents? Why should the first item be put on the front page while the latter is relegated to a humble social corner together with the news about marriage and divorce of a sex queen or a movie starlet?

• When white colonialists invaded Africa, they considered the naked women they saw there a sure sign of a primitive, underdeveloped life style (at a time when Western women wore very elaborate clothes covering themselves from head to toe except at formal evening receptions or dinner parties). The same Western people now regard nudist camps as a sign of open-mindedness and a high level of development. This means that in less than half a century the Western mentality shifted abruptly from one extreme to the other, from bias in favor of covering up to bias against it. That is why many Western women now wear revealing styles of dress and those who object to this, even from a purely aesthetic point of view, are considered old-fashioned and narrow-minded.

DEFINITION OF BIAS

Every human behavior has cultural significance and represents some epistemological paradigm and perspective. A paradigm is a mental abstract picture, an imaginary construct, and a symbolic representation of reality that results from a process of deconstruction and reconstruction. The mind assembles some features from reality, rejecting some and keeping others, rearranging them in an order of priority to make them correspond to reality. According to the nature of the paradigm, it can exaggerate those elements which it deems essential and underplay all other elements. A materialist economistic paradigm, for example, excludes non-economic, non-materialistic factors, whereas a humanist paradigm would include other elements and factors.

Each paradigm has an epistemological dimension. In other words, behind each paradigm – the process of inclusion, exclusion, reconstruction and exaggeration – there are intrinsic criteria, a set of beliefs, hypotheses, presuppositions, axioms and answers to the total and ultimate questions[1] that make up its deeply-rooted fundamentals.

The dictionary defines 'bias' as advocacy of a particular point of view. The word *mutaḥayyizan*[2] is mentioned in the Qur'an (8:16). Ancient dictionaries disregard the term and modern ones disagree on its meaning. *Al-Muʿjam al-Wasīṭ,* a dictionary published by the Arabic Language Academy, defines bias as 'joining one team against another'. It includes the meaning of adopting some people's view and rejecting that of others. It is this definition that is adopted in this paper. However, the concept of bias will be made clearer through naming some of its salient characteristics.

BIAS IS INEVITABLE

A. Bias is associated with the very structure of the human mind, which does not record events precisely and accurately, with no selectivity or creativity, as a machine would do. The human mind, as noted earlier, is not passive, but rather vital and highly selective. Perception is not random but it is a process that follows a specific pattern whose aspects can be partly identified.

B. Bias is organically bound up with language and is also language-specific. No human language contains all the vocabulary needed to describe reality with all its components. This means that choice is inevitable. It has been proven that each language is capable of describing its own reality more effectively than others. The modes of expressing the idea of time differ from one language to another. Moreover, metaphors are part of the very structure of language (e.g., eye of the needle, leg of the chair, foot of the mountain, etc.). It is noticeable that the signifier and the signified overlap; the relative constancy of signifiers (as part of the fixed linguistic system) is also observable, as well as the rapid change of many signified at a degree that exceeds that of signifiers. The significance behind all of this lies in the fact that human language is not an unbiased tool, unlike the language of algebra and geometry, which can adequately describes the world of unbiased facts and things, yet fails to express the simplest human feelings.

C. This means that bias is a basic component of the human *donnée* and is associated with the humanness of man and woman, i.e. with the very existence of the human being as a non-natural creature that cannot be reduced to the general laws of nature. Whatever is human includes within it a degree of individuality and uniqueness and, therefore, bias. If culture is defined as "all that the human being has created (in contrast with what is already given by nature)," then the cultural aspect is necessarily biased. At times, even natural objects embody bias, since it is man who discovers them, even if by chance. This is by no means haphazard but rather the result of an active human perception. When people discover a natural object, they give it a name, i.e., enter it into the network of human knowledge and transfers it from the world of nature into the world of humankind.

BIAS IS INEVITABLE, BUT NOT ULTIMATE

The inevitability of bias (and the fact that it is bound up with what is human and cultural) should by no means be a reason for grief or frustration. If disentangled from its negative sense, bias is not at all a defect. The problematic of bias can then be re-evaluated from a different perspective. Thus, instead of placing my bias over against the bias of the other, bias can be re-defined as the inevitability of human uniqueness and the possibility of freedom of choice. This implies a paradox, it should be admitted; yet such is human life. This paradox is a framework for what I term "common humanity," as distinct from the "one humanity" advocated by the Enlightenment.

Common humanity is the human potential which is part of our *fiṭrah* (instinct). However, when it is realized, its realization differs from one individual to another, from one people to another, from one period to another, and from one civilization to another, both in form and content. Hence, both potential unity and the inevitable rich variation that does not negate people's common humanity. Human beings were created by one God with a single *fiṭrah* in common. The Creator, however, wished that they not be one nation, but rather a variety of peoples and tribes, each with its particular set of choices. This does not necessarily mean that they should be in conflict with each other, nor does it mean that the one has to negate the other; after all, the possibility of communication and mutual understanding is always there. "Had God so willed, He could surely have made them all one single community" (Qur'an, 42:8); yet He wished that we be different so that we might compete and communicate. Despite its limits, human language is capable of achieving successful communication and of expressing truth that can help overcome bias and build epistemological paradigms which, though they arise from a particular cultural experience, can render communication both successful and fair to all concerned.

SELF AND OTHER

The Prophet Muhammad (ṢAAS)[3] was an Arab but was sent to the whole of humankind, and that is why he warned against pride, xenophobia and ethnocentrism: "There is no superiority for either Arab or non-Arab except by virtue of one's piety." This is a non-negotiable moral absolute. The identity of a non-Arab is different from that of an Arab and their biases are, therefore, different. Yet there is a common ultimate point of reference, namely, piety. That is what we mean by saying that bias is inevitable but not ultimate. It is inevitable in the sense that it cannot be avoided, but not ultimate in the sense that it is the final destiny; rather, the ultimate is the common humanity and the moral values that precede any form of difference or bias.

FORM OF BIAS

1. There is bias in favor of what one believes to be the truth. This is commitment. When one is biased towards the truth, one is enthusiastic and motivated, but is ready to subject himself and his judgments to the value system and to the truths that exist outside him. In this case, one is also ready to test the result of his search, for he does not believe that his (biased) judgment is the final absolute verdict, for it is, first and foremost, an ijtihad; and of this he is quite aware.

2. Bias in favor of falsehood can take different forms. Bias toward the Self is one example. When people make themselves the only acceptable point of reference, the idea of a transcendental truth is dropped, and they cannot be judged from any point external to them. This form of bias is associated with bias for power, which means that when one is victorious, one enforces one's own will; if one is defeated, one becomes a pragmatist who accepts the rules of the victorious Other, without necessarily accepting the truthfulness of the other's statements or judgments. Power is the only arbiter, and therefore such a defeated pragmatist impatiently awaits a change in the balance of power in his/her favor. Therefore pragmatic accommodation, far from bringing about peace and harmony, results in endless conflict.

3. Some biases are explicit and conscious, others are implicit and unconscious. Conscious bias is that of someone who intentionally chooses an ideology, sees the world through it, then propagates it and mobilizes in its favor. Unconscious bias, by contrast, happens when someone internalizes an epistemological system with all its premises and priorities, and unconsciously sees the world only through it.

Explicit bias manifests itself in cheap propaganda. In effect, the recipient of such propaganda can readily identify its claims. The recipient of implicit bias, by contrast, is unconsciously influenced by it. There are instances, however, when conscious bias is presented in an implicit way, with the recipient being heedless of it. An example of this is in commercial advertisements, in which the extremely conscious advertisers promote their product by, for example, forging some association between sex and their commodities, which leaves a deep impact on the innocent, unaware recipients who are treated as if they were Pavlov's dog.

The same thing happens on the political and moral levels. Western movies implicitly pander to numerous Hollywood-biased values, such as violence and suspense. Such values stem from a Darwinian perspective and would be revolting were they presented directly. Westerns and Tom and Jerry cartoons, for example, present these same values in the form of "innocent" entertainment, as if they do not embody any values or any barbarous epistemological paradigm.

4. Bias can be classified according to its degree of acuteness; it might be acute and explicit as is the case with socialist realist fiction, which always depicts the working class as victorious whereas the bourgeois hand is always declining, vanishing and being replaced by the rising forces of the proletariat. There are, nevertheless, bourgeois intellectuals who are aware of the inevitable laws of history, who shake off their class affiliations and throw in their lot with the working class. Such fiction always ends with the inevitable triumph of that revolutionary alliance between the workers, the peasants and the intellectuals, who believe in the ultimate and inevitable victory of the proletariat.

Bias is not always this explicit, of course. One might be biased in favor of a certain doctrine and support it, yet realize the difficulties involved in its application. Degrees of bias differ from one field to another. Different disciplines show various degrees of bias. It all depends on how closely related a given sphere of life or science is to the cultural identity of a community. Thus it is strongest in the fields of religious beliefs, traditions and human relationships represented in arts, literature and thought. Fields representing an average degree of bias include technology and industry. In such "pure" sciences as physics, mathematics and biology, bias is at its minimum.

5. There is also bias within bias, that is, when a researcher adopts one specific view within a comprehensive epistemological paradigm, which results in a sort of double bias. For example, great stress is placed in the Arab world on French and British theories of sociology while their German counterparts are ignored, despite the fact that all three belong to the tradition of Western sociology. The bias here is not toward Western sociological theory in general, but to one specific trend within it.

6. There is also the inverse; that is, when a researcher is biased in favor of a number of contradictory ideas belonging to incompatible epistemological systems, which are indiscriminately adopted due to a lack of any deep epistemological outlook. Some Arab poets, for example, adopt some of the central premises of the Enlightenment calling for the use of reason, adopting a very optimistic outlook. However, when some of them move from the realm of theory to the realm of literary creativity, they write pessimistic modernist poetry, stressing irrationality and the absurdity of reality. Similarly, a Western secular writer may admire some of the religious ideas of Islam, Hinduism and Confucianism, espousing all of them, yet without realizing some of the basic differences between these religious systems.

7. There is partial bias and total bias. An example of the former may be seen in a Western writer who admires a particular Oriental writer or artistic style, but who does not fully comprehend the underlying epistemological paradigm. An interesting example can be found in Arthur Fitzgerald who translated into English the *Rubāʿiyyāt* of ʿUmar al-Khayyām, the renowned Persian poet. Fitzgerald selected from Persian Islamic civilization what suited his taste as a Victorian artist and found something interesting about this Persian poet, who felt alienated from his world. Another example can be found in some Arab poets who admired Shakespeare and translated many of his plays and poems, selecting from among his ideas what matched their taste without adopting his vision of the universe; one of them, for example, appended a happy ending to Hamlet in which virtue is rewarded as it should be in a just, non-tragic world.

Partial bias may be seen in the self-confident individuals who operate within the framework of their own vision and stand on its grounds. They have specific biases and select from the world what they need to support them. They hold the scales in their hands and fear no imported ideas or objects, but weigh what they import on their scales, according to their own criteria. These people are not against borrowing from other cultures and can benefit from them. What they are really against is having their own concepts weighed for them by scales thrust into their hands by others, talking about themselves in the third person, or closing the gate of ijtihad regarding the Other. These people move within an open and flexible framework rather than within a closed and inflexible one. Their ideas stem from their own intellectual and cultural grounds and they never submit to what one Western thinker has termed the "imperialism of categories," meaning to import from the Other not only some of their views and contributions but even their basic analytical categories and vision of the universe, and therefore to weigh matters on the scales of the Other rather than on their own.

One's own ijtihad, stemming from the Self, does not contradict the scientific outlook, for natural science does not deal with totalities, absolutes, or final ends (the scales), but rather with parts and procedures (the weighed), leaving values, truth, and ultimate ends for human beings to determine according to their own beliefs. Those who submit completely to the Other are, in fact, importers of others' choices, visions and analytical categories; natural science neither encourages nor prohibits that.

8. One of the most important new forms of bias which has no parallel in previous cultures is what might be called "the bias of our material reality against us." Western colonialists have penetrated the Muslim homeland, destroyed the houses that expressed Muslim cultural identity and needs and, with their architectural designs, done away with the ancient cities that reflected the Islamic value system. In their place, other cities were built that manifested the colonialists' own values such as speed, competence, and competitiveness and that helped them control the colonized. Streets have been widened in order to cope with the many fast cars that race down them, a case which presupposes the existence of cars as a concrete necessity and final *donnée* (given fact).

Muslims might have built cities on the assumption that there are more pedestrians than car passengers and that there are more public than private transport users. Modern cities with their wide roads embody an administrative view that suggests the need for a powerful administrative center (or national central government) with control over all its subjects. This is why wide roads in European cities of the 17th Century used to be called in Latin *via militares*, i.e., meaning military roads, because they made every populated area more easily accessible to government forces which could then suppress and "re-orient" the people whenever necessary, keeping them in subjection to what the authorities deemed to be the "public interest" (which in fact meant the "supreme interests of the state or the colonialist"). Narrow roads and street alleys, let it be remembered, only allowed the passage of people rather than vehicles or military forces.

Modern Muslim houses are designed with materials which allow the entrance of a maximum amount of sunlight which, in this hot weather of ours, necessitates the use of air conditioning! Consequently, there arises the need for a large number of commodities that have become part of the "necessities of modern life." If one does not use a car, one's time (and life) is lost; if one cannot afford an air conditioner, one sweats profusely and one's productivity level plummets.

The present workday in the Arab world shows a distinct bias in favor of Western culture (from which it was adopted). For Muslim culture, it would be more suitable to start the working day immediately after the dawn prayer[4] and end at noon. People could then socialize in the late afternoon and go to bed immediately after the evening prayers.[5] I am not forwarding this proposal as "the truth, the whole truth, and nothing but the truth." I am simply suggesting that we study its feasibility, taking into consideration the resulting saved energy and the psychological comfort that is likely to result from the compatibility between biological and ecological rhythms.[6] Research should tell us whether such a working day scheme is workable. The expected result might be controversial, but there is certainly no need to give in to the imported system which is biased against our own interests and bio- and eco- rhythms. It might be an instance of liberating the Self from dependence on the Other; creativity might then flow.

BIAS IN FAVOR OF THE WESTERN CULTURAL PARADIGM

Bias toward the Western cultural paradigm is one of the most widespread forms of bias worldwide. Here are some examples.

• When I arrived in the United States in 1963 to attend a summer course at Yale University, I was invited to watch a Shakespearean play. I was dressed rather informally, but an American professor remarked that I had to wear a collar and tie. "Doesn't Shakespeare deserve it?" he whispered. Because I loved and respected Shakespeare, I returned to my room and dressed in the way recommended. The professor appreciated my good manners. However, before going back to Egypt in 1969, I happened to go to the stage again with some friends, armed with my collar and tie. They cracked a few jokes, since such formal dress had become (in the span of a few years) old fashioned and a sign of stuffiness. I realized then and there that one's clothes were not merely a covering of the body but rather a sign – a whole language. Since then I have decided to speak my own language and not just parrot others. From that time onward I was determined not to copy ready-made fashions, but rather to make up my own mind and, as much as possible, to make my own decisions.

• As a child I noticed that one of the main sources of tension for a middle class Egyptian housewife was her set of china saucers, consisting of a dozen or half a dozen matching pieces. When a servant or a guest broke a plate or a plate broke by itself, this was considered disastrous since it also broke the symmetric geometric pattern of the set. For some unknown reason, the love of such patterns was ingrained in us from childhood.

That is why I suggest that we change our strategy of impressing others by breaking away from symmetric geometric patterns, replacing them with incomplete, asymmetric patterns that are more suited to human life. Perfection is after all, God's alone. First of all, why should the set be bound to the numbers 6, 12, or 24? Why not 7, 8 or 9? Why should all the pieces be identical? Can't each plate be unique? At least this would never make the breaking of one plate a disaster because no symmetric geometric pattern would be violated. Moreover, the presence of different plate forms would imply variety and plurality. We live in the age of pluralism, do we not? This would also allow a friend to present a gift in the form of one plate with its saucer, with the result that each set would have its own character and be suffused with memorable uniqueness. I know beforehand that my suggestion will find no support among middle-class ladies. Who am I, after all, to call for a change in their tastes or to challenge such well established ideas?

Alternatively, what if a French fashion designer decided to "go back to nature" and point out, for example, that the colors of peacock feathers should be the fashion? Wouldn't people follow his suggestion? And if said designer decided that the "return to nature" meant that the skirts of women should be appended by "tails" or tail-like appendages so as to stress the human-animal continuity; would any one dare oppose the fashion? Of course not! But why should my noble human suggestion be rejected while the insane instructions of fashion designers are accepted?

• Visit an Arab middle-class household and you will immediately notice that there are dining rooms, salons with gold-plated seats and sofas, in addition to the living rooms and the bedrooms. By contrast, a traditional Japanese house might have only two or three rooms furnished with very simple mats. One room would be used as a dining room and a living room during the day and be transformed into a bedroom in the evening. It is obvious that the Arab middle class have deserted the traditional Arab house with its wide internal parlor, its high fences and its diverse furniture. The 19th century Western concept of houses has been adopted instead. This began when the Westernized Arab aristocracy (of rich landlords and court officials) wished their countries to be "part of Europe," as a result of which they deserted their heritage and became obsessed with everything Western. Western designers were thus asked to recreate the environment so as to fulfill the aristocrats' Western dreams. As usual, some members of the middle class were quick to fall in line though they had neither the knowledge nor the financial capability necessary for the change. The style was adopted to fit the limited budget of the middle class and the small space available to it. The result was a style of furniture that foreigners in Egypt used to call "Louis Farouk" (that is, neither a pure French style such as "Louis XV" or "Louis XVI," but rather, a decadent imitation thereof).

What this means is that Egyptian household furniture has not simply been transported in a truck from Damietta[7] but, rather, imported from the West through a very complicated historical process. Furniture is not mere objects positioned in one's home, but rather an embodiment of a specific conscious cultural choice on the part of the Arab aristocracy, which has adopted the Western paradigm in architecture and furniture. For the middle class, it is an unconscious cultural orientation.

It is interesting how unconscious bias can contradict an individual's daily reality. The area available for living for the Egyptian middle class is too small to provide space for such Western-style furniture. It, therefore, becomes an irritant for the family because it is too expensive and needs a larger space than is available. Hence, it is stored in a house whose inhabitants move with difficulty in the narrow lanes left for their mobility. Meanwhile, the housewife fiercely wards off the assaults of the children (and indeed other family members) on the gold-plated salon, which should stay closed except for the visits of important guests, an event that may not happen more than once or twice a year. This means that the room represents an absolute waste of possessions and an assault on the daily comfort of its owners. The dining room enjoys a better fate since the family manages to transform it into a study in which they use the table as a big desk with a place for everyone; hence the traditional paradigm enforces itself as a substitute for the imported one.

Now let us have a look at the chair, that ordinary piece of furniture made of wood, iron or plastic, standing on four legs and used to sit on (or occasionally stand on to reach for something high like an electric lamp, for example). It is believed to exist everywhere and is, therefore, taken for granted as a necessary piece of furniture.

When universities were built in the Arab Gulf states in the 1960s, it was "natural" to adopt chairs in the auditoriums and classrooms. Perhaps no one ever thought about the history and origin of chairs, their sizes, or their heights – all was taken for granted. Perhaps no one ever thought about the fact that the chair's usual height hurts one's backbone and, that therefore, it ought to be lower so as to provide more comfort and save on materials. Or perhaps no one thought of just sitting on the floor and sensing some cultural identity. Perhaps no one thought about the fact that Westerners used chairs to avoid sitting on the cold and wet ground, which explains their lack of interest in carpeting. This is, of course, the very opposite of our environment. Given the hot, dry weather, carpets are an essential cultural object. Nevertheless, chairs have come to symbolize progress despite the historical fact that until the 9th century, the Slavs offered human sacrifices while sitting on chairs. Meanwhile, their Arab and Chinese contemporaries sat on the floor and possessed civilizations of the highest sophistication.

An official in an Arab airport perhaps did not know these facts when he once saw me sitting on the rich carpets in the VIP lounge. "This is not civilized behavior," he whispered to me with certainty. Too tired to argue the point, I threw myself into an armchair, leaving him in his ignorance. This argument should by no means suggest that I am calling for the abandonment of chairs in our Eastern societies; it is, rather, a call for the opening of the gate of ijtihad concerning the use of chairs, their sizes, their heights and their possible substitutes. Is not this likely to result in discoveries that might contribute to the history of humankind? Or should we wait for some Western inventor to discover how harmful chairs are to people's backs and to the world's forests; then, and only then, would we hurry to implement his commands!

• Universities were built of stone in the heart of the desert (and were provided with air conditioners) in modern French and Italian styles (I must hasten to add, quasi-French, quasi-Italian, and quasi modern styles). Houses were built in the same fashion, but they had to be veiled since the realm of private life is still private, indeed sacred. To solve this problem, high fences were built around these quasi-Western houses, the result being that the house looked more like a prison (the traditional Arab house protected privacy by looking inward rather than outward; hence the walled-in garden). And just as the dining room conflicts with the real needs of the Egyptian middle-class family, the Western modern style of architecture conflicts with the needs of Muslim consumers. The result is alienation resulting from the enforcement of an architectural style that does not belong to one's cultural lexicon.

• In many Arab capitals one sees new blocks of flats that look like a queue of boxes or a freezer. If at all decorated, the decoration is most probably Corinthian columns, floral designs, or possibly even Arab ornamentation; however, Arabic calligraphy is never included. Even the street signs are now computer printouts. Arabic calligraphy used to be taught at school, but "progress" caught up with the Arab world and calligraphy classes were canceled, and with them was canceled the realization that calligraphy is an art form. Worse still, some calligraphers find it shameful to declare their profession, which has now become associated with billboards advertising chocolate and detergents. This may be regarded as negligence or an indifference to the heritage, and so it is. But if you look at the matter more deeply, you will realize that our vision of arts has been adopted from the West. Calligraphy, which used to be one of the most lively of Arab arts, has suffered a decline because it is not deemed a fine art from a Western perspective.

- Most of us have grown up in a "progressive" cultural environment in which it is believed that the most serious problem for Egyptian education is the stress on memorization. It is also occasionally hinted that memorization gained such centrality on account of religious education and the central status of the Qur'an. I myself believed this until 1963, when I started studying for my MA at Columbia University. There I was asked to memorize some Romantic poems. When I asked why, I was told that memorization was "one of the best techniques to build rapport between a student and a text." Later on, I learnt that the Japanese educational system does not reject memorization altogether; indeed, it utilizes it as one of its educational methods.

I came to realize that in specific disciplines the student needs to learn some basic principles and precepts by heart. Then I started to question my old and absolute "progressive" certainty. I realized then that the rejection of memorization is in fact a malicious, brazen-faced rejection of the Islamic heritage. Had such a heritage been approached with due respect and awareness, we would have probably realized how memorization could have been utilized in developing the critical sense itself.

- The modern history of Arabic drama started with tragic, comic, historical and pastoral plays translated from French and English. Then Western theories of drama (ranging from Aristotle to Brecht and Artaud) were also translated. Consequently, to us, drama meant nothing but the Western conception of it; the audience sits in front of a stage, and the show starts by drawing the curtain and ends when it is closed. Actors try to create for their audience the illusion that their dramatic world is similar to the real external world. Stemming from this, we started to write "modern" drama and failed to identify and develop the dramatic forms in our own heritage. We failed to realize that the biography of Banū Hilāl (*al-Sīrah al-Hilāliyyah*) was not merely a lyrical or even a narrative play, but was, rather a sophisticated first-class play in which the dramatic mingled with narrative and lyrical elements.

Had we studied Japanese theater (*Noh* and *Kabuki* plays), we would have discovered a completely different theater. This is a theater in which the actors mix with the audience rather than face it. Perhaps had we studied the history of the Japanese theater (and the Indian, the Chinese and non-Western forms in general), the history of the Arabic theater would have taken a very different course, and we would probably have discovered the dramatic forms in our heritage (the magic box shadow plays, the biography of Banū Hilāl, etc.). We would have taken our point of departure from these elements, developed them and thus generated new and more creative dramatic theories. Is this not better than simply mimicking the dramatic creations of the Other in a way that is pathetic at times, and ridiculous at others?

DOMINANCE OF THE WESTERN CULTURAL PARADIGM

All the aforementioned examples indicate clearly that our heritage was abandoned in favor of the Other's without realizing the implication of this behavior and without any creative critical study of our heritage and theirs, and our culture and theirs. We have adopted this cultural paradigm and avidly consumed its cultural products and transplanted them into our "alien" soil without much awareness of the implications of our deed and its impact on the fabric of our society, life-style, and values. How did this come to happen?

It is a basic fact confronting modern man that the Western cultural paradigm occupies a central position in the minds and hearts of most people and thinkers the world over. The Western cultural paradigm, by virtue of its simple and materialist approach to humankind and nature, has achieved brilliant victories on the materialist level. By the annexation and conquest of lands, the application of this paradigm initially afforded Western peoples a high standard of living. The victorious Western cultural project was translated into an ever expanding sense of self-confidence on the part of Westerners and into their solid belief that their concept of the world is the highest point of development that the human race has ever achieved. They believe that human history has thus reached its zenith in modern Western history, that Western sciences are universal, and that the Western cultural paradigm is valid for all time and place, or at least in modern times and places.

The Islamic world entered into a bitter conflict with this cultural formation right from the start. The Ottomans defended the "land of Islam" in the Arab East and elsewhere against the colonialist assault. This explains why Western imperialism circumvented the Ottoman empire, occupying parts of Africa and India and the New World. With the crisis of the Ottoman Empire, however, Western armies started to invade the Islamic East. The arrival of Napoleon's forces in Egypt (1798–1802) marked the beginning of the West's attempts to dismember this Empire and the Islamic world at large. This was followed by the annexation of the Turkish emirates on the Black Sea by the Russians and the British invasion of Cyprus (and later of Egypt). Thus the Islamic world was ultimately divided among Western imperialist powers.

For the reasons mentioned above, catching up with the West has become the essence of all so-called revival projects (called *al-Nahḍah*, or renaissance) in the "Third World," including the Islamic world.

1. This can be seen most clearly in secular liberal thought, to which "Renaissance" meant primarily the importation of Western thought and theories and the adoption of the Western cultural paradigm for better or for worse. Arab and Muslim societies, therefore, were to be "reformed" so that they would live up to the standards of the Western paradigm. This trend was represented by the liberals of the "renaissance generation" such as Ahmed Lutfi El-Sayyed, Shibli Shemayel and Salama Musa, among others. Some of these intellectuals were Westernized to the core and were so alienated from their identity that they called for such theatrical frivolities as wearing the European hat, writing Arabic in the Roman alphabet, and teaching Greek and Latin in secondary schools. Others were more moderate and kept away from such puerile antics; but representatives of both tendencies, the extremist and the moderate, were ultimately uncritical propagators of Westernization and advocates of modernization according to Western ways.

2. Another example can be found in the attitude of Arab Communists, Marxists, and Socialists. Despite their critical attitude to capitalism and economic and social liberalism, Arab leftists generally accepted the underlying cultural and cognitive paradigm of modern Western thought. Their critiques, therefore, were confined to the politico-economic aspects of the capitalist system, but never extended to the cultural cognitive paradigm itself.

3. Beginning in the 1940s, the Western cultural paradigm witnessed a retreat in the Arab world. This was represented by the rise of such Islamist movements as the Muslim Brotherhood and national socialist parties such as *Miṣr al-Fatāt* (Young Egypt). It was also reflected in the gradual crystallization of nationalist thought and in the rise of political organizations attempting to transform this thought into a concrete reality. All such movements were aware, in one way or another, of the existence of a Western

paradigm alien to them and, therefore, they stressed Arab identity and the significance of their heritage, both national and religious.

Despite the significance of such endeavors – that they form a retreat from, and a revision of, the Western cultural paradigm and greater affinity to the Eastern heritage – their target, whether declared or not, was always to "catch up with the West" and, in the meantime, retain as much as possible of Muslim identity and develop it in such a way as to make it consistent with modernity. This trend is, in reality, but another attempt at adopting the Western cultural paradigm, taking this time the form of re-modeling Arab identity along Western lines while preserving external Arab forms. Arab heritage was thus to be re-discovered from a Western perspective, and even reformulated retroactively. Accordingly, for example, the Muʿtazilites were re-labeled as rationalists, al-Jurjānī as a pioneer of semiotics and stylistics, and Islamic art as abstractionist. By the same token, alienation can be seen in the poetry of the Kharijites. Abū al-ʿAlāʾ was a pioneer of the philosophy of skepticism centuries before Descartes (or perhaps it was al-Ghazālī); and Ibn Khaldūn "discovered 80% of the rules of dialectical materialism," to use the very words of an Arab Marxist philosopher in a lecture which he devoted to a defense of the Arab heritage. According to him, Ibn Khaldūn was a Marxist even before Marx was born. It was only, therefore, due to this imperfect, latent Marxism (which later reached completion in Marx himself) that Ibn Khaldūn had any legitimacy, not because of his Arab Islamic thought or his contribution to sociological theory (a contribution whose underlying episte- mological premises are at odds with Marxist epistemology). Consequently, the Arab Islamic heritage is important only insofar as it approaches the Western cultural paradigm.

4. Surprisingly, the attempt to catch up with the West is echoed profoundly in the practices of some Islamist movements. Some Islamist thinkers accept, consciously or unconsciously, the Western cultural paradigm, or many of its aspects. They even turn this paradigm into a model to follow and a silent point of reference, so much so that, to them, the Islamic renaissance project is the shortest way to catch up with the West. Some of them even go as far as to claim that the Islamic project is the best and most effective way to adopt and apply the Western cultural paradigm to the Islamic world. This could be done after having embellished said paradigm with such additions as fasting and prayers, the separation of women from men

and enforcing *ḥijāb* (women's veil). Again, Islam is re-discovered to make it conform to the Western paradigm. So we discover that many scientific laws exist in the Qur'an. Thinkers compete to offer evidence that Islam had already given women their rights and that it had reached, a long time ago, the recently discovered rules of "modern" organization. The fatal significance here, again, is that Islam gains legitimacy inasmuch as it approaches the Western cultural paradigm. In other words, the Islamic paradigm is being subtly Westernized from within, with no cultural invasion from without.

The basic feature of all the aforementioned cultural projects – despite their apparent ideological differences – is that the West has been taken as the ultimate point of reference. In other words, they have all internalized the West's view of itself and of its cultural project. The West has therefore become the cultural formation that has outrun us, and that we have to catch up with (or, according to the aforementioned Islamist view, the paradigm that Muslims had actually founded and which they have to re-adopt in the present day). It is assumed that there is one fixed point that all societies endeavor to reach, that there is one single method for managing societies and determining the conduct of humankind, and that there is one single view of the human race and the universe. According to this perspective, the West has been transformed from a geographical area and a cultural formation that has its own specificity and individual concepts into the area from which stems modern universal and human thought, a case which has given a great deal of legitimacy to the idea of catching up with the West. Western science, consistently sought by the educated Arabs and Muslims, has thus become a "modern universal science," and the intellectual submission and subordination to the West is termed "belonging to the modern times."

Consequently, Arab intellectuals have showed a bias for the Western heritage, neglecting their own heritage and the heritage of humankind at large. For example, no one cares for Japanese or Chinese cultures and no one is genuinely interested in Swahili, the language spoken by most of the residents of Eastern Africa, despite its close association to Islam and Arabic. By contrast, everyone competes to study "world [namely, Western] heritage," never questioning its underlying cognitive categories, historical roots or the social mechanisms that led to its emergence. A researcher's job has thus become to receive the information that is termed "international," but which is in fact Western. This is then reproduced in the form of studies and books that never go beyond the scope of Western concepts and only contribute, if at all, to the development of Western science and knowledge, and which estrange the researchers themselves from their native Islamic and Arab culture.

A group of educated (as opposed to cultured) people has been formed in the Muslim world that occupies leading and important offices, such as journalists, teachers, university professors, media personnel, and translators, all of whom have completely absorbed the Western cultural paradigm without realizing its actual implications. They take it as a set of noble ideas and have become excellent propagators of its value system, sometimes consciously but quite often unconsciously, yet always without full understanding of the implications of what they propagate. Such people are always good at studying and obtaining university degrees, but show very limited critical thinking and scanty understanding of epistemological paradigms. (This is not surprising, since critical thinking requires special awareness of the Self and the Other, in addition to a high degree of self-confidence and special critical faculties; intellectual qualifications that few people possess.)

This sector of educated people is the most dangerous, for they are the most active. They reshape the value system along Western lines and propagate the Western cultural paradigm with all its biases. The Renaissance in Europe, as they were taught, was the age when the arts and literature were revived and humankind was placed at the center of the universe (rather than the age of Machiavelli and Hobbes, the beginning of the Western imperialist formation, and the genocide of millions in North America). The French Revolution, to them, is the revolution of liberty, fraternity, and equality and is associated with the Declaration of the Rights of Man (not the first truly secular revolution when humans started to worship abstract reason so unquestioningly that the revolutionaries resorted to terrorism to reshape reality in the way that would accord with this "reason." Little do they know that the French Revolution set up a central government that liquidated all ethnic and religious enclaves and invaded Egypt and Palestine). Progress, they firmly believe, is the basic fact in the history of mankind (unaware of the high price which sometimes exceeds all the achieved material benefits). They consider Nietzsche to be the greatest philosopher of humankind (rather than the philosopher of the death of God and of the human race). Finally, they believe that structuralism and deconstruction are mere schools of literary analysis (not methods of thought that reflect an anti-humanistic attitude).

Members of educated "elites," whether those who studied abroad or at home, absorb the Western cultural paradigm thoroughly, then render into Arabic all that they have read (in books or articles) without discrimination or scrutiny. Worse still, they have taken over the universities and started teaching Western science in exactly the same way native Westerners do, from the latter's perspectives and using their methods. Curricula are designed following the example of the "international" – that is, the Western – style.

BIAS TOWARDS THE MODERN WESTERN CULTURAL PARADIGM

A cultural paradigm is usually an embodiment of a full cognitive paradigm containing a value system. Here are some illustrative examples.

• Moving the hands as one speaks is a sign of enthusiasm in Middle Eastern countries, but in other countries (at least in Western Anglo-Saxon culture), it could signify coarseness and denote the lower ethnic and class origin of the speaker. Gestures are in the former case an expression of a deep desire to communicate with the Other as well as a feeling that the verbal language is incapable of fully expressing one's views and emotions. In the context of a contractual civilization, what cannot be expressed verbally should be ignored. Therefore, gestures are considered offensive or even threatening. Immigrants, for example, not yet familiar with the cultural idiom of Anglo-Saxon civilization, still move their hands as they speak. That is why people are taught to use gestures very rarely and only at a very crucial point, and they are warned against gesturing all the time. There is a whole outlook underlying the use of gesture, unconscious though it might be.

• Some Japanese and American anthropologists once studied the behavior of groups of monkeys living under the same conditions. The American anthropologists divided the monkeys into groups of equal numbers and started to record their body movements and accumulate information about them, comparing the behavior of individual monkeys. The Japanese anthropologists, on the other hand, divided their monkeys into family groups and gave names to each family and a name to each individual monkey. Each team noticed that the monkeys dipped potatoes in water before eating them. The American scientists concluded that some monkeys wash potatoes; meanwhile, the Japanese team interpreted this behavior as follows:

– Only some families, not all of them, washed their potatoes.

– Monkeys did this because they liked the taste of potatoes with salty water.

Both teams observed the same phenomenon, but interpreted it in a different way. While the American anthropologists worked within the framework of "a general, abstract monkey" or "a mere number of monkeys" with no family ties or individual features, the Japanese team, in contrast, used the family as a unit of analysis. That is why the former passed generalizations on some individual members of the species, whereas the Japanese saw the monkeys' behavior as an acquired cultural behavior (of specific families). In other words, it is a type of behavior specific to the monkey families that acquired it. Thus, whereas the American scientists studied the behavior of the monkeys in terms of the concept of utility, the Japanese saw it within the concept of security and happiness. The divergence of results emerges from the difference of presuppositions. Whereas the Americans saw the monkeys as mere objects of study and observation, the Japanese established an intimate relationship with the monkeys, which made them amenable to seeing the monkeys' specific characteristics and individual characters.

• As you walk through the market, you step on someone's toes by mistake, and immediately say, "I'm very sorry indeed." The response may differ as follows: "Never mind, Sir. You see, the market is so crowded today, you couldn't possibly avoid stepping on my toes." "God help us all!" he/she might even add. Another response might go, "In which bank do you think I can cash this *sorry* of yours?" meaning: Where on earth can I get the material equivalent of your apology? An observer might be stimulated to comment, "Such a rude reply." Another might as well think, "What a realistic response!"

• If we stop and analyze the previous utterances, we realize immediately that there is a belief on the part of the one who apologized that this is a worthy behavior that has "value," since it expresses human solidarity. Value is an immaterial quality that cannot be measured and that goes beyond the world of matter, the world of buying and selling and fixed "price." It is despite this, or perhaps because of this, "a matter of great consequence." Seekers of material equivalents of the word "sorry" have only one reference, namely, the bank and money. (What is termed in philosophy, "the material world," is not confined to money but means the world of sense perception and that which can be measured.) For the latter, value, that inner moral concept, is non-existent; to them there only exists the perceived material quantity, price, which has nothing to do with inner human feelings.

• Plutarch (ancient Greek essayist and biographer) says, "When the candles are blown out, all women are fair." This is an interesting statement which we hope that the writer meant to be a dirty joke that does not represent his world outlook. Before blowing out the candles and after lighting them again, there are many moments – a whole life – of joy, sorrow and emotionally neutral time. Thus, he who says that *all women are fair when the lights are off* is a complete materialist (pornographic in the epistemological sense) who sees the human being as a mere physical body and overlooks the moments preceding and following the blowing out of candles, when a person's complex humanity is manifested, and during which he searches for peace and tranquility. All women, in the last analysis [as the materialist would say], when the lights are off, are nothing but usable matter. This is one of the lessons of the "Enlightenment." The paradigm here is a pessimistic, nihilist one in which bursts of laughter conceal cries of pain, just as ʿUmar al-Khayyām used to curse time while getting drunk as a means of concealing his philosophical nihilism and (his sense of the) absence of meaning in the universe.

• The following conversation frequently takes place in several cultures:

> A: What work do you do, Madame?
> B: I'm just a housewife.
> A: Have you done anything today?
> B: No, Nothing at all.

This is a type of conversation that I frequently heard in the USA in the 1960s before the rise of the women's liberation movement. Such a conversation, which may still be heard here in Egypt, can be decoded as follows: "What work do you do, Madame?" "Work" means employment outside the home, and since "doing" has been defined as something performed outside one's house in the realm of public life and in return for some kind of wage (a definite price), any work in a woman's private life with a high human value (such as raising her children or looking after her family) is not "work" at all. That's because it is done at home (in the realm of private life) and wages are not paid. It cannot be measured and is not a quantity. If a woman says that her work as a mother at home fulfills her human identity, this is considered a mere appeal to defunct human values and to an outdated, metaphysical concept of human nature. These are not "scientific" things; they do not belong to the world of matter and quantity. Do not then assert that a mother's work at home might be much more useful to society than her office work, since the course of history indicates that all women have to do their work in the public realm and for remuneration; everybody has to pant in the market or in the factory. If I accept such an argument, and it has to be accepted anyway, because this is the predominant "scientific," "objective" materialist discourse, I am just a housewife. The work I do is not "productive labor."

"Have you done anything today?" Despite the fact that I have cleaned my house, cooked the meals, seen my elder son off to school, fed my younger daughter, received my husband on his return home and generated inner peace in all of them, this is mere domestic activity for which I am not paid and, therefore, I have actually done nothing at all.

In an apparently innocuous conversation of this type, the word *work* has been charged with an ideological content; it has lost its "innocence" and has become a term that cannot be fully understood except within the context of the secular cultural paradigm of modern Western civilization, which sees work as something performed in the realm of public life and for which one is paid. Man here is *homo economicus,* a producer and a consumer, nothing more, nothing less. He may also be *homo erectus,* and even *homo faber,* but he is a maker who produces without love, without hatred. No *homo sapiens,* he is nothing but *homme la machine* (Man the machine, as described by a leading enlightenment thinker).

Private life, by contrast, is the realm in which some human acts cannot be measured, and therefore lie outside the scope of objective science. Gradually, we begin to learn that the poor housewife, supposed to have done nothing from a materialist perspective, has certainly done much valuable work from a more complex perspective. However, if she has internalized the materialist cognitive discourse, she has to leave home to have "work," earn a salary and regain her lost self-respect. The whole family might collapse, the children might be juvenile delinquents or lose self-confidence and confidence in others, the specific characteristics of civilization might be lost (for it is the mother who really imparts to her children the specific values of her own culture), but it does not matter, for these are secondary issues. Or as it is often reiterated, "everything, in the last analysis, is economic." Just like the man in the market story who said, "In which bank can I cash this *sorry*?" Or perhaps like Plutarch when he said, "When the candles are blown out, all women are fair."

• An IMF official stated that large areas in Africa could be rented as dumping grounds for chemical, nuclear and other types of waste generated by Western societies in return for generous amounts of money that could be used to help the continent in its development programs. Such statements expectedly caused much consternation and the IMF denied them, but the high official himself reaffirmed his statements and added that he was expressing the key philosophy of his organization. This economistic (materialist) perspective regards the whole world as mere matter that can be utilized; the only acceptable thing is the tangible price one gets, not some pale, abstract human value.

• A friend of mine who was a high official in the IMF was sent to Egypt on a mission to implement a huge development program. When he met the young people of the village where he was supposed to carry out his project, they warned him that lots of medicinal herbs, whose medical benefits were still to be discovered by modern pharmaceutical science, and animal species, mostly unknown to scientists, would all be threatened with extinction. He was also alerted to the disintegration of the family that might result from his "development program." "So what did you do?" I asked him. "Nothing! I had a specific plan which could not be put off." My friend obviously is biased toward prompt procedural efficiency at the expense of environmental values and social balance, and did not care much for the human cost his "development" program would exact from the inhabitants of the region to be "developed."

• The following story was published in a newspaper. A journalist was on a safari with her husband in an open zoo in Ethiopia when suddenly the door of their car opened and the husband fell out, whereupon some lions attacked him. The wife tried to help for a moment but failed. She then remembered her job as a journalist with a camera and immediately recorded the unique moment. Her rare photo was later used in a photograph contest and, of course, won the first prize for the sharp wit, accuracy and speed of action. The award was biased towards the materialist values of efficiency, speed and maximal utilization of material reality, disregarding such values as mercy and family solidarity.

• An automobile manufacturer produced a new car that was considered fabulous except for one simple defect: it turned over on curves and killed its passengers. The company thus decided to recall it from the market. A smart accountant, however, by computing the matter in a precise economistic way, discovered that the compensation the company would have to pay to its victims was far less than the costs of recalling the cars and fixing them. Therefore, he advised the company against recalling the cars. The corporation, being a rational, economic entity, acted according to this sound economic advice and chose to compensate those who were killed and injured. Here again, the smart, rational, economistic means of calculation won at the expense of the less economically rational, but more humanly moral values. It did not really matter whether the fabulous cars destroyed a good number of human begins so long as the manufacturer's coffers were full (albeit a bit blood-stained).

• President Eisenhower sent a confidential memorandum to the Nuclear Power Authority (NPA) asking it to refrain from issuing any statements or releasing any data about the dangers of nuclear radiation and experimentation. I thought for a while that such a memorandum was possible only during the "dark ages" of the 1950s, but then I heard the following story.

• In December 1993, *Newsweek* reported a statement by the US Secretary of Energy to the effect that between 1963 and 1990, the USA had conducted 204 underground nuclear tests and never publicly admitted to any of them. The magazine also reported that beginning in the 1940s, the NPA had exposed 600 US citizens to radiation in experiments that aimed at measuring its effects on the human body. More than 10 people were injected with plutonium, mostly without their knowledge. The impact of this tradition of death has persisted, since there are around 24 metric tons of plutonium, used to make nuclear bombs, stored in 6 states; these represent a serious threat to American citizens and are difficult to get rid of. Six million pounds of nuclear waste are still stored in leaking basins.

- The sins of the past keep on haunting the present. Experimenting on human beings represents the most dangerous aspect of all. Eighteen people were exposed to nuclear experiments, including housewives, youth, adolescents, aged people, and even a 4-year-old boy. This study, which was conducted on a national level from 1945 to 1947, aimed at determining the speed at which plutonium travels inside the human body. If that is what is done to American citizens in their home country, think of what could be done to people of the underdeveloped countries? One of the people experimented on was hospitalized for treatment for some pains. Doctors told him he was to receive "an experimental medication," but in fact he was injected with plutonium 239, which gave his body an excessive dose of radiation equal to 46 times the total amount of radiation an ordinary person can be exposed to over an entire lifetime. This human guinea pig survived till 1984 with skin diseases, digestion problems and a state of drowsiness and lethargy that left him helpless and unable to perform any job for the rest of his life. Speaking to *Newsweek*, his cousin compared this heinous act to some of the practices of the Nazis for which they were tried and sentenced to death. He was absolutely right, for the Nazi regime was materialistic to the core and believed in the value of experimentation and the accumulation of data, regardless of absolute values or the damage that might be done to human beings. Nazi scientists conducted unethical experiments, notably on twins who were separated one from the other, after which one of them would be tortured and sometimes killed without telling the other, in order to test the latter's reactions. Apart from the entertainment value of such experiments, a great deal of "useful, very useful" scientific data were accumulated. But can we utilize this data, disregarding the fiendish method used to collect such knowledge? Should absolute moral and human values be overlooked? These are some of the questions being raised.

The automobile company referred to earlier is no different from Eisenhower or the scientists who conducted secret nuclear experiments in the USA or the experiments in Nazi Germany. Nor are they different in any fundamental way from the woman who took a photograph of her husband while he was being devoured by lions. They all share the sinister ability to transform the entire universe into useful, desacralized matter.

This is the essence of the materialistic view of reality; it denies the absoluteness and sanctity of man, stressing the primacy of matter over mind, using analytical categories derived exclusively from matter (such as length, height, depth, density, speed, etc.), and excluding all other less tangible properties.

NATURE OF THE MATERIALISTIC EPISTEMOLOGICAL PARADIGM

The modern Western cultural paradigm, utilitarian and rational-materialist, is the paradigm underlying all the aforementioned examples. It is, in fact, the paradigm underlying most of human knowledge, sciences, and attitudes. It manifests itself in human terminology, axioms, research methods, and procedures. Adopting such terminology or methods without the requisite consciousness of their implicit epistemological dimensions necessarily leads to the unconscious adoption of their underlying epistemological assumptions. This materialistic paradigm is the most dominant because Western imperialism has successfully conquered and divided the whole world and, consequently, internationalized its own cultural paradigm, imposing it on numerous societies through force, enti- cements, and natural dissemination. This has led to the misconception that this Western paradigm is universal. The most common forms of bias in Eastern societies are, therefore, in favor of this particular Western cultural paradigm. Several examples have been given of such bias and a hundred others might be added.

The following is a description of some of the salient characteristics of the modern Western cultural paradigm and the resultant biases:

1. The (modern materialist) Western epistemological paradigm is based on the assumption that the center of the universe exists within it and not beyond it; in other words, it is immanent, not transcendent. This means that either God does not exist at all or that if He does, He has nothing to do with humankind's epistemological, moral, semiotic or aesthetic systems which exist within the world of temporality. This leads to the eradication of the Creator – created (and consequently of the human-nature) duality. In other words, a metaphysics of immanence has replaced the traditional metaphysics of transcendence.

2. At first, and as a result of this world outlook, humanism emerged. It considered the whole of humankind the center, if not the god, of the universe. Renaissance literature celebrates this human centrality. Despite its immanence, humanism retained a measure of duality (humankind versus nature, though given the materialistic framework it was also humankind and nature, or even humankind in nature). However, this duality was quite tenuous, since the materialistic system is by definition monist and cannot sustain any duality. Matter is the ultimate center, anything else is a mere reflection of the movement of matter, a mere epiphenomenon. However, right from the beginning one could hear the angry rumblings of the true materialists, who knew the logic of matter, the law of nature, and the monism of the materialistic epistemological paradigms. Hobbes, Machiavelli, and later the philosophers of the Age of the Enlightenment announced that human beings are no different from vegetables or machines. Then came Darwin, Nietzsche, Engels, Freud, and Derrida, who all deconstructed humankind as we know it and reconstructed it in a way consistent with the laws of matter, the ultimate point of reference. The materialist outlook sees the universe as made up of atoms wandering in space, according to the mechanistic view, or as a coherent solid whole, according to the organic view, or otherwise of an amalgam of the two. The universe is controlled by complete, hard causality in the sense that A will always eventually lead to B. The whole universe is a continuum, whose circles are intertwined, with no gaps separating them. Creatures are subject to an evolutionary, progressive movement that is impervious to regression. That is why all creatures are subject to change since everything in the final analysis has ultimately the same essence – matter. In this world of matter, there is no substantial difference between humankind and nature. If humans were any different from nature, this would disrupt the continuum of the material natural order. That is why the materialist outlook stresses that the common features of humans and animals (perhaps even of inanimate objects) are much more important than those features that set them apart.

What this means is that human and natural phenomena form one continuous whole, the same laws applying to both, in equal degree. Human phenomena are not unique; they might be more complex, but they are ultimately governed by the same laws of matter that go beyond any religious, moral or human objectives. Human beings are thus an inseparable part of the material-natural order. Humans are natural beings (natural humans) who belong to nature, emerge from it, live within it and have no existence or will independent of it. Therefore, they are reduced to the world of nature-matter and its inexorable laws. They have no will or human purpose *(telos)* independent of the neutral motion of nature-matter, which is indifferent to them. The duality of humankind and nature, which forms the very basis of Western humanism, is thereby eradicated.

It may be noticed that this natural-material system started by drawing "natural" things from the world of humans to be placed in the world of things. Then humans themselves were drawn from the human sphere to be hurled into the world of natural laws. The modern Western epistemological materialist paradigm started by proclaiming the death of God in favor of the centrality of humankind, yet it ended with the decentering of humankind, leveling it down with nature and matter and "mute, insensate things."

This is the inner logic of materialist monism – that all creatures (human beings included) are subject to the same blind laws of things. This is the over-arching, central idea of the Western epistemological project: that there is one single law, one single culture, one single humanity, whose unity derives from the fact that it is an organic part of the natural system, having no existence outside it. This leads to the rise of the unity of science and knowledge (Muslims prefer to call it the "monism of science and knowledge") which fails to see any difference between humankind and nature.

Taking this paradigm as its point of departure, an epistemological and moral outlook was postulated and priorities were defined. Let it be noticed that the very movement of the materialist intellectual system is toward the eradication of the Creator–created duality and the humanistic human-nature duality. This is the ultimate demise of the metaphysics of transcendence and the final triumph of the metaphysics of immanence. Certain conclusions regarding the human mind follow from this initial monistic materialistic premise:

(1) The human mind is an inseparable part of nature-matter, and is able to register data received from it efficiently and objectively. However,

it is unable to go beyond it or be independent of it. Just like nature, the human mind is limitless, but it is also passive and neutral and lacks any independent boundaries. The attributes of the human mind are indeed the same as the attributes of nature.

(2) The human mind is able to register only the general, common traits of phenomena. Such features are natural-material, and they alone can guide the mind in its attempt to reach general abstract laws.

(3) Existence is material and therefore it can be perceived and understood in its entirety through the five senses. Anything else is a mere illusion. Consequently, reality (both human and natural) could be rationally gauged, and eventually subjected to a precise programming (this is the essence of technological utopia). The world becomes mere useful, desanctified matter. All things (human and natural) are seen as equal, which means that all things are relative.

(4) What is unknown in nature (both physical and human) will eventually become known through the gradual accumulation of data. The area of the unknown will diminish, and accordingly, the area of the known will gradually increase, a process which will eventually lead to a complete or semi-complete knowledge of reality (both material and human), which will lead in turn to a full or semi-full control of said reality.

(5) The human mind is able to recreate humankind and its social and material environment in such a way as to make it conform to general natural laws derived from the study of the world of nature and things. This is called "rationalization," i.e., the standardization of reality by imposing on it the monist materialist paradigm, so as to instrumentalize and control it completely, turning it into mere useful matter which can be utilized in the most efficient manner.

Leaving the epistemological system behind, let us now have a look at the moral system. Within the context of the materialist system, there is nothing sacred, absolute or teleological. The purpose of human existence in this universe is the accumulation of information leading to full control over the universe, the conquest of nature, and the maximum manipulation of its resources. In order to achieve this, everything (including humankind and nature) must be thrust into the net of hard causality so that they might be explained away and subjected to the laws of nature. Human beings, in this case, are not the vicegerents of God, nor are they honored by Him; they are, rather, mere natural, material beings.

Moral codes are non-existent, since the only purpose of life is profit and pleasure, in addition to the maximization of production and consumption. The cycle of production and consumption should go on unabated without a *telos*, in a fashion reminiscent of Nietzsche's "eternal return" or pagan cyclical history. An essential aspect of the materialist outlook often neglected by many Western and non-Western studies of modernity is that on the level of historical practice, the materialist outlook has translated itself in the form of Western imperialism. Human beings, as indicated earlier, were first placed at the center of the universe, arrogating to themselves the position of divinity. Therefore, in keeping with the metaphysics of immanence, they deemed themselves limitless, self-referential, bound by no values external to themselves. Power, accordingly, became the only criterion whereby human beings were classified. Therefore, rather than humanity in general being the center of the universe, Western (white) humans arrogated to themselves that position. Instead of a world run in such a way that it could benefit the whole human race, it became useful matter to be utilized by the white race for its advantage. Thus, humanism degenerated into imperialism. The troops of Western humans marched all over planet earth, perpetrating genocide against the native inhabitants of the American continents and transferring millions of native Africans from their homeland to be used as mere muscle power on American plantations. Thousands died in the process of this inhuman transfer and the rest were devastated after their arrival in the new world. Military forces were deployed all over the world, destroying indigenous economic, political, and cultural structures. Asia and Africa were transformed into sources of cheap labor, raw materials, and markets yielding high profits. Through direct military domination, the Old International Order was imposed on the world, only to give way to the New International Order that is being imposed through direct military domination complemented by the recruitment of the local ruling political and cultural elites in the service of Western interests.

BIASES OF THE MATERIALIST EPISTEMOLOGICAL PARADIGM

All the biases of the modern Western epistemological paradigm emanate from its materialist monism.

(1) Bias towards the material and natural at the expense of the immaterial and human is the most prominent. It manifests itself in the

attempt to explain what is human in terms of the natural and material. Humankind is thereby made amenable to control and quantification. Social phenomena are subjected to the methods of research used in the experimental and physical sciences themselves. The idea of the unity of science is an epistemological and moral manifestation of the eradication of the man-nature duality; it is the methodology through which materialist monism is imposed on all phenomena and the logic of material things is imposed on humankind; the whole world is reduced to one material dimension. The transition from the human to the natural results in a bias against teleology and in the discarding of the moral, psychological – or in short, the human – dimensions, since human beings are the only creatures in this universe known to have a free will and who seek to find a purpose in the world and the only ones who follow moral codes to organize their conduct. Then there arise deterministic theories that explain the whole universe, from humans to mosquitoes, in a scientific, deterministic manner. As for humankind's dreams, moral longings and free will, these are deemed non-scientific, and teleological.

(2) Within this framework, there is a bias toward the general at the expense of the particular. The dominant hypothesis is that the more a phenomenon is divested of its specificity and the higher the level of generalization, the more scientific and accurate we become. Phenomena have to be divested of any human or teleological specificities which form a gap in the natural continuum, till we ultimately reach a level of generalization said to be scientific and universal, where all gaps are filled and all dualities are eradicated.

This is the level at which the general may be attained. It is actually the law that links (indeed equates) the human with the natural, subjecting the former to the law of the latter. This means that the specific curve of any phenomenon, i.e., the specific characteristics that underlie its uniqueness, forms an obstacle to scientific study, since it slows the process of abstraction that ultimately leads to the attainment of general natural laws.

(3) There is a bias towards the perceptible, the measurable and the quantitative against the imperceptible, the qualitative, and that which cannot be measured. Western science has limited the scope of research to the world of the five senses. This explains its relative disregard for the complex, the qualitative and the indefinite. That which cannot be observed by the five senses, easily measured and subjected to statistical quan-

tification thus falls outside the scope of modern science. Moral and teleological issues should then be discarded and neglected, for they don't fit in that mold.

(4) There is a bias toward the simple, the mono-dimensional, and the homogeneous against the complex, the multifaceted, and the heterogeneous. Thus there is a bias toward simple interpretations that reduce phenomena to one or two variables or principles. Human conduct is interpreted via simple models. This explains the distinct predilection in favor of causal monism (explaining phenomena in terms of one decisive cause) that is inextricably bound up with the unity of sciences and materialist monism. There is, therefore, an obsessive search for a single center immanent in matter and for a single reason that would explain the universe and that can be taken as the basic core and reference of all. This center is, more often than not, identified as an economic variable (material utility [Bentham] – profit making and accumulation of wealth [Adam Smith] – the development and growth of the tools of production [Marx]). It might also take other forms, such as Freud's *eros*, Carlyle's heroes, the Nazis' Aryan race, or the promised land of the Zionists. This causal monism originating from materialist monism reflects a powerful rejection of "the different Other," since the presence of the Other necessarily means the diversity of paradigms and human laws.

(5) There is bias toward the objective against the subjective. Objectivity means that the researchers have to divest themselves of their own specificities, moral obligations, passions, and human totality, turning their minds into a blank sheet (*tabula rasa*) that registers 'facts' and observes details with complete detachment and passivity. Phenomena under investigation are turned into mere objects. This objectivity extends to human phenomena, which the objective researcher has to observe with complete detachment and neutrality. Human beings become an object of study no different from natural objects. This leads to disregarding inner motives that the human subjects, consciously or unconsciously, project on phenomena surrounding them.

It should be observed, however, that causal monism manifests itself in an oscillation between two poles. First, there is the quest for method and neutrality in procedures and a wish to arrive at simple, general laws devoid of any teleology. These laws thrust everything into the iron cage of monistic causality and absolute continuity that cannot be disrupted at any point and that leaves no gaps. Of course, such an attempt is doomed to failure, particularly when human phenomena are the subject of study. Absolute objectivity is therefore replaced by an equally absolute subjectivity which leads to a denial of the existence of general laws and to a belief in complete discontinuity, since subject is completely divorced from object. In other words, humankind moves from materialist rationalism (modernity and the enlightenment) into materialist irrationalism (postmodernism and nihilism) and what one historian of Western ideas has termed the "dark enlightenment." It is to be noted that this oscillation takes place between two varieties of monism: the monism of reason, hard causality and absolute control, and its extreme opposite, the monism of unreason, fluid non-causality, and total loss of control.

Bias against the teleological, the specific, the complex, and the subjective is necessarily a bias against distinct human features in favor of natural materialist features. Other types of bias emanating from the materialist paradigm can be seen within this framework: bias toward motion against stillness, toward accumulation and continuity against discontinuity, and toward the straight line and the full circle against curving, zigzag lines and incomplete forms.

(6) This anti-human bias is also reflected in the structure of terminology. The optimal terminology is the general, the accurate, the quantitative, the descriptive, and the non-figurative. Terms are quite often borrowed from the description of natural objects, and then applied to the realm of the human. Based on all these biases toward the precise against the ambiguous, all sciences attempt to be exact in order to fill any gaps that might disrupt the postulated natural material continuum. Accordingly, the language of algebra becomes the model, wherein there is no gap between the signifier and the signified, or the name and the named, wherein A is A, and B is B. The result is an increasing tendency toward the use of a mathematical paradigm which seeks to represent reality in terms of numbers and quantities, in both the physical and the human sciences.

The researcher has to rely on tools of quantification as questionnaires, statistical indices, mathematical models, etc. This can be achieved only by splitting up the coherent totality of phenomena, atomizing and anatomizing them, reducing them to their basic components and specifics in a way that transforms their internal qualitative uniqueness into external quantitative properties.

(7) Furthermore, it should be noted that the bias in favor of precise definitions and the requirement that a definition be exclusive and inclusive is also a form of bias in favor of Western terminology. The modern Western epistemological project is the only one in the world that has developed its theoretical framework, its methodology as well as its research procedures and tools. It is also supported by a large number of cultural, political, and military research institutions that are able to document any idea, propagate any concept, and ban or marginalize any piece of information. By contrast, all alternative epistemological projects (including the Islamic) are still in the formative stage. Despite the presence of an Islamic world outlook, it has not yet been developed into a theoretical framework for conducting research, with all the other elements concomitant with it (research tools, case studies, and a body of information investigated and analyzed from an Islamic point of view). This is the nature of the present moment in our civilization, the moment of a new birth of alternative paradigms. (The same applies to intellectual dissent in Western civilization. It is represented only by a handful of thinkers and thus still lacks an integrated theoretical system and powerful supportive research institutes to adopt, develop, and defend its theses.) Insisting on complete clarity as well as precise, inclusive-exclusive definitions (especially when it comes to human phenomena) would necessarily lead to the adoption of Western concepts and terminology. A degree of ambiguity should then be acceptable (bearing in mind that ambiguity is not synonymous with vagueness in much the same way as complexity is not synonymous with contradiction), as should procedural definitions and initial interpretive hypotheses. Once our epistemological paradigm with its terminological structure reaches a level of crystallization on a par with the level reached by the Western epistemological system, it will then be possible to demand more precise definitions (which need not be exact in the Western sense).

The bias against the teleological, the particular and the non-continuous (and in favor of the non-teleological, the general, the materialist monist, the exact, etc.) is meant to expedite the process leading to a full control of reality. For that which can be subjected to materialist monism can be readily reduced, simplified, standardized, and thrust into the network of hard causality. On the other hand, that which cannot be subjected to this reductive process resists instrumentalization and is thus usually marginalized, placed in categories such as "unnatural," "not important," "anarchist," "not a fit subject for research," etc.

MANIFESTATIONS OF THE BIASES OF THE MATERIALIST EPISTEMOLOGICAL PARADIGM

1. *Material Progress: The Central Bias*

"Progress" is the cornerstone of Western modernity. Modernization takes place for the sake of progress; development serves progress, construction and destruction projects, five-year plans, drastic changes. etc. – all are done in the name of that magical entity known as "progress." Ask a child in a narrow alley in a small town in Cairo or on a wide avenue in New York, an old man on a boulevard in Paris, or a young man driving a truck on a highway in China, all would agree that we have to progress, for without progress we would perish.

Let us have a look at Damanhur, my hometown in Egypt. There is a general consensus that some kind of progress in this small town has been achieved. Look, for instance, at the number of telephone lines used, the size of roads, the number of cars, the amount of protein consumed, the pace of life, etc., all of which point to a definite degree of progress achieved; and yet and yet … In my early childhood, children used to go out in the afternoon to make beautiful colorful kites which they would fly in the then blue sky. Mothers would make us balls from old socks that had been darned many times over. We all played together, for everyone, rich or poor, could make himself a kite or a ball from old socks. Therefore, the moment of play was also a real moment of freedom from class conflict and social inequality (even for a few moments). Nowadays, play time escalates class conflict, since poor children still play with kites and old sock balls, whereas the rich ones buy Fisher-Price battery-operated toys, then watch them passively as the toys do all the playing on their own. The toy (the thing) becomes the center of activity, and man becomes a passive recipient (a thing). With rising levels of progress, video games are being gradually introduced. They are considered the highest point of progress yet attained, but they also generate a sense of solitude and alienation never before experienced. The human being (*al-insān* in Arabic) is the one who seeks the company of others (*yasta'nis*). In other words, these games abort a very important aspect of a person's humanness.

The tension level in Damanhur was much lower when I was a young boy. Most of the people had afternoons free and were, therefore, able to communicate and socialize. Does the shortage of spare time explain the increase of tension? Or is it the pollution of land, sea, and air? Is it the gradual disintegration of the traditional family structure that used to provide people with a reasonable degree of security? Perhaps it is the noise that vehicles produce day and night. What happened to the clean and tilled parks of Damanhur (all now covered with cement) where we used to listen to music? Where is the fish park (with gold fish in some of its basins)? Where is the Municipal Club, where a gas station now stands? And the Arboretum which included a large number of rare plants? All were swept away by "the inevitable course of progress."

In the evenings, we used to sit on the roof to sing songs, tell horror stories or commit our human share of sins. We had time to watch the stars or just sit and chat. In our routine dealings, we experienced how the whole community was based on solidarity, not contract. In Ramadan evenings, along would come Mohammed al-Aʿwar, the newspaper vendor, who in Ramadan acted as *al-misaḥarātī*, the man who played his drum and sang to wake us up for the *suḥūr*, the pre-dawn meal. He sang pretty folk songs and once told me the story of a camel in Madinah the Luminous (*al-Madinah al-Munawwarah*) which ran away from the butcher who tried to slaughter it and sought asylum with the Prophet, who granted it protection. Since then the camel has become one of the images etched in my imagination. During the last ten days of Ramadan, al-Aʿwar sang his farewell song to the holy month: "Nothing is left but farewell. Nothing is left but the beautiful." My late mother would wake me up before *suḥūr* to listen to him. The man would stand on the road with his assistant holding a lantern in hand and a name list in the other. I would listen as my name was called, then go back to sleep and dream.

A realist who has lost the ability to dream, revolt, and change reality needn't tell me that I am a romantic dreamer. I know how harsh life is in Damanhur for the poor and the oppressed; but I also know that human evil cannot be overcome by material progress (as imagined by some simplistic materialists). I know that Damanhur was not a paradise, but instead of such infantile polarization of past and present, and instead of succumbing to material reality, we need desperately to open the gate of ijtihad in order to understand the epistemological biases underlying the

Western concept of progress, then count the gains and losses, the price and the prize.

To start with, it should be realized that the concept of material progress is the cornerstone of the modern materialist Western epistemological outlook. It is the ultimate point of reference, the very *telos* of existence, and the answer it provides to such ultimate questions asked by the human being as: Who am I? What is the purpose of my existence? Is it the recommendation of virtue and the condemnation of vice (from an Islamic perspective), is it moral discrimination between good and evil (from a humanistic perspective), or is it rather the escalation of the cycle of production and consumption, selling and buying, profit-making and the pursuit of pleasure? The concept of progress within the context of the modern Western outlook has a definite starting point and is characterized by some salient features.

(a) Like most other modern Western philosophical and epistemological concepts, the concept of progress is dependent on the concept of nature-matter. Progress, like natural laws, is an inevitable process that takes place despite the will of individuals and can in no way be contravened.

(b) Progress is a unilinear process that follows a natural law that applies to all societies at all times, in all spheres of life, in a homogeneous sequence.

(c) The concept of progress presupposes the existence of a single human history rather than a common humanity that manifests itself in a variety of historical and cultural forms. Hence, the belief that what is good for one historical and cultural formation is good for the others, and which we might term "historical Pantheism."

(d) Progress may take place according to various sequential developmental stages that differ in their details; however, they lead ultimately to the same objectives and achieve the same goals.

(e) Western societies, particularly those of Western Europe, are considered the peak of this universal, evolutionary, unilinear, natural process and are, therefore, the model to be imitated.

(f) The idea of progress is based on the assumption that human knowledge can be accumulated indefinitely.

(g) With the accumulation of knowledge, human control over reality increases steadily.

(h) Natural resources are not limited or finite.

(i) The human mind is infinite and limitless, which makes infinite and limitless progress possible.

However, there are dark aspects to this idea of progress that need to be pointed out:

(a) Many of the assumptions on which the Western materialistic concept of progress is based have been proven invalid. It has been discovered that natural resources are limited, the human mind is finite, and mobility could be detrimental to one's psychological health.

(b) Even on the level of theory, the concept of progress has many sinister aspects (from a human and a humanistic point of view). Like nature–matter, the process of progress has no human or teleological objective and no definite moral content. Progress, after all, is a mere movement or process. A human being usually moves from one place to another with a purpose or objective, but in the materialist Western concept, progress is merely an aimless process (or a process that leads to the production, then consumption of material goods, *ad infinitum* on the level of theory and *ad nauseam* on the level of practice).

(c) Progress becomes self-referential, which means it becomes an end in itself. We then begin to progress simply to achieve more progress. Progress, therefore, is not only a predetermined course, it is also an ultimate value.

(d) This frantic, purposeless movement is actually neither neutral nor innocent. Since a human is defined as a natural being with natural materialist (general) needs, progress (like nature-matter) is indifferent to traditional (ethnic, religious or moral) specificities and is defined as the maximization of (material) profit and pleasure (to the exclusion of other ends).

This accounts for the fact that indices of progress are defined in general materialist terms such as the number of telephone lines used, the number of cars and their speed, the length of roads and the frequency of human mobility (the more mobile the human is, the more "advanced"). Such criteria often focus on measurable and quantifiable objects; values that cannot be quantified or measured are discarded.

The idea of progress, considered a natural general law, and the West regarded as the peak of progress, both lead to the tacit acceptance of the premise that the epistemological paradigm underlying the modern Western cultural formation is superior and universal and that it is the standard norm to be adopted by all societies. The values and objectives of Western human beings, rooted in their specific historical and social experience, are projected onto the whole world, a process which inevitably leads to a wholesale application of Western theories to all sociocultural formations without regard for the specificities of each society and the rich diversity of different cultures. This results in disregard for non-Western socio-historical experiences and the significance of the non-Western Other, who is banished outside the boundaries of science and history or even outside the boundaries of existence (not in a literal material sense, but in the sense of a distinctive existence that manifests a specific identity).

The whole world, excluding Western Europe and North America, is referred to as non-Western and gradually, all the non-Western nations are adopting the Western model and using the Western paradigm to evaluate themselves. It is a form of cultural genocide that came on the heels of the physical genocide of the indigenous populations of North America, Australia, New Zealand, and some parts of Africa.

In a television interview in an Arab country, I heard the manager of the national airline say that the frequency of individuals' mobility is a sign of progress. After referring to international rates of mobility in "advanced" countries, he added solemnly, "God willing, we will reach this rate soon."

Stemming from such foolish, parrot-like mimicking of the Other's epistemological paradigms, Western technology is avidly and blindly copied without realizing the real price of this type of "progress." The close association between this technology on the one hand and the value system and culture of the producing societies, on the other, is also overlooked. It must be remembered that technology is not merely machines and equipment; rather, it is the creative generating power used to develop the methods of production and to improve the means of dealing with the environment to satisfy human needs. It is, therefore, only transferable within these narrow limits. The concept of gross national product, dominant in most, if not all, countries of the world, manifests a material concept of progress with its underlying bias against social, environmental, moral and psychological considerations. Concepts associated with the idea of progress, such as "raising the standard of living" and "improving the national income," are tied up with the Western materialist epistemological paradigm.

It is therefore time to calculate the price of progress. It should be

THE GATE OF IJTIHAD

noticed that the fruits of progress are immediate, perceptible and quantifiable. The price, however, is delayed, initially imperceptible, and cannot be easily quantified. Similarly, the fruit of progress is interwoven with its price, which is why our indices of progress have to be changed and broadened. Let us have a glance at the various ills resulting from "progress."

- trivial commodities which add nothing to one's knowledge and deepen one's sense of alienation;
- disintegration of family life;
- the way we deal with senior citizens;
- decrease of time spent with one's family;
- the shrinking of direct human communication because of the use of the computer and similar equipment;
- psychological ailments such as depression;
- increasing crime and violence in the so-called "advanced societies";
- escalated spending on armaments and other means of destruction (it is historically unprecedented that what humankind spends on means of destruction far exceeds what it spends on means of production);
- the possibility of destroying our planet either suddenly (through nuclear weapons) or gradually (through pollution);
- the impact of tourism and mobility on the social fabric of societies, on their cultural heritage, and on the environment;
- a growing sense of inability to perceive reality and change it (post-Modernism);
- a growing sense of alienation, loneliness and estrangement;
- drug addiction;
- pornography (the material cost of producing it and the moral, human, and ultimately material costs of its consumption).

Let us monitor all of these negative effects and attempt to quantify their material and moral cost. Take, for example, family disintegration and the resultant absence of adequate family care for children (especially infants). This disintegration exacts a heavy toll on society (rising levels of anxiety among children and adolescents, school vandalism, juvenile delinquency, a rising need for costly psychological therapy, etc.).

At the same time, let us undertake a radical shift by including happiness and a sense of security among our indices of progress. An immediate counter-argument will claim that such values are relative, changeable, subjective, and cannot be measured, whereas progress should be objectively measured. Does this mean that progress is one thing, and happiness and security are another? If so, then what does progress achieve for humankind – materialist expansion, or human fulfillment? At this moment, the concept of progress is revealing its true materialist nature; instead of indices derived from the human realm (happiness and security), indices derived from the world of things (speed, productivity, etc.) are adopted, without regard for whether they realize happiness or cause misery to humankind.

Even at the materialist level, there are problems. In this respect, I would like to put forward a new analytical concept which is implicit in many studies, but perhaps never named, namely, the concept of "cosmic regress versus industrial progress." Ever since the Renaissance Western humans have been propagating the idea of progress, underscoring its immediate and obvious benefits. Yet the delayed, not so clear negative results which have lately become manifest, were either downplayed or completely disregarded. Among these is the destructive impact of progress on the environment. This is but one example of "cosmic regress." The adjective "cosmic" here indicates the whole planet earth, not any particular geographical area, and the whole human race, not a particular people or race, are threatened with destruction. Therefore, rates of industrial progress must be counted against the average of cosmic regress, namely, the damage caused by industrial progress to planet earth and mankind, remembering that the West is the region that profits most from this "progress," whereas the whole world has to foot the bill. Therefore, the balance sheet of progress has to take into consideration such ecological phenomena as the depletion of the ozone layer, pollution, nuclear waste, the green-house effect, the increase of carbon dioxide, etc.

Such a complex, far-sighted method of calculating gains and losses has already been adopted in evaluating pesticides. At one point, the amount of pesticides used was an indication of "progress." Later on, however, it was discovered that the damage they cause to the environment (cosmic regress) far exceeds their immediate economic benefit. Thus, the UN Food and Agricultural Organization, which once encouraged the use of pesticides, began advising against them; the use of pesticides which once was an indicator of progress became an indicator of backwardness. Hence, the balance sheet of progress, materialistic and economistic as it is, will never be precise so long as it neglects the cost of cosmic regress.

Some statistics estimate that the real cost of an industrial project is negative if the indirect environmental costs are taken into consideration. The Western industrial project has achieved success only because others are footing the environmental bill. The fact that some countries have managed to catch up with Western levels of production and consumption accounts for the high frequency of sad news about natural catastrophes (floods, long hot summers, cancer, etc.)

The new thought of the Greens and other environmental rights activists with their theories of sustainable growth (growth that does not harm the environment and its natural resources, and which therefore can sustain future generations) is an indication of the growing recognition of the heavy price of progress. It is hoped that such a critical attitude may succeed in spurring people to discover new forms of industry that are less burdensome on human beings and their environment.

2. *Darwinism (or Nietzscheanism)*

The cult of progress reveals its materialist face through a set of governing values that control the life of the secular human being such as "the struggle for survival," "survival of the fittest or the strongest," "man is a wolf to his brother man," "ethics is a mere ploy used by the weak to undermine the strong," and the glorification of the strong man or "the superman." Values such as these stem from the materialist Western outlook that reached its peak in the works of Darwin and Nietzsche. They make no distinction between the world of humankind and the world of nature-matter; on the contrary, they underscore the fact that the materialistic biological values of conflict and struggle govern both nature and humans, both the jungle and human culture. Physical (biological) survival, according to this outlook, is the ultimate purpose *(telos)* of life on earth. The only vehicle of evolution is permanent, fierce conflict; the only arbiter for both humankind and nature is power, for it forms the overall epistemological and moral framework.

3. *The Market-Factory Metaphor*

The same Darwinian-Nietzschean materialist perspective expresses itself in the form of a key metaphor synonymous with the concept of nature-matter, namely, the view of the world as a market and a factory. It is an outlook that originates from materialist monism, where everything becomes useful matter. The whole world is like a machine and the purpose of existence is to control everything and utilize it; both physical nature, which is seen as raw material *(natura naturata)* and human nature, are seen as mere productive energy. Commodities are produced to be sent to the market, where people are seen as a mere purchasing power that buys commodities and consumes them. The mechanism of the market and commodities presupposes a predictable, standardized world and an equally predictable, standardized human who is subject to firm, inexorable laws. The best that economic humans can achieve is to produce in order to consume and consume in order to produce, serving only their own interests and struggling against others, unburdened by any ethical or epistemological values or traditions. Just like nature-matter, the market-factory is a rigid entity that moves inexorably forward, impervious to human teleologies as well as to all human values.

4. The Central State

One of the most important types of bias stemming from the Western epistemological paradigm is the bias in favor of the secular central nation or state. This bias is associated with the concepts of rationalization, progress, control and unity of sciences. With the belief in the unity of sciences and the mind's ability to accumulate information and recreate reality in accordance with natural law, the belief was reinforced that science could guide societies and rationalize them. The central state was believed to be the supreme agency to realize this objective by means of comprehensive plans to unify, standardize, and quantify social reality, eliminating all ethnic and linguistic enclaves so as to control and utilize this reality and to develop the infrastructure necessary for the achievement of all of these goals in both the material and the human spheres. In the material sphere, the market is unified, roads are built, and measurements are standardized. In the human sphere, central, specialized bureaucracies are established to orient individuals to become citizens and transcend all other loyalties, owing allegiance only to the state. In this respect, it could be said that the citizen is but a variation on the natural and economic human, a one-dimensional entity that can be explained within the framework of materialist and causal monism.

This means that the state itself stems from the concept of nature-matter and materialist monism. This is but another manifestation of the eradication of the human-nature duality and of the continuous movement towards a natural materialist monism which robs human society of its vitality, transforming it into a huge machine whose movement can be readily predicted since it follows general laws and central plans.

It is noteworthy that the state always prefers to deal with macro units rather than with the micro units of family and local groups, because bureaucracies cannot deal with specific and unique units. It can deal with humans only insofar as they are public citizens, with generalized needs and predetermined dreams, not with humans as private individuals with specific needs and unpredictable dreams. Therefore, it is understandably biased in favor of the external at the expense of the internal, the contractual at the expense of human solidarity, and the public at the expense of the private.

The so-called sovereign individual (the citizen-natural human) – divorced from any groups or institutions (such as the family) which would mediate between him and a monolithic state – becomes the only social unit. Nevertheless, these sovereign individuals gain their identity and self-image through the market, the media, or organizations (schools, five-year plans, government agencies, etc.) which carefully orchestrate needs and aspirations of human beings and plan their dreams for them. In other words, they fall an easy prey to prefabricated self-images and dreams.

5. *An International Consumerist Culture*

One of the most dangerous results of the materialist Western epistemological paradigm is what might be called "the materialist consumerist international culture." This is a culture with Western (or American) origins, but its forms are neutral in the sense that they have no distinctive color, flavor or character. This quasi-international culture has its specific products such as the hamburger, a type of standardized food cooked exactly the same way, leaving no room for personal creativity. It is a type of food that one eats alone, perhaps while walking (just like the natural human). There are also blue jeans, which consist of a piece of coarse blue cloth, preferably tattered. They are considered very practical since one can wear them for almost every occasion. There is also the T-shirt on which is printed an advertisement (Drink Coca-Cola), a statement of identity ("I Love Cairo"), an attitude ("I Love Blondes"), etc. Regardless of the content of the statement, it presupposes that the human is just a space that moves, a purely externalized creature whose external appearance is the same as his/her internal reality, whose surface and skin are the same as his/her depths and conscience. An additional example can be found in disco music, Batman and Rambo. Most of these cultural products originated in the USA but developed their own autonomy and dynamism, acquiring gradually all the traits of nature-matter with its indifference to human specificity and inner being.

The danger behind this culture lies in the fact that it panders to something latent in human beings, that is, their infantile desire to lose the very boundaries that define their identity and to retreat from the complex world of tragedy and comedy, self-transcendence and moral choices to the simple, one-dimensional world of hamburgers, T-shirts, and Batman, none of which belongs to any time or any place and all of which are devoid of historical, moral or human content. Such a consumerist culture is not only hostile to Oriental civilization; it is likewise hostile to Western civilization itself, and to any cultural forms that aspire to transcend the material and natural (which is why I term this consumerist culture "anti-culture").

MECHANISMS FOR SURMOUNTING BIAS

Having studied the various types of bias, particularly bias in favor of the modern Western epistemological and cultural paradigm, let me suggest some of the mechanisms that can help one surmount such biases.

I. *Realizing the Inevitability of Bias*

We started off by stressing the first premise, namely, the inevitability of bias. It can be argued that realizing this simple fact is in itself the first step toward overcoming it, for if we become aware of bias, we do not accept "facts" passively, believing in their absolute objectivity. Denial of the very existence of bias is intrinsically biased in favor of a specific materialistic perspective which views the human mind, and man in general, as an inseparable part of the natural system, an ineffective and passive entity, not independent from the laws of nature. The simple mind of the human being is seen as entering into a simple mechanical relationship with a simple reality.

However, this is a false image; the mind of the human being is undoubtedly limited, yet it is active. It does not transcribe reality in a passive, objective way; rather, it encounters a complex, diverse reality, then engages in a process of deconstruction and reconstruction, for it includes and magnifies some of these aspects, excluding or marginalizing others, and eventually abstracting an epistemological paradigm through which it perceives the world. As such, the human mind achieves a degree of independence for humankind from the laws of nature immanent in matter. This means that perception of the same reality differs from one person to another according to one's individual experiences, cultural heritage, historical memories, symbolic and semiotic systems, aesthetic and moral values, etc. All of this makes individual and collective bias inevitable. In this sense, recognition of bias implies rejection of the notion that reality and the mind are simple and that there are general abstract laws that can be applied indiscriminately to nature and to all human beings regardless of their cultural and social contexts. It is an affirmation of the creativity and vitality of the human mind and of the complexity of its motivation; it is a defense of the centrality of humankind against infantile materialist philosophies that proclaim the unity (and monism) of nature-matter and draw a picture of a faceless universe, not fundamentally different from a human's condition when still an embryo before becoming a full human being, a *homo sapiens*.

There is nothing new in what I am claiming. The human sciences, no matter how objective, reflect certain biases. This is a well-known fact in the social sciences, tacitly or explicitly accepted by the majority of the practitioners in this field. Only extreme behaviorists, operating in terms of the abstract general laws of nature-matter, would deny the inevitability of bias.

Moreover, it is admitted by many that the philosophical formulations of the laws of physics as well as the classification and interpretation of some of the conclusions of scientific experiments are biased. Such formulations are used in interpreting scientific experiments, after which they are considered an organic part of scientific law, even though there might be no necessary relationship between the scientific experiment and the philosophical formulation of physical laws. If physicists look at the movement of an atom and see that it moves in a way that does not follow any familiar pattern, they can then state that "the universe is chaotic and subject to chance." By contrast, they can also state that "the human mind is limited, however vital, and therefore incapable of full comprehension of the universe." Because of the materialist atheist monist paradigm underlying Western science, the first formulation, emphasizing the ideas of chaos and chance, has gained currency even though the latter has more explanatory power. It is even more "scientific" since it leaves the door wide open for ijtihad and creative thinking. Unlike the claim in the former statement, the latter does not allege that all the experiments needed for the observation of the movement of the atom have already been conducted or that the available measurement tools are the best possible.

Among the distinctive features of Western analytical categories is that they operate almost exclusively on the political, economic, and social levels; they hardly ever reach the epistemological premises underlying human discourse which form answers to the ultimate questions facing humankind such as: "What is progress?" or "What is its human content?" Such questions are hardly ever asked except in moments of crisis. Instead, people ask: "How can progress be achieved? How can it be attained?" The last set of questions assumes progress as an unquestioned category, a kind of *a priori* or absolute *donnée* which uniformly turns out, on closer scrutiny, to be the materialist monist paradigm. If our analytical discourse goes deeper to the epistemological level and if we ask questions such as, "What is the goal of progress?", "What is the ideal a given society is trying to realize?" and, "Is progress effective on both the material and human levels, or on the material level alone?", the epistemological paradigm underlying the Western concept of progress will reveal its more sinister aspects.

II. *Comprehensive Criticism*

Our theoretical effort to discover bias should never stop at the partial level of practice, but must include the whole theoretical structure of Western philosophy. We end up "patching up," that is, borrowing concepts from here and there, where the modern Western outlook is applied in one field and not in another. This sometimes takes the form of borrowing Western concepts while modifying only some aspects of their moral and epistemological content and at others, trying to prove that the borrowed Western concept has a parallel version in our heritage so as to justify its adoption. This is a process of retroactive Westernization, since it leads to a wholesale adoption of Western epistemological paradigms, though the terminology has been changed and the rationale for adoption has been altered.

The process of patching up is based on the belief that the modern Western outlook is natural, universal, and ultimate, and accordingly all that is needed is to embellish it, or perhaps rearrange some of its components. A more radical, complex and comprehensive outlook should be based on the assumption that there is no single historical or cultural course. There are, rather, numerous different historical and cultural courses, based on different premises and operating within different frameworks. Such a pluralistic outlook can only be reached through a comprehensive study of the Western cultural formation in relation to other formations.

III. *Highlighting the Inadequacies of the Western Epistemological Paradigm*

Emancipation from the hegemony of the Western epistemological paradigm requires that we highlight some of its shortcomings. The following are some examples.

1. A Paradigm Hostile to Man

It should be noticed that the modern Western epistemological paradigm implies anti-human tendencies, since it does not recognize humankind as a distinctive phenomenon in the universe or the human mind as a creative, vital force. Human beings are denied any centrality in the world (their vicegerency from God, if we were to use the Islamic idiom). This assumption runs counter not only to our view of ourselves as responsible and free beings, but also to our very concrete, existential experience. It is hard to believe that there is no substantial difference between humankind and the larva, that they are in the final analysis (as the materialists claim) one and the same, and that humankind can be reduced to the level at which one and the same law applies to all beings. When we recognize no differences, dualities or hierarchy, we should also know that we are in the leveling world of materialist monism, where the general and the natural replace the particular and the human.

All unique human boundaries collapse, along with human identity and the complex world that contains Self and Other, and wherein human beings exist as responsible creatures who choose between good and evil.

A faceless, flat universe with no boundaries emerges, for materialist monism cannot cope with complexities, boundaries, multiple levels and identities, i.e., it cannot cope with what distinguishes human beings as human beings and what sets them apart from all other beings. The Western epistemological project denies not only the existence of God; it likewise denies the existence of humankind. The death of God, so proudly proclaimed, is actually a proclamation of the death of humankind.

2. The Western Cultural and Epistemological Project is Impossible to Realize

It should be noted that the Western project for bridging the gap separating humankind from nature (so as to reach general laws that would explain all phenomena) is both superficial and impossible. Epistemologically, this paradigm presupposes the simplicity of the human mind, of the reality the mind perceives, of the linguistic signifier, of the human signified, and finally of the relation between the two. It also presupposes that the gradual accumulation of knowledge will lead to a general diminution of the unknown and a gradual expansion of the area of the known, and that the unknown is ultimately knowable. An arrogant conclusion follows from all of these simplistic initial premises: that humankind's knowledge, and therefore control, of reality will be complete at some point. It would be generous to call this hypothesis infantile and ridiculous. A desultory glance at the world at the present time would be sufficient to rebut the initial premises and the conclusions based on them.

The Western epistemological paradigm attempts to reach a level of generalization unwarranted by the level of knowledge attained at the moment of generalization. Take the concept of "social class," which Marx defined on the basis of such materialist criteria as income and the tools and relations of production. This analytical concept is an expression of the attempt to reach a so-called scientific term: precise, universal, general, quantitative, that disregards any teleological aspects and does not appeal in any way to a concept of human nature.

Marx and Engels did not know much about the rest of the world when they developed the concept of "class." Worse still, it seems that Marx's knowledge about the nature of the social and political structure in an Eastern European country such as Poland was meager. The term was, however, treated as a concept of universal applicability. Later on, when

Marx started to learn more about the Orient, he discovered social structures dissimilar to those he was familiar with. He then resorted to a Hegelian formula on the basis of which he referred to modes of production in China, India, Persia, Japan, Egypt, etc. as "the Asiatic mode of production." This ridiculous classification is tantamount to saying, "I really know almost nothing about the Orient, but I'll still go ahead and make some generalizations about it." Imagine some scholar trying to understand the long and complex history of China, India, Egypt, and Japan in light of this sweeping Marxist generalization. Would he understand anything? Would this concept be of any analytical or explanatory value?

On the practical level, the Western cultural project – based on the ideas of control of resources, maximization of production and consumption, and continuous infinite progress – has run into what I call a "cosmic wall." If the peoples of the Occident, who make up only a small percentage of the world population (20%), consume more than 80% of the world's natural resources,[8] this means that said project is a model which can be neither imitated nor repeated. To make my point clear, let us imagine that China and India adopted such a paradigm for development. It would naturally translate itself into a life style characterized by ever increasing levels of production and consumption. Imagine the cars used by one-third of the world's population, now that they have become "advanced," starting to burn fuel and oxygen! Then imagine Brazil embarking on the same course of action: the Brazilians would be obliged, in their own national interest and to sustain their own life style, to fell the rain forests which produce one-third of the earth's oxygen! This is undoubtedly a sure recipe for the suffocation of the entire human race.

3. Studying the Crisis of Modern Western Civilization

It is now imperative that we develop a general theory of the crisis of Western civilization and the Western paradigm of a materialist modernity. If the modern West has achieved its absoluteness and centrality through the material and cultural victories and successes it achieved at the early stages of its development, it is now time to reexamine critically these victories and successes, highlighting the shortcomings that became more pronounced through the varied applications of the materialist paradigm over a long period of time. It could be argued that since the late 1960s, the main features of this paradigm have more or less fully emerged and the different links of the paradigmatic sequence have been realized. It has ceased to be a mere utopian ideology or a set of ideas to be propagated; it has now become a cultural material structure whose intended, positive results in the short term have been observed, as well as its unintended, negative results in the long term. Many Western thinkers have given up their optimism regarding Western modernity, and Western civilization has lost a great deal of the self-confidence it had till the First World War. It also has lost the sense of its centrality and universality. This is quite natural and expected in view of the intensifying crisis of Western modernity (two world wars, amassing weapons of mass destruction, the ecological crisis, and an increasing sense of alienation on the part of Western man from himself and his environment). Till recently such issues were talked about only by poets in their poems, novelists in their novels, and scholars in their specialized academic papers. Since the late 1960s, however, these issues have become daily items in the media.

The crisis of Western civilization is not a figment of our imagination, nor is it a revolutionary fabrication of the "Third World". It is a theme found in the writings of such Western thinkers as Spengler, Toynbee, and many others. This crisis is manifested in all fields of knowledge and has to be studied thoroughly in its various aspects so that we may arrive at a cogent explanation of the crisis. To achieve this objective, the following questions might be asked:

- Is there a relationship between pornography (the desanctification of the human being), environmental pollution, and the amassing of enough weapons of mass destruction to destroy the world several times over (desanctification of the universe)?
- Is there a relationship between materialist rationalism and the Holocaust? Is not the Holocaust but an application of the principle of material utility to human beings such that the handicapped, the Slavs and the Jews ("useless eaters" as classified by the Nazis) were to be exterminated as useless matter, with survival granted only to the useful and productive?
- Is there a way out of this crisis, or is it "historically inevitable" given the materialist utilitarian premise of modern Western civilization?

4. The Paradigmaticality of Aberrations

After examining the Western epistemological paradigm and its crisis, its various manifestations need to be investigated. Let me here raise the issue of what are termed "mere aberrations of modern Western civilization," namely, some negative phenomena which are associated with it but which are classified as mere aberrations by historians of Western civilization. Among such aberrations are the Western imperialist formation, Nazism and Zionism.

Among the most important mechanisms for overcoming bias is to discover the paradigms underpinning these aberrations. For in point of fact, such aberrations, far from being exceptional irregularities, are actually an organic part of the underlying paradigm of modern Western civilization, and an inevitable outcome of its application to reality. In other words, the so-called aberration is actually consistent with the inner logic of the paradigm

One of the most effective ways to discover the real nature of modern Western civilization and its underlying paradigm is to study Western imperialism. Such a study might be carried out on the basis of the following question:

> Is it at all possible to separate the prosperity and continuous growth of Western societies from the Western imperialist project which divided up the whole world, then plundered it? This plundering process is historically unprecedented both in scope and method. The total amount of what England plundered from India far exceeds the former's gross production during the entire Industrial Revolution. Great Britain not only benefited economically from its colonies, it also exported its social problems to them, including its human surplus (unemployed workers), undesirable religious and ethnic minorities (notably the Jews), criminals who threatened the social fabric, and individuals who had failed to achieve social mobility. All were exported to the Orient together with a huge amount of commodities. Add to all this the manpower, expertise, cheap raw material and antiquities robbed by the colonizing powers. We can also add the oxygen burned and the carbon monoxide which accumulated in the atmosphere between the mid-19th Century (the beginning of the industrial

revolution) and the mid-20th Century (the beginning of industrialization in the Third World). This depletion of natural resources imposed severe limits on Third World countries' ability to develop themselves in the age of ecological crisis and the awareness of the limitedness of these resources. Given these and other facts, can we then separate the so-called "capitalist accumulation," considered the basis of Western progress and "take off," from "imperialist accumulation"? Studying the Western cultural and epistemological paradigm in isolation from the phenomenon of imperialism is a great bias and a fundamental analytical error that must be avoided. Imperialism should, therefore, be introduced as a basic analytical concept in the attempt to study Western society and Western modernity.

Nazism, it must be admitted, represented a rare moment in the history of Western (and human) civilization. It was unprecedented in history that millions were exterminated in such a methodical, "rational," detached manner. However, this rare moment can also be regarded as the paradigmatic moment in which the modern Western epistemological paradigm revealed its ugly face. This can be seen if we place Nazism first in the broader context of the theories of racial inequality that spread in Europe in the second half of the 19th Century and which formed the doctrinal basis of Western imperialism, and second, in the context of the systematic genocide of native Americans and the enslavement of native Africans by Westerners. If we do so, we will find that Nazism – labeled by many as a mere aberration from a humanistic Western civilization – was actually a paradigmatic moment and part of an over-all Western recurrent pattern, different from other similar phenomena only in degree, not in kind.

5. Western Voices of Dissent

We have seen that as Western civilization gradually became aware of its crises, it began to lose some of its self-confidence and started questioning some of its own central premises and underlying assumptions. Western dissident intellectuals started articulating some of this self-questioning, describing the crisis, and even suggesting ways, some radical, some conservative, to surmount it. Such dissident thought should be made use of in our attempt to develop a critical perspective on Western civilization. We should make available this rich dissident literature which extends now to all fields of knowledge, including literary criticism, linguistics, philosophy, ecology, physical sciences, history, etc. Scanning such literature reveals a rejection of materialist scientific paradigms. Availability of this literature in Arabic and other languages would set the stage for a rich and multi-faceted dialog regarding the Western cultural project:

(a) *Modernity*
There are numerous Western studies on the crisis of modernity and on the nihilism and anti-humanism of modernism. A number of philosophical and literary periodicals, some of them with Christian theological inclinations, have published revealing articles on the topic. There is valuable criticism of modernism even within Marxism, such as in the works of Lukács, Fredrick Jameson and Terry Eagleton. Despite its nihilism, post-modernist thought includes notable criticism of several aspects of the Western modernization and enlightenment project.

(b) *Development Theories and the Idea of Progress*
Several studies on the modern Western concept of development point out that it is a quantitative and materialist concept that disregards quality and the human dimensions of humankind's existence. With the intensification of the environmental crisis, several authors wonder about the limits of growth and progress. The failure of most West-based development projects in Third World countries have also given rise to a literature that demands that the pivotal concepts of growth and progress be questioned.

(c) *The Green Parties and Environment Activists*
This is one of the most important types of counter-thought. As indicated earlier, Western materialist thought is based on the assumption of the limitlessness of the human mind and its ability to conquer and control the world. It is also assumed that natural resources cannot be depleted. Environmentalists, on the other hand, believe in the finitude of the mind and natural resources and the need of human beings to maintain some kind of balance with the world of nature and with themselves. The underlying paradigm of

their thought is notably different from the materialist paradigm operative in mainstream Western thought.

(d) *Revisionist Views of Western History*
There are several revisionist studies re-examining some of the fundamentals of modern Western history and historical thought. The history of imperialism, for example, has been re-written from the point of view of the oppressed colonized peoples whose heritage has been destroyed, their way of life undermined, and their natural resources plundered. Some of these peoples have even been subjected to wholesale genocide. The French Revolution is another case in point. The occasion of its bicentennial witnessed the appearance of scores of volumes in English and French presenting a completely new outlook on this crucial event in the history of Western modernity. Some books highlighted the battle of Vendée (March 1793), in which the forces of the French Revolution launched what is now considered the first systematic extermination (holocaust) of a population in modern history. These forces massacred women and children, young and old in an attempt to eradicate "the enemies of the revolution."

One study points out that the violence and terror which accompanied the French Revolution, far from being marginal aberrations, were actually a paradigmatic structural feature thereof. Violence, according to this study, was the only available means for the new secular state, having abandoned religion, to recruit the masses and harness their vital energies in its own service.

Other studies refer to the Revolution's attitude to ethnic and religious minorities and how they were eradicated, either literally or figuratively, i.e., through the elimination of their distinctive cultural features. Another study shows that far from helping France, the Revolution impeded its economic development and slowed its growth, thereby giving England the chance to outrun France in economic growth. Other studies highlight the rise in divorce rates and the number of illegitimate children in France after the Revolution, in addition to similar social aspects which traditional, "enlightened" histories of the Revolution do not care to touch upon.

(e) *Radical Changes in Epistemological Paradigms Underlying the Physical Sciences*

Among the most notable disciplines in which Western dissident thought expresses itself is the philosophical thought underlying the physical sciences. Nineteenth century science was committed to a cumulative, non-generative view of the mind and knowledge. It was based on the belief that through a gradual accumulation of knowledge, the realm of the knowable would expand and consequently the realm of the unknown would diminish until human beings had developed full knowledge of reality, which in turn would give them control over it.

However, all this proved to be an illusion. Ironically, through accumulation of knowledge, the theories, hypotheses, and available data have become so vast, diverse, and at times contradictory, that no single individual could hope to assimilate and synthesize them all. Moreover, the illusion harbored by many that the realm of the known would expand as the realm of the unknown diminished has been completely dispelled. The realm of the known undoubtedly expands; however, the realm of the unknown expands at a far greater ratio. The more we know, the more we paradoxically realize how little we know. This realization manifests itself in scientific concepts, hypotheses, theories, and even scientific laws. In other words, human beings have paradoxically realized their limits through their many successful conquests. The natural sciences have abandoned concepts of hard causality, adopting instead concepts of correlation and procedural definition and aspiring to a partial rather than a complete explanation of phenomena. This conclusion needs to be emphasized so that researchers and scholars might be freed from the fallacy of simple causality.

It is noteworthy that an increasing number of Western intellectuals and thinkers extol multiplicity (pluralism) and denounce Euro-centricity on the level of theory. However, the materialist rationalist monist paradigm (the basis of modern Western epistemology) remains the mainstream operative paradigm that underlies the outlook adopted by the World Bank, UN development agencies, the Pentagon, etc.

IV. *Relativizing the West*

The aim of these criticisms is not to expose or deconstruct the West (an exercise worthy of nihilists and Post-Modernists). Rather, they are an attempt to sort out the Western arsenal of knowledge, dividing it into "Western," that is specific to Western civilization, and universal, expressing our common humanity. The universal elements may then be adopted and adapted to an independent theoretical framework rooted in our concrete historical reality.

To accomplish this, we need to relinquish the belief that the West is central, universal and absolute. Similarly, we need to realize that so-called "scientific laws" propagated by Westernizers are actually the product of specific historical and cultural developments and the coalescing of different elements and circumstances in a unique historical moment. Once we realize this, the West will be relativized, becoming one cultural formation among many. In other words, the West will cease to be universal. This shift requires that we retrieve a truly universal, comparative perspective which emphasizes the specific features and history of the Western cultural formation just as other formations have their specific features and histories.

The comparative perspective does not mean studying how one cultural formation has influenced another (a common practice in Arab academia); it means, rather, the attempt to arrive at a truly complex universal outlook based on the rich and diverse experiences of all human societies. Moreover, it involves an in-depth study of the historical experiences and epistemological paradigms through which human beings have dealt with the world around them and created different cultural forms with their own intrinsic laws whose humanness stems from their specificity, not from a supposed consistency with illusory "general laws" that turn out, on closer scrutiny, to be "Western laws."

The way to such a complex, truly universal perspective has been eased by the fact that Western civilization has already lost much of its presumed centrality since the rise of other, non-Western cultural centers which may be considered successful even by Western criteria. To achieve this relativization of Western civilization, the following points could be addressed:

1. Identifying the Specific Features of Western Civilization

Max Weber, the versatile German sociologist, has dealt with many issues and social phenomena in his writings. But perhaps the most important of these is the problem of the specificity of Western civilization. He argues that this specificity has manifested itself in a gradual and rising level of rationalization, a process so pervasive that it has eventually encompassed all aspects of human life. This rationalization process is the consequence of certain elements unique to Western civilization: Roman law, the structure of the Western city, some aspects of the Judeo-Christian tradition, and even the development of music. In his view, this process of rationalization is responsible for the rise of what he terms "rational capitalism" (as opposed to the "irrational" capitalism of traditional societies), which has developed objective bureaucratic administrative systems characterized by impersonal, value-free procedures.

Despite the fact that Weber at times celebrated this value-free procedural rationalization as one of the unique contributions of modern Western civilization, he eventually came to see this process as landing human beings in an "iron cage," a set of strict, blind, rational rules derived from the monist materialist paradigm to which human beings must submit so as to be standardized and programmed. Be that as it may, by underscoring the specificity of Western civilization, Weber (as opposed to Marx and Durkheim, who underscored the concept of general law) well serves us in our attempt to develop an independent epistemological project.

The specific aspects of the development of Western technology should also be investigated in comparison with other types of technology, such as the Chinese, for example, or even the technology of air and water mills in Western civilization itself. One Western historian of ideas argues that Westerners, rather than developing available, and relatively advanced, water and air technology to generate energy, opted for energy generated from fossil fuel because of the imperialist epistemology which they espoused. Whereas the former is based on balance, the latter necessitates conquest and plunder, which would yield immediate and quick results.

2. Toward a Sociology of Western Knowledge

Let us begin with a truism: It is impossible to understand any phenomenon in its full complexity without placing it in its socio-historical context, made up of a complex of elements, biases, symbols, yearnings, etc.

Therefore, a study of the context of Western concepts and ideas will undoubtedly enable us to understand them in their full complexity and specificity. Take, for example, a concept that recurs in many Western studies of the Orient, namely, "the Asiatic mode of production." This highly general and abstract phrase is obviously an expression of the centrality and universality that Westerners have bestowed on themselves. This outlook came into existence in the 16th Century and developed into explicit racism later in the 19th Century, when Westerners divided the world into two segments: Western, civilized, logical, and complex on the one hand, and non-Western, primitive, illogical, and simple on the other. This racist outlook manifested itself on the epistemological level in the Faustian desire to arrive at comprehensive scientific interpretations of the entire world, leaving no gaps whatsoever. This is manifested in the "scientific" attempt to control reality through a set of cognitive categories which are assumed to encompass all temporal and spatial human reality.

No matter how ignorant it happened to be about Asia and Africa, Western science nevertheless felt compelled to classify them, thrusting them into facile, highly generalized categories such as "the Asiatic mode of production," "tribal societies," and the like. In this way it was able to reach the comprehensiveness necessary for its claim of centrality and universality.

3. Some Jewish Sources of Modern Western Thought

Some Western ideas have a religious dimension that can hardly be detected by the "objective" researcher (such as the idea of "historical inevitability," which is more or less a secularization of the Christian view of a providential history). Let us turn first to some of the Jewish sources of modern Western thought. It is agreed upon among students of Western thought that members of the Jewish communities in the West have achieved quite a high degree of eminence within the frame of modern Western civilization. Published research has not, however, sufficiently emphasized what may be termed "the Jewish component" in modern Western thought.

By "Jewish" here, we do not mean Torah or even Talmudic Judaism, but rather that of the Kabbalah (notably the Lurianic Kabbalah of Issac Luria) which, according to Gershom Scholem, has dominated Jewish religious thought since the 16th Century. Kabbalah is a monistic, pantheistic outlook which sees the Creator as gradually coming to inhabit his creations till they form one substance, with no gaps separating the one from the other, humankind and nature becoming one with God. One might even say that they become God. In other words, the Lurianic Kabbalistic outlook is an extreme pantheistic system that leads to a form of unity (monism) of being, which is no different from materialistic monism. Lurianic Kabbalah is, therefore, a prelude to secularist thought which regards nature-matter as sacred and which defines the human being not as a unique creature but rather as an organic, inseparable part of nature-matter.

The Kabbalists developed their own outlook and view of cosmic and historical cycles, their own view of humans and their dynamism, as well as a whole system of Kabbalistic symbols. Lurianic Kabbalah resulted in what is referred to in Jewish studies as "Messianic Fever," i.e., the belief that the Jewish Savior (Messiah) is about to arrive. The Messianic tendency is hostile to boundaries, for it views the human being (or the Messiah) as a limitless human being (a god), and quite often manifests itself in licentious tendencies (which abrogate divine and human laws) and ends up abolishing the very boundaries which define human identity.

Rabbis at first confronted the Kabbalah and tried to curb the Kabbalists; indeed, they even accused them of explicit polytheism and hostility not only to monotheism but even to Judaism itself. Some rabbis pointed out that the Kabbalah was an outlook that did not originate from Judaism or the Jewish tradition, but rather from pantheistic peasant Slavic folklore. After a period of resistance, the Kabbalah won the day, and Kabbalistic interpretations of the Torah and Talmud gradually became more prevalent till they became the standard normative interpretations. Worse still, a Christian Kabbalah rose and spread, influencing many Western thinkers, particularly during the Renaissance. Kabbalah is termed "Jewish or Christian" only metaphorically, since it is in fact pagan and pantheistic.

No single study of the Kabbalah has been published in Arabic. A few books have been published about Messianism but without any thorough examination of its underlying philosophical and historical significance or recurrent patterns. The number of scholars and historians of ideas in the West studying the Kabbalah and Messianism is scanty and confined to the field of Jewish studies. Many of them make no attempt to see Jewish Messianic movements in their Western context or within the context of the Western history of ideas. Therefore, the Jewish Kabbalistic component of modern Western thought stayed implicit and nobody has yet undertaken to study the subject thoroughly and systematically.

Following are some pivotal points which may be examined so that we can identify the Kabbalistic (and, *ergo* pantheistic) component of modern Western civilization, and some of the implicit biases that underlie it.

(a) *Baruch Spinoza*

To many historians of Western thought, Spinoza is regarded as the first secular man, who abandoned his faith (Judaism) and did not espouse a new one. He advocated an extreme version of naturalism that leads to the deification of nature and the naturalization of God. It is quite important to pinpoint the relationship between his thought and Kabbalistic (Gnostic) thought. There are some studies on this topic, but they simply touch the surface.

(b) *Sigmund Freud*

Psychoanalysis, with its many symbols and emphasis on human sexuality, can only be fully understood with reference to the Kabbalah, an outlook, which "eroticized the divine and divinized the erotic." This is not an unreasonable description of Freud's outlook which transformed eros into some kind of secular absolute, immanent in matter (the body).

Consider the well-known Freudian classification of the human soul into the ego, the superego, and the Id. It would have been quite important for Arab translators of Freud to know that it is quite likely that the word 'Id' is actually derived not from the Latin *Id*, but rather, the Yiddish *Yid* (Jew). It is also believed by some to be an echo of the Hebrew word *Yesod*, meaning "foundation," one of the ten Sephirots or emanations that make up God and the Adam Kadmon (cosmic human) in the Kabbalistic system. The *yesod* in the picture of Adam Kadmon is sometimes placed at the male genitalia. This means that according to the Kabbalistic system, the Id (which is also *yid*) is the sexual basis of the universe. Several works have been published on this topic. There is even a specialized periodical titled *Judaism and Psychoanalysis*.

Significantly, a serious study was published in Arabic entitled *al-Turāth al-Yahūdī wa al-Ṣahyūnī fī al-Fikr al-Frowydī*[9] by the distinguished Egyptian psychologist Sabri Jirjis. Nevertheless, despite his meticulous and erudite examination of the topic, this excellent study has been neglected, and no scholar has bothered to support or refute it.

(c) *Franz Kafka*
Kafka is considered one of the most notable Western novelists. His absurdist, nihilist attitude can be considered an expression of the crisis of Westerners in modern times. The Jewish Kabbalistic component is evident in Kafka's art and thought.

(d) *Deconstruction*
Deconstruction is at present one of the most notable schools of thought in the West. It is associated with the name of its founder, French philosopher Jacques Derrida, who also happens to be a Jew of Algerian origin. Another prominent pioneer of deconstruction is Edmund Gabes, a Jew of Egyptian origin. The most renowned deconstructionist in the USA, Harold Bloom, is also Jewish. Derrida received some sort of Talmudic schooling with Kabbalistic trends, and was heavily influenced by Emmanuel Levinas, a leading French Jewish religious thinker. Bloom wrote a book entitled *Kabbalah and Criticism*, and a novel that he himself describes as Gnostic. Ironically, all the Arab interpreters of Deconstruction and Post-Modernism have failed to see its "Jewish" component, even though there are several studies by Susan Handelman which deal with the subject quite thoroughly.

V. *Opening up to the World*
It is necessary for us to open up to different world civilizations and benefit from their cultural and intellectual traditions which encompass a rich body of knowledge and wisdom that could deepen our understanding of humankind, society, and nature. The so-called modern Arab Renaissance opened up exclusively to the West, notably to England, France and the USA, as well as, somewhat, to Germany. By contrast, we know nearly nothing about Eastern Europe and completely disregard other non-Western civilizations, namely, most world civilizations. For example, how

much do we really know about the development of the pre- and post-19th Century Japanese economy? This paradigm has taken a course different from its Western counterpart, incorporating into its modernization project some elements derived from the Japanese cultural tradition. How much do we know about Japanese literary genres or dramatic traditions? It can be argued that the history of Arab theater could have taken a completely different course had our literary critics and writers studied the Japanese dramatic tradition, which is fundamentally different from its Western counterpart. Had they done so, they would probably have discovered that many of our folkloric epic poems (*sīras*) are actually not narrative, but rather dramatic poems, and therefore could have served as a starting point for a modern Arab theater that does not necessarily mimic Western theater.

The same argument applies to the non-Arab Muslim world. Knowledge of such "Islamic" languages as Swahili, Turkish, and Persian is confined to a small number of specialists. Our knowledge of the cultural traditions of these languages is, more often than not, obtained from Western sources, even though the history of Muslim nations, with its richness and variety, shows the possibility of establishing a genuinely pluralistic civilization whose pluralism does not necessarily lead to nihilism and absurdist relativism.

Opening up to the world can help rectify the epistemological distortion resulting from the long history of Western colonialism, which made us firm believers in the centrality and universality of the Western outlook. School curricula were rewritten so that our students would study the history of the French Revolution while neglecting the history of the Ottoman Empire which, if mentioned at all, was glibly referred to as "responsible for the decline of Egypt." The study of Muslim arts and philosophy was replaced with the study of Western arts and philosophy so that the educated Muslim now knows much more about Van Gogh and Jean-Paul Sartre than about Arab calligraphy, the structure of Muslim cities, the artistic idiom in Islamic manuscripts, or the works of al-Fārābī, Ibn Sīna (Avicenna), al-Ghazālī or Ibn Khaldūn. Even after the departure of Western colonial troops, the local, intellectual, and political elites continued to believe in the necessity of catching up with the West and, therefore, continued in the propagation of Western values and knowledge while marginalizing their own.

Realizing this underlying bias will enable us to deal more cautiously with the knowledge received from any source, be it Western cultural traditions or our own, lest we blindly and passively receive any concept in the belief that it is universal, "natural" and "scientific." After all, knowledge is the fruit of a continuous human endeavor to discover some aspects of the world. It is an endeavor that will go on forever, for humankind's limited mind cannot explain away all aspects of the universe. Aware of the fact that there is no single, universal, general law, we should employ our critical reason to discover the underlying epistemological paradigms and philosophical outlooks inherent in the knowledge we receive. In this manner, we can learn to distinguish between what makes for a better life and what deconstructs and subverts it. As a consequence, we will be freed from "facts" that claim to be solid and absolute.

Perceiving underlying biases will highlight how facts are sometimes twisted and utilized in the service of ideologies, and how the accumulation of information is not undertaken impartially but, rather, on the basis of a biased epistemological paradigm. It is this biased paradigm, moreover, which predetermines what should be monitored and what should be overlooked, what is pivotal and what is marginal.

A PROPOSED ALTERNATIVE PARADIGM

Realizing underlying biases will not necessarily lead to a philosophical nihilism which declares the end of science (and history). Rather, the elimination of bias should be accompanied by the formation of an alternative epistemological paradigm that benefits from all previous human experience (not excluding the Western), and which, at the same time, issues from our own tradition. If identifying the underlying paradigm in the discourse of the Other is not an easy matter, trying to formulate an alternative paradigm is even more difficult. It cannot be accomplished by a single individual; rather, it requires a team working at various levels (observing, classifying, criticizing, abstracting, etc.). A body of observations and insights would then coalesce; and a tentative new paradigm would emerge. Through its repeated use in explaining reality, and through modifying it to increase its explanatory power, it would crystallize, forming a new complex epistemological paradigm which could be used for monitoring reality and for the accumulation and classification of data. Since the data accumulated and classified is bound to be varied, we can then begin to see what the dominant Western paradigm has either excluded or marginalized.

I. *Features of the Proposed Alternative Paradigm*

1. Stemming from Our Own Heritage

An alternative paradigm must stem from our indigenous heritage, where the term "heritage" is used to mean the totality of a given nation's cultural history encompassing both material and spiritual achievements, whether explicit and recorded, or implicit and orally transmitted. Our heritage could be termed "Islamic," not in a religious, but rather in a cultural sense, for non-Muslims contributed to this heritage and helped in its formulation. However, it should be pointed out that the basis of the Islamic cultural epistemological paradigm is the Qur'an and the Sunnah,[10] which together offer absolute values and the Islamic answer to the ultimate questions facing the human race.

Our Islamic jurisprudence (fiqh) represents our ancestors' attempts to comprehend this epistemological paradigm in much the same way as the writings of Islamic thinkers are an attempt to comprehend the rules of the cultural paradigm. "Stemming from our own heritage" is by no means synonymous with the literal transcription of earlier contributions; rather, it denotes the ongoing, creative attempt to apprehend the paradigms implicit in different Islamic texts and phenomena. Such a paradigm translates itself into a kind of cultural grammar which can then be used to re-read the Qur'an and the Sunnah and re-examine the cultural heritage in its totality.

2. Towards a Comprehensive Theory

We are in dire need of an ambitious, comprehensive, "grand" theory. In the Western context (and within its materialist framework), a grand theory attempts to reach complete certainty, attain final explanations, and achieve comprehensive solutions. It aims at enabling humankind to have an absolute (imperialist) control over nature. When it was gradually realized that the epistemological project aiming at such full control is not possible, a shift took place from the Enlightenment dream and the promise of Modernity to the bitterness of Modernism, which in turn led to post-Modernist nihilism. The development of Western philosophical thought is a reflection of the failure of the project of modernity and the end of the illusion of complete control, resulting in the declaration of the absurdity of the universe and the end of the human race.

There is no need, however, to vacillate between these two opposite poles of total theory and final solution, on the one hand, and absurdism and nihilism on the other. We can, instead, seek to arrive at a comprehensive theory which we do not expect to give us final explanations or grant us absolute certainty. It is not a "grand theory" in the sense of being comprehensive, final or absolute, but rather a "relatively grand theory" within the limits of what is humanly possible. Such an attempt cannot succeed within a materialist monist framework, for a comprehensive absolute explanation keeps on haunting the imagination of human beings, seducing them into embarking upon an impossible Faustian course.

3. The Category of Man as a Starting Point

Let us start with the humanistic statement that human beings occupy a central position in the universe as unique and complex creatures that cannot be reduced, in their totality, to something lower (nature-matter). Amongst their most distinctive features is the human mind, which does not record nature passively; but rather, perceives and interacts creatively with it. This gives human beings a measure of independence from natural law and a reasonable range of liberty that enables them to look, contemplate and make free moral choices, and ultimately act on the basis of their choice. Human beings are the only creatures who ask about the purpose of their existence in the universe, and are never content with appearances and external realities; they are compelled to go deeper, looking for explanations, developing inner meanings, symbols and codes of communication.

Despite the common humanity that binds all of us, human beings, unlike other creatures, do not follow one universal genetic program, for there are different cultural identities and independent (individual and collective) wills. They are the only creatures capable of remodeling themselves and their environment according to their free moral choice. Their behavior is not a simple or complex reflection of the laws of nature-matter, for they are fundamentally and qualitatively different from it. That is why they form an epistemological gap in the natural-material continuum. They are not an organic, inseparable part of nature; rather, they are a part that can be separated, existing within it, sustained by it, related to it, yet remaining autonomous and independent of it. They may share in some of its features but they are not reduced in their entirety to it; they can always transcend it, and that is why they are the center of the universe and the noblest of all creatures.

4. Non-materialist Category

From a materialist standpoint, the emergence of humankind in nature happened by pure chance through a simple chemical process, which means that the materialist law of chance is ultimate. The duality of humankind and nature is thereby eradicated, all gaps separating humankind from nature-matter are filled, and materialist monism reigns. From this monism issues Western science which makes no distinction between human beings and apes, or any other creature for that matter, and which emphasizes the points of similarity between them at the expense of the points of dissimilarity. A naturalist-materialist-monist epistemology places humankind at the same level with all natural beings, whereas a non-materialist epistemology sees human beings as distinct and unique, with a gap separating them from nature, a gap that guarantees their humanness and uniqueness.

One wonders, why should one reject the category of a complex human being irreducible to nature-matter for the sake of simplicity? Rather than eradicate the humankind-nature duality in the interest of simplification and monism, it might be more in keeping with human reality to reject the materialist analytical categories because they have weak explanatory power when it comes to the category of humankind. Instead, we should adopt cognitive and analytical categories which are at once quantitative-materialist and qualitative non-materialist, derived partly (only partly) from nature-matter, yet transcending it. Such categories can enable us to explain both what falls within the parameters of hard materialist causality and what falls outside them. The non-material dimensions of these categories manifest themselves in our world, yet cannot be explained through exclusively materialist analytical categories.

Non-materialist categories in this sense complement, but do not cancel out, materialist categories. These non-materialist categories are not reducible to nature-matter, since they derive their power of transcendence from one ultimate category that goes beyond the system of nature, and which believers call "God," the transcendent center of the cosmos. He is closer to us than the jugular vein (Qur'an, 50:16) and cares about us and our world and the course of human history; however, there is nothing like Him. God's very existence is evidence of the existence of Nature and what is beyond it, the measurable and that which cannot be measured. The existence of humankind, as distinct from nature-matter, is dependent and contingent on His existence. As we said earlier, human beings became the center of this planet on account of their human distinctiveness and uniqueness, and their presence is a gap in the natural-material continuum. God's transcendental existence is the solid basis of an irreducible duality, that of Creator and created. This duality is a guarantee that the gap will never be bridged and that accordingly, the duality of humankind and nature-matter will never be eradicated, which calls for an interpretive cognitive category at once materialist and non-materialist. If the supreme duality of Creator and created is eradicated, we are back once more to materialistic monism and to the eradication of the boundaries separating humankind from nature, bringing human beings once more into the world of nature-matter and the various naturalistic-materialistic determinisms which follow therefrom. We are likewise brought out of the realm of freedom and complex moral choice. God's transcendence, in other words, is a guarantee of humankind's humanness and ability to transcend nature-matter.

5. A Generative (non-cumulative) Paradigm

This suggested alternative paradigm is generative; we believe, as indicated earlier, not in one humanity that can be monitored and examined the way merely natural-material phenomena can be, but rather in a common humanity, a generative potential energy latent in all human beings which takes different cultural forms when realized in different times and places. The multiplicity of these forms sets humankind apart from nature, one nation from another, and one individual from all other individuals. A corrollary of this is that even though there is one common basis for our humanness, there is no single ultimate point in history toward which all peoples and cultures move. The idea of one uniform, general law applying to all phenomena, natural or human, is untenable, for it is too narrow to encompass the rich complexity of humankind's historical and cultural existence. The concept of the accumulation of knowledge implies that we will eventually reach the "end of history" and establish an earthly paradise (a technological utopia). However, this concept is narrow and outdated, good for use only when dealing with some limited aspects of the world of things, but of no use when dealing with the realm of the human.

II. *Alternative Science*

A new science, different in its premises and objectives, can be developed. If the essence of the modern Western scientific outlook is the eradication of the humankind-nature duality, leading to materialistic monism, the essence of the new alternative science is to retrieve this duality by restoring humans as complex beings, irreducible to the natural-material system. Following are some of the features of this alternative science.

1. Incomplete Certainty and Continuous Ijtihad

The suggested alternative science operates within a flexible, open-ended paradigm whose aim is not to develop hard laws, final, objective answers, or simple algebraic formulas that explain it all (leading humankind to the end of history). It neither attempts to reach full objectivity and neutrality nor sinks into complete subjectivity. Objectivity means an object observed without an observing self. It presupposes a mind that is able to know everything and a simple reality that can be fully comprehended. By contrast, subjectivity means a subject that is completely absorbed in itself to the exclusion of external, "objective" reality. It presupposes a mind that cannot know reality and a reality that cannot be comprehended in any aspect. The concept of ijtihad is thus being proposed as a middle point between the two impossible poles of complete objectivity and equally complete subjectivity. Ijtihad presupposes that the human mind cannot explain everything and that the attempt to reach complete knowledge is both diabolic and doomed to failure; it likewise implies the impossibility of full objectivity and neutrality or of arriving at general, all-encompassing laws, since the human mind is both limited and creative: limited in that it cannot explain everything, and creative in that it cannot slavishly reproduce everything.

Human reality is infinitely rich and complex as a result of a latent potentiality that cannot be scientifically observed. All of God's creatures, however simple they might seem *prima facie*, are too complex to be explained away; that is what we mean when we say that every phenomenon contains an element of the unseen. By "unseen," I mean that which cannot be measured or wholly confined to the hard net of causality or materialist monism. The unlimited and the unknown (and the unknowable) are at the heart of all that is human, and of even natural phenomena (to a lesser degree).

Therefore, the paradigm of the new alternative science aspires to obtain a reasonable amount of knowledge that explains many, but not all, aspects of reality, and a reasonable level of certainty. Instead of "objective" and "subjective," other terms such as "more explanatory" and "less explanatory" might be used. These phrases alert us to the fact that there is a subjective dimension to all human knowledge ("the inevitability of bias"); at the same time, they affirm the usefulness of this knowledge and the fact that it can be tested "objectively" against a reality external to it. The paradigm underlying these phrases is open-ended, claiming no universality or finality for itself; for there will always be more to know, learn and think about. However, the incompleteness of knowledge and the impossibility of complete objectivity need not lead us to nihilism and relativism, for relativism itself will stay relative because of the existence of the absolute God, the only absolute center that transcends matter.

2. No Room for Full Control of Reality

The suggested alternative science would not aim at imperialist control of reality; nor at harnessing the whole Planet Earth in the service of human beings (as hoped by Westerners in their illusion of being a god on earth). It recognizes that all creations, people, animals, or even inanimate objects, have their share of dignity, bestowed on them by God. They have been created by Him, and are His handiwork; the essence of this alternative science is that everything in nature has some intrinsic value and that the whole universe has an ultimate purpose: "O our Sustainer! You have not created [aught of] this without meaning and purpose. Limitless are You in Your glory!" (Qur'an, 3:191). Humankind is not alone in the universe; other creatures also have their place therein. The earth has not been given to human beings in order for them to conquer and utilize it with no limitations set on them. Rather, they have been appointed vicegerents by Him Who is Greater than them; hence, they may utilize it but within limits, but they must also do their utmost to conserve it.

3. No Reductionism or Eradication of Dualities

This alternative science will not try to reduce reality to its materialist components or dimensions, nor will it try to eradicate dualities, for they are but an echo of the ultimate Creator–created duality. It will not stress the whole at the expense of the part or the inverse. It will not stress continuity at the expense of discontinuity or *vice versa*, since the world is not composed of randomly scattered atoms, nor is it formed of an organic, solid whole; it is, rather, a cohesive whole made up of smaller parts each having its distinctive character, yet which can only be comprehended with reference to the whole. The center of the whole and the source of its cohesiveness exists outside it. That is why it remains a non-organic, porous entity with consequent "gaps."

This means that the parts are as necessary as the whole, discontinuity is no less essential than continuity, and the particular is as important as the general.

Therefore, this new alternative science will try to ascertain the specific curve of the phenomenon, its diversity and personality, and its general significance. It will also attempt to relate the particulars to the general without necessarily reducing the part to the whole or the particular to the general; nor will it seek to impose continuity on discontinuity. It will, rather, attempt to reach the pivotal point where one phenomenon is related to another, yet remains distinct from it. The particular-general, whole-part, continuous-discontinuous dualities are but an echo of the humankind-nature duality (which is in turn an echo of the Creator-created duality). From the standpoint of the new science these are dualities that cannot, should not, be eradicated, which means, on the level of practice, that the individual and small social units cannot be eradicated in the interest of the state, that the past cannot be ignored for the sake of the present, and that the human cannot be disregarded in pursuit of the natural.

4. Rejecting Causal Monism

The new alternative science will not be based on the concept of materialist and causal monism or any deterministic monism. Therefore, it will reject the concept of the unity (monism) of science, and instead will underscore the fact that there should be one science for natural phenomena and another for human phenomena, though a complete separation between the one and the other is not postulated.

Instead of causal monism, the new science would operate in terms of causal pluralism, i.e., interpreting and theorizing about natural and human phenomena in light of a variety of causes. This arises from a belief in the complexity of these phenomena that cannot possibly be reduced to a single materialist element. Phenomena should, therefore, be seen as integrated and multi-faceted, not uni-dimensional. The most important aspects are identified without being placed in any *a priori* hierarchy of causes, and without giving causal primacy to one particular (usually material) element over others.

5. THE STRUCTURE OF TERMINOLOGY

(a) Given the foregoing, there is a need to structure a new body of termi-nology. The humankind-nature duality necessitates a distinction between the terms used for the social sciences and those used for the natural scien-ces. Organic metaphors, which imply that the universe is a solid, organic whole in which the part is fused with the whole and the particular with the general and which presuppose the centrality of nature-matter in the uni-verse, should be avoided, for they embody the material epistemological paradigm which reduces humankind to nature-matter.

(b) Such a new terminology aims for complexity but not necessarily precision. This does not necessarily mean that complexity leads to impre-cision; rather, it signifies an attempt to be aware of the largest possible number of the components that make up a given phenomenon, some aspects of which can be explained in terms of general laws and some of which cannot.

(c) The new terminology does not reject the use of metaphors as a legitimate means of analysis and expression. After all, figurative language is not a mere decoration, but rather, a complex code developed by human beings to describe certain situations which ordinary prose fails to com-municate. There is nothing new about that when we, for instance, speak of "economic man" or the "sick man of Europe"; we are already using metaphors characterized by a measure of complexity and high expla-natory power (from the user's viewpoint).

(d) It is necessary for the structure of the new terminology to include what may be termed "the middle term." The middle term is an expression of the awareness that reality is as complex and varied as a rainbow in which various colors intermingle with no sharp beginning or definitive end. Beginning, middle or end may be postulated as purely analytical categories, not real things. One can also postulate a point of intensity which points toward some kind of a middle, or center, while blurring at the same time the boundaries between beginning and end.

(e) The level of generalization of the term that suits the described phenomenon at issue should be carefully defined. To try to reach the highest level of generalization always lands one in the world of algebra, geometry, mathematics and the like.

(f) The validity of a term will be determined by its explanatory power rather than by its degree of precision or conformity to any specific abstract criteria.

(g) As a result of such suggested modifications, the door will be opened for the inclusion of new units of analysis, such as the family as a political unit which is no less important than the state. This, in turn, will open broad horizons of analysis by pinpointing, for instance, the cultural significance of the Palestinian intifada that managed to marshal the family to play economic and political roles in the absence of the legitimate state and under the domination of a settler state.

III. *A Nascent Project*

Even though we have so far confined ourselves to outlining the basic traits of the alternative paradigm on the abstract theoretical level, we should point out that there have been some serious attempts in concrete practice. Most notable among these attempts is the cultural garden for children built by Abdel Halim Ibrahim; Hamid el-Mously's project involving the manufacture of wood from palm tree leaves is another case in point. It might also be relevant to refer to my eight volume *Mawsūʿat al-Yahūd wa al-Yahūdiyyah wa al-Ṣahyūniyyah*.[11] It is an attempt to develop an analytical paradigm for social phenomena that goes beyond materialist monism, using Jews, Judaism and Zionism as case studies.

In this context, reference should be made to the creative contributions of pioneering architect Hasan Fathi, who resisted the so-called international style of architecture, of Anwar Abdel Malek who has endeavored to retrieve the cultural dimension in his historical and social studies, of Hamid Rabi who has developed new political concepts and terminology to help researchers discover their own cultural identity, and of the International Institute of Islamic Thought and its founding committee, notably the distinguished writings of Ismaʿīl R. al Fārūqī. The sum of these efforts forms a beginning of the alphabet of creativity.

2

Bias in Western Schools of Social Thought: Our Heritage as the Starting Point for Development

ADEL HUSSEIN

THIS WORK, in its three parts, is based on previous papers composed on different occasions several years ago. Heba Izaat Raouf has exerted substantial efforts to compile such writings into an integrated whole. May God reward her richly for accomplishing this challenging task.

I make no claim to have improved on Heba's work. However, I assume that there is a unified, structured and interrelated theme that binds together the notions treated in previous papers despite the fact that their occasions and presentations were seemingly unrelated. I have always wished to synthesize a new product that encompasses the notions and arguments which I have presented in past studies in light of my personal development coupled with changes in the world. Yet, despite the persistent urging of my dear friend Elmessiri and my own sincere desire, I have not yet accomplished such a task.

SOCIAL SCIENCES AND THE PROBLEM OF BIAS

It seems that we in the Arab and Muslim world have entered a phase of critical revision of our traditional concepts and positions on both the intellectual and theoretical levels. It also seems that the momentousness of the transformations that have taken place in our part of the world in the last few decades have been a major incentive for such a revision. On the other hand, the social sciences themselves (as a domain of knowledge) have relied for a long time on stock theories in a way that has prevented our scholars from formulating their own critical observations through practice. This moment, in our experience, coincides with a parallel moment of crisis and revision in Western thought itself. We must not, however, overwhelm ourselves investigating the various fads of Western thought as it attempts to overcome its own intellectual and existential crises. Instead, we should be conscious of the fact that we have specific reasons for our own crisis which emerge from our own experience and reality.

Most of my contribution is based on results which, due to certain limitations, cannot be fully expounded, corroborated or documented. It is not my aim here to present a comprehensive theory. Rather, the best I can hope for is to deepen our awareness and appreciation of the dangers of dependency in the domain of "social sciences," for the concepts and foundations of such a domain teem with biases. I also aim to stress the legitimacy of theoretical independence in this respect. Some points, therefore, merit explanation:

I. *Social Sciences are Different from Physical Sciences*

Our concern with what is known as "the social sciences" does not stem from the mere joy of constructing mathematical and non-mathematical models. Rather, our interest is based on the importance of comprehending the society/nation in the best possible way so as to improve its management. Such improvement is manifested, in the final analysis, through the increased balance and satisfaction experienced by the members of the society/nation, and through the integration of relations within this whole. This, in turn, implies a certain model and a certain degree of conflict.[1] All our research methods, concepts, and theoretical constructs are devoted to this aim; therefore, we should always modify and reform such methods and concepts so as to attain sound and effective knowledge. Human societies have been ceaselessly trying to perform this task, employing scientific methodology (implicitly or explicitly) to extract results from various historical experiences. Some theoretical concepts and notions are then formulated based on these experiences. This heritage has been scantily recorded (e.g., Plato's treatise, *The Republic*); most of it has not been preserved since it was orally transmitted as secrets for governing society to be handed down to the elite (a principle which, one way or another, is still maintained to date). The fact remains, however, that the practical consequences of the earlier theoretical works are unmistakably evident. Otherwise, how shall we explain the establishment and development of institutions with their well-defined interrelations? How did civilizations that embraced and utilized creativity emerge? How was stability achieved and how were conflicts and wars managed? It was the social knowledge acquired by human societies that enabled them to gain their accumulated achievements. However, the rational social concept is always interactive with some doctrine (faith). Hence, European thought (especially since the Enlightenment era in the 18th century) claimed that such a tremendous epistemological heritage was inconsistent with science; therefore, it was deemed "non-scientific," representing nothing but early attempts (fossils) of primitive peoples.

In the epistemological realm, the predominance of Enlightenment notions meant the prevalence of "secularism" (with all its variations) in social affairs; hence, the prevalence of the secular notion of progress. In this context, physical sciences occupied a place of undue honor at the expense of philosophy after the latter had been completely secularized and had ceded its lofty position to the natural sciences. Gradually, social sciences were reduced to and leveled with natural sciences. In the domain of social knowledge, this process took different forms: Classic and Neoclassic economics, Positivism in sociology, the ensuing trends in political science, then Marxism, etc. No matter what these schools were, they all aimed at the establishment of academic disciplines similar to the natural sciences. Whenever attempts failed and results remained unattainable, Western scholarship maintained that social sciences were not yet sufficiently advanced, perhaps due to their being "new" disciplines, a pretentious proposition that is clearly spurious.

In spite of recurrent failures, persistent attempts were made to impose the academic framework of natural sciences on social sciences. Being highly influenced by the West, we in the East adopted the same approach. Yet, isn't historical experience enough to prove that the objective at hand is, *ipso facto*, fallacious and impossible to achieve? The proposed methodology had previously been used in Western experimental practices. For example, the method of creating analytical units, such as "class," "elite," "institutions," "patterns," "value surplus," etc., is already used in various schools. Yet, despite the fact that a social image of the world was constructed matching the physical image produced via natural sciences, the problem has not been solved, since social sciences remain less exact than physical sciences. This problem can be attributed to the very nature of the social phenomena in question. Phenomena within a rational living society are different from those that characterize inanimate matter devoid of reason or choice. When assessing the conditions, potentials and directions of the active operators in a real (living) society, they are not subject to standard units or interrelations amongst such units. In a living society there is a great difference between discovering the rules of the game and predicting results or exercising control over it.

Apart from the impracticality of using natural science models to study social phenomena, why should anyone insist that social sciences be like natural sciences? Are we dealing here with a noble or sacred objective? Practically speaking, if we assume that we could achieve this goal, it would mean destroying the vitality of society, turning it into a huge, strictly controlled push-button machine. It would accelerate the establishment of a totalitarian state in its worst form. Would such "scientific" and "rational" achievement, with its imposed success, please us? Could we describe it as a discovery of the objective laws of social motion, or merely an attempt to impose rules and models of our own creation on social movement?

II. *Western Schools of Thought Are Not Universal Sciences*
Having criticized the Western approach which aims to merge social and natural sciences, we now move to the assessment of Western social sciences from another perspective by posing the following question: What are the geographical realms and historical dimensions which form the basis of this process (of merging natural and social sciences) and its generalizations or theoretical structure? To acquire academic legitimacy and recognition for social sciences as an objective account of human social knowledge and in order for their conclusions to be universal, reliable and scientific, they must be founded on a solid knowledge base covering all human societies and their respective histories. In reality, what are now known as "social sciences" are based solely on Western peoples' knowledge of their own societies in the modern era. Hence, the spotlight is brought to bear on a very limited sphere, historically and geographically, and all theoretical constructs are formulated according to the questions raised within this limited (Western) scope.

Though the early responses to these questions during the age of the Enlightenment were mostly simple, they grew more complex, taking the form of theoretical models in the second half of the 19th Century. There were two main trends in this respect:

(1) a trend that stressed conflict between labor and capital and aimed to precipitate radical revolutionary change.

(2) an institution-oriented trend aiming to create the institutions deemed necessary to stabilize relations between labor and capital, achieve improvement and stability, and consolidate the balance necessary for such stability.

It is noteworthy that questions and answers posed by both trends are determined by secular concepts and ideas of materialistic progress (secularism being the dominant doctrine of the modern West). Even when scientific research discovered the importance of religion to society, forms of worldly (secular) religions were – explicitly or implicitly – introduced to perform its function.

The strife between the two poles of social conflict in Europe (Capitalism and Socialism) seemed, in the past, to be a kind of a zero-sum game, i.e., a gain for one side entailed a corresponding loss for the other. At this stage, the "scientific" social theories turned into sacred symbols and doctrines (though these doctrines were only secondary in status since secularism was the fundamental religion). Nevertheless, the 1970s witnessed a rapprochement between Socialism and Capitalism; the conflict grew less tense and the ideological halo of the conflict, with its past fanaticism and its absolutes whose validity had never been academically proven, nearly vanished. Many writings proclaiming the "end of ideology" were published. This period thus witnessed the publication of many economic and social studies analyzing the gradual convergence of the existing structures of Capitalism and Socialism in the industrial countries. In this atmosphere, implicit and explicit dialog among the different theoretical schools became both a possibility and a reality. Attempts to reach common ground or synthesized formulas of theoretical paradigms were no longer disparaged.[2]

The rapprochement was reflected in a plethora of Western futuristic studies that dealt with the problems expected to arise from the scientific and technological revolution. One way or another, such studies implied that this revolution would lead to the unification of social and economic systems or to 'the Post-Industrial Society' which is (from my point of view) actually the very peak of the crisis. Western thought used to preach (throughout its internal [intellectual] crusades) that it sought to realize an earthly paradise. This false religion or ideological mirage stemmed from secular ideas. Different schools were more or less different approaches to this earthly paradise. But, if we have now reached the stage of affluence, and if the different parties have reached a similar notion of the affluent society in terms of production and distribution yet without attaining the promised paradise, what is next?

Noble values are increasingly waning. Pragmatism and individualism have reached a level where people have lost their natural desire to have children who might share their earnings or spoil their pleasures in life. There is an increasing sense of suffocation and alienation coupled with a terrible sense of insecurity. The horizons of the scientific and technological revolution not only promise prosperity, but herald mass destruction and environmental devastation. There is no theoretical notion in the Western arsenal that can solve this dilemma. Yet, this is a specific dilemma related to their own history, and their social sciences.

The problems and challenges faced by Western civilization in this contemporary era can no longer find solutions on the social and economic levels (especially after what has already been achieved on such levels), since such problems and challenges are rooted in a deeper ideological phenomenon (the predominance of secularism), i.e., in the very foundations of modern Western civilization which have yet to be seriously studied and analyzed. Here, then, is the pinnacle of the academic and theoretical crisis.

Why should we care about all this? All the above questions and answers have emerged from the various phases of Western society and experience. Based on our own historical context and our economic dependency and backwardness, we face questions (and challenges) which differ from those generated by the Western experience and which, therefore, require the development of schools of thought (methodologies and approaches) which differ from Western ones. We should understand our society, including its past and future developments, in light of Islamic principles and experience.

III. *Western Schools of Thought Are Hostile To Us*

If the first aspect of the influence of the dominant Western doctrine on Western social thought is manifested in its submission to secularism, then the second aspect of this influence is the acceptance of the axiom of Western superiority and the legitimacy of Western global hegemony over all, including our part of the world. These two aspects are closely interrelated, i.e., they are two faces of the same coin. If the West is the superior master and if the totality of its theories derived from secularism is "science," then it follows that these theories should prevail and everything else may rightly be stigmatized as backward and non-scientific and consigned to oblivion. The second aspect of the doctrinal influence, i.e., superiority and predominance, permeates all fields of Western "scientific" social thought. In studies of general history, facts are distorted to show, explicitly or implicitly (coincidentally, or for ethnic or anthropological reasons) that progress is the historical mission of the West. This trend reveals itself not only in studies of general history, but also in historically based theories and philosophies, the works of Orientalists, and the history of philosophy and science.

Throughout the last two centuries, the standard thesis has been that classical science is originally European, emanating directly from Greek philosophy and science. There may have been recognition of a certain degree of philosophical achievement or the emergence of certain sciences in other civilizations; however, this recognition was limited by the belief that they were only secondary contributions that derived their value from the "mother arsenal." All social sciences study modern Western society from this historical perspective, the outcomes of which are being felt in the present. Many economic development studies, based on the assumptions of Classical and Neoclassical Western economic schools, have been exported to dependent countries (the so-called developing countries). The discourse of competition, international trade, liberalization and development models implies (or justifies) the imposition of the superior power (the West) over the world order which is, in turn, economically dependent on a certain international division of labor. The same pattern recurs in the social and political "sciences". All forms of social organization or political management outside the West (i.e., forms other than political liberalism) are considered inferior and incapable of renewal and development. The very existence of this concept at the core of political and social schools of thought turns them into a dogma justifying imperialism and the imposition of Western hegemony in its worst forms. Moreover, the problem of these "sciences" is how to develop social and political structures in a way that enables the West more efficiently to carry out its "historical mission" of "modernizing and civilizing the world." All international (political) relations studies (as well as international economic studies) are currently based on treating problems arising from maintenance of the status quo, i.e., the reproduction of Western hegemony.

IV. *The Concept of Independent Theoretical Practice*

Practitioners of social sciences in our Eastern societies have grown increasingly cautious about the possibility of importing intellectual dependency implicit in Western social theories. This critical view has been reinforced by the detection of the bias and prejudice of Western studies (literature) against whatever concerns our history and heritage. It has to be admitted that the skepticism regarding the validity of the results of social science stems from a sense of belonging to our nation and an established confidence in its achievements. This skepticism has turned into certainty as many empirical studies conducted by our researchers have demonstrated the real value of our achievements and identified some of the specific characteristics of the course of our own history. The same thing has happened in the fields of economics, sociology, and politics (and development in general). Empirical studies have proven the deficiency in Western theoretical constructs as corroborated by the practical results of putting such theories into effect. These theories have not achieved their aims from a national perspective; they have not led to the type of knowledge that would support our decision-making. However, the critical outlook should not stop at the empirical level, thereby limiting its role to presenting the partial results of this or that experiment. Rather, it is time to use these results as the basis for challenging the totality of the Western theoretical construct. To stop at the empirical level (while keeping the theoretical construct intact) may give the impression that our empirical discoveries are mere deviations from the "norm." Consequently, we might try on and on, despite the fact that the comprehensive outlook would reveal that there is no such thing as a "norm." There is always the possibility of a different and more appropriate approach. Hence, we are facing unusual difficulties on our way to adopting the Western model; therefore, we should seek to arrive at a different (independent) model.

I believe that the increasing recognition of the notion of cultural pluralism, of a plurality of cultural centers and cultural independence is a positive development. I also believe that the terms "authenticated modernization" or "authenticity and modernity" are becoming increasingly acceptable. But, I prefer the term "self-renewal" to refer to the concept of independent theoretical practice. The increasing acceptance of this term (which is still ambiguous) indicates the growing need to start an independent theoretical practice which relies (at the minimum) on empirical results and which is supported by a general critical approach.

Independent theoretical practice[3] is an intricate task that requires ingenious and talented people; however, this should not restrain us from breaking into this field. What is not permissible in this practice is to deceive ourselves or resort to falsification. By "self deception," I mean the use of the same Western concepts while changing only the terminology, or stubbornly attempting to prove that these concepts have originated in our heritage in a way that justifies their adoption. This methodology will naturally lead us back to the "square one" of using Western models in which nothing is changed but terms, names or reasons. Dangerous falsification can take the form of adding to Western thought models and concepts related to faith in God, family or other values, for instance. We might then imagine that we have solved a nagging problem while ignoring the fact that secular Western thought models generate secondary concepts in all aspects of social knowledge, concepts which contradict the secondary notions generated by the ones that we have introduced (particularly faith in God, the Exalted). The outcome of this falsification lacks any realistic and logical consistency; thus it lacks the legitimate claim of having developed an effective theoretical construct.

In the process of constructing a theoretical basis that would inform our self-renewal, we assert that we do not reject the use of some Western theoretical constructs. Yet, this requires the sorting out of the contents of the Western arsenal to separate what is specific to the West from what can be treated as universal. The process also requires the examination of concepts so as to discover their explicit and implicit relationship to the prevailing Western doctrine, and how consistent they would be with our own prevailing doctrine. For example, concepts such as the "economic man" and "value-labor" are related to secularism as they lead to analyses and economic theoretical constructs regulated by this doctrinal bias. "Economic man" is the underlying pivotal concept in Classical and Neo-classical Western economic thought. All market mechanisms, as well as its checks and balances, would be to no avail if "economic man" were not in control of demand and supply. According to our Islamic criteria, this concept, whose characteristics are organically related to secularism, represents a distorted image of humankind. Moreover, the assumption that the value (or the exchange value) of a commodity is determined by the quantity of social labor necessary to produce it is the starting point in Ricardo's model. Marx also took this assumption as the starting point for his economic model of Capitalism. Reliance on the assumption of labor-value (according to the concept of labor used in the analysis) resulted in confusions and paradoxes in both Ricardo's and Marx's economic analyses. However, we are concerned here with the relation between this assumption (which we believe to be flawed and unrealistic) and secularism. Assessing value only through human labor with no regard to land (or nature) reflects an overstatement of humankind's status in secularism; i.e., human beings are seen here as the "creators," "doers of whatever they want," and the "conquerors of nature." It is no coincidence, then, that Ibn Khaldūn arrived at a different notion of value based on what both human labor and nature offer, which, in turn, reflects the concepts of Islamic doctrine. Based on such a doctrine, Islamic thinkers believe that human beings cultivate and enrich nature within a framework of integration. In this pursuit, which may involve conflict with nature, human beings are to avoid the destruction of the environment and seek to maintain its natural balance. Indeed, this is encouraged by Islam, which does not sanction indifference toward the destruction of the environment. The potentials and role of humankind are respected; however, such potentials and role should be seen in the overall context of subjection to God the Exalted.

In the light of these reservations, we may accept concepts and analytical units (models) such as class, elite, social hierarchy, nation, social balance, planning, etc. Such concepts or components, if used as universal ones (i.e., at a high level of abstraction), will have contents suitable to us according to our independent theoretical paradigm informed by objective social reality. This is quite natural, since our usage of such concepts in relation to a certain nation/society is at a lower level of abstraction. Consequently, the content, relative significance, and interrelations among these concepts within our theoretical paradigm are more or less different from their position in the Western theoretical paradigm. Nation and the central state in our society, for instance, attain a special connotation in accordance with the nature of their historical formation. For us, the nation-state is not a modern achievement realized by the bourgeoisie and largely related to its interests in unifying the domestic market and participating in the external dominance enterprise (as has happened in the modern West). Rather, the nation and central state were formed in our societies long ago, i.e., centuries before the emergence of the European bourgeoisie. The influence of the unifying doctrine (Islam) has accumulated to inculcate a stronger sense of unity and affinity than what is achieved, for instance, by market unification in the United States. Moreover, our social classes have imports different from those determined by the concepts of the European context. Our *multazims*, i.e., holders of commercial or agricultural concessions or monopolies, were not the same as European feudal lords, nor have our past and current "businessmen" played the same role as that played by the Western bourgeoisie. Furthermore, the conflict between our "proletariat" and our "capitalists" has not played the same major role as that performed by their counterparts in the European social and conceptual context. The role of different classes in our societies has been determined according to the logic of their unique historical development within the framework of the social continuum represented by the nation-state.

OUR HERITAGE IS THE STARTING POINT FOR DEVELOPMENT

As mentioned earlier, in order to form our own outlook for the future we must have independent theoretical practice. A prerequisite of such practice is a profound perception of our heritage with Islam at its core. This heritage is not just history; it is the conveyor of a living message and the basis of the revival to which we aspire. By "heritage" I mean our civilization's entire history in its material and moral aspects; this includes what has been written and/or published by those belonging to our culture, and what underlies or is implied in our behavior as values and traditions. The focus on Islam does not negate the influence of pre-Islamic culture in Egypt or in other areas. Rather, it means that the essential influence and ultimate point of reference stem mainly from Islam. As for modern Western civilization, it has a major impact on limited social sectors that represent a departure from the general social structure of the Ummah, since they lack a cultural link with the rest of the sectors (a fact which at times has caused severe tension in social relations). As for the majority of people (regardless of social positions), their acceptance or rejection of what comes from the West is determined by its consistency or lack thereof with Islamic principles.

Affinity with the heritage of Islamic civilization is not confined to Muslims, since this heritage has been created and lived by the entire Arab Ummah with all its various affiliations. The heritage of Islamic civilization in Egypt, for example, is a legacy shared by both Muslims and Copts (Christian Egyptians). If our secular thinkers have their own genuine thought and are not a mere echo of Western secularism, then their strong secular tendencies should reflect reverence and compassion for the culture and history of the county's national identity, i.e., the Islamic heritage.

Formulation of the future under the influence of Islam and its cultural heritage is the responsibility of independent theorization or contemporary fiqh and ijtihad. As for myself, I do not claim to have arrived at a comprehensive theoretical paradigm. There is still a wide gap between what I have reached and what I aspire to arrive at. Accordingly, I will confine myself to shedding light on a particular issue which I believe to be pivotal to the subject in question.

I. *Western Complex Development is Economic-Social*

The term "complex" development (as the literal meaning of the term "complex" suggests) emphasizes the practical impossibility of separating social from political components. Even if this were theoretically possible, it would have to be implemented carefully and as only one step of the analysis. At this point, we only seek to determine whether the economic and social aspects are dominant and constitute a determinant of the whole process of complex development. What would further delineate the issue is to review how Western practice has handled this issue. It must be noted, though, that by economic aspects we mean the rational use of natural resources in order to meet the society's needs for goods and services; however, by social aspects we mean whatever is concerned with various human relationships amongst members of any particular society. According to this general procedural definition, political and cultural practices are considered part of the social aspect.

With the Renaissance there emerged a system of beliefs known as "humanism" (we can also call it secularism or materialism). This system of beliefs spread and reached its climax in the 18th century during the Enlightenment. Humanism advocated the right of human beings to freely develop according to their "innate quintessence." This meant the recovery of the true nature of human beings as it was before their vision was blurred by Medieval ecclesiastical beliefs. The European attempt to recover what is called "innate human nature" was the basis of the targeted renaissance and the cornerstone of progress towards a rational social system. The term "innate human nature" has now been widely employed in philosophical schools and different spheres of Western social sciences ranging from psychiatry to anthropology, including economics and its "economic man" (which is a special version of the innate natural human being).

Until recently, it was a common belief that there are fixed characteristics of human instinct. After the triumph of Enlightenment ideas, schools differed in outlining such characteristics, particularly in determining the rational social system which accords with the needs of "innate human nature." Competing and conflicting paradigms emerged, each claiming to be more consistent with "innate human nature." Yet, the general framework of Europe's modern notion of human nature and instincts has governed all such differences since the 18th Century to date. After marginalizing religion or isolating it from the life of society, all Western schools of thought confirmed that human beings are by nature worldly (secular) creatures who place physical self-interest above any other consideration. However, what they claimed to be "innate human nature" is not a scientific discovery; rather, it is a manifestation of materialistic secularism. History has proven that this European concept of human nature creates devils and monsters that easily slaughter and exterminate others (individuals, groups, peoples, and civilizations).

On the level of the socio-economic system, this concept generated unanimous agreement that technical (industrial) progress was to be treated as sacred. Various notions of human development and civilization emphasize the economic dimension over other dimensions, regarding this aspect of dev-elopment as the one that squares most fully with human nature and ten- dencies. Technological and industrial development is what gratifies the material needs of human beings; thus, through this type of development, their natural disposition can be elevated and their behavior refined.

This notion might be deemed plausible if its aim is to provide human beings with their minimum material requirements before asking them to follow certain codes of behavior. This, however, is a foregone conclusion and is not subject to debate; hence, any attempt to define innate human nature must start after, not before, this point. For unless their minimal material requirements are provided for, human beings will not continue to exist. The situation here is the same whether we deal with human beings, plants or animals. We can talk about human nature as the natural code of behavior according to which the individual is judged by God and others within an appropriate framework of social organization, which is itself founded on the assumption that humankind is alive, i.e., supplied with the minimum material requirements for life.

The fact remains, however, that this is not what is meant by Western social scientists, who believe that human nature is inclined toward emphasizing self-interest regardless of the material level people have achieved in life. This explains the fact that their answers to complaints about decadent morals and manners and the deterioration of human relations and compassion is reduced, in the final analysis, to a call for an increase in growth rates. When President Ronald Reagan proposed his economic program, "Reaganomics," based on "supply-side economics," the Soviets continued to repeat slogans of raising economic growth rates as a basis for solving all problems. However, the Soviet Union collapsed while talking about the aforementioned growth rate. And the United States is doing the same thing now: insisting that economic growth is what is required by "innate human nature" despite the fact that in recent decades, it has been observed that there is an inverse relationship between economic growth rates and moral and spiritual improvement.

II. *Our Complex Development is Socio-Economic*
If we talk about dependent development in Western terms, we are talking about a modernization process which is already taking place. The degree of distortion in our part of the world may now be higher than in other dependent countries; yet, by definition, dependent development implies a degree of distortion or lopsided growth of different sectors from a national perspective.

Thus, one or two more degrees in the level of dis-tortion may be regarded as a minor problem which can be handled so long as we are conceding our dependency on an external center.

If, on the other hand, we adopt the perspective of independent development, we will be facing a real challenge. If we deal with the matter while realizing that it requires considerable calculations, our first question will be: can we generate sufficient momentum and energy for such an undertaking? And in what way? We should also take into consideration that such an understanding entails an ongoing confrontation, i.e., the possibility of "cold war" or outright hostilities.

To start with, our view of human history does not deem independent development imperative for each nation, nor does it enjoin a unified, universal pattern for independent development. What suits us is more or less different from what is suitable for others. We have to determine what suits us in terms of ends and means. At any rate, we differ from the contemporary (Western) models, especially in terms of objectives since we assign greater weight to the social rather than the economic aspect.

It is the notion of "innate human nature," *fiṭrah*, which sets us apart from the Western outlook. The two notions of *fiṭrah* are as different as secularism and Islam. According to Islam (surrender to the will of God), all wealth belongs to God, while earthly life is a path to the hereafter. We are commanded not to neglect our share in this world; however, we are to fulfill our worldly duties within the regulations according to which we will be held accountable on the Day of Judgment, when neither wealth nor offspring will be of any use to us. This Islamic notion does not accept the predominance of physical or worldly tendencies in "innate human nature." Yet, although Islam insists on the preponderance of spiritual and moral tendencies, it does not underestimate the importance of material factors. Preponderance simply means the right to guide and regulate one's behavior. The realization of such preponderance is attained through tiring struggle on the part of the individual as well as society so as to defeat, or at least neutralize, the tendencies that contradict what Islam regards as the sound and natural human *fiṭrah*.

This Islamic notion of *fiṭrah* and the objective of raising a Muslim according to the above standards is the focus of most Muslim scholars and jurists. Moreover, the fundamentals of Islam which are directly linked to civilizational studies may be regarded as an extension of the notion of Muslim character. Such fundamentals seek to make the whole social system conducive to the propagation of this human model, actualizing people's potentials and enabling them to guide the system. Whereas the secular notion of human *fiṭrah* in European civilization gave prominence to the economic side over the social one, the Islamic notion of *fiṭrah* led, by contrast, to the predominance of the social side over the economic.4 But how? And to what extent? I believe that the theoretical expression of this ultimate objective and the means to realize it will vary from one school of thought to another, as was the case in the course of our history and still is. This is normal and, in fact, desirable since what we do not want is an institution issuing arbitrary judgments about what is permitted or prohibited. The warrants for tolerable differences are numerous, and the scholars or thinkers who put forward a certain theoretical construct are required to observe the social, regional, and international conditions at hand. They should also understand the historical developments that led to the current situation on the domestic, regional, and international levels. Undoubtedly, the evaluation of all such factors and the future perspective based thereon will be conditioned by the position of the thinker him/herself. Do his/her interests identify with stability or with struggle? And to what extent? What is his/her estimate of the potentials of the situation that have yet to be revealed? Is he/she of the type that tends to take risks or not? All such questions may generate others, and all, in turn, can create various opinions.

However, we should not overlook the fact that the principle of independent development which is predicated on the prevalence of the social side minimizes differences and views different parties as members of one team. From the perspective of independent development, it is not possible, for instance, to dispute the necessity of being cautious while dealing with the superpowers dominating the world order in all fields. A nation which believes that it has a divine message to convey to the world and that it is "the best nation that has ever been brought forth for the good of humankind" should be acutely conscious of its dignity and liberty; i.e., it should not give foreigners the opportunity to dominate its economy or security. Moreover, a course of development which gives prominence to social aspects will not treat growth rates as a sacred objective whose importance surpasses that of morals, justice or values.

Islam (the religion of *fiṭrah*), as it addresses humankind on the social and individual levels, rejects oppression, exploitation and genocide (as the white settlers exterminated millions of native Americans and Canadians in North America) under the pretext of colonization, development, and the "white man's burden." Even if this was really necessary, it is utterly rejected by all Muslims who study the various models of socio-economic development. I will now elaborate on some types of developmental common ground which can help guide human social objectives and values.

CONCLUSIONS AND EXTENSIONS OF THE NOTION OF INDEPENDENT SOCIO-ECONOMIC DEVELOPMENT

I. *Criticizing the Notion of Modernization*

The West seeks to propagate its concepts of economic-social development in the Third World under the mantle of modernization. The notion of modernization itself implies that everything modern and advanced belongs to European civilization. Accordingly, the modernization process is simply the attempt of dependent countries to become "part of the West" or "part of Europe" as Khedive Ismail is reputed to have put it. So many of us have swallowed the bait that nearly anyone who would disagree is considered to be ignorant or reactionary. We find, for instance, that in Myrdal's study, he assumes that modernization is the natural and inspiring target in the "Asian Drama." Theoretically and logically, he maps out the steps required to realize the values of modernization. He then concludes his major work by observing that "the ideals of nationalism are the easiest to spread in under-developed countries in comparison to the other ideals of modernization." Unfortunately, however, he does not give much thought to this important observation, which might have made a major difference in his analytical and theoretical constructs. Careful consideration of this observation would, first, relate the restructuring of a nation to a deeply-rooted national spirit which is consistent with the complex content of the independent model and which may, in turn, repel external hegemony. Such a process would add and even transform what are known as modernization values. Myrdal's – and, naturally, others' – explanations of modernization values are confined to rationalism, development planning, higher productivity, institutions, proper policies, etc. Yet, the list of values does not include the most important one necessary for development, which is self-confidence in dealing with the dominant nations. This value is, in fact, the most important according to the notion of independent development given that the masses only respond fully within a genuine national revival in the face of strong foreign challenges.

Economic independence cannot be earned without self-confidence, liberation from the fear of the "demi-gods" of the dominant countries, encouraging the creativity of the nation, and bold rejection or criticism of foreign advice. This boldness needs to cover not only decisions regarding suitable technologies or projects, but also the whole theory of economic development and its ultimate goal. Undoubtedly, this will be reflected in determining the most suitable independent consumption patterns.

The strategy of gratifying basic needs is a strategy of independent, or self-centric, economic development. Development in general is indeed a complex process, comprising cultural, political, economic, and social components. This type of complex development is self-centric, i.e., a complete revival generated from within the nation. Obviously, this concept is not consistent with the prevailing notion of modernization. Hence, some thinkers (such as Anwar Abdul-Malik) have used the term "authenticated modernization;" however, it would be preferable to use the term "self-renewal," i.e. renewal from within the nation and its own values. Self-renewal in this sense does not overlook the broad surrounding environment, but rather interacts with it and decides what form development should take. Such self-renewal, conscious of its surroundings, is the spirit of complex independent development: the very spirit of national cultural renaissance. In fact, all we are proposing here is a rediscovery of what our own pioneers have proposed. Al-Afghānī criticized his contemporary Ottomans for the same things for which we criticize our governments today. The Ottomans established a number of schools in the new style and sent their youths to Western countries to bring back with them science, knowledge, literature and all that they call "civilization." Yet, such "civilization" is tied directly to its country of origin in accordance with its nature and social structure. In other words, civilization should emanate from within the nation itself and from the natural development of its society. Self-renewal that generates original "civilization" will lead to the formulation (revival) of various cultural centers. Such centers put forward a worldview, a self-image, and a view of others different from that offered by Western civilization. Relating the national enterprise to cultural independence is precisely what impels us to reject "modernization" as a notion and as a term.

II. *The Notion of Cultural Independence*

The issue of cultural independence requires further elaboration. Considering the treatments and approaches of al-Afghānī and Muḥammad ʿAbduh, the question of cultural independence is not a novelty in our modern intellectual literature. However, most of our political and intellectual elites are products of Western civilization. Accordingly, the objective of Arab cultural independence has been replaced by "modernization," by which its advocates mean the emulation of Western experience so as to attain what the West has realized. Thus, they construe modern civilization as a single, indivisible, global civilization, i.e., Western civilization. The notion of cultural uniqueness or independence was not on our intellectual agenda at the climax of the nationalist tide in the 1950s and 1960s. Recently, the idea has become increasingly acceptable; nevertheless, the concept is still vague for many Arabs despite their initial acceptance of it. Therefore, there is a need for more intensive theoretical efforts in order to reach a precise definition of this concept and related notions.

It may be best to term the notion in question "cultural independence," since references to the "Arab cultural enterprise" may be mistakenly understood to be Arabs' attempt to catch up with modern Western civilization, namely, a Western civilizational project carried out by Arabic speaking people. This confusion should be eliminated. I would like to emphasize that my notion of civilization comprises all that humankind has created and practiced in the past and the present to meet people's material, intellectual and spiritual needs; hence, such a notion is not confined to intellectual and spiritual creation. Naturally, as time passes, the total creative endeavor in all fields is realized through a society. At a lower level of abstraction and generalization, we can say that this process was – and is – historically realized within specific societies, their peculiar creative experiences and their environmental conditions.

Communities that preserved their common bonds until they were crystallized at some stage into a cohe-rent pattern are called nations. That is because all their cultural achie- vements (of all types and forms) were original, not from the Other. In other words, the achievements of such a nation developed into a pattern of variables and interrelations that realized cohesion and unity for the society.

Accordingly, the recognition of a nation is inseparable from the recognition of the historical and cultural achievements without which the term "nation" could not be applied to it. The term "cultural independence" is an expression of this notion. This, however, does not run counter to ongoing interaction among cultures, nor does it negate the fact that there are common characteristics of a number of nations close to each other as a result of special ties and interactions. We do not believe that there is any necessary or real connection between Western economic development and the possibility of achieving the required modification in this or that nation's cultural pattern. Accordingly, we cannot conclude that attaining such changes is an imperative (as Marx did). A wide-ranging transformation might not be possible or timely in any Western country for a number of reasons. The required change, however, is a tough struggle that Western communities should undergo even though it is tied up with the need to bring about transformation in all social spheres. Failure may result in the collapse of the whole pattern, together with its social and scientific achievements. The fact remains that whether Western societies succeed or fail in regaining what was lost during the bourgeois industrial revolution, we should adopt a different approach for revival in the East. Our success in preserving the positive core of our cultural heritage, which is based on a balance between material and moral aspects, and in establishing an economically developed society within this framework will be a real contribution toward reforming the Western cultural pattern itself, since in so doing, we will be positing an alternative cultural model and thereby contributing to human development in general.

If given careful thought, the aforementioned propositions will be seen not to be mere rhetoric. Independent economic development and cultural independence are interrelated; hence, talk about cultural independence is nonsensical without a strong economic basis, while attempts to realize genuine independent economic development will likewise be futile without cultural independence.

III. *Growth Rate and Average Income*
Our ultimate aim is cultural independence; however, the serious adoption and implementation of this aim will mean a radical revolution in all

aspects of life. That is, all development policies will have to be structured so as to cope with this process, and economic development will likewise occupy an important position. Implementing an independent cultural enterprise is impossible without substantial economic support, and sustaining high growth rates (of development) is part and parcel of the very structure of our ultimate long-term goal. However, a comprehensive notion requires reconsideration of the criterion of average income per capita or its likes (such as average quantitative shares in certain goods or services per capita). This criterion is still widely used to measure development or progress, which gives the growth rate great importance as a means by which to move from a lower to a higher average per capita income. This underlies the ability to achieve a growth that would narrow, then remove, the gap in income and living standards between "developing" countries on the one hand, and those of the "developed" countries on the other.

The narrowing and removal of that gap is viewed in Western (Capitalist and Socialist) literature as the result of the process of "modernization" and development in its quintessential sense. However, we reject the use of average income per capita and growth rates in order to assess development, since they are incompatible with our notion of independent development and its implied strategy of gratifying basic needs.

According to our ultimate long-term goal, average per capita income is not the main criterion of development (progress) or underdevelopment. The main criterion is cultural, political, and economic independence or dependence. This complex qualitative criterion is certainly not as simple and elegant as the quantitative expression represented in the criterion of average income per capita. However, if our goal is to reach a more indicative criterion, our qualitative criterion will be more effective in determining the real difference between dependent and independent or dominant countries. It is also more effective in identifying the dynamic potentials underlying various economies.

With regard to the gap between our average income per capita and that of the dominant countries, such criteria gain importance – given the conditions of independent development – to guarantee the continuous implementation of the gratifying basic needs strategy. We drop the quantitative significance of the gap that separates the underdeveloped, dependent countries from countries of the North due to the technical disadvantages involved in the calculation of average income per capita. However, we do care about the general significance (indication) of the gap insofar as it reflects a major difference in economic abilities. That is, we benefit from such criteria as an indicator of a critical qualitative state of affairs; thus, the issue is not to try to eliminate the gap at any price, nor is it to achieve the pattern of consumption and lifestyle of the North. At the same time, we are concerned about the significance of the vast gap caused by the overwhelming technological and scientific supremacy of the North. That is why the enthusiasm to have an independent lifestyle or cultural enterprise does not undermine the drive to possess modern scientific knowledge and eliminate the gap in this particular field as soon as possible. Independent economic development can never be realized without tireless efforts to break the Western monopoly on scientific knowledge. However, our economic development objectives differ from those of the North, as do our priorities and our production capabilities. All this requires an independent outlook regarding the innovation and utilization of appropriate technology. In general, we seek to attain technological capabilities that enable us to do whatever we need to meet our growing independent needs or to defend (perhaps militarily) our cultural enterprise against potential foreign assaults. This is a fierce battle, not only against the giants monopolizing this field, but also against the dangers of surrender to the temptation to be lazy and import every available technology from abroad.

IV. *The Strategy of Gratifying Basic Needs*
Development research by dependent countries has recently contributed to formulating a "production mode" suitable to the independent development model. This model is represented by the strategy of gratifying basic needs. The writings of prominent Eastern economists have explained the various aspects of this strategy. However, suffice it here to quote a general and synoptic definition offered by Ismail Sabri Abdullah: "The essence of the issue is the establishment of a domestically integrated industrial skeleton. This skeleton shall be integrated with the other national economic sectors, at the top of which is the agricultural sector. It should be consistent with the cultural and social objectives of society. Such a skeleton, which is based on reliance on a huge domestic market furnished by the gratifying basic needs strategy, will minimize dependence on unbalanced

trade with the capitalist countries. Thus, it can escape the hold of multinational corporations. Development cannot be independent and self-centric unless it is directed towards the domestic market. In the meantime, it is the type of development which can sustain itself and has the autonomous ability to proceed without begging for foreign aid." The basic value of this definition is that it understands the gratifying basic needs strategy in such a way that economic development may be employed to reach the ultimate goal, namely, the elimination of dependency and the realization of comprehensive independent development. This concept might not be as clear for some other advocates of the independence model and the gratifying basic needs strategy.

I believe that if this strategy is informed and directed by the ultimate long-term goal of independence, then its internal logic, which reflects practical needs, will lead to the integration of the following six principles in a consistent synthesis which may be briefly explained as follows:

(1) The Relationship With the Outside World

This strategy seems to be quite compatible with the aim of independence. Economically, it leads to reduced reliance on the outside world both quantitatively (by reducing imports and loans) and qualitatively (by doing without the help of the outside world in meeting most local basic needs). The logic of this strategy leads to independence through the proposed change in patterns of consumption and production.

(2) Self-reliance

This principle is naturally implied in the basic reliance on mobilizing the economic surplus and directing development to meet basic needs through labor and the use of local resources (potentials). In a broader and more dynamic sense, self-reliance is implied in what we call the spirit of self-renewal and the encounter with external challenges.

(3) The Role of the State

The role of the state in the Western experience is crucial for opening the world to its enterprise. At the same time, the role of the state in the dependent countries is essential to protect their development experience from the outside world. Unlike the Western countries, dependent countries face the outside world from a position of weakness rather than strength. Such dependent countries are in the position of strategic defense rather than offense, which requires the state to act as a centralized institution making optimal use of scarce human expertise in the scientific, technical, economic, and administrative spheres; in this way, it exemplifies the same logic of concentrating military talents in one institution. The gratifying basic needs strategy requires a highly efficient management of international relations (politically and economically), minimizing the risks and losses of probable external conflicts and making the best use of conflicts among dominant countries and blocs. This strategy cannot be implemented without war-economy institutions. This means that the very rationale of the strategy necessarily leads to control by the central authority over the national economy through explicit direction and management. Therefore, there should be central financial and resource planning to determine the directions and growth rates that are likely to support independence and that are consistent with the targeted pattern of consumption within the framework of maintaining readiness to encounter external pressures. This strategy is by no means compatible with the illusion of relying on what is known as market mechan-isms to allocate resources or the illusion of depending on the initiative of the domestic (not to mention the foreign) private sector as a decisive partner. This, however, should not be construed as a call to liquidate or undercut the private sector; we would rather call for the opposite view within the specific determinants of our situation.

(4) THE GIANT LEAP

This principle, which is guaranteed by the logic of the proposed strategy, entails maximization of the planned economic surplus (using Baran's term), its investment in accordance with the strategic objective, and the launching of a large-scale attack on all fronts (i.e. not only the economic front alone) at a particular historical moment.

(5) DISTRIBUTION

The idea of making initiatives and mobilizing humanpower to confront external as well as internal changes facing independent development requires the reduction of income differences to limits deemed necessary to spur work and creativity and eliminate schisms and conflicts. The distribution issue is not merely a compatible accessory from without the strategy of gratifying basic needs nor is it merely an internal policy. The distribution issue is an inherent part of the production skeleton itself. Yet, we can state that realizing the importance of social solidarity is a vital element in streamlining the general acceptance of the gratifying basic needs strategy.

(6) DEVELOPMENT IS A COMPLEX PROCESS

Reference to numerous concurrent changes is implied in each of the above principles. Yet, there has to be a comprehensive notion of the requisite changes which is often overlooked by many studies on the gratifying basic needs strategy. Formulating such a comprehensive notion is a formidable task that requires creative interaction between economists, sociologists, and political scientists in addition to the efforts of educators and cultural activists. However, without reaching a comprehensive notion that seems viable and consistent with the above principles, the strategy of gratifying basic needs will be impractical. Mahboub-ul-Haq is totally right when he warns of turning the talk about the new strategy into a worn-out fashion. He stresses the fact that the new strategy of development requires a balance among political, economic and social forces. Hence, unless a decision is taken on the highest political levels, with the whole political structure inside the country mobilized to support it, the planning exercise will remain little more than an academic endeavor. But how can political decisions be taken without what Myrdal terms the "strong government?" In fact, Myrdal takes all governments in dependent countries (even the strictest dictatorships) to be "soft" governments. This means that such governments are unable to enforce the laws and decisions which appear to be necessary because they are dominated by those who have interests entrenched in the status quo and who would benefit from keeping all legislation and procedures as they currently are. Strong governments are thus a prerequisite to implement the strategy of gratifying basic needs.

Moreover, the model of independent development is logically consistent with the principle of equitable distribution. Independent development does not initially assume the possibility of effecting an essential modification of distribution relations while the same international and domestic powers are still dominating production relations inside the model or the system, since the interests of these powers run radically counter to the principle of income distribution. As mentioned above, the model of independent development acquires real depth only when wedded to the strategy of gratifying basic needs which, by definition, involves a revolution in consumption patterns and a direct attack on the sources of poverty. In other words, equity of distribution is implied and assured by the very structure of the strategy. Yet, in this situation, it is more reasonable to identify the challenge that faces the strategy of gratifying basic needs, not as the re-distribution of outcome, but rather, suitable consumption patterns and the acceptance of such patterns by the different social classes of the nation. Needless to say, the targeted patterns of consumption and the commitment thereto is not merely an economic process; rather, it involves definition, persuasion, and commitment using a variety of tools. This also means that the level of currently available productive capacity cannot alone determine or develop consumption patterns.

Galal Amin criticizes economists for distorting and degrading the idea of equity by turning it into an issue of income redistribution instead of inquiring into the nature of the products themselves and whether they meet humankind's real needs. Thus, economists have been content to note the wishes of individuals to catch up economically with their neighbors regardless of whether they need what their neighbors have. This idea directs research on patterns of consumption in a way that does not allow these patterns to be a rational expression of the potentials of the national economy at a given stage. This notion remains burdened with intellectual dependency which, in turn, means that we have not changed enough to face the challenge.

If we move to the means consistent with our aim, namely, to realize the prominence of the social side of development, we will find that it is simply reliance on mobilization of the masses. This requires theoretical lucidity introduced by induction and reinterpretation of Islamic thought so as to trigger popular initiatives and to insure the legitimacy of wide participation (which implies, but is not limited to, the fundamental concept of *shūrā*, i.e., consultation) in the nation's struggle as well as all levels of decision-making. Our main means of realizing this independent development is absolute reliance on a concept of social action that seeks to mobilize diverse and competing energies within a specific society-nation via appropriate institutions.

Moreover, even if our notion does not obstruct such methods, practical requirements leave us no other choice. For example, we cannot choose reliance on the creative efforts or input of the political elite while excluding or marginalizing the masses from the struggle for independent development. We cannot opt for this choice since, as mentioned earlier, the path to independent development is open to all. Today's struggle is no longer a confrontation between two teams of knights. Modern military technologies have reduced the difference between front and back lines; everyone has literally and directly become involved in battle; besides, military efforts deplete resources with consequent effects on the level of economic development and prosperity overall. Therefore, how can we ensure steadfastness on the way to independent development without the positive, active participation of all the nation? Moreover, how can we convince the nation to participate in the process and to sacrifice on its behalf? Great revolutions and revivals are usually fueled by a solid doctrine; do we have a doctrine that can restore the Arabs' fighting spirit? Undoubtedly, Islam, in particular, embodies such a doctrine.

Lest we deceive ourselves, we have to admit that carrying out the strategy of gratifying basic needs will be very difficult. The independence model implies an unrelenting confrontation with major powers on the cultural, political, and economic fronts, with military self-defence against military invasion only as a last resort. Tough as it may be, this confrontation is considered a minor struggle. It is a struggle against external enemies with tangible dimensions, distinguished institutions and obvious interests that run radically counter to our own interests. The same perspective applies to struggling against the social classes that are associated with external enemies. None of this, however, is very difficult, given that national forces can be mobilized with high morale to confront such challenges.

The real, major jihad is self-struggle, which is becoming more difficult as the enemy has infiltrated our ranks via its consumption and cultural patterns. The record of consumers, particularly those of the middle class (or the modern sector) is not a clean one. Some habits have thus turned into a material reality which cannot be changed, let alone eliminated. As mentioned earlier, it is not enough to have a logically consistent model. Rather, one's model must be applicable to real life; otherwise, endeavors to establish it will be nothing but a sterile intellectual exercise. So, can people be changed from within? If we answer this question in the negative, we render the model inapplicable. However, I am convinced that this change can be brought about if our estimation is not based merely on ordinary calculations which favor economic or social standards exclusively.

I believe that we can induce change, bearing in mind the fact that supercomputers fail to calculate accurately the potentials of peoples in moments of historical confrontation; no doubt, cultural revival is a moment which is not subject to traditional calculations. Granted this fact, researchers' task is to envisage the major factors that ensure the success of this historical moment and the independent development model, thereby achieving its long-term ultimate goal.

3

Theories of Political Development: A Case of Biased Discourse in the Political Sciences

NASR M. ARIF

ANY ACADEMIC SCHOLARLY production emanating from the human mind and reality, i.e., based upon them and bound by their limitations, has to bear the characteristics of such mind and reality one way or another. In other words, such production is inevitably expressive – in all its manifestations – of the culture of the society in which such a human mind has been shaped and informed. Moreover, it inescapably reflects the social reality that has encompassed it and defined its key concerns, priorities, and crises. Thus, it cannot achieve full detachment even if it tries to do so; it will always be conditioned to some extent by the specificity of time, place, and people.

This understanding is closely associated with the natural disposition of human beings whose epistemological inputs are bound by time and place, not to mention the biases and desires of human beings, which might constitute serious hindrances to the acquisition of knowledge.

Generally speaking, the attempt to describe a certain human thought as universal and comprehensive in a way that makes it transcend the limits of time, place, and the potentialities of humankind is invalid and contrary to the givens of the human mind. Such an attempt is consequently unacademic, as it does not conform to the criteria of truthfulness and fairness. It is an academically faulty model governed by bias resulting in the neglect of numerous dimensions of social phenomena given that they are not in agreement with the established categories from which the researcher comes or with the findings he or she aspires to arrive at.

The essence of the concept of bias is self-centricity, and evaluating the

Other according to the criteria of the perceiving self. This implies utter negation of the Other, excluding it from the framework of history, existence, or knowledge and seeking to supplant a genuine identity with another that accords with the givens and goals of the biased/perceiving Self. This is accomplished through annihilation of the uniqueness and specificity of the Other, reabsorbing it into a system that the biased Self considers "ideal" within the milieu of its own worldview, intellectual systems, doctrines and higher ideals.

In light of this understanding of the notion of bias, we will deal with theories of political development which are considered the essence of the concept of development; these encompass all relevant theories in the domains of social, economic, and cultural development. Consequently, the following analysis will address the methodological and philosophical bases of most theories of development in the field of social sciences. The concept of political development and its philosophical, intellectual, methodological and conceptual roots will be marshaled to examine the influence of the concept of bias on the aforementioned theories and domains with the aim of finding whether bias has rendered such theories partial and exclusive, or whether these theories themselves are truly universal and applicable to most human societies regardless of their natural, environmental, cultural, religious or institutional differences.

THE SELF AND THE OTHER IN WESTERN SOCIAL SCIENCES

Science is characterized by the study of specific human or natural phenomena regardless of their details or geographical locations. It is essentially correlated with the subject matter and not with location or any particular details. For example, sociology, politics and economics are concerned with specific phenomena that are generally and ideally worthy of research. According to Western thought, science is an intellectual activity that deals with the actual and objective state of things. It is universal in the sense that it is not limited by space or time. In other words, science is not restricted to countries, nationalities or religions. This conclusion, however, is indeed questionable, if not susceptible to instantaneous refutation. A close examination of the origins and development of Western social sciences and humanities reveals that they insist upon considering theirs to be the best approaches to understanding and controlling human reality. Oddly enough, such sciences have not been successful in understanding Western reality itself. Despite their failing to provide a satisfactory understanding of the Western Self, they have nevertheless devoted specific disciplines to the study of the Other that may necessarily be different when judged from the Western social and even human points of view. The Self in this sense is represented by Europe and its extensions in North America and the South Pacific as well as the Jewish community in Palestine and historically the whites in South Africa.[1]

Since the age of the Renaissance, with the advent of the Industrial Revolution, the rise of the Western bourgeoisie, the beginning of the Age of Enlightenment, and the rise of Socialism, there has been a steadily growing academic trend that focuses essentially on the study of "non-Western societies."[2] Scholars of this trend took it upon themselves to study Oriental societies, in particular, in an attempt to understand their religions, doctrines, literature, arts, political systems, and behaviors. The purpose of such studies may well have been academic, i.e. oriented toward a real understanding of these societies, or it may have been basically political. At the same time, there has been substantial development in the methodology, tools and even the discourse of Western social sciences. By contrast, the disciplines that study non-Western societies are still flawed and devoid of any creative scholarly production.[3]

In this context, several sciences devoted to the study of non-Western societies came into being. They were mostly governed by their field of study and not by a specific subject matter. It all began with Orientalism. Controversy still surrounds the exact date of the emergence of this field, yet it is unanimously considered to be the first academic activity undertaken by the West to understand the non-Western world.[4] It may have aspired to safeguard the Western mind from the intellectual challenge of Islam, to raise doubts about Islam itself, or to detach it from the East in order ultimately to control it. Next came Anthropology as a science that studies "Neolithic" human beings who are believed to have lived in Asia, Africa, and South America. Anthropology sought to achieve a twofold purpose. The first purpose was to arrive at an alternative, fixed, and referential starting point for the Western mind after these elements had been refuted forever by the Theory of Relativity on the one hand, and the severe doubts brought about by the age of materialism on the other.[5] Its second purpose was to control the non-Western world and to undermine its culture and civilization with the aim of annexing it to Western culture.

In this connection, the relationship between anthropologists and colonialism is obvious and beyond any reasonable doubt.[6] Finally, the theories of cultural and socio-political development, to name only two, coincide neatly with the political objectives behind all other theories of Western sciences devoted to the study of the non-Western world. Thus, Orientalism came into being at a time when the "Other" meant specifically Islam or the religious East. When the West began to expand beyond the East and to colonize other regions, it was imperative for it to understand the habits, values, behavioral patterns, religions, and cultural systems of these colonized peoples, hence, the need for anthropology. This was followed by different theories of development when the non-Western worlds got rid of the direct (colonial) hegemony of the Western world. Consequently, a new pattern of domination via ideas and commodities entailed the aggrandizement of the values, lifestyle and institutions of the West as the ideal human and social model to be followed by other societies. Non-Western societies, therefore, were expected to follow in the footsteps, and behave within the framework of Western civilization.

How is it, then, that the West has devoted specific sciences to the study of the Other? It was not based on a recognition of the finitude of science and its lack of universal validity, nor on the acknowledgement of the fact that these people enjoy a certain measure of acceptable distinctiveness and difference in relation to the Western experience. On the contrary, the "Others" have been looked down upon as representing an inferior social and cultural structure vis-à-vis that of Western societies and their advanced political and economic development. Therefore, Western sciences manifest a great measure of bias and self-centricity, a "civilizational arrogance"[7] that relegates the "Other" to a position inferior to that of the "Self." Hence, it is beyond the confines of credible academia to study those societies using the same analytical categories used in the study of Western societies; rather, there have to be independent sciences for the study of such societies.

NORMATIVENESS OF THE WESTERN SOCIETAL MODEL

Scientific fields concerned with studying the non-Western world (Orientalism, Anthropology, and developmental theories) have shared the same underlying premises, concepts, methodologies, and even findings. All of these unified attitudes form what can be considered to be a grand category implying the idea that the Western societal model is the standard for all people, a touchstone against which all other human models can be measured. The sole criterion is how far those other models emulate the Western one. The foregoing assertions or "truisms" may be examined within this category:

(1) *The Simplistic Ethnic Viewpoint that Reduces Humanity to Two Groups: "Them" and "Us"*
According to the Western view, all peoples on earth may be divided into superior and inferior races. From Aristotle down to thinkers of political development, the Western, "scholarly view" of other peoples is predicated upon an ethnic classification of humanity. It looks upon all non-Westerners as one category which Aristotle describes as "barbarians," whereas Westerners themselves are seen as Graeco-Europeans. For the classical dichotomy between Greek and barbarian, Christianity proposed a more magnanimous, and more flexible measure by which it divided humanity using faith as a measure; like the Greek viewpoint, it dismissed all non-Christians as being non-civilized. Anthropologists, in turn, provided yet another classification that differentiates between the civilized, i.e. Westerners, and the primitives, i.e., all others.[8] Consequently, 19th-Century theses about Eastern backwardness and decadence and the disparity between the East and the West were linked to the then-prevalent ideas revolving around the essential bases of ethnic difference and the civilized/uncivilized dichotomy.[9] Backwardness was widely used as a description of all that is non-Western, a simplification that arbitrarily divided all peoples into two types: "us" and "them." The non-Western world was regarded as one unit characterized by a certain essence and by certain stereotypical characteristics that applied to all its constituents. This led to the promulgation of vague concepts that claimed to represent those "Other" societies. The result, however, was failure to express the true identities or fundamental tenets of such societies. They were described collectively at first as the "East," a concept that suffers inherently from ambiguity and bias. To whom is a certain part of the world the "East?" What are the criteria that allow a certain analyst to judge it as "Eastern?" On what basis have all those broad areas been called "Eastern?" And does this concept apply neatly to one unit that enjoys cultural specificity and a unified civilizational and historical experience?

In view of these implications inherent in the concept of the East, it is hard to exonerate it of partiality or the Western self-centricity that considers Europe to be the center of the universe against which other parts of the world are identified.[10] Those who define the "East" in this way risk a grave simplification, as what is also called the "Orient" or the "East" consists of a number of civilizations, cultures, religions, systems, societies, and institutions that are so diverse that they cannot be regarded as one concept or examined as a single field of study. Other concepts dealt with the Other by describing it as "developing countries" which are also classified as backward, primitive, agricultural, non-industrial, and Third World.[11] All these concepts reflect a subjective and an obviously superior Western outlook.

If the foregoing terms are re-examined from the perspective of geographical location, it will be noticed that they commonly refer to all that is non-Western. The societies in question, however, have hardly anything "social" in common. For example, from the political point of view, these countries do not constitute a single international political bloc encompassing homogeneous political systems. Political systems in such countries range from hereditary to Marxist regimes. Likewise, from the economic point of view, these countries do not share the same characteristics, as they differ essentially in terms of their patterns of production, standards of living, gross national products, and per-capita incomes. Nor do they represent a single geographical bloc, as they differ greatly in terms of geomorphology and climate. Finally, there is hardly any historical or cultural relationship among the countries under study; rather, they have been forcibly categorized by the West as one, despite their internal diversity.

PROJECTION OF THE WESTERN EXPERIENCE ON THE NON-WESTERN WORLD

According to contemporary theories of development, the Western experience is the only model to be emulated by other societies. Paradoxically, Western theorists of development have derived their propositions and theories from the history and essential content of Western progress and then tried to apply such concepts to the non-Western world. They argue that what applied to the West should necessarily work for other societies as well. This trend is a basic feature of sciences that examine the non-Western world. Since the advent of Orientalism, Western thinkers have consciously or unconsciously projected the experience of their own societies onto the non-Western world in the following ways:

(1) *Classification of History into Ancient, Medieval, and Modern*
According to Oswald Spengler,[12] the method of dividing history into such periods is senseless, fruitless, and lacking in credibility. Not only does it depict history as a static process, but it also looks at Western Europe as an unjustifiably unique and established part of the world. Moreover, this classification makes other great historical civilizations revolve humbly around the pole of Western Europe as if the whole world has been created for the service of Western Europe, or as if the remaining peoples and civilizations were just a prop to that master world.[13] In this way, the Enlightenment had to label everything before it as "Dark Ages" in order to claim the light for itself. In the period that is commonly regarded by Westerners as the Dark Ages, Islamic civilization was at its peak; and during what Europe calls the "Renaissance," "Enlightenment," and modernization, other peoples were massacred, pillaged, and dominated. At this juncture, a big question mark hangs over the criterion by which a certain period can be judged as dark and backward or as enlightened and advanced; still, are these criteria used to judge the achievements realized within a given society or those realized on a universal level?[14]

(2) *Western Political Science's Adoption of the Concept of State, Derived from the Western Historical Experience*
This concept implies that the politically integral society is the society in which the state, with its different institutions and functions, is set up in conformity with the Western historical experience. Any model that departs from this Western norm is considered far from being a real state. According to the Western definition of the concept of the state, the absence of state administration and institutions testifies to the primitiveness or backwardness of society.[15] Western thought does not allow for the exis-tence of stateless societies or of states without authority. Once again, the standard model is the way the states emerged in Europe, which is elevated to the status of a universal model. This is a result of the tendency toward self-centeredness practiced by the West whenever it attempts to evaluate the experiences of other societies, as if its historical experience were the only valid one.[16]

(3) *The Linear Development of Human Societies Across Ascending Stages*

The projection of the stages of Western history onto human development has produced several theories in the fields of anthropology, political economy, and societal development stressing the unity and linearity of human progress and asserting the fact that it must follow a pattern of ascending stages. Anthropological studies in particular have been influenced by the Darwinian evolutionism that presupposes the existence of "one line of human development that must be followed by all human societies, according to fixed, unified systems and regulations that are unchangeable anywhere in the world."[17] In other words, the diversity of civilizations is governed by the principle of evolution (in terms of quantity, not quality or kind). According to this logic, it follows that primitive peoples, in order to keep pace with developed countries, have to go through the same stages of development.

Most theories of societal development also attempt to project the experience of Western development onto the non-Western world. Karl Marx believed in five stages of human development: primitive communism, slavery, feudalism, capitalism, and scientific communism. For Auguste Comte, human development passes through three stages: theological, metaphysical, and positivistic.[18] Parsons, likewise, has posited three stages for human development: primitive, medieval, and advanced.[19] Rostow has also identified five stages: traditional society, preconditions for take-off, the take-off, the drive to maturity, and the age of high mass-consumption.[20] Karl Yosher has divided these stages into rural, urban, and international economy.[21] As for Organisky, he divides them into four stages: the traditional national union, industrialization, national welfare, and abundance.[22] According to the foregoing theories, these are the general stages of human development that must be followed by all societies. According to this perspective, non-Western countries may approach the final stage of development, but they can never achieve it. Many scholars have seriously and perseveringly attempted the application of these stages to all countries regardless of time and place, and regardless of the fact that this may lead to academic dishonesty in understanding other societies. If this vision fails at times to find correlation among the aforementioned Western stages of development and those of other countries, the problem is readily solved by reference to the particularities and irregularities of these cases. The standard here is the Western experience which has been generalized to encompass the whole world.[23]

(4) *Projection of Western Ideals and Objectives on Other Human Models*

The ideals as well as the objectives of the West have been applied, through theories of political development, to all peoples. They are considered the ideals and objectives of all humanity, i.e., the best ideal that the human mind can ever attain. To Westerners, these ideals and objectives are not mere ideals; they are a lived experience and an already established model which they seek to spread all over the world. They believe that the political goals of all human societies must be modeled after Western norms. No matter how inappropriate Western democracy and political institutions may be in the non-Western world, they have to be adopted wholeheartedly by its peoples. Likewise, the sublime economic objectives of all human beings should be securing the stage of abundant consumption. Culturally, the utmost aspirations of humankind should be the achievement of emancipation, the lifting of moral restrictions, and the dissemination of secularism. The conviction that these ideals are universal and that they should be sought by all societies has led to the emergence of short-term objectives requiring non-Western countries to "bridge the gap," to "raise the standard of living," and to "keep pace" with Western nations so that the former would perpetually follow in the footsteps of the latter. However, it is understood that non-Western countries would either need a miracle to achieve the same Western level of development or wait for Western countries to become suddenly stagnant and reachable. In other words, the world of the "Other" is doomed to chase a mirage because the circumstances that surround development in the West are totally different from those of the other world. Besides, it has to be taken into consideration that the West achieved its development partly at the expense of non-Western societies. It managed to do so mainly by plundering the resources of the Third World and through the brain drain, namely, by enticing Third World intellectuals and scientists to emigrate to the West. Consequently, the Third World has been doubly incapacitated, once through pillaging of resources by the West, and second by losing the chance to depend on the resources of its inhabitants.

In this context, some major questions have to be raised: Are the foregoing goals humankind's goals everywhere? Do all human societies consider them basic aims that have to be realized? Can they not be regarded as means rather than ends in other societies? What about societies that believe in a divine message which motivates them to regard the hereafter as an end, and this life as a means towards that sublime end? What about some people who consider abstinence and asceticism as chief ends to be sought? Are these ends or goals the best that humanity has ever achieved? What more can be done after democracy, complete freedom, and economic abundance have been realized? What will be the importance of such concepts as social integration, purity, justice, and moral commitment? Beyond all this, have all human societies been consulted as to whether these ends represent their common aspirations? Have these ends been derived from a close reading of world religions and philosophies? Is it not more human for every society to have its own ends and ideals according to its beliefs, culture, needs, and ambitions, which may certainly be different from those of other societies?

JUDGING OTHER HUMAN MODELS ACCORDING TO THE CRITERIA OF THE WESTERN ONE

Theorists of development believe the Western experience to be the standard model against which all human models can be judged. This perspective has been held true not only in the domain of development but also in the academic field concerned with the study of the "Other". This prototypical Western model evaluates other experiences according to how far or close they are to it. The following are the most important postulates of the aforementioned argument:

(1) *Western Christianity as a Standard for Assessing Other Religions*
This tendency has been particularly prevalent in Orientalist studies. It implies that other religions can only be acceptable if they correspond to the fundamental tenets of Christianity. It also suggests that whatever does not conform to the Christian spiritual model is not only faulty and defective, but indicative of religious corruption, weakness, and ineffectiveness.[24] In other words, the West believes that Christianity is the most superior religion on earth and that the development of humanity has not yet outgrown its emergence.

(2) Assessment of Other Experiences According to Contradictory Criteria Inspired by Successive Western Experiences

The history of the West progresses in terms of ascending stages whereby each stage presents hypotheses that may contradict altogether its preceding one. Accordingly, there has been considerable accumulation of concepts and criteria, most of which are not handled in the study and evaluation of Western societies, probably because they involve a great deal of contradiction. The reason could be that Western thought has passed through several stages that formed modern Europe: "there was more than one Europe. There was the Europe that grew out of the Renaissance and the Reform, Enlightenment Europe, and post-1850 Imperialist Europe. And at the heart of each of these different Europes, various circles met and overlapped, thereby creating kaleidoscopic viewpoints: those of the politician, the priest, the merchant, the intellectual and the colonist ..."[25] With this considerable accumulation of stages and angles of vision, the Western thinker has had a great number of criteria whereby he or she can judge the societies under study. This has entailed, at times, criticizing or distorting the institutions of such societies. For example, Christianity and secularism used to criticize Islam and to level hostile accusations against it such as accusing it of being deficient in spiritualism or suffering from theocratic stagnation.[26]

(3) The Study of Non-Western Societies According to Indicators Stemming from the Contemporary Western Experience

Western researchers argue that contemporary Europe is the epitome of modernity and advancement. They have consequently coined some key indicators, the presence of which denotes modernity, advancement and development, while their absence implies backwardness, primitiveness, and reactionism. From Louis Morgan onwards, there has been constant differentiation between indicators of the advanced society and those relating to the backward one. Morgan believed that a given society is advanced if the individual's place in it is determined by the criteria of achievement; if social relations are not affected by the criterion of kinship; if the individual's role is defined by how much he earns, by his position, and by his authority. If society is divided into social strata and not into clans, this society will be an advanced one and vice versa. Taylor, Fraser and Sir Henry Mean[27] proposed the same line of thought as Durkheim, who suggested that a truly advanced society is the one based on organic cohesion while the society built on mechanical cohesion is considered backward. In a similar vein, Spencer differentiated between the military society and the industrial one[28] whereas Cowley differentiated between primary and secondary communities. Max Weber, on the other hand, differentiated between the rational and irrational society, while Anthony Leader's differentiation was between the agricultural and industrial state.[29] Finally, Robert Redfield differentiated between the primitive society and the civilized society.[30]

A close look at these stock dualities and stereotypes reveals that they are built on what is called a "Teleological Bias" as well as a bias in favor of the way the West achieved its development without full understanding of the nature of non-Western societies.[31] Hence, the phenomena studied are twisted to fit certain stereotypes which are radically at variance from said phenomena, a process that results in overlooking many of their dimensions. Such concepts came to be imposed on non-Western societies regardless of their specificities. The abundance of stereotypical hypotheses about the nature of non-Western societies made it impossible for such societies to be truthfully and honestly portrayed and presented. Researchers preferred, instead, to look for evidence that would enable them to arrive at a certain idealistic pattern that ultimately overlooked, if not amputated, considerable dimensions of this phenomenon.

NEGATION OF THE OTHER AND THE ABSOLUTISM OF THE SELF

An integral characteristic of bias and self-centricity strips the Other of the right to exist and exerts strenuous efforts to expel it from the framework of science, history or even being. The notions of Self and Other in this respect are not restricted solely to social existence; they also subsume the distinctive presence expressive of identity. That is why biased science is always trying to impose its own categories, concepts, and methods. This has to do with its conflict-based outlook on human existence, a perspective that sees others only by negating them, so that the Western Self can only achieve self-realization by negating the Self of others and annexing it to its own. This outlook is an integral part of Western thought despite all that is said about diversity and pluralism, for diversity in this sense is restricted to the internal structure of a certain society within one culture or civilization. In other words, the pluralism under question is intra-civilizational rather than inter-civilizational. It does not mean the diversity of human civilizations; cultural and civilizational diversity is merely looked at from a folkloric perspective that augments the desire for supremacy and distinction. This means that the legitimacy of Others' existence and their right to formulate their own indigenous human models are not at all acknowledged. The most dramatic expression of the foregoing notion is the following quote from a native of the Solomon Islands: "You white men give orders; we no longer give orders to ourselves; we have to obey yours ... The white man has come to tell us we must behave like *his* father. Our own fathers, we must forget them... In the old days, we did this thing, we did that thing. We did not stop and say to ourselves first, 'This thing I want to do, is it right?' We always knew. Now we have to say, 'This thing I want to do, will the white man tell me it is wrong and punish me for it?'"[32]

If we consider the literature of political development in general, we will find that the process of negation and replacement emphasizes three main dimensions:

(1) *The Negation of Traditional Culture by Replacing it with Modern Culture*

To Westerners, the concept of "culture" is derived from "cultivation" which suggests planting and sowing, and which can be extended to mean the planting of concepts, values and patterns. The underlying meaning of this concept, however, is the removal of traditional culture that is prevalent in non-Western societies. Theorists of political development have emphasized this by stating that development cannot be achieved in the presence of an incapacitating culture that is against the idea of development. This traditional culture therefore has to leave the scene and be replaced with the values of modern culture. The concept of "traditional culture" applies of course to all cultures except the Western one. The characteristics of the former were traditionally formulated as directly opposite to those of Western culture. Some of these characteristics are religiosity, heredity, class rigidity, and technological inertia. Contrary to this, modern culture is characterized by secularism, equality, achievement, universality, flexible class structure, technological advancement, and ineffectiveness of subjective factors.[33] Thus, the world is divided into two spheres: that of real culture and that of folklore. Hence it is imperative to move toward one civilization representing the unity of humankind. As the present state of affairs suffers from diversity and fragmentation,[34] the cultural change of traditional societies and the destruction of existing cultural patterns in non-Western societies have to take place, since they are considered to be the real impediments to progress and development. Hence, there is almost unanimous agreement among theorists of development on the necessity of getting rid of the "traditional culture" and replacing it with the modern one, i.e., Western culture.

(2) *The Negation of Traditional Institutions by Replacing them with Modern Ones*

What has been said about culture applies also to institutions. Theories of development also stress the importance of removing traditional institutions and replacing them with modern ones fashioned after Western institutions. According to Western theorists, traditional institutions represent an impediment to development, no matter how deeply they are rooted in the culture of a given society or correlated with the society's prevalent beliefs, establishments, and system of rights and obligations,[35] as well as the predominant social equation (balance).[36] However, the fact remains that modern institutions in the non-Western world have failed to create a vital interaction between the various strata of society in the political field. Thus uprooted, these institutions have lost their credibility and effectiveness due to their alienation and aloofness from the social structure and the traditional institutions.[37]

(3) *The Negation of Traditional Economy by Replacing it with Modern Economy*

The Western experience has been chiefly based upon the Industrial Revolution. This has resulted in the increase of the role of industrialization in the economic structure and of cities in the social structure, as well as the diminution of agricultural life and the rural nature of people. Theories of development therefore argue that achievement of industrialization and urbanization – as it took place in the West – is indispensable for achieving development. Therefore, the elimination of traditional economies and societal systems mainly driven by agriculture is necessary for the establishment of a technologically advanced, industrialized society. For this industrial system to prosper, there has to be: first, accumulation of capital[38] such as that achieved by Europe when it took advantage of peoples' resources under the guise of geographical discoveries and colonization. However, the non-Western world cannot achieve accumulation of capital unless it becomes burdened with debts. The second necessary element for the industrial system to prosper is industrialization and the adoption of modern technology.[39]

It is worth noting that industrialization has had major effects on many societies. It has polluted the environment and destroyed many natural phenomena; it has spread social injustice and contributed to the emergence of exploitative, capitalistic classes that dominate all spheres of society for their own good; it has turned the human being into a mere cog in a machine[40] and caused economic imbalance among the different sectors of production. Agriculture has been neglected or at least industrialized as a raw material for other industries. Industrialization also led to the emergence of great monopolies in the field of politics and to the intervention of capitalism in decision-making and in the political process, through interest groups and tools for controlling public opinion such as information, media and propaganda.

Apart from these multifaceted problems, food is the main problem facing the non-Western world. It follows that the first priority of development in these societies is achieving self-sufficiency in food rather than industrialization. As the financial capabilities of these countries are meager and their populations are also very large, the economic model of industrialization there relies heavily on labor-intensive activities, simple technology, and scarce local resources. On the other hand, the very essence of the concepts of the world economy, with all its values and axioms, reflects the philosophy of Western society and its desire to universalize its model and to subdue the "Other". As is commonly understood by Western societies, economics is the science of the efficient allocation of rare resources to suit the diversity of needs; in other words, the scarcity of resources and the diversity of needs are well taken into consideration. This notion does not mean, however, that all countries believe in it. Islamic civilization, for example, maintains that economy means moderation, avoiding both extravagance or stinginess in food, attire, and shelter; it also asserts that a human being's needs should be limited in quantity and quality. It is the Islamic doctrine that calls for moderation and warns against extravagance, yet, it stresses that worldly resources are limitless as they come from Allah the Almighty, whose resources never come to an end. The Qur'an enjoins: "Yet if the people of those communities had but attained to faith and been conscious of Us, We would indeed have opened up for them blessings out of heaven and earth" (7:96). Besides, approaches to and methods of development differ from one society to another depending on the culture and beliefs of that society. Some of these approaches can be enumerated as voluntary work, cooperation, teamwork, etc.

(4) *The Methodology of Determining and Neutralizing Bias in Theories of Political Development*

Thus far, bias has been defined as an attempt to impose the Self upon the Other; to negate the Other and to supplant it with the Self; to generalize the particular; to absolutize the relative; to regard what is temporal and limited as constant, universal, and comprehensive; and to consider a certain human experience out of the myriad rich experiences of humankind as the supreme human model which abrogates and assimilates all other experiences.

Such is the essence of bias as an epistemological process related to the philosophy underlying methodology and scholarship. Bias often determines the method of analysis, ways of interpretation and findings of academic research. It also transforms science into an ideology or political interest by negating the value of truth that should be the only aim of any intellectual or scholarly enterprise.

As such, the impartial researcher can never define bias, let alone neutralize or remove its effects. The ultimate objective of science is to express truth regardless of the researcher's outlook, philosophy or culture; in this way, knowledge can be useful to human beings wherever they are and irrespective of their color or race. This does not mean, however, the relinquishment of specificities, for these must always be taken into account. knowledge should not claim to be universal and absolute on a particular matter. That is why the definition and neutralization of bias must comprise two fundamental methods of dealing with socio-political phenomena.

THE METHODOLOGY OF DETERMINING BIAS IN THEORIES OF POLITICAL DEVELOPMENT

The determination of bias in theories of political development is the essence of change and social evolution. This process requires some methodological approaches, most important of which are the following:

(1) *Differentiating Between the General and the Particular in Human Thought: Defining the Dimensions of the 'Common' in Human Epistemology*
It has been pointed out above that any kind of thinking is bound by time and place, and by the particularities of the human being who has originated or elaborated the idea. Therefore, the scholarly production of humankind – whether derived from empirical and intellectual principles or inspired by revelation – is characterized by a great deal of specificity and grounding in the milieu which produced it. There is invariably a close link between scholarship and the nature (characteristics) of time, place, and the human being. However, so long as there is a measure of universality and comprehensiveness, there must be common ideas and rules that apply to the whole of humankind at all times and in all locations. Thus, to define bias, one has to define the ideas, regulations, systems, or theories that generally characterize man and woman as human beings and then define particular elements that are linked with the specific details of a given culture, educational and belief system, era, or environment.

(2) *Precise Differentiation Between the Concepts of Correctness and Validity*[41]
Natural sciences deal with statements that are either true or false. In the physical domain, experiments are done to guarantee precision. As for statements about social issues, we should not be concerned about their accuracy; it is more rewarding simply to examine their time, place, and environment, for they are causally, directly and inextricably linked to their social, local, and temporal environment.[42] Social sciences are hermeneutical, i.e., they are based on understanding rather than explanation. Therefore, definition of the extent to which bias exists has to begin with a clear and accurate differentiation between the concepts of correctness and validity. Socio-political notions and theories may be accurate in them-

selves and valid in a particular environment, yet they can be inoperative in another environment since what is at issue is not their logical accuracy but their validity or capability of causing change and improvement in a certain society. At this juncture, bias is conceived of as an attempt to reconcile accuracy and validity. In other words, a clear demarcation line between accuracy and validity is required for the definition of bias in order to neutralize its effects upon analysis, theory, or action.

(3) *Forming Abstract Notions of Social Concepts, Systems and Phenomena and Separating their Reality from their Appearance*
This can be achieved through a phenomenological approach, namely, by reducing a concept, system, or phenomenon to its essence and reality, ridding it of all its forms and manifestations and even the term expressing it, i.e., purifying it of all that history has done to it, and arriving at its essence or gist so as to ascertain the exact reason why it has appeared in our world. In addition, further research has to be done into the concepts, systems, and phenomena that express this essence and how far it is achieved in all human societies with a view to explicating those concepts, systems, or phenomena no matter how different and diverse their forms and manifestations might be. Meanwhile, each society is known to have a specific way of achieving the same goals. Forms, manifestations, and terms are there to express a given cultural and civilizational experience. Confining ourselves to certain forms, manifestations, or terms is likely to make of a certain human experience a standard model through which other human experiences are evaluated. This is, in fact, the essence of bias. Abstraction, on the other hand, gives an equal chance to all societies to express the same message in different ways. A cogent example in this context is the concept of "political party" as an institution and as a social phenomenon that appeared in Europe across its historical evolution. It would be beside the point to search for the same concept, institution, or phenomenon in non-Western societies or to regard any society that does not have the party system as politically inactive, primitive, or backward.

If the necessity of the existence of the party system for the advancement of society is examined from the point of view of the determination and neutralization of bias, the concept of political party has to be stripped, first, of its institutional forms and of all manifestations and methods characterizing it. The main objective is to reveal its real essence as an organization that mediates between the rulers and the ruled, prevents the despotism of the former, works for the good of society, and provides an alternative to the political system if it deviates from the interests of society or fails to achieve them. From this standpoint, research can be done into the existence of such human activities in all societies and cultures. In the Islamic experience, for instance, the role of the political party is taken up by the Muslim scholars, professional masters, tribal chiefs, and authoritative people who act as arbiters in disputation and reconciliation. These entities perform the role of a political party without necessarily following its Western form and pattern. The same can also be said of such concepts as democracy, political participation, elitism, parliament, and such phenomena as revolutions, demonstrations, political development, etc. By doing so, the researcher can break out of the cocoon of bias which presents the Western experience as the chief frame of reference which presumably has to be emulated by all humanity.

THE METHODOLOGY OF NEUTRALIZING BIAS IN THEORIES OF POLITICAL DEVELOPMENT

If the researcher defining bias in theories of political development – which are part and parcel of political sciences – applies the foregoing three approaches, the next step is to neutralize bias in his/her own studies. He/she has to be as detached as possible lest his/her subjective vision of things overlook reality and mirror the Self's own perception. In order to help the researcher to overcome these pitfalls, the following four points might be taken into consideration:[43]

(1) *Dealing with the Phenomenon in Light of its Doctrinal Dimensions*
This is usually done through research into the system of beliefs (regarding divinity, holiness, and the unseen) behind the phenomena. Each phenomenon or socio-political theory is based on an eschatological or theological world reflected in its statements, concepts, and constituents.[44] This world comprises axioms that are not subject to discussion and are not even thought of by theorists or exponents of this phenomenon. Such axioms represent what can be called an ideational "taboo" that cannot be contradicted or examined because it is the sole foundation of the theory without which there can be no theoretical structure or phenomenon.

Thus, the researcher dealing with any phenomenon has to search for its "eschatological world" or the axioms underlying it and determining its dimensions. The definition of these axioms is a basic approach to a true and unbiased understanding of reality. As such, it is bound to put things in perspective and to interpret them according to their logical and ideological structure, not according to biased subjective interpretations.

(2) *Dealing with the Phenomenon in Light of its Historical Roots*

Dealing with the phenomenon in the light of its historical roots enables the researcher to reveal its origins and evolutionary stages, and to arrive at the best possible understanding of it. No human phenomenon or ideological theory sprang suddenly into existence without antecedents. It is the product of a historical evolution, across many stages, whereby each stage adds certain components to the phenomenon until it becomes wholly mature. Therefore, putting the phenomenon or theory in its historical context contributes to a deeper understanding. It also helps the researcher to neutralize bias, as he/she is not governed by his/her personal interpretations but by the history of the phenomenon under investigation.

(3) *Dealing with the Phenomenon in Light of its Environmental and Societal Pattern*

Social or political theories and phenomena do not exist in a vacuum. Rather, they are part and parcel of an extended social fabric; they affect it and are affected by it. The role of the researcher in this context is two-dimensional: to define the environment or the social pattern of the phenomenon, and to define the effects of the environment on the phenomenon.

This requires profound understanding of the limits of the environment and the societal pattern, that is, their nature, and their political manifestations. If we have a phenomenon or an idea from Egypt, for example, we will have to ask whether its social environment is the village, the city, the whole country, the Arab world, the Islamic nation, Africa, the world at large, etc. At this point, it has to be remembered that the envi-ronment and the societal pattern refer to the social, civilizational, and cultural spheres. Through a better understanding of the phenomenon, the researcher can thus greatly neutralize his/her bias. This also relates the researcher more strongly to his/her own reality, which is so vital in determining his/her own standpoint and frame of reference.

(4) *Dealing with the Phenomenon in the Totality of its Dimensions*
This can be achieved by combining the fragments and dimensions of the phenomenon without disproportionately concentrating on one single aspect of it. Each phenomenon has certain qualitative and quantitative dimensions. As for the qualitative ones, they are the economic, political, cultural, social, and geographical dimensions. The quantitative dimensions are the individual, the group and the community, the nation, and humankind. It cannot be said that every phenomenon has to be dealt with in all these dimensions. What has to be done first, however, is to look at it in its entirety. Thereafter, it is the turn of society to determine which dimensions are more effective and influential. A given phenomenon cannot be approached, for instance, by presupposing that the economic, cultural, social, or individual dimension is the one that defines and determines the phenomenon. The researcher should rather approach sociopolitical phenomena with all these variables in mind; then it is the reality of the phenomenon that determines which of these variables is the most effective. No single variable, after all, affects or controls phenomena in their totality. The same variable can be effective in one phenomenon but utterly ineffective in another. The economic variable, for instance, might be the major agent in one phenomenon, yet not in another. Through these approaches, the researcher can, to a great extent, neutralize his/her personal bias in an attempt to guarantee that what comes out in the end will be truth itself, or at least an approximation thereof.

There remains a basic factor that can only be controlled by learning the ethics of the scholar and the learner, for scientific research must be founded on honesty, moral probity, and adherence to the criteria of rightness and justice.[45] This truth is expressed in the verse from The Qur'an, "Do not allow your hatred for other men to turn you away from justice. Deal justly; justice is nearer to true piety ..." (5:8).

4

Modernizing vs. Westernizing the Social Sciences: The Case of Psychology

RAFIK HABIB

COMMUNITIES everywhere today are working to keep abreast of the Age of Science by boosting their technological performance and scientific activities. However, more emphasis is placed on performance than on testing scientific concepts and methods. Third World countries use science as a measure of the level of progress. Progress is essentially seen as an outcome of the scientific mode: scientific performance and the successful application of a scientific method are indicative of the community's potential, whereas the instant importation and application of new technology created and adopted by advanced countries is regarded as an achievement. The Muslims' desire for progress is satisfied by absorbing and/or imitating scientific patterns prevalent in other, more advanced communities.

Science should not be taken as an aim per se, but as a means of improving the quality of life by modifying the environment. The scientific paradigm adopted by advanced nations acquires legitimacy and importance by virtue of its ability to modify the environment in a manner acceptable to the people living in those parts of the world. In the Arab world, as well as in the rest of the Third World, the Arabs import these scientific innovations into their lives together with the lifestyle and ideals that accompany them, thus augmenting the need for more imported technology.

A number of questions arise in this context: Can the foregoing lead to scientific progress and prosperity? Can science be imported and genuine scientific pioneering be achieved on the basis of what others have invented? Can science be imported and lead to progress that surpasses what exists in the exporting societies? Can societies attain happiness and well-being through an imported lifestyle? Is what is good for others necessarily good for us?

In fact, an imitation can never pass for an original achievement. The Muslim countries have been able to import the formal and applied aspects of modern science, but not its positive social role, which is organically bound up with the social patterns and needs of its initiators. The creative concepts and methods that foster advancement in certain societies are meant to suit these societies. They are essentially different from those which may have promoted previous cultures. By copying from others the Muslim countries deprive themselves of an essential aspect of true progress, namely, the ability to develop new models of science and the patterns of life that reflect Muslim cultural identity.

It is a historical fact that during the Middle Ages, Western cultures were less advanced than their Arab-Islamic counterpart. The West benefited from Arab-Islamic achievements, but headway was not made until it began to review Arab thought in a bid to learn its lessons and then use them for further advancement. While European Christian thought was static and marred by a state of inertia, Arab philosophy and scientific thought were flourishing through the contributions of al-Fārābī, Ibn Sīna (Avicenna) and Ibn Rushd (Averroes), who had numerous disciples in Western countries, particularly in areas in proximity to the Arab countries along the Mediterranean coast. True advancement in Western philosophy and theology did not gain momentum until the West learned to outgrow Arab thought, having fully digested it in a bid to supersede it. A new, genuinely Western paradigm of thought best suited to Western needs was initiated by St. Thomas Aquinas.

By contrast, the Arab world today has still not gone beyond its awe of the thoughts and cultures of other countries. Science is acquired by imitation rather than by the creation of something new. Such an attitude is inevitably concomitant with historical periods of decline and regression whereby a more advanced community is perceived as an exemplar. However, the first step in moving past this stage of immaturity is to turn such an adolescent-like passion into a creative rebellion against the limitations of the cultural status quo. This obsession with the Other has indeed outstayed its welcome and the imitative phase has become ineffective, serving only to prolong and even reinforce the current state of backwardness.

There may be understandable reasons, but we are here concerned with the means of pulling Arab science out of this mimicking stage and overcoming the hurdles which hinder its advancement.

Mahmoud al-Dhaoudi[1] holds that in such an unbalanced relationship, the less advanced party tends to allow cultural infiltration by the dominant party with little resistance. A feeling of cultural inferiority encourages the absorption of all the incoming cultural elements in order to help one boost the image of the less advanced party. Since it is a fact that modern science is advancing by leaps and bounds, there is always the need on the part of the Muslim world to acquire more technology. Such a constant and relentless lure does not allow for a calm reassessment of the present condition of Muslims. The Muslim world has complacently admitted a good deal of foreign concepts and values over a long period of time, thereby emasculating its own identity, losing genuine criteria for sound judgment and the ability to extol and recognize its distinctive contributions. As Abdelwahab Elmessiri puts it,[2] the Muslim world tends to perceive its own reality through imported perceptual models, a state which he calls "perceptual dependency."

The moment of genuine self-awareness, the opening of the mind to creativeness, and independence from the attraction to the Other's foreign commodities in favor of reinforcing one's ego has receded more and more. At one point in time, such an attitude would have seemed to be rather farfetched. However, the present state of science in the Arab world is witnessing an attempt to restore it.

According to Burhan Ghalyoun,[3] the problems of the present state of Arab science are:

1. Basing scientific practice on the products of foreign minds rather than on local experience and experimentation.
2. The absence of genuine creativity in Arab scientific practice.
3. Adopting scientific theory, models, and methods as absolute truths, which in itself represents a violation of the nature of science.
4. Science in the Arab world does not spring from or reflect any kind of social interaction; rather, it is added to social interaction and reality.
5. Science is imported and consumed like any other commodity.

These points equally apply to the social sciences in the Arab world. While knowledge about physical and chemical facts can be safely transferred from one community to another, knowledge about social facts cannot. Even physical science requires some adjustment of the social realities of the receiving community. Adopting and applying foreign knowledge entails adopting a whole lifestyle and a social reality not rooted in the indigenous society. In the case of social science, the risk is compounded by the fact that the Muslim countries copy not only the functions and applications of scientific knowledge, but the knowledge corpus itself.

The findings of psychological and sociological research lose their significance when transported across the borders from one community to the other. This is true not only of experimentally derived results, but also of method and theory. In psychology, Arab scientists have regularly reproduced the results yielded by research in the West, using the very same methods and tools, with the claim of thereby confirming the indubitable universality of the phenomena under study. The Arab researcher's role is thus confined to duplicating experiments within an Egyptian/Arab context, using the Arabic language to rephrase foreign material. It would be more pertinent if, for example, research on extroversion in our part of the world could also attempt to Arabize the criteria used in defining the phenomenon; but it is a fact that scholars hardly pay attention to the concepts or criteria used. These are accepted as objective and impartial facts free of any cultural bias. Their alleged sacrosanct neutrality is taken for granted, causing thereby a good deal of damage and preventing the Arab intellect from revising many scientific concepts and methods. Such an assumption of objectivity is meant to confine intellectual activity within the boundaries of imitation or mimesis.

THE FALLACY OF NEUTRALITY
AND THE INEVITABILITY OF BIAS

An important issue in social science is the dogmatic concept of scientific neutrality and absolute objectivity, and even relativity, but within very narrow parameters. The Arab intellect has accepted the social sciences as essentially objective disciplines allegedly suitable for each and every community. The existing fanaticism about the utopian nature of scientific objectivity subjects any attempt at instituting a specifically Arab approach to science to serious criticism.

As such, the beginning of change must be a rephrasing of the definition of science and a careful definition of objectivity. Objectivity means the possibility of recreating facts through the separate and independent efforts of several researchers. This can only happen when a highly precise method is used in the process. In the case of importing or borrowing scientific concepts and tools, conclusions are forcibly imposed; consequently, Muslim countries are far from discovering the truth. Part of the social function of science is to discover facts. Psychological research in the United States, for example, may need to specify certain positive aspects of aggression by linking this phenomenon with the competitive nature of the society and the constant struggle between "I" and the "Other" given US values which honor this attitude as a factor in controlling the human market. Competitiveness is a human concept which may be universal. However, methods of measuring and defining its pros and cons and its possible social functions are far from being universal or neutral: these issues are necessarily community-specific. Transmitting such an attitude to other countries is one way of casting one society into the mold of another.

Heidar Ibrahim[4] is correct in asserting that objectivity and amorality in science are deceptive concepts. The transmission and application of scientific knowledge embodies the transmission of all the moral judgments and values that accompany this corpus of knowledge. Adopting a certain educational program recommended by the findings of the social sciences for another society, for example, entails adopting all the social and moral values of the source society.

The dilemma is intensified by the Other's argument in favor of scientific objectivity and the necessity of catching up with modern science as a prerequisite to progress. When we accept this as a fact, we also accept the Other's values and traditions, both scientific and social. Here lies the importance of social science: it can easily turn into an effective tool for reinforcing cultural, behavioral and moral dependency. Science may thus turn into an indirect, probably unintended, means of cultural and intellectual colonization. The incoming science brings along with it a certain life pattern and paradigm. Through modern applied psychology, new teaching techniques such as computer-aided learning have become very popular. Muslims seem to be completely dazzled by such innovative methodologies, wasting no time in introducing them into their communities. But shouldn't they first stop to ask: What does such a tendency imply?

Quantitative and continuous technological developments are important criteria of progress in the West. Machine-controlled production has turned human beings into thinking tools for inventing new technical methods as a means of providing abundance. Human beings are turning into a creative android, programmed to produce all the necessary innovations. They are taught by the computer, in a bid to evolve into some kind of robot-like creative creatures, to be used by the computer itself.

The above example represents an attempt at following an objective (i.e. scientific) but partial line of thought that is meant to serve the purpose of the community under study. Science may be objective and impartial in the sense that scientists have the ability to observe facts away from personal or external influences. However, their choice of research topics and tools of observation are not done at their own preference; they rather reflect the community-specific science-biased tendency which may push a certain society, at certain points in time, to give prime attention, unwarrantable by any topical priority, to the problems of youth, for example. Imported science and technology carry such biases along with them. A certain sector of society may unjustifiably receive more care than necessary at a particular point in time; or we may overemphasize a marginal line of behavior at the expense of another, more serious one; or some other form of bias that may distort reality for us, giving it an ugly, "scientific" face in the name of absolute objectivity. This received reality becomes irrefutable and at the same time controls social evolution.

Science, therefore, owes allegiance to those values that give it life in the first place – those values it was meant to consolidate. Science, particularly social science, is by definition biased towards the social function it is meant to implement. In the United States, for example, psychology aims at consolidating social values connected with individualism and competition, unlike the case in the Soviet Union, where it is meant to enhance a group (collective) spirit and equality. As such, various communities have different social and political aims, partly implemented and supported by the specific scientific orientation of the community.

According to Adel Hussein,[5] Western science is categorically biased because it is directly connected to state plans and prevalent ideologies. This bias is evident in the choice of a relevant topic for research and the problems it tries to solve. Bias sometimes characterizes the results themselves. Due to the special nature of each community, certain assumptions are made and certain values are given priority. This leads to scientific research favoring certain findings over others.

The history of science confirms this view. Different periods in history have witnessed radical changes in scientific theory. This is a two-way process: each change may be said to result from a cultural shift or to cause it, or both. Taking for granted the theory of objectivity and neutrality in social science, we are next obliged to admit the permanence of scientific theory, and accordingly the permanence of life and culture even though this contradicts the inevitable evolution of historical reality. The gradual and continual changes witnessed in the social sciences from year to year are not what we mean by "change" here; it is, rather, the radical change which affects theory, methodology and application, causing them to adapt themselves, in the process, to the movement of community(ies) from one cultural era to another.

EAST AND WEST

The view of psychology in the capitalist West and the (formerly) socialist East are both similar and different. The similarity springs from a common cultural framework known as modern Europe. Differences are caused by the social and cultural characteristics of the two economic systems. Each system has its requirements which science endeavors to fulfill. The common factor among capitalist and socialist countries is partly rooted in the history of psychology, one of the sources of contemporary culture. The roots of personality theory, for example,[6] can be traced back to:

1. European clinical medicine with its conception of mental disorders and its mechanistic physiological orientations.
2. Psychometrics, which has its roots in the experiments of sensory physiometrics.
3. The behavioral school that adopts the stimulus-response dichotomy.
4. German Gestalt studies which recognize the totality of perception.

The multiplicity and diversity of these elements leads us to look for the roots of modern psychology. It may be safely said that modern psychology is of European origin, both Eastern and Western, with three main sources:

1. Sensory-physiological studies.
2. Medical studies, particularly physiological ones.
3. Biological Darwinian studies, particularly comparative measurement and equitable distribution.

These are the main elements out of which grew modern psychology in Europe, both East and West, represented by Russia and the United States respectively; hence, the striking similarity between psychological studies in both societies. They both share in the same cultural assumptions of the same cultural era. Each society, however, manifested these assumptions in different forms. The noticeable similarities among these communities and the schools of research they adopt spring from a common cultural background. This common cultural background results, in turn, in shared tendencies such as an adherence to an austere scientific method, a semi-mechanistic approach, a link with other disciplines such as biology and physiology, and a set of common convictions about health and disease.

Modern psychology, namely the modern scientific study of the psyche, dominates research at the present time. This school of thought emphasizes an interaction between the social sciences and the natural sciences with their emphasis on objectivity and the ability of science to overcome human and cultural biases. Such a stance, with its emphasis on being "scientific," seems to be the outcome of an early affiliation with physiological, biological, and physical research. Early experiments in psychology, as mentioned before, were more akin to the physical sciences than to sociology or the humanities, with research topics such as finding a connection between salivating and seeing food when hungry, or the perception of color. The design of such early experiments should have included sociological and cultural variables, but it did not.

Sociological and psychological research continued in this mechanistic, biophysical trend as it moved on to further controversial and more complex topics, tending to stress its adherence to a pure scientific approach. In attempting to prove that human behavior was subject to the same mechanistic, scientific laws, science was actually undermining its own aim of objectivity. Social interaction was researched in the same manner, both theoretically and methodologically, as the effect of light on the human eye.

Mechanistic materialist determinism fully dominated psychology in both the socialist East and the capitalist West. As an outcome of their industrial and technological history, which emphasized the importance of matter in the life of humankind and at the same time humankind's struggle to control matter, both parts of the world adhered to materialism as an inevitable social value. Even though the function of the individual differs widely from capitalist to socialist societies, both underscore mechanistic materialist determinism. Humankind's very being is related to the amount of things humans can produce, the level of technological development they can attain, and the degree to which they can modernize consumer products. The role of the individual, then, is greater consumption and a better standard of living, even though the results differ when contrasting socialist with capitalist societies.

Our purpose here is not a comparison between East and West; rather, we simply wish to uncover the common ground in psychological research resulting from a common cultural and intellectual background. Psychological research in the former Soviet Union confirms this fact: academic research gives primacy to certain topics[7] such as the study of behavior and behaviorism, and attempts to establish a relationship between consciousness and behavior. Hence, Pavlovian principles that stress the functions of the central nervous system as well as physiological behavior, the application of technology to education, the development of teaching methodology and the expansion into industrial applications, are dominant.

All these topics are strikingly similar to the main features of American psychology, where the behaviorist and cognitive schools dominate. Scientific applications in the fields of education and industrial research, among others, are prevalent. However, the daily social functions of psychologists in Russia and the United States are quite different. In spite of cultural and intellectual affinities, practical application as well as pure research show that social values differ greatly. Whereas the American psychologist is inclined to stress creative freedom, the Russian psychologist may not emphasize the same values to the same degree, since the nature of systems of control differs from one state to another. The scientist, therefore, is required to perform those functions which are envisioned by his particular society.

The difference in psychological research can be illustrated by the American example, which is characterized by two approaches: (1) The quantitative physiological-mechanistic approach,[8] and (2) the qualitative humanistic existential approach. The former is connected to biological determinism, while the latter is closer to existential freedom. This dualism can be expected to affect the values and norms adopted by each approach. The mechanistic scientific school sees human behavior as an outcome of scientific determinism and strict scientific laws, though theoreticians may differ as to the source of this determinism. Skinner, for example, sees it as a product of the environment alone, while others, such as Eisnick, would also add genetic and bio-physical factors. Both schools share belief in the possibility of modifying and controlling human behavior by modifying the environment. The predominant view in the West today is thus that individual patterns of behavior can be shaped to produce the ideal individuals for their society.

Despite the apparent differences between them, both schools also share a belief in individualism, competitiveness and self-fulfillment, among other things. Within the humanistic school, self-fulfillment is a philosophical concept. The behaviorists believe in maximizing and exploiting the individual's potential. The humanistic school stresses the freedom and individual nature of the human being, while the behaviorists devise scientific means of modifying behavior to suit their model which carries the same properties of individual freedom and distinction. Each approach has its own theoretical premises and its own scientific method for creating the means by which to modify human behavior. Hence, despite the importance of the differences between the two approaches (for example, the humanistic school's opposition to the rigid mechanistic approach of the behaviorist school), they share the same goal.

Be that as it may, our concern here is simply to demonstrate that the social function of science creates a kind of reciprocal effect between it and the dominant culture. Science, in fulfillment of this social function, adopts the values of its community which may, in fact, be its *raison d'être*. Except in times of political unrest, science is given freedom of movement and generous funding by virtue of the fact that it constitutes an essential institution in the community, directly relevant to the state system.

UTILIZATION VS. EXPLOITATION OF HUMANKIND

The foregoing discussion has aimed to point out the theoretical framework, objectives and values of psychological research. Equally important, however, is the risk of importing science, which is very similar to importing technology and consumer goods. This is not a neutral act. The imported commodity cannot be neutral, because it results in adopting a distorting set of norms and values. No community can be cast in the image of another with the object of attaining the same degree of success. In importing science from the East or the West, there is no guarantee of attaining a similar degree of progress or achievement. The successful application of science in an advanced community is an outcome of the full utilization of the social potential to meet the needs of that community. When transmitted to another community, it turns into a type of consumer goods which lack the social efficacy that can produce scientific advancement.

The American model of psychological theory and research methods is widely applied in the Arab world. American psychology has influenced research in this field in the advanced Western and Eastern countries as well as in the Third World. The United States has the largest number of research projects in psychology, and therefore, the largest number of researchers in that field; it also has the most funding. Moreover, one reason for this is that American psychology celebrates the individual versus the community and claims to be able to modify human behavior to cope with modern patterns of culture by applying a scientific mechanistic approach, and as such, it is serving capitalism. Individuals are forced to adhere to an almost aggressive competitive spirit in both their patterns of production and consumption: this is one of the most revered norms of Western capitalist civilization.

If American psychology entails such dominance, then the competitive American capitalist values are also predominant. And here we can see the serious role to be played by science at an international level. Particularly in the Third World, the adoption of the American model results in reinforcing American values among developing communities. Where efforts made through media publicity and economic domination may fail, a transmitted program of distorted scientific application may actually succeed.

It is not our claim here that psychological research has any substantial presence in the Arab world. However, as the tendency to modernize by imitation and as the budgets allocated to scientific research grow bigger, the influence of foreign science, including psychology, will continue to grow, and as a consequence, scientists will be unintentionally taking part in creating a distorted image of individualistic consumer society. Moreover, because the image is distorted, it is often an image of a disintegrated individualistic society which lacks competitiveness, initiative, and productivity.

This last statement may be hypothetical. However, in view of the dynamics of contemporary psychological research and practice, it is not far from the truth. In a Western study which criticizes the current method of measuring intelligence,[9] it is made clear that this activity is geared towards academic classification, which is then promoted to professional classification and the redistribution of individuals among the various professions. As such, there is a need to improve the IQs of individuals by improving the environment, creating industrial environments and even by means of genetic engineering which aims at improving the human race.

The technical psychologist thus plays an important role in classifying and modifying human potential in a bid to fully utilize it. In the West, particularly the United States, technical psychologists are becoming increasingly important. They use precise measurements to define the individual's destiny by allocating him/her to a line of specialization, a level of education he/she can follow with success, the suitable job, and the administrative and educational rank he/she can achieve. In this way, IQs are used to develop a kind of psychological classification which defines the individual's status and place in society. And because this system of classification is far from being impartial, permeated as it is with the values and needs of society, it led to a type of scientific racism. A number of quasi-scientific studies once claimed that the black African race is less intelligent than the white European race because of biological differences. However, psychological research in the United States soon proved these findings to be unacceptable because the difference in the IQs of both races was found to be due to environmental factors.

Even so, scientific bias and racism were internalized, becoming latent in all scientific endeavors. Psychological measurements of intelligence became the criterion for the admission of school and university candidates. This means that those candidates who were privileged were likely to succeed. In other words, the socially and economically privileged stood a better chance. Science as such has created a line of social discrimination and class bias which drives the individual to aspire to life within a prescribed social frame as a prerequisite for success. Any other frame is considered marginal.

The jungle of strict criteria which determine a human being's future has turned the human being into a programmed machine for acquiring knowledge and for answering questions on IQ tests. How to pass such a test, therefore, has turned into a skill to which people devote all their time and energy so as to attain a certain status in society. Still worse, society tends through the use of such methods to stereotype its members, turning them into calculated models of mechanically educated and automatically creative individuals. This model is favored by the social setup, because it is the model required by the industrial and technological consumerism program.

The Arab individual is described by Mohammad Shakroun as a "collective" being.[10] Imported science tries to turn Arabs into individuals who strive to compete with one another and with themselves. The dilemma of the Arab individuals in Shakroun's view is their being forced to abandon their "collectiveness" in favor of an imported individualism.

Directly imposing certain norms and values on other communities may be met with resistance and failure, but when science is used to achieve this aim indirectly, it may succeed. Empiricism, scientific objectivity, abstraction and impartiality are all attractive routes for importing foreign science and foreign norms. The target is to force the Arab individual into a foreign mold, the mold of "the Other" who is completely different.

Mohammad Ezzat Hegazy[11] suggests that obsession with radical empiricism is clear insofar as the following:

1. Portraying society as a system without problems.
2. A tendency to particularize and anatomize, ignoring the totality of society.
3. An attempt to duplicate the methods of physical science.
4. Hostility towards scientific theorizing.

This may be taken as a pure scientific attitude that could be valid anywhere, anytime. Nevertheless, but the gist of the matter is not the radical empirical approach itself, but the cultural content it presents. Not all radical empirical approaches are the same. Each has its intellectual and cultural tendency as well as its own norms, values, and ethical judgments. Radical empiricism is only a general intellectual and scientific method that may be applied in any community at any time. The difference between one method and another lies in its cultural content: it may give prominence to homogeneity and socialist values, as is the case in socialist Russian psychology, or it may stress individual differences as in capitalist American psychology.

Radical empiricism, then, is a state attained by society under certain conditions, and its substance is derived from the culture of that society. What are the conditions that render empiricism characteristic of a certain society? Mohammed Ezzat Hegazy maintains that the prevalence of radical empiricism in the West can be interpreted as follows:

1. This civilization has reached a stable (universally accepted) general premise.
2. There is no need to go beyond the cultural norm.
3. There is no need to come up with a cultural alternative.
4. Civilization at this stage needs justification for its existence and continuation.
5. Civilization needs to vitalize itself to cope with the change in its present surroundings.[12]

Thus, radical empiricism is similar to political systems in times of stability. A conservative tendency automatically affirms itself when the majority is fairly satisfied with general conditions and attempts to preserve them. Under these conditions, science turns equally conservative in a bid to prolong and enhance the status quo as well as to effect the desired degree of change. Radical empiricism does not promote a scientific revolution or a means of radical social change. The question now is: Have Arab communities reached a stage of development which allows them to introduce radical empiricism?

Arab communities today are still at a preliminary stage of scientific progress. They may be standing at the threshold of a long-awaited era, with new hopes for social change. They therefore need a speedy recovery program, with radical changes and regular upward curves of development, not excluding scientific and intellectual leaps, imagination and creativity. The question is: Are they at this stage in need of a radical empirical approach, or do they actually need some other scientific approach which differs fundamentally from radical empiricism and the pseudo-political function it performs?

The crisis of this rigorous imported objectivity is most evident in psychology and the social sciences with its endemic belief in medical therapy which reduces crises to symptoms and alternatives to sedatives. Salem Sary[13] finds this concept in keeping with the implication that the social system is at its best and does not constitute any problem: the problem lies in a number of patients. Such individual limited cases represent a deviation from the norm. The general state of affairs is taken for granted, and the simple solution is to typify and normalize the deviant few. The question is: Is the social system sound enough to sustain the concept of health and disease at the individual and group levels?

The situation in the Arab world today shows that it is still far from attaining progress. It is still looking for the content of progress, for what constitutes progress. The very social system needs to change. The negative attitude of its society is clear in that social and psychological diseases are attributed to individual causes and treated with sedatives and painkillers. It tends to rehabilitate the individual rather than change the social setup, even though it may be desperately in need of change. Imported science thus assists it in wasting all chances for change and the ability to diagnose its diseases as social rather than individual or group diseases.

THE FALL OF IDEOLOGY

This expression is widely used at the present time. But has it really failed? Has ideology lost its role and standing? Mohammad Abid al-Jabiri[14] notes that in the 19th century there appeared a number of theories claiming to be scientific, but which in fact used science to mask their ideological reality, hiding behind scientific objectivity. Mechanistic and biological Darwinism is one of those theories. From 1950 onward, in the absence of philosophy, the world was divided between ideology and science. Today, in al-Jabiri's words, the world is divided between science and technology with no room for ideology or philosophy. He adds that Gorbachev's *Perestroika* was a stage in the fall of ideology.

The same opinion is offered by Ghaly Shoukry,[15] who holds that this age has seen the end of ideology. In the West, the ideological struggle between the individual and society has disappeared. In the East, under the rule of socialism and the mechanistic Marxist system, ideology has been defeated. The present conflicts in these societies are not ideological, but rather concerned with the demands of daily life and peripheral systemic details, with differences dictated by the nature of each society.

Ideology is not a choice or a probability: it is a historical, social and natural inevitability. After all, ideology simply means thought. There is no individual or society, no social, political or academic system without thought. Every group and every act implies an ideology or a philosophy. Hence, the rise and fall of an ideology does not negate its presence. Ideologies are not completely wiped out. Rather, the human life cycle involves ideologies which stabilize for a period of time, then destabilize and become dysfunctional. The end of the age of ideology is only a phase of destabilization. It has not disappeared, because its presence is natural and a part of the permanent structure of society.

The beginning of a new cultural era is marked by a new ideology and philosophy which give new definitions to life, humankind, politics, science, etc. These definitions are the foundations of the new era. The society undergoing this change witnesses the dissemination and consolidation of the new ideology to the detriment of old thoughts and ideas. The new ideology, therefore, gains importance and attention. As the society draws closer to its aim of realizing the people's dreams, the role of ideology gradually diminishes. The people's concern over the established ideology wanes during the stage of stability. There is no more need for propaganda or controversy, as it is now an integral part of the social structure. This state may last until problems arise and the people are dissatisfied with the system. Ideology and philosophy then return to present a new picture of society. In the making of a new cultural era, the intellectual potential is revitalized and routine research is abandoned in favor of more original work.

Cultural progress and development result from intellectual and ideological creativity, which is itself contingent on scientific revolutions emanating from the social structure. When transmitting science from a foreign source, the Arab world is not aiming at the kind of scientific revolution which results in progress and development, but as Ali al-Kinz puts it,[16] it stops at the stage of copying static intellectual frames which it holds in greater esteem than its innovators.

Psychology in the Arab world is individual to the core. However, American psychology, from which we have copied a good deal, has outgrown this stage to a new stage characterized by a social and historical emphasis. Logically, psychology should develop in the importing countries because it requires a substantial degree of modification and reformulation to cope with the new social environment. But this is not the case. When the Arab world copies, it copies faithfully under the pretext of sacred objectivity and cultural neutrality in spite of the shortcomings that were admittedly found by its creators.

The combined problem of adhering to a sacrosanct empirical objectivity and the fall of ideology has resulted in halting the scientific movement in the Arab world and the Third World today. The irony lies in the fact that a radical empiricism tends to preserve the status quo which the Arab world is trying hard to change. With a falling ideology, it is destined to drift further away from the desired philosophical and ideological model of life which could be the key to the realization of its dream. It insists on preserving the status quo because it prefers to import science with its alleged objectivity.

THE ALTERNATIVE OF HOPE

The picture is neither rosy nor hopeless. It all depends on the attitude we are willing to take. The present condition of Arab science requires the abandonment of the illusion of neutral scientific objectivity in favor of a new ideological stance. Such a shift will enable the Arab world to devise a new cultural threshold to end its crisis and its "third" position before it turns to a fourth or worse.

A new dynamic outlook is needed and serious attempts at change have to be made, some of which may fail while some may succeed, until the Arab world attains the alternative that gives genuine expression to its aspirations. The stages of such a process can be visualized as a set of radical mental operations which may lead to an acceptable and appropriate solution:

Stage One
This stage is marked by outgrowing the present state of scientific and intellectual adolescence and cultural fanaticism. All previous attempts have failed because the Arab world could not see a better way than the imported one, and will continue to fail if it insists on seeing everything foreign as evil and wrong and to be avoided. The beginning, then, is to outline its attitude towards the Other, which must involve accepting the Other's successful experiences without being obsessed with them. It should be able to make use of these experiences without copying them

blindly. It should be able to follow up the Other's efforts without adoration. It can learn from the Others if it is able to interact with them. The Arab world does not need to be like them and it can converse without a feeling of inferiority. By learning a critical mind it can pursue the road which it has begun by absorbing the Others' experiences and by following up on that.

Stage Two
The Arab world needs to develop its own concepts and methods, using them flexibly and critically in order to arrive at a relatively specific approach which can assist it in seeing the phenomena under research in a new light, different from the approach presented by the current static, idealized methods. By making new discoveries, it can rephrase theoretical methods and approaches in a gradual and cumulative manner. A case in point is class struggle and its relation to religious movements, where the concept of class struggle can be used in a flexible way, allowing an effective handling of the phenomenon and thereby discovering its characteristics. This discovery has led to the knowledge of the various inter- and intra-aspects of the struggle and the different types and levels of this struggle such as the so-called socio-economic conflict or the socio-cultural conflict. The various structural aspects of class and class struggle can be described, including social, economic, and cultural features.

Stage Three
The scientific revolution becomes a fact through new findings and discoveries in theory, method, and thought. The phenomenon under study can be envisaged through a better perspective. These requirements should stir in the Arab world some degree of anxiety concerning the present status quo in scientific research theory and method. This anxiety should lead to a new scientific vision, which is what the Arab world is hoping for.

Stage Four
The new scientific perspective is completely envisaged and the substitute ideology is conceived, both leading to an alternative cultural state and a new cultural stage. This account may seem a little too theoretical or idealistic, but at the same time it represents an attempt at a constructive, polemical review of the Arab world's present dilemma in scientific research.

REFERENCES

Rafik Habib, *"al-Taṭawur al-Nafsī Lī al-Shakhṣiyyah al-Maṣriyyah"* (Psychological Development of the Egyptian Personality). Unpublished Ph.D. Thesis, Faculty of Arts, Ain Shams University, 1997.

Rafik Habib, *al-Iḥtijaj al-Dīnī wa al-Ṣirāʿ al-Ṭabqī fī Miṣr* (Religious Dissent and Class Conflict in Egypt) (Cairo: Sinai for Publication, 1989).

J. Brozek, "Soviet Psychology," in M.H Marx & W.A. Hillix, *Systems and Theories in Psychology* (New Delhi: Tata McGraw-Hill, 1973).

A.H. Maslow, *Toward a Psychology of Being* (New York: VNR, 1968).

C.R. Rogers, *On Becoming a Person* (Boston: Houghton Mifflin, 1961).

S.B. Sarason, *Psychology Misdirected* (New York: Free Press, 1981).

5

Bias in Curricula and Course Contents

HODA HEGAZY

EDUCATIONAL INSTITUTIONS are considered the prime media for transmitting a cultural tradition. In modern times, knowledge has ceased to be a relatively stable body of information and ideas, as was the case in the past. Rather, knowledge has become vast in volume and is subject to a continuous process of evaluation and reevaluation at an extremely rapid pace. Against this backdrop, it has become almost impossible for educational institutions to transmit the totality of the body of knowledge available. Thus, it has become imperative for such institutions to select from an almost limitless amount of data and ideas, and to define for the student a certain set of values that society at large has adopted. This matter raises a methodological issue, namely, that of selecting from the body of knowledge available a limited number of subjects which students should learn, then deciding on the proper content to be taught in the different educational stages.

Curricula are usually formulated and set based on a number of factors, the most important being the prevalent ideology in a given society, its educational philosophy, its value system, and its concept of human nature. Moreover, the curricula are determined in accordance with the needs of the individuals and their stages of development. Inevitably, all educational activities raise questions pertaining to the values on which is based the totality of the educational process. This means that developing a curriculum inevitably necessitates a process of inclusion and exclusion. Certain elements from the cultural tradition are excluded or marginalized, others are reinterpreted or given centrality, then transmitted to the student as though they constituted the whole tradition.

It is not expected, therefore, that school textbooks be "neutral" or "objective," especially considering the fact that the school, by its very nature, is an educational institution founded by society. It is society which provides it with the human and financial resources needed for the upbringing and socialization of young generations. Thus, society has every right to ask for the school's help in carrying out its philosophy and in achieving its goals and future plans. Biases in textbooks might differ, both in degree and in explicitness, from one educational stage to another. Expectedly, they are more explicit in primary school textbooks, and less explicit in university books and reference works. But whether explicit or implicit, epistemological bias is always present. Therefore, to try to define the epistemological paradigm underlying curricula is something of the utmost importance. When a professor decides to prepare a certain course about history, geography, reading or even the physical sciences, there is bound to be a paradigm of some sort. The objectives of the course, the principle of inclusion or exclusion of material, what should be emphasized and given sufficient centrality, and what should be marginalized or omitted, are all decided on the basis of a particular paradigm.

Ideological bias resulting from the process of inclusion, exclusion, marginalization, etc., is quite manifest in history books. History textbooks in the USA, until very recently, disregarded the contributions of Afro-Americans (to American society) and mentioned next to nothing about the indigenous population of North America before the arrival of Columbus or about their extermination. Egyptian history books see the history of modern Egypt in relation to European history, neglecting the history of the Ottoman Empire or its historical, administrative, and cultural achievements. If the Ottoman Empire is mentioned at all, it is in the context of it being "responsible" for the prolonged dark age that enveloped Egypt, only to be brought to an end by Napoleon's cannons and troops which brought Egypt science, light, reason, and technology, all of which led eventually to the development of an Egyptian national self-awareness.

Obviously, the writers of Egyptian history books see Westernization (called "modernization") as the most important and beneficial element in modern Egyptian history, and therefore, it serves as those writers' principle of inclusion and exclusion.

Through a comparative study which I conducted to gauge the values and attitudes manifested in Arabic reading books used in Egyptian primary schools prior to 1952 and those taught in 1972, it became apparent that each set of readers has its own biases.[1] For instance, readers before 1952 dealt with Egyptian history through its various historical epochs. One finds references to Pharaonic Egypt, to Arab/Islamic Egypt and to modern Egypt (after 1800) without underestimating or belittling any epoch. The 1972 readers, however, view Egyptian history in a different manner. The Pharaonic era, though still viewed as a great one, is not given the same centrality it enjoyed in readers taught before 1952. Egypt's Arabic/Islamic past is glorified, while its importance and direct relation to present-day Egypt is emphasized. Egypt's modern history, though frequently referred to, is usually regarded as a dark epoch (till the 1952 revolution) and its significance is belittled. Conspicuous differences are also found in the concept of identity found in the two sets of readers. While the readers taught before 1952 emphasize the various aspects of the Egyptian national identity, the 1972 readers stress only the Arabic/Islamic national identity.

Analysis of the recommended references in a course on "the Jewish history of education" in an American university yielded very dramatic results. These references, considered basic works in this field of study, stressed the common aspects between different Jewish educational institutions in different countries and eras, disregarding some basic differences. This was done in a way that seemed "objective," "neutral," and unbiased, for an impressive amount of data was marshaled to support the hypothesis that there is one "Jewish educational system" that derives its oneness from its Jewishness. Upon closer examination, however, one discovers a biased presupposition, namely, the belief that Jewish educational systems are independent of the civilizations in which the Jewish communities live. Another presupposition follows from the previous one, namely, that the scholar in this field should study what Jewish educational institutions have in common to the exclusion of all else. Most references recommended in this course are, not surprisingly, dedicated to the study of the common aspects, though they might have very little explanatory value when compared with those aspects that set one Jewish community apart from others, or what distinguishes one Jewish educational system from others in different times and other places.

The impact of the educational systems of the societies in which the

Jewish communities lived on their respective educational institutions and instruction systems was either marginalized or disregarded altogether. Jewish educational systems were thus viewed as having emerged either *ex-nihilo*, or out of a hypothetical, quintessential Jewish religious and cultural tradition. In other words, the bias underlying the initial presupposition was given an air of objectivity and neutrality through a biased selection (inclusion and exclusion) of data.

The same could be said of a sociology course which I once studied in the USA. This course attempted to explore the relationship between Islam and Capitalism using Max Weber's thesis pertaining to the relationship between Protestant ethics and the spirit of capitalism. There is a complex, perhaps unconscious, bias implicit in the very choice of topic. This is the case because it postulates rational (Western) capitalism, which is specific to Occidental civilization, as some kind of ultimate, though silent, point of reference, and a yardstick by which all economic and cultural developments are judged. Once this Occidental perspective (or paradigm) is adopted, certain questions are raised to the exclusion of others and certain issues are underscored to the exclusion of others.

But these questions and views might be of marginal importance, or even completely irrelevant, obscuring more fundamental and relevant issues in case a different perspective (or paradigm) is adopted. Once the perspective is changed, other issues move to the center and other questions become more relevant and important. Economic developments and different modes of modernization are then judged according to different criteria and seen in a completely different light. This might be anticipating things, so let us begin at the beginning.

Rather than take a simplistic economistic view of the world of ideas, reducing it to the level of mere epiphenomena (the real phenomena being modes, forces, or relations of production) German sociologist Max Weber saw the world of economy and ideas as closely intertwined. In other words, he recognized the irreducible complexity of the human phenomenon. For instance, his introduction of the category of religion in sociological studies has surely helped to dispel any illusions about the simplicity of social phenomena. It is no longer possible to explain society in terms of one factor or another, nor is it possible to rest content with an atomistic view of society that regards it as an aggregate, not a complex, of different elements (as is the case with economistic models of analysis). Even though religion is a set of ideas and beliefs related to the sacred, the transcendental and the timeless, it has a deep impact on humankind's temporal, social life.

Weber's thesis about the relationship between the Protestant ethic and Occidental capitalism is a case in point. It is a seminal and controversial idea. In his book *The Protestant Ethic and the Spirit of Capitalism*, he tries to account for the rise of an economic system by considering the formative influence of a non-economic factor. By evolving a view of an inscrutable God whose will is unknown to the believer yet Who predetermines the fate of everything, Protestantism creates a unique state of mind comprising two antagonistic tendencies: an urge to be certain about one's salvation, combined with a complete lack of any evidence concerning it. In the absence of any mediating processes such as church or ritual (or tribe, or extended family), the loneliness of the believer is intensified and a deep contradictory sense of chosenness and dereliction sets in. This dualism, though impossible to eliminate, had at least to be mitigated. The strategy was to make it incumbent on the believer to have unquestioning faith in the fact that he has been saved and elected, but at the same time, in order to strengthen that faith and to support it with evidence and signs, he had to follow a certain life style. For instance, he should not withdraw from this world in the manner of monks and mystics, but rather remain in it yet without getting involved with it. Mastery of the world is the goal, which means working very hard, accumulating wealth, and by succeeding, the believer serves God.

This inner-worldly asceticism, this attempt to master one's impulses and to control one's world, is a state of mind that Weber found as having an "elective affinity" with "*one* of the fundamental elements of the spirit of modern capitalism." Nisbet underscores the fact that Weber never tried to ascribe causal primacy to the Protestant ethic; he was primarily concerned with showing its role, as one factor among many, in forming Occidental capitalism.[2]

Weber's range of interests, however, was much wider than mere speculation on, or explanation of, the origins of Occidental capitalism. His scope and intent were far broader: the Protestant ethics theory is part and parcel of his endeavor to discover and define that element which, according to Weber, sets Occidental civilization apart from other civilizations: namely, the whole process of rationalization, of intimately relating means to well-defined ends. In this sense, Weber's classic work is just one premise in a wider, more comprehensive intellectual structure. In order to fully grasp the depth of Weber's imagination, the true complexity of his vision, and to view the Protestant ethics theory in its wider context, one has to examine his other works concerning seemingly unrelated subjects such as the religions of China and India, the origins of the Occidental city as opposed to the sacred and imperial cities of the Orient, and the development of laws and legal institutions in the West and elsewhere.

Weber traces the origins of Occidental rationalism to the very beginnings of Western civilization. Even though the process of rationalization reached its full fruition in the 19th and 20th Centuries, it is an organic process inherent in the very seeds of Western civilization. Roman law, for instance, with its concept of property as an absolute right for use or abuse, is one prime source.[3]

In Weber's view, the Christian churches in the Occident, rather than legislating for the here and hereafter in the manner of Islam, Judaism and Confucianism, remained content to legislate the moral behavior of the individual. Matters of state were regulated by secular law, leaving what is Caesar's to Caesar. This relative autonomy of secular law was essential for the development of a "formal juristic theory,"[4] at the expense of law oriented towards material principles such as utility and equity, the law typical of theocratic and absolutist regimes. This formalistic jurisprudence was in turn crucial for the development of an Occidental capitalism of the modern, rational variety.

Closely linked with the concept of autonomous and formal law is the structure of the Occidental city. Unlike the Oriental city, the Occidental city developed as an autonomous unit, with an independent class structure, burghers and guilds, an autonomous military force, be it a standing army or a militia, and an autonomous law. Though encircled on all sides by the feudal order, the Occidental city maintained its autonomy till it grew strong enough to assume power and reorganize society along more capitalistic, rational lines. The Oriental city, on the other hand, remained an organic part of the society, never developing a separate dynamic.

The religious traditions of both Judaism and Christianity were yet another tendency in Western civilization that proved conducive to the development of a rationalist outlook. Unlike the immanentist-pantheistic religions of Asia, so runs Weber's argument, the transcendental-monotheistic tradition implies a rupture between Creator and created, between the here and the hereafter, and between the real and the ideal. In an immanent-pantheist context, the aim of the believer is either to withdraw completely from, or to achieve harmony with, "the world," whereas within the transcendental-monotheist frame of reference, the goal is the mastery of this world in the name of another. This attempt at mastery of a world in flux in the name of a unified ideal is already one step on the road to rationalization, dealing with the infinite flux not on an ad hoc basis, but rather, in a total manner. This is a value-oriented rationality which paved the way to, and was eventually replaced by, goal-oriented rationality. The systematization of religious life also led to the elimination of such ad hoc methods of control as magic and crude forms of soothsaying. The prophet replaced the magician, and the process went on until eventually the bureaucrat replaced all.

Weber's arguments are all interconnected and the way in which they are presented in this paper does not do them justice. For instance, the salvation-oriented religious outlook helped reinforce the autonomy of the Occidental city by breaking kinship ties, and by replacing family or tribal groupings with broader religious ties. So whereas the Oriental city remained clannish or tribal in character, the Occidental city became an autonomous professional grouping of believers. If the salvation-oriented religious outlook helped in the origination of the autonomy of the city, some of the autonomous urban classes, in turn, proved to be the only possible carriers of one variety of the ethics of this religion. Weber argues that neither the landed, nor the military aristocracy, nor the peasantry could have developed a religious outlook that stressed individual responsibility and accountability. It is only small tradesmen who have the time to meditate, whose very occupation forces them to engage in the processes of calculation, and who are quite conscious of their status. Only this urban group can espouse a world outlook based on an inner-worldly asceticism.

It may be observed that the interrelations between the various aspects of this argument are such that it takes a spiral form, one aspect leading to another which, in turn, begins to act on the original causal factor. Some commentators on the work of Weber (*The Protestant Ethic and the Spirit of Capitalism*) suggest that his work represents a dialog with the ghost of Marx. In some important aspects, Weber was seeking to emphasize the complexity of social phenomena and to show the inadequacy of any conception of the causal primacy of one specific factor in contradistinction to others. But to conclude on the basis of the preceding argument that Weber attributed to ideas causal primacy and that he denied socio-economic formations any powers of determination, would be to miss the point. As indicated earlier, his account of the rise of modern capitalism does not envisage it as being *caused by* the Protestant ethic nor *vice versa*. Rather, he saw an elective affinity between the economic system and religious belief. If this is true of the specific Protestant ethic thesis, it is even more so of the wider thesis about the process of rationalization in Occidental civilization. It seems the distinction between Occidental rationality and what he classified as non-rational civilizations is correlated with another: the distinction between feudal and patrimonial socio-economic formations. It seems there is an "elective affinity," if we may use the term in this new context, between rationalism and feudalism on the one hand, and non-rationalism and patrimonialism on the other. Without going into the details of the distinction, it seems that Weber argues that patrimonial societies such as China and the Islamic state – where there is no individual property to speak of (or, when it exists, it is precarious and not hereditary), no self-equipped military owing fealty to a feudal landlord, but rather a military force recruited and paid by the state, and no formal law but rather general principles of justice or a set of laws tailored to specific situations – were not conducive to the rise of the rationalist impulse.

The preceding account is not meant to be a synopsis of the Weberian thesis about the rationalism of Occidental civilization; it simply tries to underscore some aspects of that thesis which are relevant to this study. Perhaps the most important conclusion from the standpoint of this chapter is that the Protestant ethic thesis is a part of a whole. When engaging in a comparative approach, only complete wholes can be subjected to comparisons. It is a worthless mental exercise to try to compare two component parts belonging to two different systems or structures. In that sense, the Protestantism-capitalism thesis cannot be divorced from the wider context of the rationalization thesis. Weber tried to study this specifically Occidental phenomenon of rationalization as manifested in what he considered to be specifically Occidental phenomena: the city, secular law, feudalism, inner worldly asceticism, etc., and it was this specificity that concerned him most.

Any specificity can be viewed in two distinct ways: from the viewpoint of its uniqueness, or from the viewpoint of its universality. If they are concerned with defining uniqueness, the researchers try to discover the features that set one culture apart from another. If, on the other hand, they want to discover the universal in the specific, they try to discover what is common between one culture and another. To reach this level of generality, one needs a language not reducible to the specificity of any one single system or structure, or else one would be reducing the laws and language of one structure to another, thereby missing both the uniqueness and specificity, and the universality. That is why nobody has asked the question: Why did the medieval European artist not use the Arabesque? Or, why did modern art in China not produce impressionist or post-impressionist paintings? "Arabesque" and "impressionism" are terms specific to the culture[5] that produced them and therefore cannot serve as terms of universal applicability. The question should be formulated in terms of concepts of symmetry, unity, and beauty, because such terms are on a level of generality that makes for their applicability to almost all systems. All cultures have a sense (consciousness) of symmetry, but not all cultures have an Impressionist school of painting.

What I am suggesting here is that the very terminology of the problematic of capitalism and Islam is misleading. Occidental capitalism, if we accept the Weberian viewpoint, is specific to Occidental civilization. But to try to envisage Islam using this category of capitalism would be to lapse into Euro-centricity, or what two American scholars on India once termed the "imperialism of categories."[6]

It was entirely appropriate for Weber to use the phenomenon of Occidental capitalism to further explore his culture and its specific and enduring relationships, but to use the same set of terms to explore the specific nature of another culture is quite misleading.

This is the basic flaw of Russell Stone's "Religious Ethic and the Spirit of Capitalism in Tunisia"[7] where the author concludes, after some empirical research, that the Jerba sect, a Muslim religious sect with what may be termed a Calvinist state of mind, has a definite orientation toward capitalist enterprise. This demonstration of the relationship between the religious ethic and capitalist activity, the author argues, "again suggests that Weber's hypothesis generally applies to many societies. Just as the Protestant ethic led to capitalist development in Europe at the time of the

Reformation, likewise a similar religious ethic among Jerba merchants in Tunisia in the 19th and 20th Centuries resulted in successful capitalistic activity."[8]

Stone's conclusion is diametrically opposed to the spirit of Weber's scholarly works and his preoccupations. Whereas Weber was concerned with specificity, precisely to loosen the grip of the idea of a general law applicable to all social phenomena, Stone wants to demonstrate the universal validity of the "Weberian law." But even within the confines of his own thesis, Stone demonstrates implicitly the very opposite of what he has set out to prove. If the ethic of Calvinist Geneva helped bring about an economic system (or pattern) that prevailed all over Europe, the ethic of the small tribe of Jerba did not lead to similar developments. Therefore, the original question remains more or less the same – why there, and not here?

Maxime Rodinson's *Islam and Capitalism*[9] is not as limited in scope or argument as the preceding work, but nevertheless it suffers from the same constricting empiricism. This very erudite work sets forth to demolish many sacred myths and long-established certainties in the West concerning the "Arab mentality" and the submissiveness of the Islamic mind. Rodinson ably demonstrates that Islamic civilization had some seeds of rationalization. There is a great deal of appeal to human reason in the Qur'an and an exhortation to reflection. He also shows that there was an Islamic world market[10] and a strong commercial sector during certain periods in medieval Islam. Rodinson likewise indicates that the "coefficient of magic" was no higher in Islamic society than in any other.[11]

But Rodinson, despite the usefulness of his work in some respects, misses the essential point and operates on a strictly economic level. As a self-avowed materialist, he denies religion any autonomous role, and denies its absolute role in history. One justifiably wonders: Can a true materialist write about the sociology of religion without reductionism? Would not the very assumptions of the discipline run counter to his view of humankind and history? That is why in a book on Islam and capitalism, Rodinson, in a facile manner, writes off "the process of systematic idealization to which the Caliphate of ʿUmar has been subjected in Sunni tradition."[12] But it is precisely this process of idealization that matters most on this level of analysis, and to write it off as a mere "illusion" is to miss the point. Rodinson concentrates on legislation, economic figures, sayings and maxims to prove that nothing in Islam or Islamic civilization would inhibit the development of capitalism. But then figures, like maxims, can be interpreted in many ways, and it was probably the general orientation of the culture, a socio-economic formation that buttresses an outlook – and an outlook in turn that reinforces the formation – that made Islamic civilization take its particular form and no other.

Bryan Turner's *Weber and Islam*[13] is perhaps the only work I know of that tries to encompass the problem in its totality. For instance, he does not confine himself to religious ethics as Russell does, nor to economy and general principles as Rodinson does, but deals with the Islamic city, Islamic law and other related subjects with breadth of vision and knowledge of and respect for Islamic civilization. Turner does not lapse into Euro-centricity. However, rather than presenting a sustained argument, Turner lapses into mere comparative vignettes of various tenuously related subjects such as Allah and humankind and the difference between Shaykh and Saint. Each study in itself is very illuminating, but they do not interconnect and rather than answer the question about the relationship between Islam and capitalism, or even Islam and rationalization, the author tries to reconcile Weber's thesis about Oriental patrimonialism with Marx's thesis about the Asiatic mode of production.

The level of research in the area of Islamic civilization was, till very recently, monopolized by colonialists or by zealous missionaries sure of their cultural and religious superiority and unaware of their epistemological biases. Such Orientalists and missionaries produced excellent scholarly editions of the classics of Islamic civilization, but their work was inordinately ideological and ethnocentric. The work of Gustave E. von Grünebaum is an excellent example. His study of medieval Islam is a brilliant, erudite work made up of dehistoricized statements which give no explanation of the phenomenon at hand. For instance, "Islam," von Grünebaum says, "did not follow the West in changing the purpose of conduct from the static ideal of happiness to the dynamics of the pursuit of happiness."[14] This is a descriptive statement that adds nothing to one's knowledge. Moreover, by abstracting the trait of staticism, it turns history into a battlefield of allegorical absolutes, with an Islamic absolute always lagging behind. In another statement, von Grünebaum claims that "the West is ready to sacrifice the present for the future."[15] Any researcher knows that in the West, the ideal is no longer one of sacrifice or renunciation, and only totalitarian societies are "stigmatized" by this virtue. Only recently have we begun to read works by young European social scientists who look at Islamic civilization not as an antique to be admired or condemned, but as a social process susceptible to the universal laws of change. However, most of the members of this group are materialists and reductionists who, like Rodinson, are busy exonerating the ghost of Marx.[16]

The level of available research and the ideological burden of the researchers might represent some impediments in the attempt to deal with the issue of Islam and capitalism, but the major hurdle is the very way in which the issue is formulated. If we accept the argument that there are no "natural" economic systems,[17] then capitalism, like Faustianism or futurism in the field of literature, is part of a language specific to one cultural formation and therefore does not have universal applicability. Occidental civilization, along with its cultural idiom, cannot be used to describe or examine another. What is needed is a general language and analytical categories, external to all systems and structures, but applicable, in some way, to all. Rather than capitalism, rationalization might be a more general and more appropriate term, in relation to which the issue can be rephrased as "rationalization and Islam."

Yet, despite the more general nature of the term "rationalization" we still have problems. If we were to speak of "non-rational civilizations," it would be like talking of "prelogical societies," a notion that has been completely discredited. Every society has its form of rationalization, of matching means to ends. Weber himself detects in the Chinese empire forms of value-oriented rationalization. The issue is probably best phrased as "Islam and modernity." It is an incontrovertible fact of our "modern" age that modern technology and science are global phenomena, and that any society that does not adopt them, in one form or another, perishes. A course on the subject would deal with relevant issues and ask questions such as: Can Islamic society adopt science and technology without losing its unique identity? How can Islam, or the reformist Islamic movements, mobilize the masses to achieve the transition from societies based on agriculture and low levels of technology to those bent on mastering nature? Phrased in this way, the issue becomes a question asked by the Muslims themselves from within, yet it is a question of universal significance. Then, rather than try to demonstrate that the Islamic city cannot produce capitalists, we can begin to ask what type of outlook the Islamic city generates. In this way, the whole structure, because it is approached from within, can begin to yield its secrets and give us its laws, which will no longer be considered defects to be corrected or wrongs to be righted. The fact that Islamic society never distinguished between secular and religious law – or at least even when there was a distinction, the ultimate legitimacy of law was religious – will not be a major drawback but simply a trait, a *donnée*, to be interpreted and explained, and probably evaluated. But when evaluating it, we should not accept as a criterion the degree of proximity to Occidental civilization. The totality of humankind's experience in the East and the West, past or present, should be the only standard.

Given our knowledge about the crisis of legitimization in secular society, coupled with our awareness that Occidental world mastery has led to world imperialism, two world wars, and a world about to be depleted of its natural resources, the idea of a religiously guided society might not be that unpalatable or non-rational after all. The concept of a Confucian accommodation with the world, be it the world of nature or the human-made world of history, might not be necessarily negative.

Adopting some aspects of such a Confucian perspective, or any non-Western perspective, would lead to posing a set of questions completely different from those questions that result from adopting a Western perspective. The way Western capitalism, forms of economic development in the Orient, and the varied forms of modernization in the world are studied would then take a completely different course. Each school curriculum would then posit its own questions based on a common universal human concept.

6

An Exploration of the Nature of Human Artificial Intelligence and the Qur'anic Perspective

MAHMOUD DHAOUADI

THE ONGOING CONTROVERSY over artificial and human intelligence is characterized by open disagreement. Some researchers believe that artificial intelligence has the potential to become equal to or even superior to human intelligence, while others say that such a development is impossible. The thesis of this chapter is that the gap between human and artificial intelligence is bound to remain considerable, both in the short term and in the long term. The concepts of human cultural symbols and the Qur'anic vision of human intelligence are introduced in support of this thesis. Humanity's ability to manipulate cultural symbols, upon which the phenomenon of human intelligence depends, is a uniquely human characteristic. And this uniqueness, according to the Qur'an, is the direct result of a divine decision, not of evolution. Many of the mysteries of this uniqueness are hardly accessible to humans; hence, how would human researchers be able to include them in the design of artificial intelligence machines?

In the last two decades, research in the field of artificial intelligence (hereinafter referred to as AI) has made considerable headway on both the theoretical and the applied levels. The input into the field has not been restricted only to cybernetics and information process experts; neurophysiologists, cognitive psychologists, philosophers, and sociologists[1] have also been interested in human intelligence (hereinafter referred to as HI) and AI. As AI infrastructures and authority continue to expand in modern and postmodern societies, specialists in other areas will also have to become involved.

For scientists, basic and applied research into AI constitutes an exciting challenge for two reasons: (a) Continued improvement of AI will relieve individuals of many tedious tasks. Furthermore, the increasing speed and quality of numerous human actions and transactions are bound to become major characteristics of those societies that have entered the Information Age. For example, the widespread use of credit cards has improved and eased all financial transaction services. (b) Basic research into AI will force researchers and others to follow Socrates' admonition to "know thyself," for AI and HI are intimately linked. AI enthusiasts such as Feigenbaum[2] and Simon state that AI could eventually be a real match for, if not actually superior to, HI. Opponents, such as Dreyfus[3] and Searle,[4] view this as wishful thinking.

The issue of human intelligence remains central to both sides. As AI machines today are manifestly inferior to HI, researchers are forced to ask: Why is HI superior? What does HI have that AI does not? Answering such questions will ultimately lead to a better understanding of ourselves. A good knowledge of ourselves, and of HI in particular, should be of great help in designing more intelligent machines.

THE ARTIFICIAL INTELLIGENCE CONTROVERSY

The causes of AI's inferiority to HI are the subject of heated debate. Searle believes that AI will come close to HI only if biochemical hardware is actually placed within the AI hardware itself. He also argues that plain symbol manipulation (he calls this strong AI) by machines, computers, and robots cannot raise AI to the level of HI, for while they can manipulate the symbols, they cannot attach any meaning(s) to them.[5] This, in his words, is the big difference between AI and HI.

Enthusiasts such as P.M. and P.S. Churchland believe that AI machines do not necessarily need biochemical hardware (infrastructure) to bring their intelligence up to the level of humans. What is needed, they claim, is to design machines that can function like a human brain. This raises another fundamental, and still unanswered, question, which has been the subject of debate for the last three decades: Can a machine think? Church and Turing defend the thesis that AI machines can think if they are provided with certain infrastructures: "... a standard digital computer, given only the right program, a large memory and sufficient time, can compute any rule-governed input-output function. That is, it can display any systematic pattern of responses to any environment whatsoever."[6] To prove their point, Church and Turing argue that such AI machines can think, because they are able to pass the so-called Turing Test for Conscious Intelligence. The test in question consists of entering conversational questions and remarks into the symbol manipulation machine (SAM). If the AI machines' typed responses cannot be distinguished from those of a real person, the machine is said to have passed the test and therefore to possess conscious intelligence.[7]

Simon and Feigenbaum have suggested that thinking machines can solve problems and adopt a rational manner in formulating a solution to them. But they and others have also discovered that certain elements intimately associated with HI (i.e., intuition, mood, and emotions) have no place in an AI scheme. Thus a rational thinking machine does not "think" in the human sense of the term. Feigenbaum admits that for a machine to think like a human being, it must possess (a) learning competence, (b) common sense experience or general problem-solving skills, and (c) a natural language that permits it to understand and manipulate its environment.

Many scientists and scholars, such as Dreyfus, Searle, and Penrose, assert that machines cannot think like human beings. They oppose the idea that a computer is a metaphor of the human brain. Dreyfus believes that an individual's knowledge cannot be broken down into a finite number of facts and rules, for a mind knows unutterable truths that are not algorithmic and therefore cannot be programmed.[8] Searle argues that as computers simply follow algorithms, they cannot deal with important factors like meaning and content. Computers are, for him, syntactic and not semantic beasts. Penrose views the idea of AI with suspicion and contempt, for he seems to be strongly convinced that there is something special about human thinking.[9] His key argument is that there are "nonrecursive" problems in mathematics, by which he means that they cannot be solved through the use of algorithms. Yet people somehow are able to solve them, which means that the human brain must be doing something non-algorithmic. He therefore insists that the human brain possesses a "mysterious quality" giving it a direct link to eternal truths which have some kind of prior ethereal existence. Penrose's "mysticism" has not pushed him out of the scientific orbit. Johnson describes Penrose's situation this way:

So, going way beyond Dreyfus and Searle, he tries to find some conceivable scientific explanation for what amounts to communicating with a kind of Platonic planton zone. Instead of invoking Heidegger and Wittgenstein, Penrose calls on Niels Bohr, Werner Heisenberg, Max Planck, Erwin Schrodinger, the inventors of quantum theory. For quantum theory shows that at the roots of reality things are acausal, indeterministic, nonlocal – *everything a computer is not.*[10]

Thus, scientists and scholars are faced with two issues: (a) the dispute over whether AI could one day equal HI, and (b) that HI, the human mind, and human thinking are still little understood and therefore remain a mystery for modern science and knowledge. Given that symbol manipulation by AI machines and human beings is the crucial factor on which depend the level and quality of intelligence, research into the nature of human cultural symbols can lead to a better understanding of HI, the human mind, and human thinking. Humans are, after all, the most distinct and sophisticated cultural-symbol manipulators.

THE CONCEPT OF CULTURE IN THE SOCIAL SCIENCES

What distinguishes humanity from other species and from AI machines is the phenomenon of culture. According to White, "Man is unique: he is the only living species that has a culture. All peoples in all times and places have possessed culture; no other species has or has had culture."[11] However, it has not been easy to define culture, for, as Ogburn has stated, "... culture is one of those large concepts, like democracy or science, a definition of which seems very bare and inadequate to convey its rich meanings. Different students will emphasize different aspects of culture as most significant, and in the future important new ideas about culture may be discovered."[12] The definition most often quoted by social scientists is still that of Tylor: "Culture is that complex whole which includes knowledge, belief, art, morals, custom, and other capabilities and habits acquired by man as a member of society."[13]

There is a consensus among scholars of culture that humanity's use of symbols is human culture's most striking feature. The sociological school of Symbolic Interaction bases its premises, as well as its explanations of human individual and collective behaviors, on the symbolic skills of social actors.[14] The symbolic abilities of humans are the yardstick by which White defines the nature of humanity: "... we thus define man in terms of the abilities to symbolize and the consequent ability to produce culture."[15] He identifies language as the most important cultural symbol: "But perhaps the best example of all is articulate speech or language; at any rate, we may well regard articulate speech as the most characteristic and the most important form of expression of the ability to symbol."[16]

These observations enable us to assert that (a) the human species is decisively cultural-symbolic by nature, and (b) this ability to use cultural symbols makes it radically different from all other species and AI machines. Those behavioral social science theories and paradigms that fail to take these claims into account are doomed to failure. However, many Western researchers still ascribe HI's superiority to a human being's possession of a biochemical body, emotions, common sense, and the ability to behave according to illogical and irrational laws. Others say that what is really missing is an efficient neural network. But can the development of an artificial neural network really raise AI to the same level as HI?[17]

Hardly any philosopher or social scientist has raised the issue of culture and its relationship to artificial intelligence. If one seeks a true understanding of HI, the realm of human cultural symbols must be studied. Morin,[18] a leader in the scientific exploration of the world of ideas and the creation of thought, has elaborated a sort of ecology of ideas. Among the many questions he raises is: How do we create ideas and how do they, in turn, create us? In an earlier work,[19] he dealt with the complexity of human thought and its subtle mechanisms and dynamics.

The ability to manipulate cultural symbols in thought-complexity or idea-creation processes is more than crucial; it is fundamental for the acquisition of reliable knowledge about the processes of cognition and semantics. Cognitive psychologists and other specialists agree that there is currently little knowledge in this field. It is our contention that this partial absence of a corpus of solid knowledge on cultural symbols constitutes the missing link in the ever-growing body of knowledge on human and artificial intelligence. Building a solid foundation in this domain is imperative, for how can researchers speak of the shortcomings of AI machines as regards learning (i.e., no common sense and no natural language)[20] without reference to why HI is superior? Such disinterest is a major weakness that can only confuse the researcher's understanding of HI's originality and render many of his/her hopes and promises illusory.

CULTURAL SYMBOLS AND THE MAKING OF THE HUMAN MIND

Philosophers, thinkers, and scientists, despite their persistent efforts, have not yet been able to fully disclose the nature of the human mind. Descartes, Leibnitz, and Kant viewed it as made of something incorporeal: spirit, pure thought, or soul.[21] By 1950, psychology began to liken it to an intellectual machine, seeing it as an extremely sophisticated information processing mechanism.[22] Further exploration established a distinction between the brain and the mind: the mind is the brain's programs or the brain's total set of symbol manipulation. Put another way, the brain is what is and the mind is what the brain does.[23]

Studies on the mind continue to explore its numerous activities and components. Memory has been looked at as an intellectual muscle, as a writing-recording department, and as a working reference encyclopedia.[24] Research by modern cognitive scientists shows that logical reasoning is not the usual practice of humans. Wason and other cognitive scientists have concluded that human beings tend to find it much more natural to look for proof and to look for disproof.[25]

The mind's advanced thinking cannot materialize without the use of cultural symbols. This conclusion is explicitly stated by Hunt:

> Advanced thinking depends on the mental manipulation of symbols, and while nonlinguistic symbol systems such as those of mathematics and art are sophisticated, they are extremely narrow. Language, by contrast, is a virtually unbounded symbol system capable of expressing every kind of thought. It is the *prerequisite* (our emphasis) of culture which can't exist without it or by means of any other symbol system. It is the way we human beings communicate most of our thoughts to each other and receive from each other the food of thought. In sum, we don't always think in words, but we could do little thinking without them.[26]

Any discussion of the mind's mental activities raises the question of the origin of intelligence and its relation to the culture-mind connection. In the case of a computer, its so-called intelligence is the result of an information processing system run by a flip-flop (on-off) system.[27] A human brain, however, consists of innumerable neurons, each of which has thousands of linkages to other neurons. It is thus far from being limited to the on-off system. Hunt summarizes the difference in information processing between the computer and the human brain by saying that, "the computer deals with information serially, in a single line. The brain does so via millions (even trillions) of parallel channels, each capable of acting at the same time as the others."[28] Compared with other beings and AI machines, the human mind is a super mind,[29] for only it has the ability to manipulate the cultural symbols found, for example, in language, thought, knowledge, values, and religious beliefs. Modern psychological and sociological studies have highlighted the negative effects of social deprivation on human intelligence, thereby indicating that intelligence is strongly dependent on the cultural symbols that permit the socialization of human beings to take place. As pointed out earlier, Searle argues that the human mind is partially a biological phenomenon.[30]

TWO VIEWS OF HUMAN THINKING

Contemporary studies by cognitive scientists of culture, the mind, and human ideas have adopted two points of view: (1) the enlightenment view and (2) the romantic rebellion view. The first holds that the mind is "intentionally rational and scientific, that the dictates of reason are equally binding for all regardless of time, place, culture, race, personal desire, or individual endowment, and that in reason can be found a universally applicable standard for judging validity and worth."[31] The romantic rebellion view states that "ideas and practices have their foundation in neither logic nor empirical science, that ideas and practices fall beyond the scope of deductive and inductive reason, that ideas and practices are neither rational nor irrational but rather non-rational."[32] Voltaire, Spinoza, Frazer, Tylor, Chomsky, Lévi-Strauss, and Piaget belong to the enlightenment perspective, while Goethe, Schiller, Levy-Bruhl, Whorf, Sahlins, Feyerabend, and Geertz are associated with the romantic rebellion view. The latter group says that culture, the mind, and intelligence should not be measured by the yardstick of empirico-positivism, reasoning, logic, and rationalism alone, for, claims March, ambiguity, apparent inefficiency, and apparent inconsistency are "not necessarily a fault in human choice to be corrected but a form of intelligence."[33]

Cognitive research inspired by the romanticist outlook has opened new vistas by replacing the rigid, narrow, and uni-dimensional vision of empiricism, positivism, logic, and rationalism. Shweder writes:

> Don't knock the mystical, the transcendental, or the arbitrary. In recent years, cognitive scientists have advanced our understanding of the type of ideas underlying non-rational action, and it has become more and more apparent that language, thought, and society are built up out of ideas that fall beyond the sweep of logical and scientific evaluation, ideas for which there are no universally binding normative criteria.[34]

The enlightenment and the romantic rebellion views are extremely relevant to the AI debate. Simon and Feigenbaum believe strongly that the basis of HI is rational, logical, and step-by-step. Basing themselves on this enlightenment view, they believe that the creation of machines that think (i.e., follow rational, logical, and step-by-step procedures) either at the same level or above that of humans is only a matter of time. Adherents of the romantic rebellion view regard human intelligence and thinking as not having a purely rational and logical nature, for they are affected by irrational and non-rational human factors. Prime examples of this are emotions and intuition, which are basic components in human intelligence and thinking.[35] According to Dreyfus, "the best performing computer and the most powerful of all can't understand a story which a four-year-old child can, because the latter has common sense, while the computer functions only through logic. Having no physical body, no emotion, no language, the computer can't understand even those things which are considered by us the most simple."[36] In this view, human intelligence is a combination of rationalism, order, logic, irrationality, intuition, non-rationality, imagination, and disorder. Only a technique which incorporates those elements can unlock the secrets of human intelligence, the mind, and thinking.

Since AI's inferiority as regards HI is due to its narrow logical-rational-logarithmic structural design, a design that does not take into account any points raised by the romantics, there are serious questions raised. For example, how credible is the empirico-positivist paradigm, as two of its fundamental elements are logic and rationality? Two implications of such a realization are that humans are more than just logical and rational thinkers, and that HI's superiority comes from such intangible and subjective traits as irrationality, emotionality, and intuition. In other words, researchers studying this phenomenon need to move beyond the traditional empirico-positivist view by beginning to consider the transcendental dimensions of cultural symbols – studying human cultural symbols and their manipulation from within.

CULTURAL SYMBOLS AND THE MEANING OF TRANSCENDENCE

Human cultural symbols, as defined above, have metaphysical-divine characteristics. This transcendental character does not seem to have captured the attention of modern social-behavioral scientists. This situation persists despite the tremendous theoretical and empirical explorations of anthropologists and sociologists, beginning in the 19th Century, of the phenomenon of culture. Consequently, the following reflections are but the result of a continuing personal research effort on the nature of human cultural symbols.[37]

Human cultural symbols are, in their own way, eternal. The symptoms of the latter can be displayed in tangible and measurable terms: (a) human language, preserved through writing, permits an individual's symbolic existence to survive beyond his/her physical death. In the absence of a written language to preserve human thought, the ideas of Aristotle, Ibn Khaldūn, Shakespeare, Marx, Einstein, Sartre, and others would never have come down to us intact; (b) on the oral level, human beings often use the spoken word in their meditation, contemplation, and their addresses to their gods or to anything else they believe is eternal or sacred. Thus, unlike other living organisms, human beings can establish contact with the metaphysical realm; (c) on the audio-visual level, increasing technological sophistication has made it possible for an individual's image and voice to last forever.

McLuhan's famous statement, "The planet has become a small village," requires some qualification in this regard. What has brought about this development is the attainment of a level of technological innovation that allows the almost instantaneous transmission of human cultural symbols (i.e., the written word, speech, pictures) to almost any place in the world. This transmitability makes cultural symbols unique, because other elements, such as smell or the physical body, cannot be handled in the same manner. Thus cultural symbols, no longer bound by time and space, have taken on a quasi-metaphysical quality and are now part of a world whose logic and order defy the logic and order of the sensory world. Cultural symbols also possess intrinsic aptitudes for freedom and independence, which non-cultural symbols do not, as they are not confined to the boundaries of the human body. Based on the above discussion, it is clear that language, the most important human cultural symbol, is transcendental in nature and fundamental to the development of human intelligence. Attempts by positivist researchers to deny or marginalize its role is counter to the true neutral scientific spirit and also hinders the establishment of a credible scientific corpus on language.

Given the strong relation between language and HI, the study of language might help to explain some of the non-rational components of human intelligence (i.e., irrationality, intuition, illogic) which are at least partially affected by language's transcendental (non-rational) nature. One example is the study of consciousness, which, according to Penrose, is determined by non-algorithmic ingredients.[38] If researchers are to understand such transcendental phenomena, they need to go beyond their faith in the unidimensional causality of such phenomena. All specialists have largely confined themselves to algorithmic, rational, and logical materialistic structures, a limitation which has allowed them to produce AI machines that remain vastly inferior to HI.

Some true believers, such as Simon and Feigenbaum,[39] insist that AI can equal or surpass HI by maintaining the logical-rational principles in the new or modified designs and structures of AI machines. This rigid stand reminds us of Russell and Whitehead, both of whom tried to place mathematics on a completely logical basis. Godel's incompleteness theorem came as a response, for he believed that there would always be mathematical results that could be constructed but not deduced within the system of axioms and logic. The same is true of human cultural symbols. Modern psychology and AI research have accomplished very little in their attempts to explain and understand the nature and the functioning processes of HI, for they do not give due importance to the cognitive process as a fundamental feature of human behavior.

Research on AI HI must not follow a rigid and narrow formula, for human behavior is a complex phenomenon whose roots are to be largely found in HI itself. This makes HI, by definition, a complex phenomenon.

The concept of intelligence has undergone substantial transformations since Binet's time. Gardner's recent findings on HI are just one example.[40] The growing participation in the field of AI/HI by specialists in physics, cybernetics, neurophysiology, cognitive psychology, philosophy, linguistics, and sociology, for example, ought to be considered a healthy and promising sign.

THE MAKING OF HUMAN INTELLIGENCE IN THE QUR'AN

Revealed texts are hardly consulted on the subject of HI by modern researchers. This is due to the West's experience of the Renaissance, which bypassed the Muslim world, and the usually hostile relationship between religion and science. As such a situation is unknown in Islam, it is logical for a Muslim researcher in the field of AI/HI to consult the Qur'an, where he/she learns the following:

The Transcendental Nature of Human Intelligence. The term "intelligence" is of modern origin and is strongly associated with modern psychology. With Binet (1857–1911), intelligence became a measurable phenomenon. In the Qur'an, HI is indicated by other terms and particular traits: "Verily We honored the children of Adam. We carry them on the land and the sea, and have made good provision of good things and have preferred them above many of those whom We created with marked preferment" (17:70). The phrases, "honored the children of Adam," "preferred them," and "whom We created with marked preferment" all appear to refer directly to HI as a distinctly human thought ability (skill) possessed by no other creature. There is a striking similarity between the old and the new definitions of HI: both stress that thinking is the characteristic distinguishing humans from nonhumans. Classical Greek philosophers described humans as rational (thinking) beings, while more recent definitions of intelligence consider thought processes as the basis of intelligence: "Intelligence has gradually come to mean the higher level abstract thought processes, as opposed to the simpler sensory or perceptual processes."[41]

A second, less direct Qur'anic verse is, "We have indeed created man in the best of moulds" (95:4), in other words the best of forms. In anthropological terms, the "best of moulds" or forms is the upright stand and the greater size of the human brain. Obviously, the second is far more important than the first, for the human brain's larger size is the crucial determinant factor that has made humans superior to nonhumans: "But above all man owes his astonishingly rapid evolution to the growth of his brain. It would not be too much to say the history of mankind is the history of the human brain."[42] The Qur'anic verse means that humanity is superior only because it can think.

A third verse specifies HI's roots and its very nature: "And lo! Your Sustainer said to the angels: 'Behold, I am about to create mortal man out of sounding clay, out of dark slime transmuted; and when I have formed him fully and breathed into him of My spirit, fall down before him in prostration!'" (15:28–29). While interpretations of the meaning of the breathed divine spirit may differ, there is a strong consensus that it should include the thought processes, which includes human cultural symbols, that apparently separate human beings from all other creations, including the angels. According to these Qur'anic verses, it is HI (i.e., the ability to think and to manipulate human cultural symbols) that sets humanity apart. The Qur'an's strong emphasis on the thinking process as the fundamental pillar of HI is compatible with the findings of modern AI and HI research. However, the origin of HI is sharply disputed. The Qur'an views HI as deriving from a divine, metaphysical source, while Western science remains staunch in its belief that HI is the result of sensory and tangible objective factors. This view is then subdivided into the neuron connectionist and the information process models of the brain, both of which see HI as the outcome of a long evolutionary process. There is no room in such a view for any subjective, spiritual, or metaphysical dimensions.

As HI is transcendental, a methodology recognizing this fact must be employed if researchers are to gain an accurate understanding of this phenomenon. As the Western empirico-positivist method does not recognize HI's transcendental nature, it is hardly a suitable approach. What is needed is a thoroughly nonbiased approach, one that considers all possibilities, be they logical, rational, empirical, or otherwise.[43]

Thinking and Human Intelligence. The mystery of human thinking, despite its primary place in modern scientific research, is still a great puzzle for modern science. The Qur'an attaches a great deal of importance to thinking, for it views thinking as the most important component and indicator of HI. Many verses emphasize the need for humanity to ponder and think: "… who remember God when they stand, and when they sit, and when they lie down to sleep, and [thus] reflect on the creation of the heavens and the earth: 'O our Sustainer! You have not created [aught of] this without meaning and purpose. Limitless are You in Your glory!'" (3:191); "And He has made the night and the day and the sun and the moon subservient to you; and all the stars are subservient to His command: in this, behold, there are messages indeed for people who use their reason!" (16:12); "Have they never learned to think for themselves? God has not created the heavens and the earth and all that is between them without [an inner] truth and a term set [by Him]" (30:8); and "Have they, then, never journeyed about the earth, letting their hearts gain wisdom, and causing their ears to hear? Yet, verily, it is not their eyes that have become blind – but blind have become the hearts that are in their breasts!" (22:46).

Human Intelligence and the Act of Creating. The capacity to create and to invent is seen in the Qur'an as a strong manifestation of intelligence. The superiority of divine intelligence over all other forms of intelligence lies in God's ability to create what humans and nonhumans cannot create. The creation of living beings from the most simple to the most complex strictly falls within the range of the divine power; "Behold, those beings whom you invoke instead of God cannot create [as much as] a fly, even were they to join all their forces to that end! And if a fly robs them of anything, they cannot [even] rescue it from him! Weak indeed is the seeker, and [weak] the sought!" (22:73). This verse ridicules the worship of nonintelligent idols by intelligent human beings, portraying such an act as an affront to the dignity of human intelligence. How can an intelligent being worship that which has no intelligence? This is unacceptable. As God is the most intelligent being of all, only He is fit to be worshiped by intelligent beings. Human beings are practically the only living beings that can "create" in the larger sense of the term. The phenomena of civilization and culture are uniquely human, for they are the outcomes of the human act of creation. Nonhuman living creatures and AI machines are involved in very limited acts of creation, but they can do this only because of their instincts and genetic programs, not through any conscious decision making or choice on their part. The role of HI in a human being's act of creation is essential, a fact recognized by the Qur'an but largely ignored by current AI and HI research. As previously pointed out, researchers commonly measure intelligence by such things as the ability to deal effectively with abstract concepts and to learn and adapt to new situations.44

From a Qur'anic outlook, the act of creating must be viewed as a fundamental and crucial component of intelligence. An articulate understanding of the differences among the divine, the human, the animal, and artificial machines cannot be achieved without taking this into account.

Humanity's Status as God's Khalīfah and Human Intelligence. Like the human act of creating, humanity's role as the *khalīfah* (vicegerent) of God, which entails the management of the material realm, is another indication of superior intelligence. According to the Qur'an, such an intelligence comes from the divine breath that endowed humanity with thought, reasoning, and the ability to use symbols and create. All of these are needed in order to carry out this task successfully. The Qur'an singles out human beings, who possess this intelligence, as the only suitable candidates for this role: "Verily, We did offer the trust [of reason and volition] to the heavens, and the earth, and the mountains: but they refused to bear it because they were afraid of it. Yet man took it up – for, verily, he has always been prone to be most wicked, most foolish" (33:72).

CONCLUSION

The concept of HI as developed in this chapter allows us to settle two thorny questions: Are humans responsible beings, and are they God's representatives on earth? As to the first question, both religious and secular doctrines agree that only human beings can be held responsible for their acts, for the responsibility of action requires, by definition, that the actor have the ability to behave freely. It has been emphasized throughout this chapter that HI gives humanity this ability, and thus whether human beings can be held responsible (i.e., if their intelligence is not impaired) for their actions is no longer a matter of purely religious-philosophical speculation.

As far as the legitimacy of human beings' role as God's vicegerent, the issue is decisively settled by their high level of intelligence. Of all of God's creation, only humanity has been able to develop, modify, and transform the earth and the world at large. As no other part of creation can do this, humanity is God's representative. The key to this position is the divine spark of intelligence which God breathed into humanity. Thus it is inaccurate to say that a human being is an animal-angel; he/she is an animal-divine entity.

The issue of HI is central throughout the Qur'an. The first verses of the first revealed surah addresses this issue directly: "Read in the name of thy Sustainer, who has created – created man out of a germ-cell! Read – for thy Sustainer is the Most Bountiful One who has taught [man] the use of the pen – taught man what he did not know!" (96:1–5). Reading, learning, and writing abilities are distinct skills associated only with HI. The verses that invite and urge humans to acquire knowledge and science are estimated to constitute one-sixth of the Qur'an. Without the presence of a well-developed HI, it would be unrealistic to ask human beings to pursue knowledge and science. Likewise, there would be no need for the Qur'an to exhort them to think, ponder, and meditate if they did not possess a level of intelligence that would enable them to carry out these tasks. Such tasks were not assigned to other living and intelligent beings, because their level of intelligence was not symbols. Hence, the beautiful linguistic Qur'anic text stands as the perfect example to stimulate HI through its authentic Arabic text in style, expressions, metaphors, analogies, and eloquence. The Qur'an clearly states that Adam's creation would have meant nothing without the gift of a correspondingly high level of intelligence. In the absence of such intelligence, there would also have been no need to celebrate the event by ordering the angels to prostrate before him, for he would be just another creation.

From the Qur'anic perspective, the phenomenon of HI did not develop through time and space, as claimed by evolutionists. Rather, it was there at the beginning of creation. It was not the end result of a long process of evolution, but was instead the outcome of a deliberate divine choice and decision. Thus, since the beginning, HI has been the determinant force on which depends everything in this world, including the very existence and destiny of humanity. As outlined above, HI is a central Qur'anic theme and preoccupation. As modern Western scientists and scholars do not accept information provided in revealed texts, they and Muslim scientists and scholars active in this field have major differences. The root of these differences is epistemological, for Muslims see intelligence as the result of the divine breath imparted to humankind, while their Western counterparts view it as the result of a long evolutionary process. These two views are so far apart that they are, essentially, irreconcilable.

The implications of this epistemological split make the Qur'anic stand as a close ally of those modern scientists and scholars who do not believe that it is possible to raise AI to a level which is either equal or superior to that of human beings. This rapprochement is not, however, exactly for the same reasons. Searle asserts the need for biochemical structures in the design of AI machines, while Feigenbaum and Simon's logical-rational settings claim that the intelligence standard of AI products can eventually be made at least equal to that of HI. Both of these views ignore the main assertion of the Qur'an: AI can never be equal to HI, for God has not imparted to it His divine breath. But just as AI can never reach the level of HI, a human being's level of intelligence can never approach that of God: "And they will ask thee about [the nature of] divine inspiration. Say: 'This inspiration [comes] at my Sustainer's behest; and [you cannot understand its nature, O men, since] you have been granted very little of [real] knowledge.'" (17:85). Thus complete knowledge about the origin of intelligence lies with God and out of human reach. While the Qur'anic perspective can help us to understand this, the empirico-positivist approach, the most favored of the West, is of no use due to its refusal to recognize the transcendental nature of intelligence.

7

Confronting Bias in Third World Culture

FERIAL J. GHAZOUL

THE CREATIVE WRITER often senses – before a researcher – a given problem such as prejudice or bias in perspectives or methodologies. This concern gets translated into creative expressions which attempt to reveal and deal with a particular phenomenon. Bias against the Third World – a legacy of colonial world views – in intellectual spheres and methodologies is common knowledge: it is the theoretical translation, complement and correlative of racist practices and subordination of citizens in the Third World. Literature offers resistance to such biases and prejudices, sometimes even before a cultural movement of resistance is articulated; literature functions as a precursor for theoretical pronouncements addressing and combating such a destructive phenomenon. In artistic fields battles are fought without military weapons and cause no human casualties; rather, they offer an arena for the struggle over consciousness and values. Unlike military warfare, the literary domain does not need advanced technology, which is often monopolized by the stronger party and thus gives it a ready-made advantage over the Other, as we see in confrontations between unequal parties in the history of colonization. Literature, generally speaking, depends on stylistic techniques and artistic strategies which are not based on technological superiority of one over the other, but on equal access to the verbal and the conceptual. Literary expression does not correspond to the so-called dichotomy between advanced/backward or developed/underdeveloped. On the contrary, the oppressed and the marginal seem more creative and more productive on the artistic level than the oppressor and the powerful. This is because art is linked to the profundity of human vision rather than power mechanisms and methods of control.

Creative resistance against ingrained bias takes different forms, according to the circumstances of the writer in question. This chapter deals with three writers from the African continent – which has been a victim of racism – who have written in three languages: English, Arabic, and French. They are, respectively, the Nigerian Chinua Achebe, author of *Things Fall Apart*,[1] the Sudanese Tayeb Salih, author of *Season of Migration to the North*,[2] and the Moroccan Francophone writer Tahar Ben Jelloun, author of "I am an Arab, I am Suspect."[3] I shall deal with these works in their chronological order.

In his novel *Things Fall Apart*, Achebe presents the unfolding of the tragedy of its protagonist Okonkwo from the Obi ethnic group, who ends up committing suicide before the onslaught of the conquering colonizer and the imposition of foreign values – a seemingly inevitable consequence, given his attachment to tribal traditions and indigenous African heritage. The protagonist ends up broken by the colonial advance. It is the story of a proud man from the Third World, attached to his traditions in an unwavering individual commitment to them, yet unable to mobilize the same degree of commitment from the rest of his community. The lack of collective resistance, among other things, leads to defeat before such a formidable enemy. The novel reveals the modalities of penetration, suppression and defamation of Nigerian tradition with the combined efforts of foreign institutions – military, economic, and religious – to deliberately dismantle the African cultural base by infiltrating it through its more vulnerable aspects. This novel strikes us as convincing and realistic because it does not present the struggle by pitting the African hero against the European villain or by presenting the drama as the opposition between good and evil. Instead, it analyzes the process of conquest step by step and on the many levels on which it is enacted – its synchronization and manipulation of gaps and weaknesses in African culture. This penetration is undertaken in order to dispossess and reappropriate the natives, not in order to interact with or learn from them; it dismisses their culture, and does not recognize its value to the world at large.

The changes that take place in Nigerian society following the British conquest and Christian missionary activity render the continuity of old values impossible. Okonkwo, the protagonist, is besieged: he can neither give up his own cultural traditions, nor can he adjust to the givens of his time or adapt to the values of the Other. When he resists the colonizer who violates his sacred beliefs, he finds himself encircled, as he cannot mobilize others to join him in resistance, and he ends up using individualized and spontaneous violence against his enemy. This in turn leads to his punishment and humiliation; not finding a way out, he ends up seeking escape and resolution through death. Here opting for death is not martyrdom, sacrifice or resistance; it is a recognition of impotence and failure. This novel may be considered a parable of individual resistance that would not lead to liberation because it is now aware of the complexity of the task. It is also a condemnation of tribal society that is not able to achieve solidarity and cohesiveness leading to mobilization against the imperial tide. One of the most important features of ruling by dividing a community is the conqueror's use of weak points in the group and his appeal to the subaltern among them.

The novel uncovers African impotence while stripping bare imperial mechanisms to anchor its hegemony, disseminate prejudice, undermine and condemn the culture of the Other, and fragment lifestyles in the Third World. The distinguished novelist Achebe uses a variety of strategies and techniques in deploying creative resistance to such imperial culture. To start with, he does not respond to the colonizers by drawing an imaginary vision, painting an idea of indigenous African culture in contrast to a conquering European one. Armed with a high degree of critical consciousness, Achebe presents the imbalance inherent in the equation, and this is why his novel carries a realistic dimension and distances itself from simplifying binaries. From this perspective, there is a fundamental difference between the ethos of this novel and that of the Orientalist or exotic novel which uses the Other as a backdrop for the desires of the colonizer, a framework of sorts in which the colonial obsessions unfold. In such Orientalist tales, even when the Other from the Third World is present, his/her presence is depicted as incomplete, deformed or less human than that of the European. We often encounter Third World settings in Western literature used to create a fantastic ambiance that will charge and incite the imagination of the Western reader rather than introduce the Other in a humanizing way.

In *Things Fall Apart*, Achebe contrasts African ideology with European ideology, and in this way he exposes and liberates both. By situating them on the same horizontal level, the author allows a fair comparison and dismantles racial hierarchy. In addition, Achebe subjects relations and practices to painstaking scrutiny. He, for instance, subtly pits African institutions of justice against their parallel colonial institutions of justice. In African courts the administration of justice, which has local and religious dimensions, leads to peaceful compromise and settlement between the opposed parties, while in the English colonial and secular court, collective punishment is violently imposed to "teach a lesson" to the colonized. As for the symbolic and doctrinal differences between missionary European Christianity and the local African religion, the author presents them through an oblique contrast: while the Africans sacralize the snake, considering it an emanation from the God of water, the Christians do not hesitate to kill it. The author presents the two religions, the Christianity of the colonizer and the Animism of the Africans, as two manifestations of practically the same essence despite differences in dogmas. We gather from this that the author – through his fictional spokesman – finds religions to be varied formulas revolving around the principles of sacred and taboo, of Creator and creation. Akunna addresses the Christian missionary, for instance, by saying:

> You say that there is one supreme God who made Heaven and earth ... we also believe in Him and call Him Chukwu. He made all the world ...[4]

This comparative approach makes it impossible for us to classify religions hierarchically or deny to some belief systems the attribute of religion, for all these faiths are to be found in the domain of the sacred even though they may differ in their formulation of the relation between the Creator and the created. In this approach we find the seeds of refutation of colonialism, which not only claimed racial and economic superiority, but spiritual and cultural superiority as well.

Among Achebe's techniques which lure the foreign reader, only to lead him or her later to question his or her cultural presumptions, is his manipulation of intertextuality. The author borrows the title of his novel and his epigraph from the Irish poet William Butler Yeats' poem *The Second Coming*. The title of the poem refers to the coming of Christ at the end of Time, when "things fall apart":

> Turning and turning in the widening gyre,
> The falcon cannot bear the falconer.
> Things fall apart; the center cannot hold,
> Mere anarchy is loosed upon the world.

In this poem, written in 1920 following the horrors of World War I, the Irish poet points to European civilization and its disintegration. But Achebe uses the citation to show how the invasive expeditions of the colonizers brought catastrophe to his homeland. Here intertextuality works, not to confirm the intention of this citation as it appeared in the Yeatsian poem, but in order to transfer it elsewhere and thus reveal the destructive role played by imperialism, presented as the White Man's Burden (i.e., Europe's putative responsibility to bring welfare and enlightenment to the dark continent).

This borrowing of a citation to use it for another objective corresponds to Achebe's use of a literary genre developed in Europe, namely the novel, to reveal African concerns. For *Things Fall Apart* is an African novel – African in topos, ambiance, and style – representing what may be called the "regional novel," which uses local color, not to create a sense of the exotic, as in Orientalist literature, but to manifest a cultural identity. There is rich ethnographic data in it depicting customs, traditions, beliefs, practices, musical instruments, agricultural lore, and rituals – all of which make the novel a reference work and a document of a traditional culture threatened with extinction. The transfer of a literary genre, such as the novel, from one culture to another, may seem like an easy matter, but it is far from it. Literary history creates certain genres which relate intimately to the poetics and aesthetics of a certain civilization or culture, and to transfer such a genre from one place to another is no less difficult than transferring a plant from one soil to another. Achebe succeeds, however, in "Africanizing" the novel. By giving it an African ethos, he causes its structure, plot, dialogue and oral character to become an extension of African poetics and Nigerian civilization, even though it is written in English. Achebe does this by emptying the genre of one ideological content and restructuring it to accommodate another. The novel – as Lukács has said – is an epic of the middle class, but Achebe succeeds in making it the epic of African peasants; and this is no minor achievement. It goes beyond the writing of a novel about an African theme to Africanizing its form and the style.

Although Achebe writes his novel in the language of the colonizer rather than in the local Ibo language, he manipulates English syntax to conform to his own will and creativity without surrendering to its traditional rhythms; and as has been said of writers like him, he molds the

CONFRONTING BIAS IN THIRD WORLD CULTURE 179

language rather than allow the language to mold him; thus he "writes-English" and not simply "writes-in-English."[5] He transforms the foreign language into a radical weapon serving his own culture, as other African writers have done by writing back in the appropriated language of the colonizer.[6] Achebe makes frequent use of words and terms common among the Ibo which have no equivalent in English. Thus, his novel is replete with local idioms and expressions. At the end of the novel, we find a glossary of local idioms that will be unfamiliar to readers outside the culture. This appended glossary includes more than thirty frequently recurring words. At times, the author uses a local expression not because it is impossible to translate, but in order to hybridize English and charge it with a foreign touch. It is as if the colonizer has been invaded in his very language. Sometimes, Achebe uses the expression "nana aye" which means "our father" (p.18), easily rendered in English; at other times he uses terms such as "chi" which means something akin to a personal god, spiritual double or guardian angel, which is almost impossible to find an equivalent for in English (p.44). At other times, Achebe uses entire sentences in Ibo which make the dialog credible (p.97). There is also in the novel a song written in Ibo (p.54).

Here we find an attempt to Africanize the English language, a counter-offensive reversing what happened in Nigeria where English invaded local culture. The English language was imposed on the colonies; as such, it became the official idiom and the language of written literature, all the more because the local languages tended to be oral rather than written. This is why the Africanization of English carries the significance of poetic justice, that is, getting even culturally with the invader, so to speak. The novel, for instance, points to the white man's bicycle as an "iron horse" (p.125), that is, it is described from the African perspective, and is expressed in terms of what can be apprehended by a countryside African. Furthermore, the novel refers to the passing of time through an African frame of reference, namely the harvest, which is calculated in lunar months:

> He was very good on his flute and his happiest
> Moments were the two or three moons after the
> Harvest when the village musicians brought down
> Their instruments, hung above the fire place. (p.4)

This mode of narration situates us within the local group and its worldview. Achebe also makes successful use of popular proverbs and animal fables, as, for example:

> When the moon is shining the cripple becomes hungry for a walk. (p.10)
>
> The clan was like a lizard, if it lost its tail it soon grew another. (p.155)

In other words, Achebe superimposes African signifiers and signs onto the linguistic fabric of the colonizers' language.

Resistance to cultural bias is distilled in Achebe's work through his effective deployment of metaphoric language to lay bare prejudice, which ultimately reveals itself for what it is. When Achebe makes comparisons, he elevates the "inferior" (in the context of a biased worldview) to the state of parallelism with the "superior." And when both are put on the same level, superiority is demystified and inferiority is revealed as no more than a projection by the colonial beholder. In this, he uses a mechanism of metaphoric language which binds and links what is separate and isolated, and thus he deconstructs hierarchy. Metaphor is nothing but a transfer from one domain to another, just as Achebe transfers the idea of "falling apart" from the European continent to the African continent, and as he transfers the expression of local complaints from Ibo to English.

When we turn to the Sudanese novelist Tayeb Salih, we find that his novel *Season of Migration to the North* exudes opposition to both colonialism and neo-colonialism. The novel resists northern prejudices and misrepresentation of the African through caricature-like exaggeration and *muʿāraḍah*, or literary countering,[7] which takes up the essential drama but reinterprets it in a different light in order to go beyond the earlier mode of stating it. Tayeb Salih wrote his novel in Arabic to counter the Shakespearean tragedy of Othello, the Moor of Venice. Shakespeare presented the Moorish hero as separated from his roots and thoroughly assimilated in the expansive European Christian culture. His only problem was his marital jealousy and a rash temperament which led to the destruction of conjugal harmony. The problem of Othello, according to Shakespeare, is not a cultural dislocation or a crisis of coping with two types of cultural ethos, but rather, the primitive rashness, emotionality and mindless rage which characterize the African hero and which ultimately lead to his undoing and to the destruction of his marital life, as he is convinced that his loyal wife Desdemona has not been chaste. It is true that Iago, who stages a mean intrigue to do Othello in, is responsible for the tragedy. However, Othello in the Shakespearean tragedy has a vulnerable spot and a weakness which the villain Iago uses to trap his chief, namely, his gullibility. This is the gist of the tragedy and the crux of the problem according to Shakespeare, who knew about Africans and Moors from varied sources and used Leo Africanus – who became a European citizen – as a model from which he drew the exceptional character of his Othello.[8]

What cannot be dismissed is that Shakespeare depicts the African as a hero in this drama and grants him nobility and bravery. However, despite his assimilation of Venetian culture, Othello remains a rash, primitive man who is swayed by the magic of the handkerchief given to him by his mother and believes whatever he is told without any attempt at verification; in other words, he is naïve and superstitious.

What we can gather from reading Shakespeare's drama is that Othello's acculturation to European life has not fully erased his simplistic, spontaneous dimension. Naiveté and rashness are attributes associated with southerners in European thought. It is no mere accident in Shakespearean tragedies that the contemplative and reflective hero is an educated Danish Prince (Hamlet) while the naïve, rash hero is a Moorish military leader (Othello). This stereotypical image of the Moor in Shakespeare's work is confirmed by the attributes that are associated with him in Iago's description of Othello's attachment to and love for Desdemona:

> Zounds, sir, y'are robbed! For shame, put on your gown!
> Your heart is burst; you have lost half your soul
> Even now, now, an old black ram
> Is tupping your white ewe. Arise, arise!
> Awake the snorting citizens with the bell,
> Or else the devil will make a grandsire of you.
> Arise, I say![9]

Iago also uses animal imagery to depict Moorish kin relations:

> Zounds, sir, you are one of those that will not serve
> God if the devil bid you. Because we come to do you

> Service, and you think we are ruffians, you'll have
> Your daughter covered with a Barbary horse, you'll
> Have your nephews neigh to you; you'll have
> Coursers for cousins, and gennets for germans.[10]

And while Desdemona is also depicted through the use of animal imagery (a white ewe), the difference in the two images is striking. The ewe connotes humility and innocence, while the lamb specifically is the symbol of purity in European traditions (related to Christ's association with, and comparison to, the Lamb). Furthermore, white also signifies purity, while the ram or horse and especially the black ram and the Barbary horse imply the beastly and the savage. In this imagery, then, there is an implicit confirmation of the racial inclination in European civilization whose roots can be detected among the early Greek thinkers who thought all Others savages and used the term "Barbarian" for non-Greeks. Ibn Khaldūn quotes the Greek physician Galen as explaining the black men's rashness and light-headedness as being based on "a weakness in their brains which results in a weakness in their intellect" – a statement which, according to Ibn Khaldūn, is baseless and impossible to prove.[11]

Tayeb Salih wanted to oppose and correct this image of the African in Europe; he wrote his novel to deconstruct the image of Othello which was current not only in Europe, but in the Arab and Islamic worlds as well. The tragedy of Othello was the first dramatic work to be translated and performed on stage in the Arab world (in Cairo in 1884).[12] The drama has remained alive and has inspired Arabs from the Mashriq and the Maghrib, as well as Iranians, to express their concerns.[13] In an interview with Nadia Hijab, Tayeb Salih himself declared that one of the most important reasons behind writing his novel was to negate the image of Othello and to offer a rebuttal to Shakespeare's play:

> One person will write a poem, and another will retaliate by writing along the same lines, but reversing the meaning – this is called *muʿāraḍah*. I did the same with Othello. From the beginning I thought Othello did not make sense. He was probably an Arab – they called him a Moor – someone very like the Sudanese. He came to Venice – the greatest European center at that time – and he was accepted completely. A man whose skin was dark was accepted by the establishment of Venice, became a general and married. Can you imagine an Arab becoming commander of the British army? Then

along comes Iago and tells him all those things; he believes him and kills Desdemona. This only makes sense if you hold the view that Othello never really accepted the Venetians, nor they him. Only then is his rage understood – it is a nationalistic rage, a clash of cultures. Mustafa Saʿeed (the protagonist of *Season*) is how I feel Othello should have been, and I use the same terminology and the handkerchief in my murder scene.[14]

In the novel, references to Othello abound, sometimes explicitly and sometimes implicitly:

Professor Maxwell Foster-Keen continued to draw a distinctive picture of the mind of a genius whom circumstances had driven to killing in a moment of passion (p.32).

There came a moment when I felt I had been transformed in her eyes into a naked, primitive creature, a spear in one hand and arrows in the other, hunting elephants and lions in the jungles. This was fine. Curiosity has changed to gaiety, and gaiety to sympathy, and when I stir the still pool in the depths the sympathy will be transformed into a desire upon whose taut strings I shall play as I wish.

"What race are you?" she asked me. "Are you African or Asian?"
"I am like Othello – Arab-African," I said to her (p.38).

I knew she was unfaithful to me; the whole house was impregnated with the smell of infidelity. Once I found a man's handkerchief which wasn't mine.
"It's yours," she said when I asked her.
"This handkerchief isn't mine," I told her.
"Assuming it's not your handkerchief," she said, "what are you going to do about it?" On another occasion I found a cigarette case, then a pen.
"You're being unfaithful to me," I said to her.
"Suppose I am being unfaithful to you," she said.
"I swear I'll kill you!" I shouted at her.
"You only say that," she said with a jeering smile.
"What's stopping you from killing me? What are you waiting for? Perhaps you're waiting till you find a man lying on top of me, and even then I don't think you'd do anything. You'd sit on the edge of the bed and cry" (p.162).

The Sudanese protagonist in *Season of Migration to the North* expresses his vision of the Western rape of his world and their bias against him in an interior monologue, as he stands in the courtroom, having committed the crime of murdering his wife when making love to her:

> The ships at first sailed down the Nile carrying guns not bread, and the railways were originally set up to transport troops. The schools were started so as to teach us how to say, "Yes" in their language. They imported to us the germ of the greatest European violence, as seen on the Somme and at Verdun, the likes of which the world had never previously known, the germ of a deadly disease that struck them more than a thousand years ago. Yes, my dear sirs, I came as an invader into your very homes: a drop of the poison which you have injected into the veins of history. I am no Othello, Othello was a lie.[15]

The protagonist in the novel of Tayeb Salih is a Sudanese student who travels to England to study. Women fall in love with him, throw themselves at him, and eventually are destroyed by this passion: Ann Hammond, Sheila Greenwood, Isabella Seymour and Jean Morris – all fall in his trap. Despite their different temperaments and backgrounds, they all became easy prey and are engulfed by this African. Even Mustafa Saʿeed's relationship with Mrs. Robinson – who is old enough to be his mother, and who embraces him as a small child and stands by him after he commits his dreadful crime – is not presented in the novel as that of an empathetic type exuding motherly concerns, but is marked by an erotic dimension:

> Then the man introduced me to his wife, and all of a sudden I felt the woman's arms embracing me and her lips on my cheek. At that moment, as I stood on the station platform amidst a welter of sounds and sensations, with the woman's arms round my neck, her mouth on my cheek, the smell of her body – a strange European smell – tickling my nose, and her breast touching my chest, I felt – I, a boy of twelve – a vague sexual yearning I had never previously experienced.[16]

Tayeb Salih uses a complex strategy to deconstruct the ready-made image of the African. First he uses hyperbole and satire to depict the attributes which Europeans associate with the African, namely, his sexual virility and his rashness. He presents his hero as if he were an erotic animal with no objective other than to penetrate the Other and engage sexually with foreign women. This image is exaggerated in order to satirize the

Orientalist mentality. Often the women confess their feelings, which confirm that they are victims of the preconceived image of an African man:

> She would tell me that in my eyes she saw the shimmer of mirages in hot deserts, that in my voice she heard the screams of ferocious beasts in the jungles...
> "Come here," I said to her imperiously. "To hear is to obey, O master!" she answered me in a subdued voice.[17]

We see in the novel how the protagonist, Mustafa Saʿeed, plays his role superbly, telling the English women what they want to hear. He lies and turns his bedroom into a stage so that it will have Oriental, Shahrayar-like associations. He decorates it with carpets and incense and all the stereotypical details of the South and the Orient, of the Arab and the African, of the Muslim and all that excites a foreigner. The author lays bare, through props and dramatizations in the relations, the reciprocal making up and deformations. By depicting Mustafa Saʿeed's sexual triumphs in this exaggerated manner, Tayeb Salih satirizes the unrealistic, imaginary model constructed by academic and literary Orientalism. Needless to say, this sexual conquest in England leads only to crime and prison. The implied moral lesson in the novel is a by-product of the satiric deconstruction of a false image.

Tayeb Salih presents Mustafa Saʿeed as a false hero; his falsehood is the product of a cultural union between oppressor and oppressed, between authority and dependency, and this is why the result is a hybrid who belongs neither to his homeland nor to the foreign land and culture. Despite Mustafa Saʿeed's academic excellence, he fails to achieve psychological balance, as a result of which all his relations end likewise in failure. Even when he decides to leave England and go back to the Sudan to start a new life as a farmer in a Sudanese village, he is unable to get rid of his wound and his foreign strand. He conceals it within himself; this is exemplified in the secret room which he constructs in his village house, and which is filled with artifacts from the colonizers' culture. The secret English room in his home in the Sudan, with its fireplace and walls lined with English books, takes on a symbolic dimension, pointing to the impossibility of ridding oneself completely of the foreign element. It is the mirror image of the Oriental room which he had so proudly exhibited in his home in London. The difference between the two rooms is that the Arabic room in England was on display, while the English room in Sudan remains a secret. In both cases, we find the room either locked up or staged, either dark or false, displacing reality and not representing a natural extension of its owner, as if it were below consciousness or above it. The novel's ending in murder and suicide is the literary equivalent of Frantz Fanon's vision of the inevitability of violence among the oppressed and against their oppressors. Through this the author confirms that there is no possibility of creative human interaction between oppressor and oppressed, between colonizer and colonized. Even the attraction which binds Mustafa Saʿeed and Jean Morris is nothing but the drive to suppress, control and erase the other; it is not the drive of complementarity, symbiosis or correspondence.

In addition to parody and satirical irony which pit hypocrisy against truth, image against reality, we find the author employing *muʿāraḍah* (literary countering) by presenting a reverse parallel of Shakespeare's Othello in the character of Mustafa Saʿeed. Tayeb Salih presents the details of the Desdemona-Othello relationship upside down. Instead of love and empathy, we find hate and provocation between Mustafa and Jean. While the tragedy of Othello is the result of his gullibility concerning the handkerchief which is falsely reported to him to have been given by his wife to her lover, we find Jean openly bragging about her lovers who leave their traces in the conjugal nest.

The conjugal murder in *Season of Migration to the North*, then, is not triggered by jealousy which has been engineered by an intrigue as in the play *Othello* but, rather, arises from an accumulation of resentment between two cultures, one of which is invasive. The issue is no more a matter of jealousy and misunderstanding on the part of a husband who commits a crime of passion, but is a violent crime intended and planned by a protagonist who has experienced a history of hostility. Mustafa's revenge, however, cannot be considered a liberating violence; on the contrary, it is an individual vengeance which leads only to further violence that crystallizes in his eventual suicide. Othello, too, commits suicide after murdering his wife, but in his case there is recognition of error and a guilty conscience. As for Mustafa Saʿeed, he does not regret his crime, but concludes at the end of his life that his trajectory was erroneous, that his effort to replant himself in his own land is virtually impossible after his having been transplanted abroad. This is why he advises the unnamed narrator within the novel to protect his children from migration.

What Tayeb Salih is doing in his novel *Season of Migration to the North* is thus multi-faceted: he parodies Orientalists' characterization of the African/ Arab/ Muslim, revealing its falseness and demonstrating how practices and actions get based on such false images; the author also redraws the sick relationship between the subaltern and the hegemonic from the perspective of a citizen of the Third World.

In his moving story, "I Am An Arab, I Am Suspect," Tahar Ben Jelloun uses structural irony in which the reader knows more than the protagonist does. We find irony on the level of narrative structure which contrasts the simplicity of the subaltern with the meanness of society and the deviation of the world – all of which can be read between the lines of the work.

The title of the story summarizes its significance. The Arab is guilty until he proves his innocence in a Western world that is so prejudiced against him. The narrated story of Ben Jelloun opens with a first person account: "My name is Mohamed Bouchaid ..."[18] The narrator mentions his profession: window cleaner in Paris, then his nationality: Moroccan. He comments on how people make fun of his name, then describes himself as a dark man with a beard and wavy hair. He is the father of three sons, ranging in age from 15 to 20 years. The police are constantly after him, checking his identity and identification papers, as he is suspect everywhere and at all times.

> I'm an Arab, a poor Arab, and I'm not at home. I'm also the classic type. I get checked systematically at the entrance and exit to the Metro. There's always a finger to point me out in the crowd. You'd think they were waiting for me wherever I go.[19]

The police are disappointed when, after searching him thoroughly, they find no explosives or drugs on him. Despite the fact that he has a beard only because he's too lazy to shave, a lot of people ask if he is a fundamentalist or an extremist: "I've often been asked, 'Are you a fundamentalist?' as if it were a race or a nationality,"[20] as he says. He is surprised, as the term was not part of his daily lexicon before he migrated, and he does not understand why he is called an Islamic extremist: "Before I came to France I didn't know the word 'fundamentalist'. I think I heard it for the first time on TV."[21] It is true he fasts in Ramadan and abstains from eating pork, but from time to time he sips a glass of wine, and he does not pray regularly.[22] This sense of surprise in itself indicates to the reader how the evaluation of the Other does not necessarily spring from the behavior of the Other, but from preconceived accusations and ready-made condemnations.

This innocent worker asks himself why he is always suspect, and as he poses this question, the reader is moved to disapprove, if not condemn, the present set up with all its racial, sectarian and class prejudices:

> So is it because I'm a Muslim that they find me suspicious, or is it because I'm not nice-looking? They say we wear beards to frighten them. Is my face frightening? Maybe it is! It's odd, the more care I take, the more I look after my appearance, the more I arouse the cops' suspicion. They say "I don't like the look of him." But what kind of guy would they like the look of? A well-dressed guy with white skin? What color eyes do we need to have to be nice-looking?[23]

The speaker goes on to describe French doubts and their asking him (just before the Gulf War) if he is one of Saddam's soldiers. The sparks of this destructive war moved from the Mashriq to the Maghrib and encircled this poor Moroccan worker at his very home and his livelihood; his boss insisted on preventing him from working in these circumstances, out of fear or malice:

> Like a lot of people, I thought the war was going to happen on TV. I was wrong. The war was going to reach right into our workplace. On the day the war started I was due to be part of a team that was cleaning the windows of the Montparnasse Tower. The job had been arranged a long time before. There were two of us from North Africa and two Europeans, a Portuguese and a Frenchman. The foreman told me and my Algerian colleague, "No, not this time; you're going to stay put at the office. There's work to do here, like cleaning the toilets." I was surprised, especially since Martin's a pretty nice guy. That morning, there was nothing nice about his expression. He had some reason to take exception to us. Only we hadn't done anything wrong. My Algerian pal told me, "See, the war's really started now."[24]

This racism spreads even in schools as this Moroccan worker remembers what a school supervisor said to one of his sons, namely, that Arabs are insects that should be exterminated; and he comments by asking what crime they have committed:

> Are we vermin? I didn't know they called us that. Sure, they use "little rat" for the Arab, and "rat hunt" for an assault on an Arab. But what have we done to God and his Prophet to deserve all that?[25]

These disturbing interrogations abound, depicting the reality of treatment of the Muslim Arab minority in France, and portraying an extreme and deeply rooted racism projecting its own terrorism onto the Other.

Mohamed Bouchaid describes his feelings as he listens to the news from the Gulf War:

> According to the radio – I always carry a little transistor with me – American planes have dropped 18,000 tons of bombs on Iraq. How many deaths is that, 18,000 tons of bombs? They didn't say on the radio. It must be so many people that they prefer not to say. I'm not an Iraqi, but it does something to me: I feel like there's a pain or a weight on my stomach. Those were Arabs, Muslims like me, under the bombs. On the radio and the TV they say we're fanatics. They're tough, these Americans: from high up in their planes they spot fanatics and send them greetings stuffed with bombs![26]

In a splendid shot, the prayers and supplications of the Christians join the prayer of Mohamed Bouchaid to God and His Messenger for peace on earth and fairness to the Arabs, which demonstrates the spiritual magnanimity of our Moroccan worker and his humane opening unto the Other despite religious differences:

> Notre Dame was crowded that day. Men and women were praying in small groups. They assembled in silence, begging God for clemency and mercy. It was moving. I felt like praying too. But I had to get to work. On the radio they were talking a lot about missiles and Israel. Up there on my scaffolding I prayed to myself. I invoked Allah and his Prophet Mohammed, that they might bring about the Kingdom of peace on earth, that we Arabs might be given greater consideration, treated with less suspicion, not necessarily loved but at least respected.[27]

The response of the French political institution to Hussein Scud rockets falling on Israel highlights the uneven reactions to victims and draws attention to double standards and moral schizophrenia. The story ends with the Moroccan worker hearing on the radio that the President of France has called by phone to give condolences to an Israeli settlement's residents, expressing his solidarity with "the Jewish people in their predicament."[28] Our worker thinks to himself that a parallel solidarity with victimized Arabs is on its way and that he, too, will be receiving a message of support. So he goes home to wait for a phone call from Francois Mitterrand. Here the reader recognizes, first, the absurdity of such a wait, second, the double standard in behavior, and third, the innocence of this Moroccan worker.

Ben Jelloun does not come up with a conclusion or sermonize, but presents in a juxtaposed way the two faces of treatment, leaving judgment to the reader, while basing his narrative on the technique of dramatic irony. Ben Jelloun thus brings together what is normally viewed separately in order to reveal the reality of duplicitous standards. This juxtaposition between two modes of behavior moves minds and consciences, making the reader rethink what is taken for granted in his or her daily life. Although the double standard Ben Jelloun presents is a familiar practice, he nevertheless renders it unfamiliar and unacceptable by presenting it from the viewpoint of this simple worker. The shock which confronts the reader cannot be ignored or explained away. Here the technique of alienating the common and joining the separate makes the reader reflect and feel the shock of prejudice. Racist society attempts to normalize this prejudice and adjust the reader to its reception, while the creative writer attempts a reverse process placing racism in such relief that it cannot go unnoticed.

Thus we see how African writers have contributed to resisting bias, not only by denouncing it in critical essays but, in addition, by formulating it fictionally and creating identifiable strategies of resistance. These techniques of resistance and opposition can be summarized in three modes: (1) bringing together and comparing what usually is viewed as intrinsically different; (2) reinterpreting a master narrative by juxtaposing the motivation of an established hero onto that of a new one; (3) defamiliarizing the familiar and projecting it, thereby highlighting the grotesqueness of its bias. If we were to analyze what takes place in these modes, we would find two essential processes: (1) negating a vertical hierarchy and turning it into a horizontal relation which allows comparisons, contrasts and balanced judgments, and (2) displacing the center of the dominant discourse by illuminating its peripheries and pockets, thus foregrounding the biases beneath its surface in such a way that they can no longer be covered up or neutralized. In this way, the creative writer presents a comprehensive view of existing biases while simultaneously deconstructing the grounds from which prejudice derives and on which it thrives.

8

Beyond Methodology: Forms of Bias in Western Literary Criticism

SAAD ABDULRAHMAN AL-BAZIʿI

THE FOLLOWING remarks attempt to substantiate the thesis that the methods of literary criticism in the West are in essence biased in favor of the cultural context that engendered them. In other words, as literary theories, or approaches to the study of literature, such methods carry cultural implications that are in keeping with their Western cultural milieu. Consequently, if the non-Western critic, such as the one whose culture is essentially Arabo-Islamic, is to apply any of these methods to the literature produced by his/she Arabo-Islamic culture, he/she is faced with two choices:

1. To apply such methods as they are, thus adopting involuntarily the implications and ideologies that formed them. Such an application will inevitably lead to misunderstanding of the literary material which is to be critically analyzed.

2. To cause radical change to such a method whereby the resultant applied method departs dramatically from the original one.

The claim that methodology can be stripped of its context with little or no change is rendered groundless by a historical analysis of the cultural and philosophical background of such a methodology. The context for this argument is to be found in the situation prevailing in many non-Western cultures, including the Arab world, where Western literary criticism, among other Western cultural forces, has been exerting an impact which is at once attractive and hegemonic. Ready-made and easy to adopt,

Western literary theories and methods offer themselves in easy-to-swallow, large chunks that are rarely subjected to the scrutiny or revision displayed by Western literary critics themselves. Under the banner of universal unity, many contemporary Arab critics argue that what is used (and applied) in the West is good for all places. Their polemics are better understood in view of what an opposing party of conservatives has been arguing. These conservatives are against almost all types of cultural interaction with the West. Yet if the argument of these conservatives is difficult to justify, neither is the opposing stand of opening up indiscriminately to Western methods.

It should be noted that this argument is not completely new to the ancient or modern Arabic critical consciousness. In fact, it is one of the fundamental tenets of the longstanding Arabo-Islamic dialog with Western civilization. In the 7th Century, Ḥāzim al-Qarṭājannī stated that the critical premises in Aristotle's *Poetics* were not fit subjects for Arabic literature, as the Greek philosopher "only cared for poetry in so far as Greeks cared for it."[1] In the modern age, the Egyptian critic Mohammad Mandour has voiced a similar viewpoint by emphasizing that when we "study Arabic literature, we must be diligent to avoid applying to it the points of view of Europeans, who formulated them with other literatures in mind."[2]

The problem with these recurrent opinions is that they are scarcely substantiated, which is a good reason to reconsider the whole question and to check its justifications as a significant cultural issue that affects the humanities generally and not merely literary criticism. Some contemporary Western critical methods such as structuralism have cast their shadow on more than one of the human sciences. The general complexity inherent in such methods also makes it difficult to pass absolute and hurried judgments about them. Yet it is not only the simplicity with which this topic has been dealt with that makes reconsideration so urgent. As I have already indicated, there are those critics and scholars who do not even believe that some methods are biased; rather, they believe that methods, which are in this case Western, are neutral tools which can be used unproblematically to study any literature, whether it is Arabic, French or Chinese. Abdallah Laroui, the well-known Moroccan historian and novelist, locates this problem while differentiating between methodology and epistemology: some critics, says Laroui, jump from one to the other: "... what really happens is that a given program may yield satisfactory results in studying a certain subject, after which its author looks into its logical bases, thus jumping from the first to the second level." He exemplifies this by adding that "historicism or structuralism can be at once rejected as a philosophy and manipulated as a method of analysis within certain limits."[3]

This differentiation between methodology and its philosophical content is adopted by one of the most active contemporary Arab critics in his use of the structuralist method. In his book *al-Khafā' wa al-Tajallī* [Covertness and Overtness], Syrian critic Kamal Abu Deeb goes so far as to abrogate any philosophical content in structuralism by maintaining that "structuralism is not a philosophy but a vantage point and a method of exploring the universe."[4] Therefore, his argument goes, structuralism remains a neutral critical method that can safely be adopted and applied.

An important point here is that Abu Deeb believes that the application of structuralism enables Arabic critical thinking to arrive at a stage where it can "enrich world thinking" and through which the entire Arab nation can be "uplifted to the ... level of cultural contemporaneity." This is in view of the fact that "enrichment is not to be achieved by translation and representation, but by participation in the process of exploration, in exerting strenuous efforts, and in personal initiative on the level of thinking and analysis." Abu Deeb's outlook is predicated on a comprehensive humanist tendency that looks forward to the unity of human thought through overcoming the barriers of difference in cultural contexts. This is a sufficiently familiar viewpoint in the history of Arabic thought and literary criticism, a view that has almost as strong historical and ideological roots as the contrary viewpoint. Those who called for making use of Greek thought, such as Mattī ibn Yūnis, al-Fārābī, and Ibn Rushd [Averroes] adopted such a view in the past. Later on it came again to be emphasized by modern scholars, whether the pioneers of the contemporary Arabic revival in the nineteenth century, or those who followed them like Taha Hussain, Elias Abu Shabaka, Muhammad Ghonaimi Hilal, and, to some extent, Mohammad Mandour.

The Egyptian Muhammad Ghunaimi Hilal presents an overview of Western critical approaches in his *Dirāsāt fī Madhāhib al-Shiʿr wa Naqdihi* [Studies in the Schools of Thought and Criticism of Poetry]: "[These approaches] have become universal artistic currents, a common resource fulfilling the needs of the talented from all nations, and a common heritage for all mankind which can quite safely be consulted ... Our being affected by these currents is not a novelty in the history of world art and criticism, for world cooperation in the history of literature and art is just like world cooperation in the history of science. Both are a way of achieving integration and revival of the national heritage so that it can keep pace with world progress."[5]

Evidently, the concepts dominating the foregoing statement – "world thinking," "cultural contemporaneity," "world cooperation," and "keeping pace with world progress" – derive their referential power from a Western context first and foremost. The "world" in this context is the West rather than the East: America, England, France, etc., rather than China, Japan, India, etc. Universality itself connotes evolution according to the cultural standards charted by the West. It is no wonder then that Western methods of criticism have allegedly become universal and have gained a measure of impartiality that exceeds the boundaries of location. All other alternatives – and one has to admit that there may not be many of these – are, consequently, not taken into consideration, and the non-Western cultural heritage shrinks accordingly. The critical discourse employed in these statements reveals bias in favor of the West, not only through adoption of its methods and abrogation of other ones, but through identification with a Western critical discourse which speaks for itself and for the whole world from a purely pro-Western perspective. It conceives of the world in much the same way that critics like Matthew Arnold in the 19th Century and T. S. Eliot in the twentieth have done, both having been affected by the notion of European supremacy and Western cultural centrality in general.[6]

The decisiveness and simplicity with which Western critical methods are sometimes dismissed by ultra-conservatives, at other times characterize the acceptance of the same methods. If it goes without saying that rejection cannot weaken the presence of these methods in cultural contexts other than their original ones, it can similarly be decided that acceptance of such methods will not endow them with the impartiality which might enable them to be harmonious within frameworks different from the ones where they developed. We are faced here with two attitudes that can be regarded as all too easy solutions to a highly complicated and important question. Nor is it enough to call for selectivity and syncretism, for adopting what is "appropriate" and rejecting what is not. For this attitude frequently develops into a ready-made excuse for surmounting all complications so as to arrive at a group of ideas that have no logical justification other than the mood of their author. In most of these cases – whereby the critic manages to select certain methodological elements which he/she considers valid – the character of the selected elements will have changed to the extent that a question mark rightly hangs over whether anything remains of the essence of that method which would justify calling it by the same label. A cogent example in this respect is talking about an "Arabic" structuralism or Marxism and the like, and the concomitant question of what is left of structuralism or Marxism after "Arabization" whereby they can still be termed as such. This does not preclude, however, the relative success of sporadic attempts to adapt Western methods.

Nevertheless, there remains an inevitable and nagging question as to the degree of distortion afflicting literary works and even the cultural structure as a whole no matter how much success is achieved. The following pages attempt to reply to this question in light of the initial thesis that the Egyptian Salah Fadhl aptly recapitulates as follows:

> [When we] began to be acquainted with these [critical] methods, when some of us were affected by them, such methods lost their two most important characteristics: their being directly rooted in their cultural reality, responding to its internal development and the details of its history, as well as the quality of succession along a straight time sequence. Therefore, these methods have entirely dominated our thinking; they have changed from doctrines relying on integral philosophical bases and finite theoretical principles into individual *tours de force* and limited ventures. They have thus simultaneously led to the re-arrangement of our literary field and the redirection of its production and output.[7]

However, the present study will not deal with the effects of applying Western critical methods as glimpsed by Salah Fadhl. For, though examination of these effects is necessary to uncover the bias of methodology, this has to be preceded by a reading of the methodology itself so as to reveal bias in its origin prior to its actual manifestations. Beside this methodological point, I should also define the outlines of my vision and the epistemological framework behind the whole argument. In other words, my questioning of bias has to involve the argument of this paper also, even more so than the arguments being discussed.

To say that the methods developed in Western criticism are biased is to describe critical methods developed everywhere, and not only Western ones, in the same fashion. The bias I have in mind is the one implicit in such concepts as cultural specificity, a concept without which no one can talk about a Western or an Arabo-Islamic culture or any other of the concepts, based on the assumption that human cultures are significantly, though not totally different.

My second point is that assuming the bias of method or the significance of cultural specificity does not necessarily mean that methods as a whole are rendered entirely irrelevant. It does not preclude the possibility of mutual benefit or the presence of common characteristics. To abrogate all this is to risk naiveté and to run counter to the development of human thought throughout history. What bias of method means here is simply the presence of a high degree of homogeneity among the various elements of a given culture, which makes it difficult to make such elements function in another culture for the same purpose or to have the same significance. To accept the validity of such an argument suggests, in the first place, the preclusion of direct translation or free borrowing of such elements as theories and methods to contextualize them in a foreign framework, and working instead with full awareness that a greater degree of revision and reworking is needed to achieve cultural interaction.

This brings me to a third theoretical point with which the nature of cultural differences can be clarified, and which is an implicit touchstone of this chapter. My exploration of the para-methodology of Western criticism is in fact based on an implicit view of the specificity of Arabo-Islamic culture, a view which I rely on in my discussion of bias in Western methodology. It is difficult to expatiate upon the outlines of this view, as this in itself is a huge, self-contained issue. But I may refer in passing to the profound and comprehensive studies on this subject undertaken by a group of contemporary Arab thinkers, such as the Moroccan Mohamed Abid al-Jabiri in his critique of the Arab mind.[8] Al-Jabiri highlights the specificity of the Arab mind, or rather its ancient cultural output, mainly in relation to its Greek counterpart. Other examples include the analytical explorations of those who have studied the role of basic concepts such as "heritage," "society," and "home" in shaping our thinking and culture. It suffices to go back to the roots of some basic critical and cultural terms to realize the sometimes great degree of difference between the Arabo-Islamic culture and its Western counterpart.

The concept of "text," for example, has been decisive in forming some contemporary Western critical methods. It is one of the major keys to understanding Western cultural specificity. Simultaneously, the same concept infuses Arabo-Islamic culture with an important difference. There is almost unanimous agreement among Arabic dictionaries on the view that "text" implies "specific reference and definition" (*isnād, taʿyīn*). Al-Azhari states that "the origin of the text is the far end and ultimate goal of objects; the texts of the Qur'an and that of the Sunnah [the Prophet's sayings or traditions] are the judgments indicated by the overt terms of those texts" (*Lisān al-ʿArab*). In *Tāj al-ʿArūs*, "the text suggests specific reference and clarity. Consequently, the text of the Qur'an and the prophetic traditions can be understood in terms of this definition as consisting of words having specific significance ..." This is quite remote from the etymological implications of "text" in modern European languages such as English or French, which derive from the Latin *texere* the meaning of "weaving" and "fabrication," a link which eventually led to the emergence of the theory of textuality or rather the process whereby texts interlace with one another to constitute the post-structural concept of "intertextuality".

It is true that the contemporary Arabic concept of text differs from that found in old dictionaries. Whereas some still see the old semantic content prevailing, there are those who wholly embrace the modern, i.e. Western concept, or perhaps the fusing of the Western concept and the one which has come down from ancient Arabo-Islamic culture. Whatever the case may be, it does not justify projection of the Western concept, or even our amalgamated one, onto a culture produced in essentially different circumstances. Concepts remain different so long as their cultural contexts are different. No matter how relative this difference may be, the Arabo-Islamic world is required to be fully aware of it and even to reject it whenever necessary. There is a major emphasis in the Arabo-Islamic philosophical and critical heritage on the importance of this awareness and on the necessity of illuminating some aspects of methodological bias. This represents one of two major reasons why the Arabo-Islamic world needs to take a look, though cursory, at this heritage, as I propose to do here. It is a need rendered even more urgent by the fact that this inherited sort of thinking involves a historical model that may be unprecedented in the history of thought, one which is badly needed so as to reinforce the Arabo-Islamic world's critical attitude toward the Western thought which surrounds it from almost all directions and in a manner that is much more intense and deliberate than before.

In the ideological encounters of such Muslim thinkers as Ibn Sīna, al-Ghazālī, Ibn Rushd, and others, there is a reminder that philosophical and literary borrowings are too sensitive to be indulged in freely. This does not necessarily entail suspicion of the "Other"; rather, it merely helps the Arabo-Islamic world to realize the existence of difference and to be more concerned for cultural integrity, no matter how fictitious such a concept may be for Western post-structuralists. Despite some significant differences among them, the ancient Muslim thinkers offer a model which largely supports such an interrogative attitude by problematizing the relationship to the West. The Arabo-Islamic world is bound to feel this, despite the inadequacy of its reception of that model and, more importantly, despite the difference in historical circumstances. For its relationship to the West is not identical to the one crystallized in the 3rd, 4th or 5th Centuries AH (roughly the 8th, 9th, and 10th centuries AC). The West itself is not the same as before, and the Arabo-Islamic world has come a long distance from where Ibn Sīna and Ḥāzim al-Qarṭājannī once stood. However, the cultural encounter remains as intense as ever. Nothing is more illustrative of this hypothesis than the fact that contemporary Western thought deals with the problem of bias and with its relationship to the "Other" in much the same way that was once adopted the length and breadth of the Islamic world.

The Western critical output discussed in this paper is understandably not concerned much, if at all, with Arabo-Islamic elements interwoven into its culture (i.e. Western culture). Rather, some of that output is significantly conscious of another sort of bias: its limitation and self-involutedness. There are Western critics who in recent years have shown sensitivity towards the limitations of Western patterns, articulating an uncomfortable position towards their prevalent cultural models, and looking forward to breaking them. Numerous Western thinkers and critics have expressed a desire to overcome Western self-enclosure. And some of these have been highly effective in the formation of contemporary Western critical methodology, such as the French Michel Foucault, Roland Barthes, and the American, Fredric Jameson. What their argument implies is a serious questioning of the universality and neutrality hastily claimed for such methodology by some non-Western critics who think that only by adopting Western methods of thinking and analysis could they ascend the ladder of cultural "progress".

BIASED LOGIC: A TRADITIONAL PARADIGM

In his introduction to *Logic of the Easterners*, Ibn Sīna (Avicenna) presents the problem of methodology as one that belongs in the realm of logic. Like many of our ancient philosophers, Ibn Sīna defines logic in a way that endows it with many of the characteristics of what is currently termed methodology. He states that "the science of logic is but a tool permeating all sciences; it attracts attention to the bases with which the unknown can be distinguished from what is known by manipulating the latter in such a way as to enable the inquirer to be acquainted with the unknown ..."[9]

The problem Ibn Sīna refers to here is that the bases of the science of logic, or the methodological bases of what we know now as epistemology, consist of a comprehensive philosophical outlook. Consequently, the difference in this philosophical outlook hinges, of necessity, on the difference in methodological or logical bases. In other words, if philosophy changes, there have to be concomitant changes in the methodological bases of inquiry and epistemological deduction on which such a philosophy is based. Ibn Sīna is aware of this problem in his attempt to establish a philosophical outlook that is different from Aristotelian philosophy or, rather, from the philosophy of Ibn Sīna's contemporary Aristotelians, the peripatetics. For Ibn Sīna, the logic of the Easterners, which for him meant a mixture of Indian, Persian, and neo-platonic elements, can be a viable alternative to that of the Greeks. The methodology he followed in distinguishing the true from the false is that of comparing two dissimilar alternatives so as to undermine the halo surrounding a given method and stressing the numerous potentialities of selectivity. He sums up his stance as follows:

> As for us, it became easy to understand what [the Greeks/the Aristotelians] said, and what we worked on. And it is not unlikely that we recei-

ved some sciences from nations other than the Greeks. That was when we were still young, yet God's help made it easier for us to shorten the period of learning what was handed down. Then we carefully compared all that with what the Greeks called "logic" – and it is not unlikely that the Easterners know the same by a different label – and realized what was similar and what was not. Following that we evaluated the entire matter, and realized what was right and what was wrong.[10]

Ibn Sīna's epistemological encounter with the Greeks can also be traced in the field of literary criticism. In his summary of Aristotle's *Poetics*, he emphasizes the importance of selectivity and creativity in dealing with Greek literary criticism. He declares that his objective in summarizing this work is to "select whatever sciences can be of use." Still, he exhorts us "to be creative in order to produce – in pure poetics and the poetics of this age – work which is very knowledgeable and very detailed." Yet his achievement in this respect is still regarded as marginal. He left the more solid work to an important critic who was to follow.

In *Minhāj al-Bulaghā' wa Sirāj al-'Udabā'* [The Method of the Eloquent and the Lantern of the Men of Letters], Ḥāzim al-Qarṭājannī says that the details in his book aspire to embody the kind of details about poetics that Ibn Sīna was looking forward to.[11] He states that though Aristotle talked about poetry in some detail, he operated under the influence of Greek poetry, which was rhyming and limited in scope. Unlike Arabic poetry which teems with wisdom, proverbs, deduction and creativity, Greek poetry was "flawed by the prevalence of superstitions and unreal suppositions."[12]

Al-Qarṭājannī's criticism of the bias in Aristotle's *Poetics* calls to mind Ibn Rushd's argument as the latter – though a great exponent of Aristotelian philosophy – points out that some of what Aristotle says about poetry may not be applicable to poetry from other cultures. Thus, for both al-Qarṭājannī and Ibn Rushd, the examination of Aristotle's book reveals the Greeks' bias towards their culture and the limitation of their assessment as one that fails to apply to non-Greek cultures. Ibn Rushd is known to be among the most enthusiastic proponents of Greek thought in Islamic civilization, but his assessment of the limited applicability of Aristotelian poetics is a strong indication of a general sensitivity with regard to the potential bias engendered by cultural difference. This sensitivity naturally increases in the case of those on the other side of the argument, the people known to be conservative among ancient Muslim intellectuals such as Abū Saʿīd al-Sīrāfī, Ibn Taymiyyah, and al-Ghazālī who, at different times and places during the evolution of Arabo-Islamic civilization, resisted the call for a cultural open-door policy. In a famous debate with al-Mattī ibn Yūnis, Aristotle's translator in the 10th Century (the 4th Century AH), al-Sīrāfī objected to the claim that logic in its Greek form is an accurate criterion for distinguishing truth from falsehood. He supported his objection by referring to cultural bias. "If logic," he argued, "was invented by a Greek thinker who mastered the language, terminology, and structure of Greek thought, then it would be hard for Turks, Indians, Persians, and Arabs to regard it as *the* criterion governing their thought."[13]

Though it is likely that historians have been biased in favor of al-Sīrāfī against al-Mattī ibn Yūnis, the latter's opinions were adopted and elaborated by many. Ibn Rushd, for instance, disagrees in his treatise *Faṣl al-Maqāl* (the Decisive Statement) with the argument elaborated by al-Sīrāfī over the bias of philosophical methodology and calls for a vision that transcends ideological and religious differences "on the basis that the instruments used for slaughtering [animals] are not judged to be usable on the basis of whether or not they are used by people who do not share our religion, as long as they can be used."[14] The problem with this argument is the difficulty of defining the conditions of usability. According to the American philosopher John Dewey, logic is naturally biased in favor of a certain philosophical principle; logicians are strongly affiliated with, and often base their analyses and conclusions on, a given philosophical doctrine.[15] To say that methodology has to be dissociated from its epistemological objective is to call for a separation between form and content. Similarly, the presence of common human objectives does not preclude the diversity of means leading to such goals.

FROM THE SACRED TO THE PROFANE: THE FORMALISM OF ARCHETYPES

According to Northrop Frye the harmony between the methods and objectives of criticism could only be achieved if critical principles and hypotheses were to issue from the art dealt with in criticism. "Critical principles cannot be taken over ready-made from theology, philosophy, politics, or any combination of these."[16] For literary works represent an organic unity based on common symbols, traditions, or models, the latter contributing to the close connection between one poem and another, thus unifying all literary experiences.[17] By way of these denominators, Frye's method shares common ground with formalism whether it is Russian formalism or its American counterpart, the New Criticism. They all converge on the principle that literature is independent from other forms of linguistic discourse, as the referentiality of literature is held to stem from within literature itself and not from social life or the movement of history. In this context, Frye[18] agrees with Eliot's assertion in "The Function of Criticism" that fundamentally criticism regards "the existing monuments of literature [as they] form an ideal order among themselves..."[19]

Frye's methodology remains different, however, from other formalist tendencies in that it attempts to be comprehensive by studying types as symbolic or typological connections among literary works. His great achievement in this project represents a viable bridge between the New Criticism and Structuralism, a vantage point which makes his extremely important work one of the most appropriate for launching this assessment of the cultural specificity of Western literary methods.

To begin with, modern Western culture is characterized by its general and strong inclination towards secularity. This is a commonplace, but it has to be restated as a point of special relevance here. In modern Western intellectual output neither is God present, nor does the Bible have any credibility outside its symbolic, mythic or literary significance. The mainstream of Western thought, including its diverse philosophies and theories, is secular. This secularism has, since the late Middle Ages, but more so since the Renaissance, been gaining increasing dominance over the whole of Western civilization. M. H. Abrams sums up this phenomenon by stating that "it is a historical commonplace that the course of Western thought since the Renaissance has been one of progressive secularization."[20] The increasing authority of secularism, however, does not necessarily mean the disappearance of religion, which is in this case the Judeo-Christian tradition, from Western thought or culture as a whole. There is, rather, a conscious rationalist rejection of such a tradition accompanied by an informing conscious, or unconscious, presence of what Michel Foucault terms "the codes of culture."[21] Harold Bloom, in response to a question about heresy, sees this unconscious presence in the form of assumptions which go unchallenged: "... there is no such thing as religious heresy anymore because there is no such thing as religious orthodoxy anymore. What exist in fact, are unchallenged assumptions, unchallenged metaphysical assumptions, unchallenged epistemological assumptions, unchallenged procedural assumptions in every field of academic study, but particularly in the study of literature."[22]

Frye's typological criticism provides a clear example of the unchallenged assumptions Bloom talks about. Religious doctrines and secularist tendencies coexist in the critic's belief at once in the mythological nature of the Bible and the independence of literature. Frye's statements carry this confluence, though in terms that carry some measure of vagueness: "I *feel* that historical scholarship is without exception 'lower' or analytic criticism, and that 'higher' criticism would be a quite different activity. The latter *seems* to me to be a purely literary criticism"[23] (my italics). The traditional Christian interpretation of the Bible, as Frye reminds us, symbolically conflates the Old Testament and the New Testament in that the events and people of the former foreshadow those of the latter (Adam is a forerunner of Christ). This typological interpretation is highlighted by Frye as a model methodology already established by "typological" criticism and is now fused into its contemporary secularist version: the literary criticism performed by someone like Frye himself.

Meanwhile, Frye rejects the historical analytic study of the Bible as embodied in the kind of criticism that prevailed in the 18th and 19th Centuries and constituted the secular link between the religious criticism of Augustine and the secular criticism of Frye. However, Frye does not refer to this linkage, and he may be right in attacking it. Yet this does not lessen its importance in the development of Western literary criticism, especially the formalist approach. The methodological assumption about the mythic nature of the Bible, the assumption emphatically adopted by Frye, began in 18th-Century European criticism, as did also the basic formalist hypothesis about the autonomy of the text.

Towards the middle of the 18th Century, propelled by the Enlightenment, which was generally antagonistic to religious orthodoxy, there emerged a religious critical movement which attempted a defense of religion through a new interpretation of the Bible that emphasized its literary and mythological nature as Oriental poetry, Hebrew in particular. This in turn was expected to stop people from literally interpreting the Bible and consequently from stultifying the rational, scientific mind. The objective of such critics was to show that the poetry of Hebrew sacred writings was a fit subject for appreciation and criticism.[24] The religious text was thus read anew in the context of poetry. According to Robert Lowth, the greater part of the Old Testament is poetry, and it should never be read in light of rules other than those applying to poetic language.[25]

It has to be remembered that such developments paralleled the rise of Romanticism, and that Coleridge – the pioneering critic of formalism in the Anglo-Saxon tradition – was an important contributor to the crystallization of the new sacred/secular criticism combination, which is part of the secularization process. As critics of the Bible tried to defend their scripture, they employed a formalist defensive methodology that led to the marginalization of such a scripture; that methodology turned out to be no less secular than the stance of many extremists in the non-religious Enlightenment movement. Eventually this led to the profanation (desacralization) of the religious text in Western literary criticism and to equating it with human, worldly texts. As E. S. Shaffer says, "if in our time 'text' has been liberated from 'writing' and become a system of signs, so in that period text was liberated from the letter of divine inspiration and became a system of human symbols."[26]

Liberating the text from its sacredness at the hands of formalist critics was not unprecedented. In the mid-17th Century, Spinoza's *Theological Political Treatise* (1670) played an important role in the development of Biblical criticism,[27] which, as we have seen, adopted a more or less formalist approach. Spinoza's interpretative methodology suggests that "Scriptural interpretation proceeds by the examination of Scripture."[28] The sacredness of the Bible, according to Spinoza's suggestion, should not be an *a priori* stipulation; rather, it should result from intensive research. Spinoza himself does not reach this conclusion; rather, he announces that the application of his methodology will lead the interpreter to such a conclusion. His warning is simply against the hypothesis that all that God says to anybody in the Bible is a prophecy or revelation.[29]

Spinoza's conclusions, therefore, call to mind the historical terminology underlying some of the chief principles enunciated by Northrop Frye, such as Biblical mythology and the necessity of deriving the principles of literary criticism solely from literature. The only difference is that literature has replaced sacred religious texts. This is a long story of replacements that involves the emergence of Romanticism, William Blake's prophetic books, Wordsworth's revolt against classical poetry, and Emerson's call upon his countrymen to be on a par with the masters of the ancient world. Every age, exhorts the American sage, has to write its own books, and the books of the ancient ages are not necessarily appropriate for later times.[30]

All of this is part of the background explaining Northrop Frye's archetypal/formalist approach. An important component in that background is pinpointed by Geoffrey Hartman:

> The value of Frye's system is that it methodologically eliminates the last obstacle barring art from spreading its influence: the qualitative distinction between the sacred and the profane, or the popular and the aristocratic. His general sense of art is extremely Protestant: every man is a priest of the imagination ...[31]

Needless to say, the Protestantism Hartman refers to in connection with Frye is not the dogmatic adherence to religious principles, the "religious orthodoxy" Harold Bloom refers to. Frye is far from that; rather, it is the cultural context informing the critic's ideas, the totality of criteria and rules affecting his principles and worldview. Prominent among these criteria and rules is the traditional Protestant iconoclasm that, for instance, informs the title and content of one of Frye's books: *The Secular Scripture*.[32] Literature is thus presented as an alternative, a semi-alternative to be more accurate, to religion, an essential backdrop, as Terry Eagleton saw it, for the failure of religious ideology.[33]

These "unchallenged assumptions," to use Blooms' words again, only highlight the difficulty involved in trying to part with metaphysics in contemporary Western culture. It was this difficulty that Martin Heidegger summed up in his conclusion that "yet a regard for metaphysics still prevails even in the intention to overcome metaphysics."[34] Frye's approach to metaphysics is predicated on his concept of the archetype with its structuralist, linguistic, and transcendental connotations. The *arch* or "beginning" in Greek gives the last part of the work, the *type*, its transcendence. It is as if the archetype is a religious type devoid of its verbal habiliments.[35] Frye's apparent overlooking of these latent metaphysics does not, however, prevent him from agreeing with Heidegger's conclusion regarding the impossibility of getting rid of the metaphysical dimension in human thought. In *The Secular Scripture*, he points out that the use of orthodox terminology is part of a dilemma: "Not all of us will be satisfied with calling the central part of our mythological inheritance a revelation from God ... I cannot claim to have found a more acceptable formulation."[36]

In other forms of critical methodology like structuralism and Marxism, both secularism and metaphysics (here synonymous with religiosity) are variably correlated and perhaps conflated. What this suggests is that there are attempts to dethrone metaphysics or at least to supersede its concepts. Despite Nietzsche's declaration of the death of God and the consequent prevalent conviction that religions are mythological and traditional values are delusive, there has been constant tension in Western thinking resulting in, among other manifestations, a perpetual attempt to purify language of metaphysical presence. Contemporary Western culture has long been characterized by the absence of the sacred; its chief criterion has therefore been the degree to which thinking has gotten rid of the effects of the metaphysical. A striking example is Tzvetan Todorov's statement in the introduction to a book announcing a shift of critical stance on his part: "... this book will deal both with the meaning of some twentieth-century critical works, and with the possibility of opposing nihilism without ceasing to be an atheist."[37]

STRUCTURALISM: COLLAPSE OF THE DREAM

According to Todorov, post-Spinoza critics are no longer preoccupied with whether what the text says is correct or not; they are rather concerned with exactly *what* the text says. He justifies this shift in the following terms:

> ... in the absence of transcendence, each text becomes its own frame of reference, and the critic's task is completed in classification of the text's meaning, in the description of its forms and textual functioning, far removed from any value ... Earlier, people believed in the existence of an absolute and common truth, in a universal standard (for several centuries, absolute truth happened to coincide with the Christian doctrine). The breakdown of this belief, the recognition of human diversity and equality led to relativism and individualism, and finally to nihilism.[38]

In the past also, but not the remote past, this statement, which sums up a great deal of what this discussion argues, would not have been articulated by one of the most active structuralist critics in the West. Now it has become all too clear to Todorov that nihilism is the logical conclusion of limiting the critic's role to the discussion of the meaning of a text, its forms, and its performance, far from value-judgments; it is the conclusion, that is, of the preoccupation with a critical method such as structuralism. The philosophical implications of such a method become now clear to the author of *The Poetics of Prose*,[39] who has now shifted to a method he calls: critical humanism.[40]

It would, however, be fair to say that the Bulgarian/French critic did not write his book to announce the abandonment of structuralism. His method is rather to make a counter-statement to some of the theses constituting the new era of post-structuralism. Proponents of the new era are, needless to say, in disagreement with what they might regard as Todorov's "regressive" attitude. Roland Barthes, Todorov's mentor and the one whose works form a large curve showing the appearance and decline of critical structuralism, is one of those proponents.

Roland Barthes's works are in fact closer to demonstrating the decline than the emergence and prosperity of structuralism. His equivocal role as at once founder and deconstructer of structuralist methodology is one strong testimony to the fact that structuralism, like other methods, is full of variables that render it less objective than it claims to be. For Barthes has revolted against the very ideology he espoused when younger, and later on came to call for the very nihilism that his disciple was afraid of. Though more radical, Barthes's attitude is still more in harmony with the logic of its cultural climate than that of his student.

In his famous essay "An Introduction to Structuralist Analysis of Fictional Texts,"[41] Barthes defines the outlines of the structuralist method and suggests that linguistics should be the chief model for structuralist analysis. Only one year later did Barthes decide to follow another totally different critical course by calling for the presence of an analytical tool which, instead of appraising structures, would be concerned with the illogical play and reversion of such structures.[42] The following stage in Western critical thought, namely post-structuralism, has been characterized by the rebellion of structuralists against unchallenged premises in the realm of science.

One of the most important issues addressed by structuralism is how literary criticism, with the help of the linguistic model, can be so scientific that knowledge itself - as Northrop Frye put it - moves from accidental to the causal.[43] The synchronic aspect of language is transmitted, through the structuralist analysis, to the structure of the literary work, ultimately producing a perennial entity that is divorced from the movement of time, sociological and economic factors and all that is outside the text. Finally, the text is seen as a self-contained structure that is completely independent of outside elements.

In a dialog with a number of French intellectuals, Claude Lévi-Strauss, the pioneer of structuralist methodology, conceded that structuralism may be described as a materialistic philosophy.[44] In response to Paul Ricoeur's observation regarding meaning, Lévi-Strauss highlighted an aspect of the philosophical underpinnings of structuralism by indicating that his method had little room for meaning: "In my perspective meaning is never the primary phenomenon: meaning is always reducible."[45] In this sense, structuralism appears to have developed a secularist stance not very different from the one articulated by its later, staunch critic – deconstruction.

Other aspects of the philosophical basis or bias of structuralism are revealed by others such as Jean-Paul Sartre,[46] who criticized it from a Marxist, materialistic perspective, describing it as the last ideological setback to Marxism that is presented by the bourgeoisie. Paul Ricoeur, on the other hand, sees in structuralism an "extreme form of modern agnosticism."[47] The critic whose critique of structuralism seems more probing and effective, however, is the American Marxist Fredric Jameson.

In his *The Prison-House of Language: a Critical Reading of Structuralism and Russian Formalism*, Jameson begins with the premise that "the history of thought is a history of its models."[48] He points out the structuralist emphasis on linguistics in its historical perspective so as to examine the sociological and economic circumstances leading to its emergence. It soon becomes clear that the model used here is not only different from the organic model which dominated 19th-Century thought, but is here to displace that model. The new model of linguistics depends for its meaning on the social system of contemporary Western societies:

> It lies in the concrete character of the social life of so-called advanced countries today, which offer the spectacle of a world from which nature has been eliminated, a world saturated with messages and information,

whose intricate commodity network may be seen as the very prototype of system of signs. There is therefore a profound consonance between linguistics, as a model, and that ghostly, systematic nightmare, which is our contemporary culture.[49]

Ten years after these words, Jameson reconsidered the relation he had charted between the model and culture in order to put on one end the ideology of Western modernism, the ideology responsible for the formalist currents in general, and, on the other, the capitalist culture dominating post-industrial societies of the West. In so doing, he found that Modernist ideology imposes a distorted model of literary history through its aesthetics and conceptual limits. This conceptual and aesthetic domination is the consequence of the capitalist system being able to spread out like any trademark. "For we all know," writes Jameson, "capitalism is the first genuinely global culture, and has never renounced its mission to assimilate everything alien into itself."[50]

As for the way out of this domination and the resulting isolation, which Jameson compares to that of the cave men in the well-known Platonic analogy, Jameson prescribes a comprehensive and far-reaching reformulation of "our" economic and social system.[51] Yet it soon becomes clear that the new model being suggested is not only a part of Marxist theory, but is highly reformulated, with the deconstructive climate overshadowing the entire critical and ideological scene at the time.

JAMESON AND MARXIST DECONSTRUCTION

As Marxist criticism falls under the impact of deconstructive thinking, it becomes difficult to talk about Marxist theses in the traditional sense. For Marxism is itself touched by the deconstructive skepticism, and the end result is what Jameson calls "post-Marxism." This is the stage which represents the equivalent to what is known as "post-structuralism," and all the other "posts" dotting the contemporary Western cultural landscape (postmodernism, post-capitalism, post-colonialism, etc.). As is well known, deconstruction is at the heart of these "posts," particularly post-structuralism.

If deconstruction is at the heart of post-structuralism, nihilism is at the heart of deconstruction. Nihilism here is understood in its original Nietzschean sense, which is articulated in the introduction to *The Will to Power*. Here Nietzsche asserts that nihilism implies a full conviction that life has no meaning in the light of the highest values known, that humankind has no right to assume that there is a supernatural or sacred level of existence.[52] The way deconstruction relates to this nihilist conviction is of course to be sought in the major work of the authorities in the field: Derrida, Paul de Man, and J. Hillis Miller. Roland Barthes lends the authoritative voice of a kindred spirit when he expresses his conviction that "nihilism is the only philosophy possible in our present situation."[53]

Barthes is not usually linked to deconstruction, but he was always aware of a link that came directly from Nietzsche. This was the link bringing him, along with Derrida, to the older philosophy of nihilism. Both he and Derrida, he said, felt the need to partake in a stage of history that Nietzsche called "nihilism."[54] This stage of history is, of course, what we now know under different "posts": post-structuralism, postmodernism, etc.

In his *The Political Unconscious*, Jameson highlights his own role as pioneer of post-structuralist thought. He states:

> *The Political Unconscious* ... turns on the dynamics of the act of interpretation and presupposes as an organizational fiction, that we never really confront a text immediately, in all its freshness as a thing-in-itself. Rather, texts come before us as the always-already-read... This presupposition then dictates the use of a method (which I have elsewhere termed 'metacommentary') according to which our object of study is less the text itself than the interpretation through which we attempt to confront and to appropriate it.[55]

Jameson's use in this book of the word "fiction" instead of the more familiar "thesis" or "point of view" is in keeping with deconstructive criticism, which emphasizes the literary and imaginary character of *all* texts. For criticism is a kind of literature, and both criticism and literature are a kind of writing or "écriture".[56] Jameson's method in this context is parallel, if not identical, to that of semiotics, which "attempts to identify the rules and conventions which, consciously or unconsciously are assimilated by members of that culture [and] make possible the meanings which the phenomena have."[57]

Jameson's ideological stance rests on a post-structuralist conviction that acknowledges the literary nature of criticism and the fictitious character of scientific discourse. Nonetheless, his interpretation of literary history is Marxist in so far as it looks at class conflict as implicit in literary texts. Political interpretation of texts, therefore, is given priority over other different interpretations.[58] In other words, Jameson's deconstruction is bent on undermining the interpretations that claim to be innocent of political purport; he has even attempted deconstruction of Marxism itself by rejecting some of its tenets so as to make it harmonious with the reality of contemporary Western thought. In his view, traditional Marxism can itself be seen as fraught with metaphysics, especially in its utopian vision of a classless society.

However, Jameson's attempt to modify his Marxism has naturally led to contradiction and to the criticism of deconstructionists whose method he tried to adopt. An example of this is his description of the approach which he calls "immanent analysis":

> ... the ideal of the immanent analysis of the text, of a dismantling or deconstruction of its parts and a description of its functioning and malfunctioning, amounts more to a wholesale nullification of all interpretive activity than to a demand for the construction of some new and more adequate, immanent or antitranscendental hermeneutic model which it will be the task of the following pages to propose.[59]

Jameson's proposal here is to adopt a deconstructive approach which he describes as "immanent" and, elsewhere, as "metacommentary." The only problem with this proposal is that it remains faithful to a Marxism that insists on being second to none. This double stand becomes ironically incongruous once Jameson's description of his approach starts deploying terms more familiar in the description of traditional approaches. Jameson, for example, refuses to compare Marxism with other methods: "Marxism cannot today be defended as a mere substitute for such other methods, which would then triumphantly be consigned to the trash bin of history."[60] This becomes even more interesting when the same critic who describes his method as "antitranscendent" moves on a little later to rely on the implications of 'transcendence' to describe the method itself: "In the spirit of a more authentic dialectical tradition, Marxism is here conceived as the 'untranscendable horizon'."[61]

Deconstructionists are likely to see Jameson's efforts to reconcile his

Marxist approach, with all its "untranscendable" claims, as nothing but another instance of the inevitable succumbing to the potent forces of metaphysics. Eventually one would find the term used earlier by Marxist critic Pierre Macherey to describe structuralism likewise appropriate for his fellow American's method, namely: "... a variant of theological aesthetics."[62]

DECONSTRUCTION: RECONCILING THE IRRECONCILABLE

The religious and philosophical bias which I have set out to outline here should now be clear: Northrop Frye highlights the mythological nature of the Bible yet holds to a metaphysical concept of the archetype; Claude Lévi-Strauss describes structuralism as materialistic, yet sees it as divorced from history and causality. On the other hand, Fredric Jameson believes in historical materialism and rejects metaphysics, yet he describes his Marxism in terms highly fraught with transcendence.

This doubletalk is one of the very significant dilemmas of a culture embracing the secular yet unable to break away from its religious and metaphysical roots. The deconstructionists were the last to try to accomplish what they call a cultural "free play," the attempt initiated so vigorously by Nietzsche who early on saw the inevitability of this happening as Christian morals harbored their enemy: nihilism.[63] More recently, American critic J. Hillis Miller quotes Nietzsche and moves on to highlight the role of deconstruction, "of which Nietzsche is one of the patrons," in tackling the problem of metaphysical domination of culture.[64] Miller argues that deconstruction is as old as the Greek sophists and Plato; however, he does not explain why such an ancient critical method has acquired such a strong momentum at the present time, and in the United States in particular.

It is difficult to come up with a definite answer to this question. The history of secularism glimpsed might, despite its vagueness, be the only answer possible. American critic Robert Scholes, in an unsympathetic discussion of deconstruction, suggests that deconstruction is strong among "us" because "we deserve it." Western history as a whole, in other words, prepared Western culture for such a rationalist "invasion."[65] Scholes does not clarify exactly what he means, but he seems to have in mind the entire history of secularization since the Middle Ages, and the ceaseless efforts to overcome the metaphysical over the centuries, especially in the work of Nietzsche, Freud, and Heidegger.[66] The confrontation of the problem in the work of deconstructionists such as Derrida, Paul de Man, and Miller would thus seem to be only the latest episode. In *Writing and Difference*, Derrida highlights this ongoing confrontation: "Nietzsche, Freud and Heidegger, for example, worked within inherited metaphysical concepts. Since those concepts are not elements or atoms, since they are taken from a linguistic structure and a system, each metaphor pulls with it all metaphysics."[67]

In terms of literary criticism, Derrida's statement translates as follows: metaphysics is another name for such concepts and values as "truth," "reality," "meaning," etc.; on the other hand, nihilism becomes shrouded in "language," "literature," and the labyrinth of texts that are recalcitrant to all kinds of conventional rationalism. Paul de Man states that poetic language constantly names this vacuum (the presence of nothing): "This persistent naming is what we call literature."[68] In other words, literature is the awareness of nihilism; it is the constant realization of whether there are meanings in as much as there are readers and that it is impossible to agree on one transcendental meaning or criterion. For meaning ultimately evaporates into sheer absence and the quest for it becomes a sort of critical absurdity. Yet as Edward Said has observed, these de Manian "intellectual hobbles on the possibility of statement have not ... inhibited de Man from stating and re-stating them ..."[69]

What is especially important here is the cultural context that led de Man and other deconstructionists to define the impediments to speech and abstract communication and even to believe in them. It is a consistent and interdependent context that explains the inevitable (not to say logical) tendency to deconstruction in Western culture, a fact that has motivated a prominent non-deconstructionist critic such as George Steiner to admit that deconstructionist theses are beyond refutation. Steiner's suggestion for transcending deconstruction is to assimilate what he calls the ambiguity of existence, an element that is essential to literary creativity whereby characters remain alive even after the death of their author. Steiner's other suggestion is that we read as if the text in question yields meaning.[70] Of course these suggestions turn out to accept deconstruction instead of going beyond it. Like the ideas offered by critics such as Abrams and Todorov, they draw attention to the presence of meaning and acknowledge its absence in the same breath, a type of contradiction that always calls for deconstruction.

Deconstructionists hardly need any of their opponents to remind them that their direction harbors a latent, radical metaphysics.[71] They are keenly aware of their problems; hence, they themselves are perhaps the best place to go for an understanding of the contextual developments leading to their type of thinking and procedure. A self-diagnosis by J. Hillis Miller on his intellectual link to Derrida is so significant in this regard that it should be quoted in full:

> I've thought about why someone (with my Protestant background) like that American would have been attracted by, let's say, Derrida. I think I have an answer. There is a similarity between a certain aspect of American Protestantism, or even Protestantism generally, and the Jewish tradition, or the Jewish, intellectual European tradition, which has a suspicion of icons, signs, of graven images, and a suspicion that things may not be for the best in the 'best of all worlds,' a kind of instinctive darkness of view, and a kind of conflict that I have in myself between a commitment to truth, the search for truth as the highest value, and moral values on the other. They may be in conflict. That is to say, you might reach a point where truth was challenging or dangerous to values.[72]

It would be difficult to find a testimony more emphatically direct than this to the inherent prejudice of Western critical methods. To elaborate on it a little one could recall the old Jewish Spinozian connection and the development of sacred into literary criticism. It is with this connection that I would like to bring these remarks to a conclusion.

In *Writing and Difference*, Derrida contemplates the work of the Jewish/French poet Edmond Jabès, and finds that a distinctive Jewish view regarding truth, interpretation, and meaning characterizes this poet's work. This view emphasizes an atheistic perspective which does not seek truth or origins as it engages in the poetic interpretation of the world. It issues from a common experience of Jewish Diaspora and continuous journeying from one place to the other with no hope of return, without, that is, a dream of meaning, truth or any metaphysical structure that provides comfort. The French Jewish philosopher Emanuel Levinas places this ongoing one-way journey in contrast to the Greek cyclical journey: "In contrast to Ulysses going back home, we would like to place the story of Abraham leaving his country to an unknown country forever."[73]

In a study that contextualizes deconstruction within the Hebrew tradition, Susan Handelman argues that the idea of the death of God in contemporary Western thought can be traced back to the Jewish concept of godhead. In the Jewish concept God appears other, distant and absent in Jewish lore,[74] in contrast to Greek gods who are always present. The Jewish concept thus became an important factor in the deconstruction of Christian religiosity, "and in the long run instated a different god: the book. According to one commentator on Jabés, the long period between the Diaspora and the return of the Messiah witnessed the transformation of the 'people of God' into the 'people of the book'".[75] Levinas, however, who "deconstructed" theology from a Jewish point of view, chose to articulate the centrality of the book in the Jewish secular conception with an expression drawn from the Talmudic Midrashian tradition: "You should love the Torah more than you love God."[76] A more poetic articulation of the same position can be found in Jabés: "So, with God dead, I found my Jewishness confirmed in the book ... Because being Jewish means exiling yourself in the word and, at the same time, weeping for your exile. The return to the book is a return to forgotten sites."[77]

There is nothing outside the text, goes one Derridean conclusion,[78] and in Jabés this conclusion finds its home: "We are not free. We are nailed alive to the signs of the book. Could it be that our freedom lies in the word's vain try to cut loose from the word?"[79] Critics working outside this home of cultural meaning are unlikely to be aware of what is inside. They will be transferring the words to a different context where they won't quite fit. They will revel in the discovery of textuality, endless meanings, and other post-structural concepts, unable to see the full significance of what they are using. They will be nailed to the signs of a book they never read, denying that structuralism or deconstruction has any philosophical meaning or cultural specificity that limits or qualifies its free circulation.

Ultimately, the remarks I have made above regarding the cultural contextuality of Western critical methods may amount to no more than a gloss on one of the two positions articulated in an earlier century by Arab grammarian Abū Saʿīd al-Sīrāfī in the debate concerning the attitude Muslims should adopt towards Greek logic. Western critical methods, like Greek logic and like critical methods used anywhere, enjoy a considerable degree of universality. Yet there will always remain another considerable degree in them that is culture-specific, which is home-bound, which cannot be transferred. It is this latter quality which makes it imperative for people not sharing the Western cultural context to thoroughly revise such methods before using them, if they have to – if, that is, they can't be more original than that.

9

Theories and Principles of Design in the Architecture of Islamic Societies: A Ceremonial Approach to Community Building

A. I. ABDELHALIM

WHAT I HOPE TO SHOW in the following pages is that the values of excellence and beauty are needed to overcome the underdevelopment, alienation, and apathy now prevalent in most communities in the Islamic and the developing world.[1] I will also suggest that the central cause of that underdevelopment lies in the separation of the means of production, especially of the built environment, from what is germane to their cultures. Despite this separation, however, there still exist cultural mechanisms which are capable of linking the construction of buildings to the culture of the community. The "building ceremony," in which the order of the community is identified, the creative energy of the people is released, and community resources and skills are regenerated, can be such a mechanism.

Until recently, rituals and ceremonies have taken place around particular building operations. In many communities today, however, building operations are under the exclusive control of formal institutions such as law and management. Whether recognized through rituals and ceremonies or controlled by law and management, the inner nature of these building operations suggests that a regenerative process similar to that which takes place around life crises, transitions, and growth may also be present.

A class of events in which the process of the community can be regenerated includes the definition of boundaries, the establishment of centers, and the connecting of the building to the community. If the regenerative process of the community is channeled into these building operations, then the building's construction can contribute to the vitality of the people and to the creative development of their community. If removed from the production of the building, the urge for regeneration does not die, but breaks out instead in violence, alienation, or apathy.

In many communities and in a variety of social and economic contexts, I have observed rituals and ceremonies centered on activities considered vital both to the process of building and to the life of the community. The similarity between these events led me to examine the relation between rituals in building and this sense of vitality and regeneration that takes place in them. Building, both in theory and practice, has thus far viewed these instances of regeneration as, at best, ancillary to the rational process of building.

Over the past few years, I have been using theoretical work as well as actual building to try to examine ways of using building ceremonies as mechanisms that can channel activity into the regular building process. My purpose was to understand whether building ceremonies are a part of building that can be the source of creative action or are simply blind reenactments of traditional rituals. These questions are important because the majority of the world's population live in communities in which custom and tradition are the only available means of organizing them. Whether one calls such communities informal, marginal, underdeveloped, traditional, or primitive, any development therein must fundamentally rely on local abilities and resources. The building ceremony, regardless of the community or culture, is the mechanism that links building with the community.

On the island of Mactan in the Philippines construction day is called *bayanihan*, which means "laughter." In Upper Egypt, the Nubian women of Kushtamna Garb dig deeply in the soil of the streets to reach a layer of fine sand, which reminds them of the ground in their old village. They move rhythmically, chanting the name of the occasion, as they spread the sand to repair the streets and the floors of their houses. In the fishing community of Kameshima on Wasaka Bay in Japan, the Yoimiya, or "night festival" is held on the second night of August each year. The young people of the community reconstruct a miniature shrine to house the "awakened gods" and carry it to the village. Then the boats, streets, plazas, and buildings are repaired, and platforms are built as resting places for the awakened gods.

Mosque repair in Mali, house decoration in Nubia, barn-raising in rural America, land subdivision in Mexico, community gardening in Niger, and roof construction among the Berbers are only a few of the many examples that indicate how building has always been intimately connected to the people and their creative instincts that have produced both buildings and artifacts of great interest. The stark beauty of house decorations in Nubia and the majesty of a mud-brick mosque in Mali are just two examples of the products of these events.

All these instances are indications that a basic regenerative process similar to that which embodied the rituals and ceremonies of many societies and to the vital process which guides the growth and forms the identity of individuals may now in fact be operating in the building process. The fact that a great many societies have devised ceremonies around building – laying the foundation, constructing the main beam, laying the cornerstone, raising the roof, subdividing the land, establishing boundaries, and the sale or exchange of property, for example – suggests this. Today, however, the building ceremony has all but disappeared from building construction. The phrase "building ceremony" in itself suggests some kind of contradiction since building involves construction, finance, and law, while ceremony is associated with ritual, festivity, and regeneration.

Today it is fashionable to argue that building should remain separate from ceremony in the name of economic necessity, efficiency, or rationality. At most an appropriate integration between culture and production must remain on the symbolic level. Such an argument is, however, false and misleading. The integration of culture and production is both essential and possible. Evidence suggests that ceremony increases productivity, improves performance, and enhances the quality of the things that are produced. Building, more than any other productive activity, can combine economic growth with the vitality and creativity of the people and add to the accumulation of capital, knowledge, and authority, the regeneration of identity, creative energy, and community solidarity.

An actual community building project in Egypt – a cultural park for children near the Ibn Ṭūlūn Mosque in Cairo – gave me the opportunity to test out my theories. It well illustrated the advantages of this combination. The park site is a few hundred yards north of the Ibn Ṭūlūn Mosque. The project, whose design we were awarded as a result of a national competition held in the fall of 1983, was financed by the Ministry of Culture in Egypt. Among its facilities it included a children's museum, an open-air theater, a library, playgrounds, and gardens. The site was about two and a half acres with clusters of trees and the remnants of an older park called El-Hod el-Marsoud, which had occupied the site in the late 19th Century.

The community around the project is called al-Sayyidah Zaynab. It is one of the oldest, most densely populated, and poorly maintained quarters in Cairo, but also one of the most vibrant and lively. Its population is over a million, and it is rich in history. It is named after al-Sayyidah Zaynab, the granddaughter of the Prophet Muhammad. The mosques of Ibn Ṭūlūn and al-Sayyidah Zaynab are among the many great buildings from various periods that embody in their form some of the power, vitality, and meaning of the community's life there. More important than these monuments, however, is the lively festival of al-Sayyidah Zaynab held every year, during which the identity and the culture of the community are reenacted and regenerated.

When we began working on the scheme for the park we concentrated primarily on order. How were we going to conceive its geometry and organization, its images and symbols, in such a way as to capture the community's spirit? We were convinced that a project built right in the heart of the community had the potential to restore its creative capacity.

Every community has its own concept of order, a way of relating its existence to the universe. In al-Sayyidah Zaynab today, as in many other poor but vital communities, this concept is based on myth and belief but also has a scientific and ideological aspect. Design in such a community must strike a balance between analysis, abstraction, and rationality, on the one hand, and faith and submission to the community's ideas about order, on the other. We found an expression of the concept of order to be found in ceremonial processions and the rhythm of the folk dance (*zikre*) and music, in the structure of the oral poetic tradition, and in a few building rituals such as the foundation sacrifice and the laying of the cornerstone. We also used landmarks – the minaret of Ibn Ṭūlūn, the domes of several mausoleums, and land patterns – as messages that could reveal something about the configuration of the social order. The configuration of a procession and the structure of poetic rhythm reflect belief and ideology in their relationships in space. The task of the designer is to disentangle these containers of order and discover their underlying geometry.

In our case, the point of departure was to find links between the growth of a child and the growth of the park, and we searched for events, objects, and symbols in the culture that could give this idea expression. The Ibn Ṭūlūn minaret was clearly visible from the site, and it too became an inspiration for our order. We reconstructed the spiral form of the minaret in a series of geometric operations, informed by the shape and the elements of the site and organized in terms of the project's requirements. The first formulation involved the movement of two intersecting circles. The center of the first circle is a point at the intersection of the axis of a palm tree promenade on the site, with the main street leading from the entrance to make a significant visual link to the minaret. The center of the second circle was a large tree at the end of the promenade axis. The progression of each movement's intervals roughly followed the spacing of the palm trees along the two sides of the promenade. Program requirements and the patterns of activities within the different fields defined the final arrangement of the scheme.

A large fountain, modeled after the traditional fountains in Cairo, marked the center of the first area. A small café, playgrounds, playing fields, and platforms for observing these activities completed this first area.

Around the center of the second area, a cascade of spiral walls and terraces suggested the setting of the children's museum. Animals and birds were placed around it. The intersection of the two areas created a third set of geometrical relations where a variety of activities were located. The theater was placed so as to form two interlocking spirals around a triangular group of large Bengali trees. The border between the geometrical order of the park and the surrounding streets and alleys provided a setting for a café at the corner, an outdoor fountain and ablution place, a small *zāwiyah* (a little corner for people to meet) and an outdoor prayer area, several shops, workshops, and a very large outdoor community space made by including the alley within the walls.

After the competition awarded the scheme to our firm, a contract was signed for design development and construction, funds were allocated for the building, and then ... nothing happened. The project had been blocked by political interest groups in the parliament. Several confrontations with officials, including the prime minister and the minister of culture, resulted in an official go-ahead, but still nothing happened. Something was wrong. We soon realized what it was. We had been trying to defend the project through public meetings and through the media, but the people in the community, the real supporters of the project, had no contact with either. They were cut off from the press and from the power structure, which in any case were confused about the image of the project and argued against its order and character. We realized we would have to mobilize the community to get the project moving, not just to defend the project but to build it. We looked for an opportunity to do this.

The opportunity came when the minister of culture decided to lay the cornerstone of the project during the National Festival for Children, a celebration held in Egypt in November of each year. Some officials, the architect, and representatives of the local community were scheduled to attend.

Normally a cornerstone laying is completely detached from the life of the community, but we proposed to the minister of culture that in place of drawings and working models that were usually displayed in a tent on these occasions and which to most people were meaningless, a real, life-size model of the scheme could be displayed to give the whole community a glimpse of what the project was to look like. The spiral geometry of the fountain, exhibits, museum, and theater would be constructed in a tent, and the platforms and terraces would be marked on the ground by colors. Each element would be mocked up full scale in its actual place on the site.

In our memorandum to the minister we also suggested inviting artists, musicians and dancers to participate. They could propose works suggesting the scheme, which could then be performed by school children from the local community. In this way we sought to restore the age-old function of the building ceremony that had been traditional in Egypt from the Luxor Temple and the mosque of Ibn Ṭūlūn almost up to the present day.

The minister was eventually won over to our scheme, though mainly because the ceremony was to be attended by the President and his wife and would draw attention to the significant role it was playing in the development of local communities. The image of hundreds of children playing and dancing around the mocked-up part and the full-scale model, while tens of thousands of citizens looked on, appealed to the minister's political instincts, and he approved. We were given seven days to execute our plans.

We began by making a set of drawings that would enable the tent builders to produce a tent overnight. Tent builders work in two teams of four each. One man works from the top of a very long ladder, which he holds onto with his legs, moving the ladder about like a circus performer. The others on the ground deal with the ropes and spread the canvas over the poles that structure the tent. Our drawings had to follow this method of construction. On the site, local officials prepared the grounds for the tents and contacted schools, artists, and musicians. Within eighteen hours a two-and-a-half acre lot had been transformed from a deserted, rundown site into a fabulous scene of tents that beautifully, if not altogether accurately, reproduced the arrangement of the proposed scheme. The neighbors hung out of their windows, and peered off of rooftops and out of the tree tops to see the emerging event. Cheers like those heard at weddings and other festivities came from every direction. The children began to arrive to rehearse on the temporary stage that had been set up. For three or four days hundreds of them gathered in groups to practice, while a choreographer and the musicians worked out the performance to follow the configuration of the scheme. When they could not, we changed the scheme's arrangement. This happened several times and each time it did, the scheme was improved. Instead of the original plan disappearing from sight, it continued to evolve before my very eyes. I came actually to believe what I had claimed to the minister, that the great buildings of Egypt were always the result of ceremony. Certainly the performance of this festival added something to the plan that rational designing could not have conceived. The action of the community added a sense of wholeness that would otherwise not have been there.

Combining crafts with technology is a difficult operation because it comes into conflict with current modes of building. But in the case of our park it could not be built entirely with modern methods and still involve the entire community as the building festival had done. Working drawings, order forms, spec sheets, and legal documents seemed oddly out of place after the festival. The elements of the scheme remained the same, but the participation of thousands of community members in the festival had introduced ideas and images that did not lend themselves to inclusion in working drawings. Nor would minor modifications remedy the situation. Rather, the static geometry of the original had to be transformed into a lively order for which the dimensions and specifications of working drawings were not only limiting but inappropriate. Like any community project, this one had to be capable of retaining its original order while at the same time constantly changing and adapting as the process of building continued.

The central question was how the orthogonal system of measurement and dimension could render the non-orthogonal geometry of our scheme and retain the tremendous variety of space and expression that had turned up in the festival. We devised a system of drawing based on proportions and not on dimensions. The logarithmic spiral which was used to organize the scheme was now developed into a system of proportions based on rhythm and harmonics, which allowed us to develop or change a particular element without losing the general order.

We selected stone for our construction as best suited to an environment, which included the stone and brick construction of the Ibn Ṭūlūn mosque and a few Mamluk and Ottoman buildings in the neighborhood along with the reinforced concrete of most of the rest of the buildings. We thought that stone would represent a meeting point for the carpenters, farmworkers, steelworkers, and surveyors of the typical Egyptian general contracting crew and any traditional craftsmen who might still be found in the community. The wall-bearing construction which we chose utilized arches, vaults, and domes which allowed for freedom and liveliness in the general order.

In Egypt the law requires that publicly financed projects be assigned to general contractors through public bidding. This means that contractors' crews usually will not include craftsmen. To surmount this difficulty we divided the work up into two categories of operation: ordinary work – including the foundations, damp-proofing, and regular walls – that would strictly adhere to the dictates of the drawings, and extraordinary work – arches, vaults, domes, and curved walls – that would require both technical work and the expertise of craftsmen. For the extraordinary work, we required the technician to prepare a full-scale model of each element, with the craftsmen present to advise on the materials and techniques involved. These models were then used as patterns for carving stone and building vaults and arches. This way we were able to combine the skills of the stoneworker and his instinctive knowledge of geometry and measurement with the technician's ability to work from written instructions and drawings. The combination also made it easier to introduce innovation. It allowed the craftsmen to rescue lost skills with the aid of the technicians and the technicians to add advanced skills to their ordinary tasks of steel reinforcement and waterproofing. (Incidentally, some of them revived the ancient ritual of animal sacrifice before reinforcing some of the foundations.)

Contractors are supposed to be accountable to the architect, who in turn should be accountable to the client. Contractors subcontract out particular jobs to a chain of other subcontractors in such a way that the interplay between the technicians and the craftsmen that we had proposed would have been impossible to manage. Public clients, whether government or corporations or cooperatives, are not really interested in construction innovation. Our park was no exception. The bureaucracy had its representative on the site, and this required a basic change in procedure. Instead of the contractor, the architect assumed responsibility for relations between technicians and craftsmen and left management in charge of supplies and the hiring, training, and organization of unskilled labor.

I cannot be a judge of my own work, but there is no doubt that it has already forged a link between the activity of building and the culture of the community at al-Sayyidah Zaynab.

10

Reflections on Technology and Development: A Cultural Perspective

HAMED IBRAHIM EL-MOUSLY

MY MOTIVATION in writing this chapter is my feeling that I possess a certain ability to live and to view the universe, the people and the hereafter in a distinctive way. My need to express such an ability gives me a sense of meaningfulness and fulfilment, not only in this life but in the afterlife as well. I also feel that my identity and my culture are now in danger. It is my duty to mobilize all my abilities to proceed on the way of self/cultural realization. To me, this is the aim of life.

INTRODUCTION

Why does the problem of bias (in terms of worldview, methods of research, and disciplines of knowledge) lie at the heart of our cultural and scientific interests? In spite of their "scientific death," many terms related to modernization, development, and technology are still commonly used. They are employed equally by Western governments and world institutions as well as by some of the Muslim heads of state, ministers, technocrats, and bureaucrats working in Muslim sovereign bodies, research centers, and universities. It has been demonstrated that such terms cannot be used in different political and cultural contexts without there being a change in their meaning. Attempts at development that are based on Western concepts have failed in Arab and Muslim countries, as well as in Third World countries across Asia, Africa, and Latin America. Insisting on the continued use of such terms is indicative of only one thing: they are intended to replace religion. Muslims are expected to *believe* in modernization and Western technology. It is presumed that this religion endows

Muslims with the hope of achieving welfare and luxury in the "paradise" that Muslims will enjoy if they follow the Western model of development. What is required, then, is to reveal or unveil this "new religion."

Furthermore, Muslims and their readers (who are assumed to represent the intelligentsia) are part and parcel of the crisis of Muslim societies. Muslims have all been subjected to the Western winds of change to varying degrees in the course of their cultural, scientific, and/or professional formation, whether at home or in Western societies. Assuming that the issue of choice is related more to society than to individuals, then Muslims have admittedly made many wrong choices under the deteriorating cultural, political, social, and economic conditions of our societies. They have opted for themselves rather than our societies. They have surrendered to the Western winds of change. They have turned into mere vessels into which various Western values, customs, attitudes, and disciplines are poured. Thus their minds have become a heterogeneous mixture of the modern/Western and traditional/Arab-Muslim cultures. The idea of mixture in itself is not hazardous; however, randomness and heterogeneity are, since they have obliterated the Muslim character and hindered Muslims from achieving their most sublime aim, which is to rebuild their nation based on an Islamic cultural perspective. Muslims have to change themselves first before they can change the world around them. They have to rebuild themselves before they can think of rebuilding their nation/society. They have to re-examine all the axioms, criteria and values which have governed their cultural, scientific and practical activities and which have been subjected to Western cultural bias.

The issue of bias is closely linked to the urgent matter of cultural independence. Time adds a dramatic dimension to the Muslims' treatment of both issues. The more time elapses, the higher the price they have to pay. As time passes, Muslims become increasingly subservient to the West, culturally, politically, and economically and are faced with more and more restrictive terms and conditions in their independent cultural enterprise. There will be more lost chances as long as they serve as clients of Western civilization, which further destroys their abilities to realize a cultural enterprise in the future. In short, Muslims are in one of the most serious and critical situations that they have ever encountered.

BASIC CONCEPTS

In this section we shall discuss some of the basic terms and concepts used in the chapter.

Culture is the totality of meanings, values, and relations that distinguish a given human group and that may be conveyed from one generation to another. In this sense, any culture is based on a certain view of life and the universe, and has its own justification for existence. It stems, in short, from a distinctive existential option. Culture is formed round a core of basic values and a distinct concept of the relations between human beings and the universe (the beliefs dimension), human beings and themselves, human beings and others (the patterns of social relations), humankind and the environment, humankind and time, humankind and knowledge, and so forth.

Though human communities may be similar in many aspects, they generally form distinct cultural structures.[1] The main differences among such structures do not stem from the elements composing them, since it is possible for distinct cultural patterns to have many elements in common. The main difference stems from the relative importance of each element within each culture, the function it performs, and the way it interacts with other elements in the same culture. It is possible for two cultural patterns to share a given element, though it may be dominant in one of them and recessive in the other. For instance, it may be argued that as a behavioral determinant, piety is present in Western culture just as it is in Arab/Muslim culture. However, it is hard to claim that such a feature has had the same pivotal role in determining the behavior of individuals in the West as it has in the Arab/Muslim world. Similarly, two cultures may share a certain element, though it may perform completely different roles in each of these cultures. What is of paramount significance, then, is the core of the culture concerned, i.e. the basic values and principles that govern and define life in that culture.

It is extremely difficult for the individual, group, or society/nation to be totally detached from its original cultural pattern and to adopt a foreign one.[2] (The degree of difficulty, in this context, increases as we move from the level of the individual towards that of the nation.) The process of a cultural shift requires the constant operation of a large number of foreign cultural elements for prolonged periods of time. If cultural alienation is the process in which a sector of society/nation is impelled to adopt externally imposed behavioral patterns, then it is too complex a process to take place completely. It is difficult to bring about total or basic transformations in all the behavioral characteristics of an individual so that he may adopt the incoming culture. In this context, a number of questions may be posed. How deeply are such behavioral transformations rooted in the individual's psyche? How long can they withstand various circumstances? How long can they endure?

It is usually the case that superficial behavioral changes spread faster than the corresponding changes in the individual's inner world or reality. It may be easy for a person to adopt the material manifestations of the Western way of life, represented, for instance, by styles of dressing, eating, housing, and transportation (the private motorcar). However, it would be difficult – even if one consciously desired it – to adopt the dominant values and principles governing Western life in the same way.

There are two possible explanations for this. First, there is what anthropologists call the "instinctive transferability" of some cultural elements.[3] Elements of culture, in this view, differ as regards their amenability to being transferred to other cultures. The elements that can be publicly expressed and imitated (such as action patterns and, to a lesser degree, production patterns) are the most transferable of cultural elements. These are followed by the dominant concepts at the conscious level in the foreign culture, which are hard to express directly in external behavior (even though they may exist through verbal behavior, such as the values and frameworks that organize relations among individuals and the different classes of society). The most difficult elements to transfer are, in this view, cultural values which are latent in the subconscious and "which the ordinary individual rarely attempts to express verbally, even to himself."[4] However, it is such values that form the point of departure for behavior in society. This latter category includes the basic philosophical biases which determine the relationships between human beings and the universe, nature, and other human beings, as well as the meaning and the aim of life. Diagram (1) is a simplified illustration of the levels of cultural structure in society/nation (note the direction of change from top to bottom, which is related to the ease of transferability).

Second, there is the method of transferring foreign cultural elements. The basic assumption here is teleology. The foreign culture imposes certain elements upon the conquered culture with a view to achieving a number of gains. This leads to a situation in which the conquered culture has contact only with selected elements of the incoming culture rather than with the whole set of elements. It is not logical for the incoming culture to give the conquered culture access to all its elements so that it may choose whatever it wishes.

Cultural invasion is the process by which a dominant culture attempts to subordinate another culture and deprive it of its independence. In this way, it can control and exploit that culture for the sake of its own pernicious development. Looked at from the inside, this process is a means of destroying integration and creating gaps in the structure of the conquered culture. Apart from any temporary gains that cannot survive any crisis, this process leads to the elimination of the vital creative potentials and the auto-dynamic abilities of the conquered culture, which increases its subordination to the dominant culture.

[*Diagram* 1]
LEVELS OF THE CULTURAL STRUCTURE IN SOCIETY/NATION

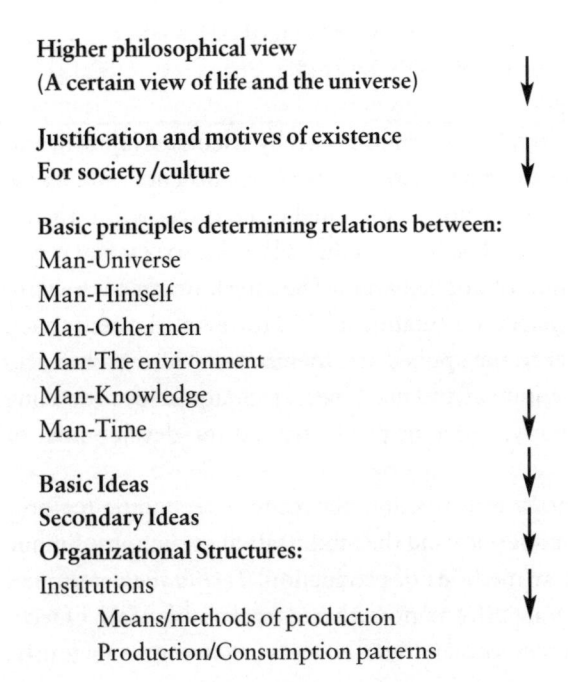

Higher philosophical view
(A certain view of life and the universe)

Justification and motives of existence
For society/culture

Basic principles determining relations between:
Man-Universe
Man-Himself
Man-Other men
Man-The environment
Man-Knowledge
Man-Time

Basic Ideas
Secondary Ideas
Organizational Structures:
Institutions
    Means/methods of production
    Production/Consumption patterns

As used in this chapter, the term "Western" does not refer to the geographical or geopolitical sense of the word. It is a common practice to describe capitalist European countries as "Western" and socialist countries as "Eastern."[5] However, the capitalist "West" and socialist "East" have much more in common than what is generally assumed (e.g., the philosophical view at the highly abstract level or the values governing the individual's life). Perhaps the only difference between them, in fact, lies in the social mechanisms used and the distribution of social roles for realizing the Western model of modernization as well as the mechanism of distributing social resources. (The point can be illustrated by comparing the historical role of the class of capitalist entrepreneurs in Western European countries with that of the state in Eastern European countries in spreading modern technological achievements and "revolutionizing" the methods of production.) In either case, the term "Western" means applying the dominant principles and values as they appeared within the context of Western culture looked at from a historical perspective (in ancient Greece and the Roman Empire) and which were revived in Europe after the Renaissance.[6]

WE AND TECHNOLOGY: A CRITIQUE OF SOME COMMON TERMS

The Term "Technology"

Since the term "technology" is commonly used by scientists, laymen, and politicians alike,[7] its meaning has grown increasingly obscure[8] and its use associated with a kind of "halo," which makes its discussion difficult. This term appeared in English as early as the 17th Century,[9] when it was used to mean "discussion of applied arts." The Greek origin of the term *technologia* means "systematic treatment."[10] However, the term soon came to be used to refer to the applied arts themselves. The term has also been used to denote equipment and machinery, techniques for producing equipment and machinery, different products, and the development of such techniques.

It is necessary to draw a distinction between the technique for producing a commodity or a service and the modification of such a technique in order to arrive at new methods of production. *Technique* determines the method of production performance, whereas the modification of technique and finding new methods are referred to as *technology*. Obviously, technique in general is a product of technology. It seems that the high speed at which production techniques change in the industrial Western countries has contributed to blurring the distinction between "techniques" and "technology" (which is the activity that produces techniques). This is particularly true with the gradual disappearance of the social/professional barriers between those working in the field of technology (research and development of human resources) and those who prepare work systems according to the new techniques for pilot operation and production of the first prototypes.

It is similarly necessary to distinguish between *technique* and *equipment* (whose definition is sometimes extended to cover all the material elements that are necessary for production, such as previously prepared raw material, machinery, tools, installations, and buildings). In order to be applied, any technique needs material media that are prepared in accordance with the requirements of the technique itself. With the rapidly growing scientific and technological development, an increasing number of the components of technique are being incorporated into equipment/machinery, and even in previously prepared material. Technology, then, is an activity that aims at modifying production techniques or developing new techniques.

TECHNOLOGY: A HISTORICAL LOOK

The previous section was intended to show, first, that there is a difference between technique and technology. Technique is strongly linked to the activity of production itself (any production activity is performed through a certain technique). Technology is an activity that takes place in the mind and in the physical reality at a level higher than that of production, with a view to modifying or developing other techniques of production. Second, I wanted to emphasize that the suffix *–ology* in the word *technology* does not necessarily mean that technology is related to the scientific experimental method which has been dominant in the West for the last three centuries. Such a misconception may lead some to think that technology, as a human activity, is foreign in character and in origin. In many popular conceptions, technology has become a foreign "commodity" that can be purchased and imported. This latter point is elaborated below.

Let us begin with what is general to humankind as a species, or as one of God's creatures. It is known that one of the main differences between humankind and animals is that animals are controlled by a strict genetic program that determines their actions and activity, while human beings are born with a very flexible genetic program. It can even be said that man, unlike animals, does not have any fixed action patterns. The only role of heredity is to transfer general features representing the raw materials for an individual's abilities, skills, and character. Man's behavior is primarily determined by his interaction with the cultural environment.[11] Here comes the role of awareness (or consciousness) in determining man's actions. While animals lead only an external life, man leads both external and internal lives. Man interacts with the concrete world, apprehends external stimuli through his senses, classifies and stores them in his memory, then deals with them through his mind and imagination, thus developing new concepts that do not exist in the world of reality. Then he turns to reality and reorganizes it according to such new concepts. Here, in particular, lies the technological component in man's mental activity, both at the conscious and the subconscious levels. Technology, in this sense, has always accompanied human development in all its stages.

The above concept may become clearer if one contemplates the relationship between man and his body. For instance, the great developments that accompanied the appearance of different languages and the perfection of the pronunciation system (a process which was completed over several centuries) could not have occurred without the presence of an important technological component. Where there are tools (the tongue and the oral cavity), techniques (mechanisms of pronunciation), and modification of such techniques (development of languages), there is technology. Similarly, we cannot imagine the great development of primitive folk arts, such as dancing, in many cultures without an accompanying technological component (in the broad sense of the word *technology*).

Let us follow the path of technology or technological activity over the ages. We may regard the Industrial Revolution and its ensuing massive technological innovations as the threshold between two distinctive periods of technological development. Before the Industrial Revolution, technology had been an accidental activity mainly governed by mere coincidence. Some techniques had remained without any significant change for long periods of time. Technological development had been based primarily on the experience accumulated over long periods of production activity and gained by some natural experiments, some of which were planned while most were the product of coincidence. The period of the Industrial Revolution witnessed rapid acceleration in technological development in which science played no role. The economic and political conditions at that time (the colonization of the New and Old World and the availability of unprecedented financial resources, services, and markets) offered great impetus to technological development. At the same time, it was technology that provided impetus to scientific activity. The enormous increase in the production of textiles that resulted from technological innovations in equipment caused a demand for artificial dye, thus using science as an aid to increase productivity. Similarly, the appearance of the steam engine coupled with the development of new important fields for its application provided impetus to scientific research in the areas of gas dynamics (discovering the general law of gases).

Science continued to play the role of a catalyst until around the mid-19th Century, when industries owing their existence to science began to appear (such as the chemical and electrical industries). Such industries established a new pattern for the science-technology relationship. Since then, scientific activity and its products have become important pillars for technology. With accelerated progress, there is more reliance upon science. Technological activity turns into planned activity performed by specialized institutions, which are based mainly on science, as well as accumulated experience (though coincidence may still have a role in this system).

To sum up, just as some projects are delivered to us ready made, so it seems that some concepts are passed on to us in the same way. They are exported to us readily packaged for political and social use rather than for technical use. In any case, we need to learn to distinguish between "technique" and "technology." Technique is strongly linked to the production activity itself, representing, as it were, its "neurological system." Technology is a more abstract pattern of human action, which is independent of production activity and of science. For science, in the final analysis, aims at reaching the truth, whereas technology aims at changing reality. This is not to deny that technology underwent a qualitative change in its relation to human activity after the Industrial Revolution, which brought it closer to science. We can clearly distinguish between traditional technologies and modern, Western technology.[12] The former are governed by the accumulation of acquired experience and are based on an ideology that revolves around considerations of balance, settlement, and survival. The latter is governed by scientific research and is based on a rationality that revolves around profit and capital accumulation. In this way, we can conceive of technology as a basic feature of culture and of human progress (Diagram 2), as involving potential for the individual and the group to interact creatively with the surrounding environment (in the broad sense of the word "environment"), as a method of dealing with reality, and as a special kind of human activity.

Such a conception of technology leads to a number of conclusions. First, there can be science without there being technology; there can be intensive scientific research without any technological outcome relating to changing and interacting with the reality of production. Second, there can be technologies without science (with some reservation), i.e. without a consciousness of the abstract scientific theory or general scientific laws governing the phenomenon concerned. It is hard to believe that those unknown technologists, who innovated many important techniques without which the great achievements of civilizations would not have been realized, were not aware of at least some aspects of scientific theory through the accumulation of observations and experiences in addition to intuition. The trouble may be that the scientific vision of those ingenious "old technologists" was personally associated with them. It was not written separately in the form of laws or theories. Third, the discovery of scientific facts that explain the operation of a given technique (as in the case of the general theory of gases and the steam engine) or the converse situation, where the technique is based on science (as in case of the chemical industry), allows a higher degree of control of the production activity. This in turn allows a qualitative transformation in productivity and in the spread of the technique applied. It also permits us to make full use of the potentials made available by the technique applied.

As a society and as a nation, the Arabo-Islamic world has not yet been socially or culturally prepared for the scientific and technological changes required for entering the 21st Century. Therefore, it needs to prepare itself for the hard task of undertaking changes, beginning with its members changing themselves until they change the reality around them. It follows that the Arabo-Islamic world ought to form its own concept of technology as an axis of social and cultural change that operates synergistically with other axes, rather than a ready-made "ticket" which it buys to catch the train of Western modernization, leaving behind the luggage of the past. Does it not sometimes perceive modernization in such a simplistic way?

TECHNOLOGY TRANSFER

The term "technology transfer" has been one of the most commonly used terms in the field of development and in discussing the relationship between the North and the South, the former being technologically advanced and the latter technologically backward. (The "South" refers mainly to Asian and African countries, though admittedly the position in Africa is interim. Asian countries have made considerable progress, which began with Japan and China. Now we have what are called the "newly industrializing countries" or "the four little dragons," i.e., South Korea, Taiwan, Hong Kong, and Singapore.) As used today, the term is associated with two serious fallacies:

(1) The term assumes a one-way transfer relation between two parties, one active (the giver) and the other passive (the recipient). It also assumes that the process of transfer is similar to filling up an empty vessel whose shape is unchanging throughout the process. The most serious implication of such an assumption is that the recipient does not possess any technology. The common understanding of technology transfer does not take into account the idea of interaction with given local technological capabilities. Rather, it assumes that there is a technological "vacuum" that has to be filled.

(2) The term assumes that technology is an "object" that can be transferred from one social-cultural context to another. This is totally untrue. Many experiments in several Third World countries confirm that technology is non-transferable. According to an important piece of research,[13] technological ability is divided into four stages:

1. Acquisition (looking for and evaluating available alternatives, negotiating purchase, designing the factory, manufacturing equipment, installing, and pilot running).
2. Operation (operating the factory, maintenance, product quality control, stock control, and human resources training).
3. Adaptation (assimilating technology or having the ability to

[Diagram 2]
VIEW OF LIFE AND THE STRUCTURE OF VALUES ASSOCIATED WITH A PATTERN OF WESTERN MODERNIZATION

- Man as the center of the universe

- There is no life except the one we are living (Secularism)

- Existential refusal of death; evading death as a truth, a process, and a natural end to the individual's life

- Symbol as a quantity only – as a measure of productivity, self-accomplishment, and mobility. Time as a commodity that can be consumed or exchanged.

- Desire to evade the pain associated with realizing the truth of death (the death of an individual or the ones he/she loves). Hence the loss of desire and ability to identify with others, which may cause pain. Falling in love with oneself: self-worship

- The worship of life as an idol, and hence the worship of youth, strength, and vitality.

- Tendency to compensate as a mechanism for adapting to the above situation. Speed as virtue. Tendency to overestimate pragmatism: power, material profit, material luxury, sensual pleasure, and intense consumption.

- A way of life that ignores death and acts for distracting humankind from its truth by all possible means; its priority is to achieve the highest degree of material luxury. Resources, however, are limited by nature.

- Competition and conflict as basic values; Strength (violence) as a basic means to settling conflicts; Aggression as a favourable moral feature and value.

- *Collapse of relations of dialog, co-operation, social solidarity, and mercy.*

imitate products and make minor modifications in the process of operation).
4. Innovation (performing research and development, making substantial modifications in products or creating new ones, making substantial changes in processes, innovating new processes, inventions).

The above research affirms that it is possible to transfer elements of technological ability only at the stages of acquisition and operation. Unless great effort is exerted by the Arabo-Islamic world to build its own technological abilities, it will never be possible for it to reach the stages of adaptation and innovation, which are decisive for technological independence. It seems that the confusion between technique and technology is one of the causes of the fallacy of technology transferability.[14]

Before the Industrial Revolution, the dominant trend in Europe had been the transfer of techniques (which are indeed transferable with varying degrees of precision) from one culture or society to another. They had been transferred through acquired knowledge, through tools and machines, through the products themselves sometimes, and through the semimanufactured raw materials. In most cases, the transfer of such elements did not have any detrimental effect on the recipient cultures. The local socio-cultural fabric usually assimilated the external elements so that they ultimately became integral parts of it. It seems that the development, transfer, and assimilation of techniques occurred so slowly that the homogeneity of the recipient cultures was not affected. In this way, many technical innovations were transferred among different societies and cultural arenas. Examples of such innovations are the military carriage (from the Hyksos), the mandolin (from the Greeks), and the water wheel (from the Romans). There are also different techniques of production in different fields, such as construction and agriculture.

Sometimes, however, the technological abilities themselves were transferred through the movement of individuals and groups from one society to another. But the recipient socio-cultural fabric was generally able to absorb the incoming elements so that they worked according to its own laws and in harmony with its cultural structure.

The new variable that accompanied the Industrial Revolution, which became more effective with the scientific technological revolution, was the enormous acceleration in technological development. New techniques appeared, then were quickly replaced with even newer ones. The process occurs so dynamically that the assumed age of any technique (its appearance, spread, and moral obsolescence)[15] is continuously decreasing. In this context, the dominant attitude in Third World countries (especially Arab and Muslim ones) is to formulate and implement development plans that are based on the transfer of techniques from the industrial Western societies or from Japan. This attitude leads to a two-fold dilemma:

- The social and cultural effects of transferring huge production structures, such as agricultural, industrial, and service production systems which have not been adapted to fit the socio-cultural fabric of the recipient society.

- The "nihilistic" attitude, which adopts the Western pattern of development and considers it possible to realize Western goals in our societies by imitating the industrial Western societies. This attitude establishes cultural, political, and economic subordination to the West. It can be illustrated diagrammatically as follows:

Sense of cultural inferiority
↓
Adopting the Western pattern of development
↓
Fascination with all that is produced by the West and all new ways of life
↓
Cultural subordination to the West
↓
Loss of self-confidence

As for the technical aspect of this attitude, the fast-changing rhythm of production techniques in different fields turns what is generally called "technology transfer" into a sort of addiction. This is exactly the relationship between Third World countries, particularly the Arab and Muslim ones,[16] and the industrial Western countries as well as the world capitalist market in general.

There is another important conclusion yielded by the above treatment of the terms technology and technology transfer. If the Arabo-Islamic world considered the failure of its development plans, it would stop asking itself questions such as: Have we succeeded in transferring Western technology to our societies? Or rather, have we succeeded in transferring sufficient Western technology to our societies? How do we improve terms of negotiation regarding technology transfer? How do we secure the financial resources necessary for transfer? Questions would then take a different direction. The Arabo-Islamic world would ask itself: If technology in the final analysis is a human ability that aims at changing the world, then where are our technological abilities? Why have such abilities abated in our case and flourished in the case of other nations? Why do we not feel endangered by the widening chasm between the technological and scientific abilities of the world's dominant cultural powers and our own abilities? What does this signify to us? Why do we not sense this imminent danger?

If, on the level of institutions, groups, and individuals, technology depends on examining the conditions of production and modifying the techniques used, then questions such as the following arise: Why do we not innovate technology? Does the problem lie in disloyalty (failure, or rather unwillingness, to identify psychologically or mentally with the conditions of production, whether in the factory, the field, the service institution, or the governmental department)? What are the reasons? Does the problem lie in the fact that we do not possess the motivation necessary to develop the conditions of production and which are simultaneously compatible with the cultural structure of society? Is it that the individual's behavioral motives are contradictory?

However, these questions could assume a more positive orientation, represented by the following: How can we assimilate technology as a potential and a feature of our cultural structure? How can we revive such motives and values as "love of work," "perfection," "learning," "diligence," "innovation," and "creativity," which are essential to technological vitality? How can they be incorporated into our cultural structure? What are the policies that the state should adopt in order to build up the technological abilities of our society/nation? What are the necessary resources (e.g., capital, knowledge, information, equipment, abilities, and skills)? What is the role of factory, farm, school, university, mosque, and family in this context?

THE "ARABO-ISLAMIC WORLD" AND THE WESTERN MODEL OF DEVELOPMENT

The 20th Century witnessed the spread of the notion of development as a prerequisite to the progress and welfare of peoples. In the 1950s, following World War II, this idea gained much ground in industrial Western societies.[17] There arose a concept of development which made economic growth, in the quantitative sense, the highest goal of society.[18] In that same decade, many Third World countries gained independence and embarked on development. The common feeling at that time was that "all roads lead to Rome" and that there was only one model of development for all countries irrespective of where to begin or how fast to proceed. The following decades (since the 1960s) have witnessed intensive endeavors by many Third World countries to achieve development according to the Western model. The term "developing countries" has been commonly used to refer to those Third World countries which adopt the Western model of development. Compared with the term "developed," which refers to the industrial Western countries, the term "developing" reflects the view underlying it. It is one way and one goal; the Third World's present is the Western countries' past. All the Third World has to do is to follow the ready Western model.

Such attempts have obviously not achieved their goals.[19] Most Third World countries are now suffering from large debts, not to mention the enormous socio-cultural and environmental problems resulting from such development attempts. Therefore, many countries that tried the Western model of development have decided to take the opposite approach and return to their indigenous cultural norms. Some countries have already taken such a stance. It is also being adopted by an increasing number of intellectuals as well as members of many Arab Muslim societies.

There are important responses on the part of some international organizations concerned with development (such as UNESCO and other UN agencies).[20] Such responses come under the label of "taking into consideration the cultural dimension of development." However, the attitude toward "others" (i.e., toward societies not belonging to the Western culture) is not clear. There are justifiable fears that the increasing concern with the cultural dimension may be confined to areas such as the following:

- Employing the mechanisms and specific features of the other cultures to articulate social models of modernization according to the Western model.
- Supplying Western cultural powers with information about other cultures, assimilating such information to support Western models and thus enabling them to further destroy such cultures.

As for the view that rejects Eurocentrism, it admits other cultures' right to live, flourish, coexist and positively interact with other cultures, recognizing that this is the true path to human progress, peace, and civilization. However, this orientation has not yet crystallized into a clear stance.

Factors and mechanisms associated with adopting the Western model of development
If one considers the Arab/Muslim societies over the last four decades, one will observe that they have undergone enormous changes. New social, economic, and political institutions have appeared. Lifestyles and consumption patterns have changed dramatically. These changes, however, have not occurred within the framework of a modernization process that is endogenously initiated, but rather within the framework of adopting the Western model of development and subordination to the West (be it socialist or capitalist). This poses the following questions: *What factors have facilitated the adoption of this model? What are the mechanisms through which this model with its various dimensions has spread in Arab/Muslim societies?*

(1) Loss of self-confidence in the cultural sense. Such a loss of self-confidence leads to indiscriminate fascination with Western civilization and all its symbols. It may even result from Arab/Muslim societies having a sense of inferiority towards the West and in having passive feelings towards themselves. It may also lead to a desire to deny all that is traditional or inherited[21] while flocking toward all that is "fashionable," provided that it is a "Western" product.

It does not matter what the nature of the product is; it could be a consumer good, a production tool, or even a computer. What matters is to purchase Western goods, not because of their original function, whether as production or consumer goods, but because they function as "Western makeup" or Western cultural symbols associated with concepts such as modernization, modernity, and progress.

(2) The presence of certain cultural elements or tendencies in Arab/Muslim societies[22] that represent a propitious cultural background for the predominance of the above stance toward Western culture. This stance, in its turn, fosters such elements or tendencies. It can thus be argued that the spread of such products supports some values and behavioral patterns that reinforce their dissemination. This need not be beneficial to the society/nation's development. On the contrary, it usually acts against such development, if its historical dimension is taken into account. For instance, the Western consumption patterns may result in supporting the values of individualism in a society that urgently needs the values of collectivism to effect drastic changes in it. They may support the values of pragmatism, earthly pleasure, and welfare while the society in fact needs the value of self-sacrifice. They may support the values of power centralization at a time when decentralization is needed. They may create acute social differences at a time when social rapprochement is needed. It is not hard, then, to see how this can be detrimental to society. There are many examples that illustrate this point:

- The way in which Arabs/Muslims receive many Western technological products in their society can be regarded as a revival of the traditions of magic in their heritage. Many words and expressions, such as *the latest achievements in science and technology, electronic, automatic,* and *by computer,* are used in mass media, by many officials, and by lay people, in a way that suggests that there is a magical power that can very easily serve humankind. All that one has to do is to press a button to launch that giant magical power. Such a "magical" reception of the products of Western technology, accompanied by a lack of understanding of their design and performance, is indeed a revival of the tale of *Aladdin and the Magical Lamp.* Contrary to what many people think, the current stance towards Western technology supports irrationality in the Arabs/Muslims' views of life and their economic choices.

- The rapid growth of industrialization in Egypt in the 1960s, and particularly during the first (indeed, the "only") five-year plan (1959–1964), which was associated with establishing the industrial public sector on a modern basis and accomplishing giant projects using Western technological products, can be regarded as a revival of ancient Egyptian traditions. The concentration of hundreds of industrial installations with their Westernized organizational patterns in the suburb of Helwan represented a powerful move towards centralization of power in the political and social sense. Furthermore, the shift in the socio-cultural structure of Egypt, which was associated with the domination and support of technocrats, led in its turn to accepting more Western technological products in the fields of production, infrastructure projects, and services that suited the process of centralization in management and administration. From this perspective, the industrialization plan of Egypt in the 1960s can be viewed as a revival of the tradition of centralization at a historical moment when society was looking forward to effecting more changes in its structure. Therefore, it was in need of decentralization and democracy rather than centralization and technocracy.

- The spread of many Western technological products in the areas of consumption, communication, and transport is associated with assigning new forms to some of the dominant values of the socio-cultural fabric of the local society. Such values are thus expressed differently in order to cope with the spread of new Western technological products. For instance, one of the values that are dominant in the community of Arish in North Sinai is vainglory. Before the Israeli occupation of Sinai in 1967, when the community of Arish consisted of a number of large families bound together by strong ties, this value was commonly expressed through generosity, which was translated socially into redistribution of wealth and social solidarity.[23]

During the Israeli occupation, the value of vainglory took different forms. It was expressed through intensive, individualized consumption of products such as private cars, consumer durables, and clothes. These new forms of expressing the same value were more compatible with the Israeli technological products in the field of consumer goods. Looked at from the inside, however, these new forms of expressing vainglory were not well-suited to the socio-cultural structure of Arish; in fact, they led, together with other factors, to the disintegration of that very structure.

(3) The fallacy that imported capitalist products and equipment represent the main path to progress and enhancement of production has led to a lack of compatibility between human beings and machines, whether at the stage of selecting equipment or at the stage of training in operation and maintenance. This situation has resulted in the absence of a positive relationship between the technicians and their tools of production. Such a relationship, if present, would make them more careful about using and maintaining their tools. As a result, many scientific and technological achievements incorporated in the imported equipment have not been truly assimilated by our society. Similarly, the potentials of the techniques used in production are normally not exhausted before moving to more modern techniques,[24] a fact which has reduced the technological revenue – or surplus value – of the process of importation, which in turn has reinforced the Arabs/Muslims' position as "consumers" of Western technological products.

There are a number of factors that have contributed to the spread of Western technological consumer products and the Western consumption pattern as a whole. Among these is the adoption of this pattern by the higher social classes, as a result of which it has become a symbol of social distinction that can be easily purchased by the lower classes. Let us assume, for instance, that some Western commodities (say, clothes) have started to spread in some of the Egyptian poorer areas, such as Boulak al-Dakrour, Imbaba, and Matariya. Would the adoption of such commodities by the lower social classes help in their spread among other classes of society? Another example is the spread of the popular "galabias" made in the village of Kirdasa among the higher social classes in Egypt after they became popular among the foreign tourists visiting Egypt, which seems to have been a "certificate" of the validity of such products. History is replete with examples like this, the clearest of which is perhaps the spread of the European style of furniture in Egypt.[25]

There are two factors that led to the domination of the Western pattern of consumption in the societies of the area. The first of these was the call to reduce differences among the classes in a non-revolutionary atmosphere, yet without originality and creativity on the part of those who adopted this slogan. An important example here is the 23rd July Revolution in Egypt, whose view of social freedom was rather superficial. According to this view, the poor should obtain the same commodities as the rich, however low their quality may be. The Revolution coined slogans such as the "popular dwelling," the "popular suit," the "popular refrigerator," and the "popular car," which on the whole flirted with the consumption aspirations of large classes of the populace and ultimately led to tying the people to the Western lifestyle and consumption pattern in general. In fact, it helped achieve this goal with greater efficiency than any Western propaganda could have hoped to. The distribution of popular flats on a large scale entailed putting an end to the "large house" that had contained an extended family and which represented an authentic cultural formula characterized by several advantages.[26] Moreover, it accustomed people to the Western housing pattern and the lifestyle of the isolated nuclear family with all its psycho-social disadvantages and consumption patterns that are nationally inappropriate. It also stimulated people's ambition to have a similar home but of a better quality. The same applies to the clothes, the refrigerator, and the car, which led to the spread of the Western consumption pattern among all classes of society.[27] This may be one of the main disadvantages of that phase.[28] The second of these factors is the income increases that accompanied the oil price rises beginning in 1974, and which had a strong impact upon all the societies of the region through temporary and permanent emigration of labor. This in turn led to the spread of the Western pattern of consumption in the whole area.

SOME EFFECTS OF ADOPTING THE WESTERN DEVELOPMENT MODEL

The adoption of the Western development model in Arab/Muslim society created unbalanced exchange relations that turned its members into customers of all the consumer goods, durables, tools of production, techniques, and services produced by Western culture. It is interesting to observe not the change itself, but the way in which it was effected. Change did not take place through people's self-development, awareness, and participation. Rather, it was a kind of replacement of the established native-cultural structure, which led to the disintegration of the socio-cultural fabric of the nation. Here are some examples:

The fast spread of Western consumption patterns, particularly since the 1970s (represented, for example, by the modern flat, the private car, and European furniture), has led to the disintegration of the socio-cultural fabric in very large sectors of the countryside and local communities in small towns. This, accordingly, has destroyed the rich production potentials of that fabric. The materialistic components of the Western consumption patterns could not be competed with by the local consumption pattern that was provided by the local production structures. Furthermore, the process of replacing the local component of the consumption pattern with the foreign component was in fact a replacement of a multi-functional component with a mono-functional one. A ready example is the traditional home that had been dominant in Arish, North Sinai, before the Israeli occupation. That type of house, which was inhabited by an extended family consisting of many nuclear families, featured abundant craft activities that included weaving, pottery, and the making of palm-leaf products. It also provided a rich socio-cultural life. However, when the Arishi house was replaced with a house of the Israeli type (during occupation) or a modern flat in a flat block (after the return of Egyptian administration), it lost its rich productive and socio-cultural functions for a mono-functional component (only for non-productive nuclear family living). Since the process of replacement is in one way or another exogenously imposed (i.e., from outside the local community) rather than stemming from the local society within the framework of a comprehensive process of transformation, there was no attempt to find new forms to perform the vacant functions resulting from the above replacement process. The result was many voids in the socio-cultural structure of the local society, ultimately leading to its disintegration and the destruction of its productive potentials.

Nature is among the victims of this replacement of the local consumption pattern with the Western one. As a result of rushing towards Western alternatives, dozens of elements of the flora of the local communities, which used to play a major role in the production of locally manufactured commodities, are ignored. The result is the total destruction of flora in the area (the palm beach of Arish, North Sinai, for example, is on the verge of disappearance). It is not simply a matter of losing important economic resources. What is more serious is that the natives of the area are alienated from their cultural identity, for the psychological association with nature is one of the most important dimensions of cultural affiliation.

A similar situation holds when foreign production systems replace local ones. This kind of replacement is usually associated with a process of socio-cultural disintegration of the local community. For example, land in the areas adjacent to Mersa Matrouh (north of Egypt) is not only a factor of production, but also a source of socio-cultural equilibrium for the local community. The whole of the Western Desert can in fact be viewed as a chessboard of tribal formations. Land there is distributed with precision among different tribes according to established rules that have been applied for many generations. Land is thus not considered the private property of the individual or even of the tribe; rather, it has a socio-economic function. The rules governing the distribution of land there are very important for the preservation of the environment.[29] Water in the Farafra Oasis in the Western Desert of Egypt is not merely an economic resource; for the socio-cultural fabric of the community of the oasis is strongly tied to the water springs there. The distribution of water is one of the most important functions of the socio-economic fabric in Farafra. Thus, the introduction of Western systems of production, which have a narrow, strictly functional view of the resources of the local community, deprives the socio-cultural fabric of some of its vital roles without offering alternative forms to perform such roles.

Mass media, particularly TV, have destructive effects on the socio-cultural fabric of the local community. The problem lies not in the scientific principle used,[30] but in the socio-cultural model represented by TV as it is currently used, i.e., as a means of transmitting information, and hence of forming human beings' awareness. Human beings in this case are viewed as individuals or rather as objects that are completely manageable by the socio-political system controlling TV. The relationship here is a vertical, mono-directional one, where information is conveyed as ready-made packages to individuals in the form of monolog. When family members sit in front of the TV, the live dialogs between them turn into monolog relations between the TV and each one of them in isolation. At the same time, the disintegration of the social fabric leads to the spread of an isolationist pattern of social life, which in turn creates a new need, namely, the need for the TV set. Individuals who spend a great deal of their time in isolation, be they mothers, fathers, or children, establish strong relations with the TV (or the video, the radio, etc.), which gradually turns into an alternative to live communication with other people.[31]

Western means of transportation usually have a detrimental effect on the socio-cultural fabric of local communities, especially in the countryside. Place in such communities, be it the house, the road, etc., is an expression of a particular socio-cultural logic. Such logic is extremely sensitive to considerations of privacy and therefore it allows a gradual movement from private to public space. When wide asphalt roads are extended through any village, this logic is mercilessly destroyed. In addition, asphalt roads lead to the presence of private cars, which are associated with a strict division of the road between those who possess private cars and those who don't. Moreover, the function of the road changes as well. Instead of being a place of work, learning, fun, social gathering, and interaction with nature (as in many rural or desert areas, e.g. the Farafra Oasis in the Western Desert of Egypt), it turns into a mono-functional place. Thus the asphalt road eventually represents a place where individuals compete by force (expressed by speed, headlights, and horn sounds).

The ability of a society to defend itself against any form of cultural invasion (one of which being the spread of Western technological products) depends on the strength of the social solidarity that allows society to control its individuals' behavior. On the other hand, the control functions performed by the socio-cultural fabric are balanced by other functions – those of satisfying the basic material and spiritual needs. However, the replacement of local means of satisfying material needs with foreign ones (e.g., consumer products of Western technology) deprives the socio-cultural fabric of the local community of its means of satisfying both material and spiritual needs. According to the holistic approach of the local community and traditional technologies, the satisfaction of material needs is strongly linked to that of spiritual needs; there aren't clear boundaries between them. Thus the equilibrium between the control and the satisfaction functions of the socio-cultural fabric collapses. This in turn leads to the collapse of the legitimacy of the control functions of that fabric, which weakens the society's solidarity and its ability to resist the further spread of Western technological products.

Official education is one of the main factors that lead to the disintegration of local communities, the loss of their cultural distinction, and the destruction of much of their traditional knowledge and technological experience. For instance, the organizational structures of the official university education in Egypt are mostly distorted copies of those of Western societies. Similarly, courses and methods of teaching are literally copied from their Western counterparts. Perhaps the main difference between them is merely due to a time lag; the current courses are old compared with the Western ones. It is not strange, then, that our official university education institutions do not benefit from the rich heritage of education in our culture (e.g., al-Azhar, the first university in the world). Therefore, it is not surprising that there is no reference to the nation's heritage in the fields of science and technology in an educational atmosphere that glorifies Western achievements and abilities in such areas. Furthermore, scientific research in its current form in educational institutions is mostly isolated from the problems of society and imitates Western institutions in the selection and conduct of scientific research. This pattern of education has produced a kind of educated people who are unable to interact with their socio-cultural environment. For the language of science, which is often one of the signs of social distinction in Egypt, is the wall that isolates our educated people from the reality of their nation and society. The educated people's failure to communicate with the ordinary people in a comprehensible language is not simply a formal issue. Rather, it is the issue of the legitimacy of science in Egypt. The chasm between the educated and the uneducated in our society will remain unbridgeable as long as the educated people carry out their scientific activity within organizational and cultural frameworks that are alien to their local counterparts.

Official education, with its extreme centralization (at the school and university levels), is also unable to sense the cultural differences between different provinces and areas. The ideal that such education establishes is the bureaucratic or technocratic personality rather than that of the social reformer, which is probably more suitable for our socio-cultural fabric. Thus, from the local perspective, official education (at the school and university levels) represents a centrifugal force that alienates the educated youths from their cultural environment and pushes them to large cities, where the Western lifestyle, which is more compatible with the official education structure, is dominant. The rich scientific and technological cultural heritage of local communities is never examined, modified, or revived over different generations. This increases the gap between the stagnant traditional technology and modern Western technology, making the former inferior to the latter. This in turn creates an increasing need for Western technological products.

In this way, life according to the Western model of development represents continuous training in alienation due to:

1. Working with individuals who have one-dimensional work relations with each other in a market-oriented production activity;
2. Living in isolated nuclear (and birth-controlled, of course) families, in identical small flats in high buildings;
3. Hectic rushes on consumer goods and durable, which vary more with each passing day;
4. Diminution of the time allocated for maintaining social relations and learning;
5. Gradual captivation by mass information media, which continuously feed citizens with news and events without giving them any real opportunity to participate in such events;
6. Walking in crowded streets full of strangers and cars, which intensifies one's sense of helplessness and reinforces one's condition as an indifferent viewer of life.

All the above leads to the ongoing disintegration of the local communities in the area under the influence of Western technological patterns.

The disintegration of the socio-cultural fabric of society under the influence of modernization in the Western sense, together with the loss (or dissolution) of cultural identity, simply means that the moral and spiritual foundation of life, as known in that society, has been demolished. This creates a profound lack of self-confidence and loss of inner security, which leads to a hectic search for external means of self-assertion. In the absence of a real sense of identity (which is necessarily cultural), and given the disintegration of character, individuals are inclined toward compensatory rather than integrated action patterns. In such a case, individuals do not seek harmony and coordination in all areas of life, but rather seek compensation for what they have lost in one area with what they can gain in another. This behavioral pattern, which is an expression of "cultural schizophrenia," lies behind the spread of some extravagant and illogical

Western consumption patterns and new patterns of delinquency (e.g., drug addiction and the spread of crime) in many societies in the area.

DEVELOPMENT OR CULTURAL RESURRECTION?

It is obvious from the above that adopting the Western model of development means, first, accepting the formula of Western modernization as it is, including Western political, social, economic, and cultural institutions and the dominant division of labor and lifestyles regardless of the resulting social, cultural, and environmental cost. Second, it means taking the industrial Western countries as the only model to follow, and thus turning Arabs/Muslims into followers, rather than students, of Western culture. There is a major difference between the two positions. The student's position is a temporary one (some students even surpass their teachers). The follower's position, on the other hand, is assumed to be permanent.

What does this signify at a higher level of abstraction? It is known that one of the main functions of cultures is to produce and reproduce values (i.e., to revive old values and give them new content which is in harmony with new spatio-temporal contexts). In addition, one of the main criteria for judging the originality and vitality of social and cultural changes and revolutions is their ability to produce values. Given the above, what does the follower's position (that of following the Western model of development and imitating the West) mean? It simply means deprivation of one of the main functions of culture, i.e. production of values. Such deprivation not only leads to the loss of cultural distinction and originality, but also entails the loss of the vital energy that is necessary for great achievements. Values are the keys to great social and cultural potentials. Deprivation of the opportunity or ability to produce values will have a direct impact on material and intellectual production in various fields. This will ultimately turn us into a mere spatial extension or suburb of Western culture.

NEED TO ABANDON THE WESTERN MODEL OF DEVELOPMENT

There is an urgent need to abandon attempts to adopt the Western model of development. Such a model is undesirable because it is closely associated with the Western formula of modernization, which stems from a secularist view of life that puts humankind at the center of the universe and denies the afterlife.

The existentialist motives behind the Western model of development aim at achieving maximum luxury for humankind as the highest goal of life. According to such motives, the inevitable conflict between the above goal and scarcity of resources is not settled through self-control or reconciliation, but through employing science and technology to further control nature, and also through competition at the social and international levels without regard for environmental or socio-cultural problems which arise as a result. Perhaps this view is reflected in the terrifying polarity between countries that possess enormous scientific and technological abilities, in addition to nuclear arsenals that could destroy the world several times over, and other countries whose populations are threatened with starvation. Indeed, income levels in developed countries are a hundred times more than those in developing countries.[32]

In addition, the Western development model represents an unrepeatable phenomenon. The success of this model depended on unrepeatable historical conditions: the spread of European imperialism, the colonization of the old and the new worlds, the unprecedented accumulation of material wealth,[33] the availability of labor and raw materials at cheap prices, and the presence of large markets for European products with almost no competition. At the same time, it entailed a high social and cultural cost which has been paid by some social strata of Western society itself as well as many Third World societies.

Furthermore, this model, as scientific research increasingly affirms, is incompatible with the biosphere. Western technology, with which the model is associated, uses natural cycles only marginally. At the same time, it unjustifiably exhausts many non-renewable resources.[34] On the other hand, the employment of such technology results in waste that is incompatible with the biosphere.[35] As such, they threaten some natural cycles that are necessary for preserving and reproducing the conditions needed by vegetable, animal, and human life.[36] Scientific evidence increasingly affirms that the Western model and technology are not compatible with the biosphere, whether as regards the use of natural resources or environmental pollution. Therefore, the Western model lacks the conditions that are necessary for its survival and reproduction.[37]

CONDITIONS OF CULTURAL RESURRECTION

When we consider the problem of backwardness in Arab/Muslim societies, whose cultural contribution has been absent for a long time, we realize that it cannot be attributed simply to the absence of one or more of the factors necessary for development in the Western sense (capital, human resources in the field of research and development, information systems, etc.). It is rather an existential crisis, if I am allowed to use this term here, embodied in the decay of the socio-cultural values in these societies and the collapse of their cultural cohesion. This leads as a consequence to the loss of their motives for existence and for achieving growth and prosperity. This is due not only to external factors (different forms of Western imperialism), but also to the deterioration and decay of such societies. This raises new questions: *How can the Arabo-Islamic world restore its cultural unity and efficacy? How can it rebuild itself in the cultural sense?* The following is a discussion of the necessary conditions for such cultural resurrection:

The essence of modernization consists in self-realization in the cultural sense, i.e., bringing about the cultural and social changes necessary to fulfill scientific and technological imperatives. In other words, it consists of the ability to meet "the necessary preconditions for survival in the international economic and military spheres."[38] It is important to benefit from the fulfillment of such imperatives and, at the same time, to transcend them culturally. This cultural realization requires the employment of the power of faith, nurturing a sense of cultural affiliation, and the awakening of the unifying forces in the socio-cultural fabric of society. Moreover, the above view of modernization implies that we ought to begin with human beings, in whom we must put our trust, and on whom we must rely for the fulfillment of these socio-cultural changes.

Those who view their lives as a sacred mission to be fulfilled, as a mere drop in a current of cultural revival which transcends their individuality, extends across different ages and generations, and transcends even our worldly time, who are self-confident, inspired by a deep sense of meaningfulness, and satisfied that they belong to their mother culture – only these people have the ability to participate consciously in the attempt to awaken their societies and nations. Here the strength of faith represents a way to resist one's greed, to sacrifice one's own interest for the sake of collective goals, and to resist all forms of allurement related to the Western cultural invasion, which aims at the gradual subordination of others by persuading them to adopt foreign habits and behavioral patterns.

Cultural integration and coherence (i.e., consistency and continuity of cultural identity and its capacity for self-rejuvenation over the ages) depends not only on productive abilities, but also on the efficacy of the different cultural systems and symbols and their capability to express and impart cultural contents within and across generations. The role played by such symbolic patterns[39] may be summed up as follows:

First: During the span of one generation, these symbolic patterns help bring up individuals as cultural actors. This task can only be achieved by making them fully understand the significance of their own culture and the meaning of its different aspects and features. In this way, they can participate in building and renewing their culture, relying on its own potentials and inherent capabilities.

Second: They help transfer cultural heritage – which is the sum total of the experiences of successive generations' interactions with nature, with themselves, and with other cultures – to the forthcoming generations. Without such transfer, cultural continuity would be violated and hence the ability for self-development and regeneration would decline.

What is required then is a cultural revival rather than development in the usual sense. Such a revival would be essentially different from the revival which occurred in the West. For the Western model, from the Renaissance and the Industrial Revolution up to the technological and scientific revolution, is quite undesirable for Arab/Muslim societies, since it is inconsistent with the governing principles and basic values of their culture. It is also impracticable, since it is disharmonious with their environment. The cultural revival we are talking about is different from that of the West not only in its ends, but also in the means to achieving these ends, such as the role to be played by science and technology, teaching methods, and socio-cultural transformations.

In Arab/Muslim culture the dream of achieving paradise on earth, the dream of attaining material welfare as a supreme goal has never been a genuine one. Arab/Muslim culture does not place humankind at the center of the universe nor does it view worldly life as separate from the other, eternal life. Even its material needs and wants are not regarded as separate from its spiritual needs. Furthermore, Arab/Muslim culture stresses the need for restraint and moderation with regard to the pleasures of life. This concept of cultural revival consists of the liberation of humankind from thralldom to the various false idols, be they political, social, economic or even intellectual. Let us go back to Diagram (2), which illustrates the view of development from a Western perspective, and consider what characterizes the Islamically based cultural vision.

Muslims view the universe only through their faith in God. According to the teachings of Islam, God is manifest in everything in the universe – in the distant galaxies, in humankind, and in the minute particles constituting everything on our planet. By virtue of their faith in God, Muslims have a sense of belonging to the whole universe. Faith is their great homeland, their ultimate haven which contains whatever other lesser affiliations or homelands they may belong to. Islam teaches that the Muslims' sense of belonging should not be confined to those lesser circles of belongings. Human beings tend through our human instincts to be tied to earth and shut out from the larger realm of their existence – that realm of time and space which religion refers to as "the world of the unknown." It is the realm of time in its eternity. Compared with that eternal light, our life on earth is but a fleeting glimmer, a tiny speck of light which will soon fade away and die out. It is life and death. It is this life and the afterlife. It is God Almighty and all His creatures. It is true that human beings prefer to be shut inside this shell of their earthly material world, which they can perceive and bring to some extent under their control. We give in to the allure of this limited, concrete existence. The quest for faith is a journey from darkness to light in which Muslims renounce this confined, spiritually arid world. It is a quest for the greater realm of the spirit, which is the realm of truth. Seeking faith implies a quest for spiritual maturity that takes place through actual experience of this broader realm, just as one experiences the secular world. One should witness God, feel His eternal presence, recognize Satan and the angels, witness death, the life-hereafter and the Day of Judgment as one witnesses the various manifestations of the restricted secular world. Only through such experience can the soul be changed. This leads human beings to reconsider their relations with their environment and the people around them, and their attitude to the spatio-temporal world of the unknown. Consequently, such an experience will define human motives and goals in this world, as well as the amount of dedication needed for their fulfillment. In this way one can simultaneously experience the two worlds: the secular world, the world of the "here and now," and the world to come, the world of "there and then."

THE CONCEPT OF TIME IN THE ISLAMIC VIEW

- Secular worldly time as human beings perceive it is closely related to the human concept of time in its eternity. In fact, there is an organic relation between these two concepts of time, a relation established by the indisputable fact of judgment on the Day of Judgment in the Hereafter, namely, "that no bearer of burdens can bear the burden of another; That man can have nothing but what he strives for; That [the fruit of] his striving will soon come in sight: Then will he be rewarded with a reward complete" (53:38–41).
- Time, as conceived by Islam, assumes a certain open pattern; it is not viewed as a mere quantity, measured in hours and minutes, to be bought or sold or consumed.[40] Islam views time as full of meaning and significance: "I have only created Jinns and men, that they may worship Me" (51:56). Time is quality rather than quantity. It is collective rather than individualized.[41] The Qur'an here addresses the whole nation, though each individual will be judged separately on the Day of Judgment.
- The concept of the individual in Islam is distinct from that of the Western view. For only within the context of judgment in the afterlife are there verses addressed to the individual. This means that what distinguishes individuals relates to their social function. Individuals in Islam are not viewed as separate beings with distinctive skills, abilities, and desires. They are the vicegerents of God on earth, entrusted with the proper use of all God's endowments in the form of abilities, skills, material potentialities, emotional faculties, senses, and time. The "self" in Islam can never be one's sole frame of reference as is the case in Western culture. Human beings are asked to enter into a heated debate with the self as long as they are relying on their relation to God. This argument is dictated by their belief in God. The self, according to Islam, has good and evil motives. Human beings are enjoined to make the good in themselves prevail over the evil. Thus the Western saying "to be myself" has no meaning in Islam.

- The human act in Islam, the act of a believer, must never be viewed as being separate from the act of God. Mysticism in Islam, in its profoundest sense, consists in the attainment of such a degree of harmony between human beings and their Creator that human beings become an instrument for the fulfillment of God's will, thus effecting a unity between their limited power and God's supreme power.

Human beings are enjoined not to perform any act or adopt any attitude which might alienate them from God: "Nay, but man does transgress all bounds, in that he looks upon himself as self-sufficient. Verily, to your Lord is the return [of all]" (96:6–8). Hence, the motives behind Arab/Muslim activity in the field of scientific research and technology are different from those in the West. Scientific research, like technology, is a cultural component, and scientific knowledge is, in its turn, a cultural product. Science in this sense is neither neutral nor universal.[42] The issue is not whether these structures of knowledge are universally correct, but whether they are legitimate, i.e., it is a question of the legitimacy of each discipline within its socio-cultural context.[43] The reason why Western science cannot touch the soul of the ordinary person in Arab/Muslim societies is that it lacks legitimacy within the Arab/Muslim distinctive cultural context.[44] Science has derived its legitimacy in the West through its role in effecting those technological changes which fulfill the human inclination to control and dominate nature as well as other cultures. Its motive is to achieve the greatest degree of material welfare and prosperity as well as to curb the power of the church and prevent it and religion in general from interfering in the affairs of life and society.

This kind of scientific legitimacy is alien to a culture like that of the Arabo-Islamic world, which views science as a means of attaining truth and as a point of departure for the recognition of Divine power. Arab/Muslim culture sees no contradiction between the role of science in that sense and belief in God. There thus arises an urgent need for an alternative approach to science. Arabs/Muslims need to formulate their own model of rationality that defines their course of action and their motives for the use of scientific research and technology. The intellectual Western attitude to science and technology has acquired certain features due to the particular relation existing between it and Western culture with its specific features and traits. These are exemplified by exaggerating the importance of profit as an incentive, glorifying the value of conquering nature, dominating it at the expense of achieving harmony with it, and the assumption that nature is a means, a mere object to be exploited. Nature is seen as mere scattered elements rather than well-knit systems connected by a network of complex relations. The natural resources are seen as elements with no intrinsic value, which acquire value only through their service to human beings. Therefore, a need arises for a Arab/Muslim pattern of rationality which defines the Arabo-Islamic view of scientific research and technology.

Arabs/Muslims have to restore their self-confidence and the staunch belief in their ability as a nation to be creative and build their own technological capabilities. They have to free themselves from enthrallment with Western technological and scientific achievements. They should always be aware of the fact that the supremacy of the West in the field of science and technology is a relatively new phenomenon when measured against the long span of human history. Human history has witnessed a long series of great technological and scientific feats which testified to the great debt that human culture owes to Arab/Muslim societies.[45] Moreover, the scientific approach which prevailed in Europe during the 16th and 17th Centuries was well known to the peoples of Islamic countries (from the beginning of the 9th Century to the 15th Century AC).[46]

The dominant pattern nowadays of the importation of the achievements of technology from industrial Western countries is quite a new phenomenon.[47] Until the emergence of the Industrial Revolution in Europe during the 18th Century, the world had witnessed the transfer of technological inventions from one civilization to another. They were then assimilated to fit in with the spirit of the recipient culture. There were dozens of cases[48] where such a spontaneous and successful transfer of cultural components took place. Moreover, it is an indisputable fact that the borrowing and consequent adaptation of cultural components constitute one of the most important conditions for the development and prosperity of different cultures.[49]

The subjection of the Arabo-Islamic world to Western technology has two aspects which may be considered as two sides of the same coin. The first is its dependence on Western technology for the fulfillment of many tasks in Arab/Muslim society, e.g. extractive industries, manufacturing, consumption, transportation, communications, defense, etc. The other side reflects the dependence of the West on Arab/Muslim societies as markets for their technological products in various fields.[50] This means that the West does not have the upper hand; for the Arabo-Islamic world has the ability to influence the West and international affairs by rationalizing and limiting its needs for Western products in all fields.

If Arabs/Muslims are to regard themselves as the natives of a distinguished culture which reflects its character in all fields of human activity, they should consider their societies in the same light. For any society is in fact a mosaic of socio-cultural structures, each having its distinctive features and traits. This distinctiveness arises from a difference in the bio-sphere of each community and the diversity of historical experience over thousands of years. Such diversity – whether at the national or local levels – must be considered as the rule rather than the exception. In fact, it is standardization that represents the exception. By standardization, I mean the elimination of any differences between the various socio-cultural structures as a step towards integrating them into one universal culture. This, in turn, means stripping these cultural entities of their potential for development. Here in Egypt, for example, we have various environmental conditions and environments ranging from the oases in the Western desert and small communities of Bedouins in the Eastern desert (on the northern coast of the Sinai Peninsula), to the two parts constituting the Nile Valley, namely, Lower and Upper Egypt. As for their inhabitants, they vary amongst themselves as concerning temperament, habits, religion and historical experience. Thus we can say that there are distinctive traits even on the level of cities. Damietta, for example, is distinguished by its historical experiences and the habits and customs of its inhabitants. And national identity is the outcome of these local features and traits. This kind of cultural diversity enriches cultures. In fact, there is no contradiction, as it is sometimes claimed, between unity and diversity. The realization of diver-sity within unity means that unity was attained voluntarily and not by force. Let us consider an example of this diversity-within-unity and how it is related to the use of technology. The types of dwellings dominant in the different geographical areas in Egypt vary. Such variation is determined by: (1) environmental differences: differences in the climate and the kinds of natural resources available, and (2) differences in the socio-cultural structures of local communities. In the north of Sinai, for instance, the inhabitants of Arish use the mud found in Arish Valley to make adobe (unburned bricks) after mixing it with hay and sand. The ceilings of their dwellings, which house extended families consisting of several nuclear families, are constructed of boards of tamarisk wood and palm-leaf fronds. Such houses are fit for habitation for a period of time ranging from 150–200 years. On the other hand, the Bedouins in the east of Arish use the naturally growing *al-ader* plant in building their extremely beautiful dwellings and huts for their animals, using tamarisk wood as pillars.

In the southern Sinai, the Bedouins build their dwellings using igneous rocks which they obtain from the surrounding mountains as well as the clay deposited by the freshets. The inhabitants of the northern coast west of Alexandria follow the Islamic Arab model in the construction of their houses, using limestone found in abundance in the nearby quarries. For mortar, they use the local clay. The people of Siwa construct their houses using rock salt called *korshif*, which is available in abundance there, and so on. Thus, a recognition of diversity would lead to the exploitation of the human and natural resources available in every local community so as to fulfill the needs which may differ from one community to another. Moreover, the means of fulfilling the same needs might vary from one local community to another as environmental conditions as well as historical experiences might vary.

Half of wisdom is to have the right dreams; the other half lies in the use of suitable means to realize these dreams. This saying is most true when applied to the techniques used. A technique is not only an answer to a *how*-question (how to make or produce something or perform a certain service), but it is also and most often an indirect answer to a *what*-question (what to make, produce or perform). The techniques of construction dominant in the West imply a definite choice of dwelling, the techniques of the soda-water industry imply social acceptance of soda water, and so on. Technology in general is not impartial in its application, whether socially, politically or culturally. In fact, any technological choice has cultural, political and social implications. Western technology, for example, has evolved and developed simultaneously with the emergence and development of the Western way of life.

The problem facing Arab societies as well as most Third World ones is the erosion of the natural link between their social needs and the suitable means for their fulfillment. It is natural for new social needs to arise and for society to decide on the best means for their fulfillment and the right techniques for their production leading to the emergence of new social needs, and so on. But in the Arab world things happen differently. What is dominant now is that certain means of satisfying certain needs are imported (e.g., all consumer and durable goods). Such means are often imposed in one way or another from the outside (or from within, if they are apt to fulfill the interests of certain social strata). With the prevalence of such means, corresponding needs evolve and gradually prevail. This means that in such societies, needs no longer define the means. On the contrary, it is the means which define the needs. There is a sacred duty which is as yet unfulfilled. This is the duty of deciding on a way of life and patterns of consumption which are in keeping with the priorities set by the prevalent values and principles governing our culture. Such a way of life and such patterns of consumption will thus be quite different in their quality from those adopted in the West.

However, such a choice does not take place in a vacuum. It is an indisputable fact that in the field of technology we are but satellites revolving in the orbit of industrial Western countries. They are the acknowledged masters in this field, over which they have full control. The flow of Western goods is endless. Moreover, rate of obsolescence is accelerating. Every day, if not every hour, there are new inventions and developments in the West, which cover all aspects of public daily life and which can fulfill human beings' basic needs[51] as well as their desire to lead a luxurious life, whether reasonable or not. There also exist the mass media, which relegate the ordinary people in Arab/Muslim society, as well as in all Third World societies, to the position of passive receivers who admire whatever the West produces in the fields of science and technology. In this way Arab/Muslim subordination to the West deepens at the psychological level while the confidence of Arab/Muslim societies in their own strength declines. Moreover, their attempts at choice, not to mention their attempts at development and invention, are rendered useless and futile. For what is the use of inventing what has already been invented? What are the prospects of catching up with the West, not to mention surpassing it, if scientific and technological achievements in the West are accelerating at an astronomical rate? Of course, if Arabs/Muslims think in the same way as the West does (that is to say, if their dreams, aspirations, conceptions of their needs and their lifestyles are identical with those in the West), our efforts to compete with the West by seeking other ways and means will be vain and useless. The West will always be our Makkah from which Arab/Muslim societies derive their means as well as their ends, and their subordination to the economic Western powers will be complete. Thus, in order to achieve distinctiveness from the West, Arab/Muslim societies have to choose their own way of life and patterns of consumption. These are, in fact, two facets of one and the same coin, namely, cultural independence.

Thus, it is clear that the issue of appropriate technology is not primarily a technical or economic issue, for it has a bearing on cultural, political, and social aspects as well. Much of the Western literature on appropriate technology or "intermediate technology"[52] suggests that technology is equivalent to the means and methods of production, i.e. it is a commodity that can be readily imported from the industrial Western countries. The essential precondition for appropriate technology as we view it is that it should be based on the society's real potentialities, be freely and independently chosen, and be potentially developed by using local resources and means.

It is argued here that no real Industrial Revolution can be achieved without the participation of all parties involved in production. For instance, the basic achievements in the textile industry during the Industrial Revolution in England[53] were not the result of scientific progress alone, but, more importantly, were the result of favorable economic circumstances and skilled labor. Yet there are different forms of Industrial Revolutions. The Industrial Revolution in the West witnessed the collapse of the feudal system, the decay of the countryside and the establishment of new communities around the new cities, the then evolving industrial centers in England. But within the cultural context of Arab/Muslim societies, and because of their present circumstances, it is inconceivable to imitate this kind of revolution, which was primarily motivated by economic incentives with all its socio-cultural environmental costs. Within Arab/Muslim socio-cultural contexts, technology must develop in conformity with the ultimate aims of its culture and society as well as with the environmental and socio-cultural conditions defined by these aims. This attitude towards technology is essentially different from that adopted in the West.

Thus, the Arab/Muslim Industrial Revolution must take place all over the Arabo-Islamic world, and not be confined to cities only; industry must have a bearing on other production activities in local communities, be they rural or urban. Finally, this revolution must rely primarily on local potentialities and resources.

Local communities, whether rural or provincial, have rich resources and potentialities for developing their endogenous technological capabilities. These resources and potentialities consist of:

1. The vast majority of individuals in local communities who have wide knowledge about the environment in which they live. This knowledge has accumulated over thousands of years of creative interaction with and experience of their natural environment.[54]
2. A wide range of abilities and experiences in all fields of human activity (agriculture, varied handicrafts, construction of houses, methods of storing water, irrigation, popular methods of curing diseases and various ailments, prediction of climatic changes, etc.).
3. A high degree of social coherence and solidarity and well-developed structures capable of exercising social control over individuals and highly reliable in conducting the affairs of the local community in all fields of life.
4. Values specific to the local community which represent their mode of adaptation to the environment as well as to the outside world over generations. This mode of adaptation defines their way of life (patterns of production, consumption, recreation, etc.) and makes it not only acceptable in their eyes but also highly desirable,[55] however unacceptable it may seem to other local communities. Thanks to such values, this local community can achieve stability, psychological balance and security.

Many of the traditional technological capabilities that abound in local communities in Egypt have died an unnatural death.[56] This is due to the spread of Western patterns of consumption and the invasion of Egyptian local communities by the products of Western technology which such communities do not make use of in their endogenous development. The real loss arising from the decay of these technological capabilities is not a material loss, which can be made up for. Rather, it lies in the collapse of value structures and the symbols related to them, which may lead to the eventual extinction of all potentialities for developing these structures from within and according to their inherent logic.

The view we have adopted here maintains that in order to derive the greatest benefit from the rich possibilities of building up our traditional, endogenous technological capabilities, we must achieve as much integration as possible between the cultural structures within which these technologies function and the corresponding modern structures which make use of Western technological components. Such integration can be effected through division of labor between them in the different fields of goods and services production.[57] Networks of various production structures would then carry out distinctive production projects according to the techniques applied and within unified production patterns. Attention should also be given to the internal transfer of technology[58] among the different patterns of production by virtue of which the methods of production, evaluation, quality-control, planning, scientific research, marketing and advertising are transferred from structures using modern techniques to others using conventional or modified conventional techniques. In this larger context, the traditional technological capacities of local communities allow the following:

First: True potentialities for fulfilling many of the basic needs of local communities (as in the fields of housing, food production, the clothes industry, or medical treatment), thus contributing to the achievement of self-reliance[59] on the national level. Generally, these abilities were decisive tools for the fulfillment of the basic material needs of the vast majority of individuals in all human societies until perhaps the beginning of the 19th Century. Moreover, conventional technologies which were widely used and which relied on renewable natural resources were not hostile or detrimental to the environment. The tendency of some of these technologies not to change with time is sometimes considered evidence of stagnation and backwardness; in fact, however, this feature is an indication of such technologies' having attained a high degree of perfection[60] in adapting themselves to the environment. Many of the conventional techniques used in building houses and making clothes or agricultural tools or equipment are good examples in this respect.

Second: Potentials for developing these traditional technological capabilities through the use of modern technological components (e.g., the development of handicrafts by using modern tools and equipment). There is, in fact, a process of conversion towards automation and modern equipment in many handicrafts, while the organizational structure remains intact.[61] Such a process is needed in order to cope with the changes in demand for the commodities produced by these handicrafts.

Third: Developing many such techniques so as to choose new products that can cater to prevailing demands on local and international markets and improving product quality while keeping production methods basically manual. Such development aims at the production of goods with high cultural content, some of which may be exported.

In order to achieve a cultural revival in Arab/Muslim societies and make full use of their potentialities in building their technological capabilities, it is necessary to pave the way for wide participation on the part of producers and consumers in all fields of activities in general. The kind of knowledge prevailing in any socio-cultural context is related to socio-cultural sovereignty. Thus, many components and aspects of technological knowledge in this sense lie in a state of dormancy and captivity within socio-cultural systems which lack the capacity for prosperity or self-fulfillment. Releasing these repressed potentials can only be effected by liberating the systems containing them and providing opportunities for the positive participation of these structures in all the aspects of life. Thus, the issue of building up Arab/Muslim technological capability is closely related to the issue of the cultural, social, and political liberation of the individual.

However, a true rendering of this concept of liberation requires Arabs/Muslims "to deepen [their] vision of the citizen, not as an individual but as a member of a social entity."[62] Individuals' sense of belonging can be best achieved in the light of their sense of affiliation with socio-cultural structures which are open-ended and constantly expanding. They begin with the nuclear family and move on to the extended family, to one's neighbors, to the village, to the small community, to the tribe one belongs to, to the province, and on to the wider society and the nation. Each of these social systems derives its own criteria of performance from its identification with the larger and wider system which encompasses it.[63] The larger system must respect the privacy and independence of the relatively smaller system, providing it with circumstances favorable to its flourishing and prospering. There is essentially no contradiction between the sense of belonging to one of these systems and the sense of belonging to a system smaller than it. On the contrary, it is the only right way to broaden one's sense of belonging to include one's whole nation. This normally starts from one's sense of belonging to the family and small community, just as universality starts from one's sense of national belonging.

The problem lies not in the diversity and multiplicity of the systems to which the individual belongs, but rather in their isolation from each other. If it is common in the Western literature on this topic to describe traditional entities such as the extended family, the village community or the tribe as inherently "backward" or "reactionary" and as obstacles to development which must be eliminated,[64] the criterion the Arab/Muslim society should adopt to judge these social systems should be the role they fulfill within the framework of the mother culture rather than their role within certain isolated systems. If Arab/Muslim society judges these patterns from the viewpoint of their ability to transcend themselves and adopts the values of the mother structure to which they belong, it may find that an extended family capable of participating positively in an independent cultural project is more progressive than a nuclear family less able to transcend itself. Hence it is necessary to review the theoretical framework of traditional socio-cultural systems prevalent in Egypt.

ATTITUDES TOWARDS WESTERN SCIENCE AND TECHNOLOGY

The prevalent practice of transferring technological components to Arab/Muslim societies is accompanied by the transfer of their technocratic frame of reference[65,66] This reduces all problems facing contemporary societies to one problem, namely, a shortage in resources; similarly, it reduces politics to economic policy and economics to science. It introduces science as the panacea, the miraculous cure to all the problems of society. It further claims that science can lead, through its technological application, to more accumulation of wealth; in other words, it can solve the resource shortage. Within this framework, politics, in its broad sense, becomes meaningless and purposeless, and it appears that the truly happy country is, by definition, "apolitical." Morals likewise become unnecessary, since science – which has been surrounded with a false halo of objectivity, justice and infallibility – concerns itself with the problem of right and wrong (the forbidden and the virtuous). The danger of adopting such a technocratic attitude[67] in the Arabo-Islamic world lies in the consequent, unquestioning adoption of the Western value system, which is inimical to the cultural structure of Arab/Muslim societies.

The true challenge facing Arab/Muslim societies, whose contribution in the fields of science and technology has been absent for centuries, is to benefit from Western technological and scientific achievements within the framework of their own independent cultural vision. The challenge is, in other words, to transfer and assimilate technological and scientific knowledge to the exclusion of Western values. The Arabo-Islamic world might actually need to borrow certain tools of scientific research and production, as well as technological and scientific knowledge pertaining to specific fields based on the priorities it has set for itself. However, it does not necessarily need to borrow the language of scientific research, its contents (i.e., Western priorities), or its products (which should be defined according to the social needs of Arabs/Muslims). Nor does the Arabo-Islamic world need to transfer the structures and organizational frameworks related to Western scientific research, development and production or the motives and values underlying these activities. The Arabization, or Islamization of science and technology thus means the ability to make use of foreign cultural elements in the fields of science and technology as the basis for an Arabo-Islamic structure with its own unique values and organizational principles. What the Arabo-Islamic world must reject is not all foreign elements and structures, but rather, the transformation of these elements and structures into "islands"– foreign bodies within Arab/Muslim culture, as it were, which reproduce their mother culture in the Arab/Muslim cultural environment.

A highly significant model in this respect is presented by Japan, which has achieved an industrial transformation relying on Western technological and scientific input by assimilating such input into purely Japanese organizational structures. Thus Japan has succeeded in achieving what most Third World countries, including India and Egypt, have failed to achieve. It has managed to introduce modern, capital intensive production techniques without detriment to its traditional production sector. These modern production methods have led to the slow but continual mechanization of the local industrial sector[68] through the establishment of cooperation, rather than competition, between large and small scale enterprises (primarily via subcontracting). In this way, Japan has been able to effect its industrial revolution while continuing to depend primarily on labor-intensive production structures.[69]

If we wish to benefit from the Western model, we must bear in mind that the West achieved its own scientific progress by borrowing profusely from Arabic Islamic science as well as the technological achievements of other cultures (printing techniques and gunpowder production from China, for example) within the framework of an independent cultural project.[70] Thus, the Renaissance witnessed the reconstruction of Western science, which changed according to the requirements of each period and in conformity with the other axes of activity in Western culture.[71]

The Arabo-Islamic world is in need of no less than a cultural revolution in the field of education, where current methods of instruction lead most often to cultural alienation on both the national and local levels. There needs to be a reconsideration of the educational process as a whole, and particularly its cultural content, the principles and values it conveys and the character-forming pattern it adopts such that in order to establish a system of edu cation which conforms to our cultural structure. Such a system must, in essence, uphold a model of social work. Its motto should be "learning through dialog with the living socio-cultural fabric of society and the local environment." It is also necessary to abandon the mass production approach to public education. There must be complete decentralization of education at the school level, and to a lesser degree at the university or higher-institute level (e.g., by establishing technical schools for handicrafts and small-scale industries in Damietta, and agricultural schools on the Northern Coast). The needs of local communities must be taken into consideration in defining syllabi and building schools, higher institutes and universities. This would mean the adaptation of syllabi to meet the needs of each local community within the general framework of the public interest. In this way, school programs can serve to help pupils choose, affirm and apply the vast knowledge they acquire as members of their local community.[72]

11

Philosophical Beliefs Underlying the Formulation of Physical Laws

MAHJOOB TAHA

ON THE LAWS OF PHYSICS

A NUMBER OF POPULAR concepts of the essence of physics and its purposes are shared among most intellectuals and even among some of the people engaged in scientific research. The roots of these concepts are buried in schoolbooks, popular newspapers and scientific articles which describe the "ideal" world of physicists. In a nutshell, this popular outlook regards the laws and theories of physics as a unique product that no two could differ on. The premise underlying this outlook is that all disputes on scientific matters may be settled in the lab, and that the scientific experiment is the final arbitrator. In fact, however, this applies only to a single aspect of natural science, namely, that which is concerned with gathering a list of observations from a given experiment. Such observations, whether they are recorded by human beings or a machine, represent nothing more than a starting point. The true scientific work, however, is the result of the interaction between the human mind and the list of observations, and what the human mind adds to it by way of causality and logical unity. This human theorization is essential and represents the true spirit of scientific work. Hence, physics is just another human experience, and like all other human experiences, its meaning, purpose and use are subject to dispute and disagreement.

Take gravity,[1] for example. It would be possible to record lists upon lists of observations, which in due time would fill thousands of pages containing information on bodies falling to earth: on the shape of the body, its volume, its density, the kind of material it is made of, the height from which it fell, the time of flight, the type of soil it fell on, the depth of the hole it caused, etc. In other words, we would have lab books filled with facts, but no science. Science emerges only when the human mind comprehends such facts and views them from every conceivable angle, relating them to each other in such a way that the information can be compressed into a single statement (mathematical or verbal). After centuries of organized research, humankind finally taps into the science of gravity when it is announced that objects falling to earth do so at the same rate of acceleration. Decades later, the general law of gravitation is announced and a connection is made between bodies falling to earth, the moon orbiting the earth, and the planets orbiting the sun. Then centuries go by and the general theory of relativity is unveiled along with the role that gravity plays in shaping galaxies and nebulae. Yet, the science of gravity remains "open" and researchers in the field disagree on its underlying theories. This is due to the existence of more than one theory and philosophy to explain the lists of observations. The superiority of one philosophy over another cannot be tested by experiment or astronomical observations. In addition, we do not have any concrete idea of what gravity really is; hence, our endeavors are limited to finding a mathematical formula that gives an accurate description of how particles move under its influence. The methods currently available for scientific research fail to explain the nature of gravity, its essence and its source. In fact, it appears to be impossible to define such concepts in a way that would incorporate them into the realm of empirical research. This also applies to other known phenomena such as electric, magnetic and nuclear forces. In general, one can say that at the fundamental level, science does not seek to define the "reality of things," nor does it specify the essence of the forces that dictate things' behavior. Instead, the goal of science is to discover the most fundamental building blocks of which things are made as well as the laws which govern the forces that dictate their behavior. The foregoing discussion naturally leads us to the following question: What is a physical law and how does one discover it?

It is clear that empirical methods have greatly evolved over the centuries. The progress they have witnessed may be attributed not only to technological breakthroughs but also to the theorization and methods of scientific thought, which have proven to be effective in organizing and correlating the experimental facts. The aforementioned progress has allowed us to establish a methodology leading to the formulation of general laws from experimental observations. This applies at least to those studies that have reached a high level of maturity and precision like modern physics. The first step is to specify the state of the system under investigation by recording the experimental values for certain dynamic variables pertaining to the system. Experiments are then carried out to measure the values of these different variables while the system evolves. As it so happens, some of the system variables take on the same value throughout the course of the experiment, i.e., they are unchanged or constant. These constants lead to the "conservation laws" for the system. By scrutinizing the conservation laws for a set of identical systems one may be led to postulate a general law that conforms to the conservation laws. This law is then thoroughly tested against experiment and attempts are made to deduce them from more fundamental and comprehensive theories. These comprehensive theories are mathematical models for a large class of physical phenomena, which fall under the same type of fundamental interaction.

From the foregoing discussion of the strategy leading to useful scientific generalization, there appear to be three different levels of abstraction:

The conservation law level, which is a generalization akin to the experiment and is deduced directly from observation and measurement. The form of the conservation law is characterized by a specific function that depends on the measured variables and that retains the same value while the system evolves from one state to another. Because of the direct relationship between the conservation law and the experiment, it represents the frontline on the battleground for theory and experiment. The conservation laws are the foundations upon which theoretical constructs are built. The discovery of a physical process that does not abide by the conservation laws will therefore have a strong impact on the existing physical theories. This happened in 1957 when the law of parity conservation broke down and again in 1964 when the law of space inversion-charge conjugation was violated.[2] Physicists are currently engaged in a number of experiments to test the integrity of baryon[3] number conservation, which predicts the stability of protons against radioactive decay.

The general law level, which is a postulate formulated in such a way as to guarantee the validity of the known conservation laws. This level represents a mathematical foundation for discussing several phenomena that participate in the interactions affecting the phenomena that lead to the formulation of the conservation laws. The transition from the conservation law level to the general law level is not unique. There are often several mathematical postulates that lead to the same conservation laws but which differ outside the realm of experiment. The postulates that survive are only those which are not invalidated by experimentation.

The comprehensive theory level, which gives a unified mathematical formula for the fundamental interaction being studied in all the pertinent fields. The interaction is usually represented by a specific term in a Hamiltonian function that satisfies the required conservation laws. This level also provides the form of the general laws governing the set of phenomena it seeks to explain. The comprehensive theory contains a lot more than the bulk of experiments that instigated it. It is an artifact of the human mind constructed for the purpose of reproducing the various experimental results and possibly explaining the concepts emanating from it. Perhaps it is best to give an example from the field of electricity to illustrate the aforementioned levels of abstraction. At level (A), we find the law of conservation of charge: The net charge in a given process is constant. At level (B), we find several general laws, which describe reactions in which photons appear like photon-proton interaction or photon-electron or positron interaction. As for level (C), we find the theory of electromagnetism, which describes the behavior of material particles in an electromagnetic field and includes in a concise and precise mathematical formula all the known experimental properties of electric and magnetic phenomena.

Having demonstrated that human thought is a major factor involved in the generalization of experimental facts, we now move on to discuss the role of philosophical beliefs in the formulation of scientific laws and theories.

THE PHILOSOPHICAL BACKGROUND INVOLVED IN THE FORMULATION OF PHYSICAL LAW

There is a fundamental assumption upon which natural sciences are based, namely, that we live in a rational universe. In other words, the assumption that natural events are causally connected. Without it, science as we know it would be impossible. This assumption is natural and is perhaps even a part of human nature and its mental structure. In its extreme form, it is the belief in causal deterministic correlation, i.e. the belief that a specific state of a natural system necessarily leads to another specific state. The belief in causal deterministic correlation was prevalent till the beginning of the 20th Century and had such a strong hold on the scientific method that a great many scientists continued to believe that humankind's sense of freedom is nothing but an illusion. With the turn of the century, however, it was discovered that absolute determinism contradicts experiment. Causal correlation, in one way or another, remains an essential ingredient of the scientific method; however, the modifications which occurred in the postulate of determinism were tailored precisely to agree with the results of experimentation. So at the onset of the special theory of relativity, it was postulated that there is a causal connection between different events, i.e., that every event leads to a set of subsequent events independent of the existence of an observer. With the rise of the quantum theory of matter, it was postulated that systems evolve from one state to another in a deterministic fashion but that these states do not completely determine the values of the quantities being measured and only provide probabilities for obtaining specific values. The retreat from absolute determinism made room for some indeterminism and coincidence and allowed for a bit of "freedom of choice" for subatomic particles. The community of physicists, however, were left with a sense of discomfort since they had grown accustomed to the assumption that initial conditions along with the laws of dynamics precisely determine the evolutionary path of particles.

This view of the natural world necessarily entails the adoption of a philosophical standpoint, although is impossible to defend such a standpoint by means of a completely persuasive logic. At the same time, one cannot dismiss the possibility that we live in a chaotic universe with no rhyme or reason in the occurrence of events; however, a certain degree of implicit indeterminism need not prevent humankind from comprehending nature and reaping its fruits.

Sometimes it happens that a scientific theory is rejected on philosophical grounds despite its accordance with experimental results. For example, Newton's law of universal gravitation was criticized – even before the discovery that it disagreed with observations – because it allows for action at a distance, that is, particles separated by a distance are allowed to interact without a mediator. Also, researchers considered that one of the advantages of the general theory of relativity is that it somehow fulfills Mach's idea that remote bodies in the universe are responsible for giving massive particles their inertial properties. However, Mach's idea is nothing but a yearning to find a strong connection between that which is distant and that which is near – an idea meant to give meaning to the concept of mass and to make our perception of it more attractive.

This discussion leads us to conclude that at the level of fundamental interactions, scientific research has always been associated with philosophical premises or beliefs that do not emanate from experiment. This association is of paramount importance as it gives an intellectual and cultural dimension to the efforts put into research in the natural sciences. Furthermore, it could possibly contribute not only to the domain of technical applications, but also to the realm of human thought that aspires to a deeper understanding of life and its order. Consequently, we find that the formulation of many basic scientific laws leans toward sweeping generalizations, thereby giving the impression that certain philosophical standpoints are the fruit of empirical science and that any other standpoint must be false. This point can be illustrated by means of a few examples.

The first example is from the field of thermodynamics. The traditional forms of the second law of thermodynamics were sweeping and all-inclusive from the very beginning: "It is impossible to construct a device which converts all heat into useful work;" "The efficiency of the device which converts heat into useful work cannot in principle attain the maximum value of one which corresponds to the complete conversion of heat into work," or, "There is no natural process whose sole effect is the transfer of heat from one object to another at a higher temperature." To achieve this level of generality in a statement is no easy matter, especially when the statements are based on a limited number of experiments that were performed at a specific place and time on our planet earth. These are universal postulates about the nature of things. They fulfill the ambition of human beings to see their thoughts soar over the horizons of space and time. These universal statements are much preferred over the more humble statement that "a group of researchers performed certain experiments on specific materials under certain conditions in an attempt at achieving perfect efficiency in the conversion of heat into work but failed!"

The huge difference between this modest statement and the statements before cannot be attributed to experiment, but is the result of human thought and the adoption of a philosophical standpoint whose implicit claim is that, "What we failed to accomplish must be impossible." The assumptions that were "deduced" by such elaborate means allow us to apply them to the universe as a whole on the assumption that it represents an isolated thermodynamic system which abides by the laws of our labs, thus allowing us to predict the "heat death of the universe"!

The second example is from quantum theory. There is a corollary to the famous uncertainty principle which places an upper bound on the precision of a simultaneous measurement of a particle's position and momentum.[4] This corollary relates energy to time in the same way that the uncertainty principle relates momentum to position. This relationship between energy and time can be deduced from the first principles of quantum theory and does not require any additional postulates. The mathematical statement that relates the uncertainty in a measurement of time to the uncertainty in a measurement of energy is very simple and unanimously agreed upon as was the case for the laboratory experiments in our first example. If we restrict the interpretation to the mathematical statement, we find that it is just a statement of the degree of incompatibility of a simultaneous measurement of two incompatible observables, in this case energy and time. So whenever these two variables crop up (possibly among additional variables) in the description of the state of a system, they must appear in such a way as to satisfy the energy-time uncertainty principle. In particular, they must appear in the form of average values as opposed to exact values. Basically, this is one of the principles of quantum theory. If we assume that quantum theory is a representation of the reality of natural phenomena, then it must be considered an inherent property of the observed natural world. We then place a limitation on the precision of measuring the values of incompatible observables whenever they appear together in the description of the state of a system. However, the sweeping universal postulate which was founded on the aforementioned principle has far surpassed its strict meaning: "It is possible for a certain amount of energy to appear from nothing and disappear again within a given time interval provided that the amount of energy and its lifetime abide by the given mathematical relationship."

We are no longer talking about the properties of an explanatory theory for experimental observations or the limitations on measurements of variables used for specifying the state of a system. Rather, we are discussing emergence from emptiness, demise, and conservation. The subject, which originally was the limitation of humankind, has shifted to the extent of what is possible: the possibility of sudden creation and sudden annihilation.

Thus we can explain the emergence of energy from nothing since we have a physical law defined by a mathematical relation that makes this "emergence from nothing" possible. Moreover, a philosophical conclusion can be drawn about the basis of empirical science: Physical laws are not necessarily bound by "causality" as a mathematical relation relates the two variables of energy and time whenever they are. If we expand on this and say that energy can emerge from nothing, we can say that this can happen at any time and place without a cause-effect relationship between the event in question and events prior to it. Though a mathematical relation allows a tiny chance for arbitrariness or defiance of causality, and though the aforementioned postulate is apparently sweeping and undiscriminating concerning what humankind can observe and study, a number of researchers did propose theories based on this postulate. They intended to explain the emergence of the whole universe out of nonexistence with no cause or reason.

Our third and final example is from the field of cosmology, specifically, the "general principle of cosmology". Astronomical observations indicate that the galaxies and the faint background radiation reaching the Earth from every part of the sky are all regularly distributed up to the distance that astronomers managed to observe and record. This "fact" has been made the basis of a comprehensive postulate/assumption which is, in turn, a major principle in contemporary cosmology: "The universe seems regular and harmonious from any point in space and at any moment in time." This assumption is a sweeping generalization and an expansion based on limited observations carried out at a given spot of the universe. Yet, it is taken to be universally applicable and is the basis of every mathematical paradigm of the appearance and the evolution of the universe. The established philosophical point of departure is too obvious: perhaps we cannot see the entire universe, but what we cannot see must not be any different from what is already seen. This implies that the things and phenomena that draw our attention and set our minds working are those that have been proved to exist by our observatories and what is beyond that involves no mysteries or has nothing which is not known to us. This conviction makes it possible for researchers to propose theories about the whole universe and not just the world they can observe. These theories encompass the unique, huge universe from end to end rather than the limited observed world whose bounds taper off into an unseen and unknown realm that might be governed by factors that are not subject to human reasoning and experimentation.

The limits of experimentation and observation have obviously been overstepped in the three previous examples. This is consistent with an established philosophical proposition that gives the human mind full rein in the attempt to comprehend and explain natural phenomena. It is only natural that scientists tend to express their hypotheses in terms that give them the broadest possible applicability. These hypotheses are then tested by more experiments to adapt, alter or narrow down their scope. The intention here is not to criticize this method – for it may well be inherent in humankind. Rather, we simply wish to show that it is not really governed by the activities of observation and experimentation. We mean to show that the setting of laws and the formulation of propositions can take different forms that express different philosophical frames of reference, i.e. different presumptions that have nothing to do with scientific pursuit. The three examples cited here illustrate similar philosophical frames of reference revolving around the belief in the apparently endless capacities of the human mind: "What is humanly impossible is absolutely impossible" (the first example), "the human mind can comprehend everything including a natural law that governs the emergence of energy from non-existence" (the second example); "human knowledge encompasses the whole universe and there is very little that is beyond the cognition of man" (the third example).

These frames of reference share the belief that human reason, thought and work reign supreme in the entire universe and that there are no secrets or dark corners that human inventions and devices do not recognize. It is not surprising, then, that those who hold these beliefs should come out with generalizations and propositions shaped in a way that spontaneously echoes these beliefs. At this point, it is worth noting that a person who believes in the absolute superiority of human thought and actions and who believes that it was not humankind who set the rules and laws of the universe is not disturbed to find any aspect of irregularity or chaos in the course of nature.

However, to show that this philosophy is not dictated by science and that it has hardly any influence on its evolution and expansion, we propose to reconsider these same three examples in light of a philosophy that does not place human thought "above" existence.

FROM A DIFFERENT FRAME OF REFERENCE

Suppose that a researcher believes that there is an all wise Creator for this universe: Almighty God. He/she also believes that He created all creatures and sent them messengers and by means of revelation, via His messengers, He taught humans many facts of existence. He taught them that God is one; that His creatures are far more than people's eyes and observatories can see; that human beings are distinguished from other beings by their free will, freedom, and knowledge, and that consequently, they are required by God to worship and obey Him. They are also aware that it is possible to acquire knowledge by experimentation and calculations, because these teachings state that God has made the conduct of beings regular and disciplined. By study and research, human beings can discover the laws that govern this conduct. When they do, life on earth is made easier and human beings are better informed about God's Greatness and Might and the beauty of His creation. Accordingly, our empirical science and theories are nothing in comparison to God's knowledge, and are not enough to recognize the secrets of existence and its Creator. The room available for human beings to live, experiment, and reflect is limited, and so are human mental capacities. Indeed, human beings' earthly lifespan is fleeting, and human beings' knowledge is not meant to unveil what has been concealed from them by God.

Such a researcher – who may be termed the believer-researcher – believes that human beings' free will is a reality and not a psychological illusion. Therefore, unlike other physicists who hold that the behavior of particles is predetermined, he/she believes that this determinism must stop at a certain degree of complexity, such as the degree of complexity of a mature human mind.

At present it seems that the choices that individual particles make are always arbitrary and accidental, but statistically they tend to agree with the expected frequency of occurrence. The faith-based position of the believer-researcher rejects the very notion of accident as incompatible with the laws of God. The notion of accident rather reflects humankind's blindness to the causes and reasons beyond the phenomena in question. This ignorance relates either to the finiteness of human knowledge in general, or to lack of knowledge at this particular stage. This faith does not rule out the possibility of particles having their own sense of determinism and their own volition with which the individual "choices" of these particles are accordingly made. This has to do with the belief in the existence of a special relation between these beings and their Creator to which we are impervious. Perhaps the behavior of these beings is too subtle and profound for our minds and experiments to unravel. In social studies we normally accept statistical predictability concerning human collective conduct, standardizing "general tendencies" and possible patterns of development for groups of people. At the same time, we admit that these norms cannot help predict the behavior of a certain member of society in the very general circumstances shared by his/her fellow citizens. However, we do not describe the behavior of individuals as haphazard or accidental. Ironically, the same phenomenon is found in the behavior of electrons; their collective behavior is fairly disciplined and their individual behavior is almost chaotic, which leads to the description of the individual electrons as accidental. A believer-researcher has an explanation for the disparity between collective and individual behavior: he/she believes that, unlike electrons, humankind has volition, will, and responsibility to God. Nevertheless, this researcher might see in the existence of electrons a significance that no labs can find.

This line of thought is rejected by many researchers as a self-contradictory scientific method. This very rejection implies a belief in the uniqueness of human mentality and the superiority of human reason to everything else in the universe. A believer-researcher sees nothing in his/her belief contradicting the scientific method. On the contrary, he/she finds that the success of the scientific method proves the permanence of God's universal laws. Such a faith-based outlook by no means prevented believers from contributing to scientific research even within the context of absolute determinism when that was prevalent, or the probabilistic interpretation of quantum behavior when it was dominant. Such a researcher believes that all human knowledge is limited, temporal and approximate, and that it is based on the most infinitesimal part of existence as a whole. This summarizes the position of the believer-researcher concerning the three above examples and others.

In the first example we find that the second law of thermodynamics expresses an observed property of thermodynamics systems examined in labs: these systems do not convert all heat into useful work. It would be scientifically profitable to develop such a property into a general principle that would regulate the conduct of these systems. If we could further apply this principle on a wider scale, provided that it did not contradict empirical observations or better established principles, then this would be an undisputed success and would provide material evidence of the validity of the theory used. This method of theorizing is undoubtedly better than stating that the researchers could not realize their ends. However, this principle should not be made into a universal postulate eliminating the mere possibility that something different might occur. To be more specific, it cannot be thought of as applicable to the entire universe and made into a premise from which we can jump to conclusions about how human existence will come to an end. Humankind's environment, which includes everything that the human-made devices can detect, is not the whole universe. It is not a closed thermodynamic system. It is no more than a negligible part in a creation that only Almighty God fully understands. This limited (human) environment might interact with the rest of the universe in ways that are beyond humankind's recognition and means. The believer-researcher, backed by the solidly established teachings of a God-revealed religion, places this conviction on a much higher scale than empirical and uncertain methods. By means of it, he/she holds his or her imagination in check.

The point of departure for the believer-researcher in the second example is the limitedness of human experience in time and space. His/her basic position is that our lab experiments can tell us nothing about "absolute nonexistence," for it does not exist in our environment. It is logically impossible to realize how this world – this bubble of time, space, and energy – could have emerged out of no time, no space, and no energy. Human beings are imprisoned in this bubble by their body and mind. It is thus absurd that they should think themselves able, by means of experimentation and theorization, to transcend this status, look at existence from the outside, and get to know how things were shaped out of absolute nonexistence. However, there is no philosophical problematic concerning the explanation of the relation between the uncertainty in energy and the uncertainty in time. Energy and time are, according to the quantum theory, two incompatible variables. If we accept this theory's account of physical reality, it follows that when we have to describe the state of a physical system using variables including energy and time, we must allow for a degree of uncertainty in their values so as not to contradict the quantum theory that describes them as incompatible. This allows no room for the use of the expression "absolute nonexistence" or the possibility of the emergence or the disappearance of energy. A believer-researcher rejects the notion of arbitrariness which allows the emergence and disappearance of energy for no reason for any amount of time, however short it might be. Causality is the basis of empirical science, and this mathematical relation casts no doubt on the validity of this postulate.

The cosmological principle in the third example is in itself an embodiment of a philosophy that rejects the possibility that anything of significance might be beyond the grasp of human recognition. To think that unobserved aspects of existence might not be a mere extension of the observed world and that, instead, they might have decidedly different properties, is to shake the established certainty that the knowledge acquired by experimentation is final and adequate as far as the human pursuit of knowledge is concerned. It is, of course, of great importance to know that the observed part of the universe is harmonious and regular. It is a basic step for building mathematical paradigms that explain the evolution of the universe from its very early phases. However, these cannot be built without detaching the observer from the observed in accordance with the strategy followed in natural sciences. The study of a hydrogen atom, for instance, is based on the assumption that there is nothing in the world beyond the interaction of an electron and a proton. This makes the properties of the hydrogen atom a type of microcosm of the wider universe. This is true in relation to cosmology just as it is in relation to all natural sciences. The properties of the cosmic paradigms, which are inferred from the cosmic principle, pertain to the observed part of the universe. The cosmological principle is that this part could, to some extent, be isolated. Part of the assumption is that the cosmic paradigms do not indefinitely expand in existence. This makes it possible to induce the properties of the universe from a single part thereof.

However, many contemporary cosmologists have realized how naïve it is to think that the observed part of existence is the whole existence; they no longer look at their field as confined to the established properties of observed existence, i.e. the three spatial dimensions. The observed dimensions do not exclude the possibility of the existence of other spatial dimensions that our experiment–based devices cannot see. Apart from the implications of these theoretical paradigms, which are still in their primary phases and have no distinct physical content, the belief that the basic properties of the observed world are essentially local agrees with the accumulated experiences of the natural sciences, and especially astronomy. In this discipline we move from the Earth to the Solar System, to the galaxy, to the constellation of galaxies and then to the regular distribution of galaxies within view of our observatories. Each of these levels of observed existence possesses local properties that do not apply to other levels. It is thus only natural to believe that differences among the various levels might vanish at the point where human astronomy cannot see further. A believer-researcher sees the origin of this belief as humankind's fear that existence might be too vast for human beings to see for themselves. In the approximate harmony of observed existence, a believer-researcher finds support for the study of his/her local environment by the use of mathematical paradigms. This study deepens his/her appreciation of God's Creation, of which his/her own environment is only a tiny part.

CONCLUSION

What is normally called the empirical method is only a more developed and regulated form of the method used by ordinary people to acquire information about their surroundings. The profound knowledge which has been attained by the natural sciences of the behavior of particles and the forces affecting them has not come about by waving a magic wand called "the empirical." When a physicist phrases physical laws in a way which is incomprehensible to the ordinary man or woman, he/she, in fact, oversteps the bounds of the scientific method. This method is rather too narrow – neither broad nor sublime enough – for human ambition. No researcher can approach his/her work with his/her personal feelings and psychological make-up completely neutralized. He/she approaches his/her work with ambitions, views and expectations that have been formed in relation to a certain philosophy or frame of reference.

The failure to accurately observe the limits of the scientific method in the formation of discovered laws is perhaps inherent in man, be it a deliberate or an unintentional act. Many distinguished researchers over ages of scientific evolution have been moved by the desire to introduce "daring" propositions. Such exciting propositions, which do not observe methodical restraints, have been of prime importance to the evolution of all sciences. It is these daring propositions which have attained the status of established laws, and which are encountered in scientific journals and specialized publications. Thus it can be seen that the human aspect of scientific pursuit is what enriches and energizes it. However, we must not lose sight of the fact that scientific writings do reflect their writer's philosophies and beliefs and that they are not completely governed by the findings of their experimental work. With this in mind, it should not be hard to follow what is written and said cautiously and critically. In so doing, it should not take long to acquire the experience necessary to distinguish between purely scientific content and the writer's philosophy and beliefs.

At this point we have to distinguish between philosophical-social and moral speculation based on or inspired by the findings of natural sciences on the one hand, and on the other, a comprehensive belief system espoused by researchers before they engage in the process of scientific research, since such beliefs tend to dominate research and influence the formulation of scientific laws. In this article, we are concerned only with the latter aspect. Some philosophical positions can undoubtedly change as a result of experimental work and the facts it reveals. Some philosophical issues have thus been resolved by experimental facts. Examples of these are mechanical determinism and the timelessness of the universe. However, the resolution of such issues has led in most cases to a slight modification that would ensure that the researchers' philosophical convictions would not be invalidated by the new facts. This casts doubt on the alleged objectivity of natural scientists. The professional objectivity of scientific research requires that we do nothing but record facts and observations as they occur. However, it is not necessary for researchers to confine their speculations, conclusions, and statements to the body of facts they possess. Indeed, as we mentioned earlier, this would in no way benefit science. Nevertheless, if it is taken to extremes we might be presented with an exciting philosophical view which is devoid of real science. In such cases, the scientists make use of their scientific reputation to convey a message that has nothing to do with their field of expertise, though perfectly disguised in it. A case in point is a series of articles published recently by a contemporary cosmologist in specialized journals. He introduces what he calls the "chaotic universe." Briefly, he argues that the initial state of the Creation allowed several values for certain variables that were randomly distributed. The result was a great number of universes, the evolution of each of which was determined by the specific initial value from which it evolved. Our share is the universe we now live in.

These ideas were presented in the context of an answer to a question that demanded an explanation of the values of the known fundamental constants. The author said that the question was pointless, as there were universes with all possible sets of values. My argument in reply to this is that this kind of statement echoes a belief-based philosophy devoid of scientific content. It reflects an essentially "non-experimental" position which rejects causal thought. If other sets of values exist in the unobserved world, it is of no use to wonder about the specific values of the fundamental constants actualized in the observed world. The author's response is similar to the popular quantum mechanical interpretation of the multiplicity of universes which claims that we observe an electron to "choose" a certain path from an infinite number of possible paths because of our inability to observe the many unseen worlds. These philosophies are beliefs devoid of intellectual content. They add nothing to real science; they are, in essence, a type of preaching that distracts people lest they raise certain taboo questions.

To recapitulate, every effort exerted in the natural sciences, from outlining lab experiments to the wording of general laws and basic theories, is a human pursuit that bears the features of those engaged therein. It reflects ideological, intellectual, and philosophical positions which are by no means essential to the relevant field of scientific work. This should be borne in mind when we read scientific writings and when we train young scholars and scientists in all fields of the natural sciences.

NOTES

CHAPTER ONE
Based on Abdelwahab Elmessiri, ed. *The Problem of Bias: An Epistemological Perspective and Call for Ijtihad. Introductory Volume: Scholarship of Bias* (USA: The International Institute of Islamic Thought, 1997), Monograph 9. Translated by A. El-Ezabi, who has a PhD in Linguistics and is currently a full time Associate Professor of Linguistics at the College of Translation, Al-Azhar University in Cairo and a part-time instructor of translation studies at the Arabic Studies Division in the American University in Cairo.

1. Such questions include queries about the purpose of creation, the nature of humankind (material, spiritual or both) and the center of the universe (immanent or transcendant).
2. *Mutaḥayyizan*: A term used in Islamic theology to denote the use of independent reasoning, as opposed to a strict application of the letter of scripture or a reliance upon tradition, to arrive at answers to questions of dogma.
3. ṢAAS: *Ṣalla Allahu ʿalayhi wa Sallam*: May the peace and blessings of Allah be upon him. This prayer is said by Muslims whenever the name of the Prophet Muhammad is mentioned, or whenever he is referred to as the Prophet of Allah.
4. About ninety minutes before sunrise.
5. About two hours after sunset.
6. Most of my foreign friends tell me that they usually wake up at dawn but then go back to sleep afterwards.
7. The North-coastal Egyptian town most renowned for its flourishing furniture industry.
8. The total amount of American consumption in the last hundred years is estimated to equal the total consumption of the human race throughout its entire history.
9. Sabri Jirjis, *al-Turāth al-Yahūdī wa al-Ṣahyūnī fī al-Fikr al-Frowydī* (The Jewish and Zionist Tradition in Freudian Thought) (Cairo: ʿĀlam al-Kutub, 1970).
10. The whole tradition of the Prophet Muhammad, whether in the form of his sayings, his acts or his approval of others' behavior. For the majority of Muslims, the Sunnah is considered complementary to and explanatory of the Qur'an.
11. *Mawsuʿat al-Yahūd wa al-Yahūdiyyah wa al-Ṣahyūniyyah* (Encyclopedia of the Jews, Judaism and Zionism: A New Explanatory Paradigm) (Cairo: Dār Elshurūk, 1999).

CHAPTER TWO

1. The Qur'an describes this disciplined degree of conflict in (2:251): "And if God had not enabled people to defend themselves against one another, corruption would surely overwhelm the earth: but God is limitless in His bounty unto all the worlds."
2. This study was authored before the collapse of the Soviet Union and the communist camp in the early 1990s. However, such a stunning transformation

does not undermine the analyses or conclusions provided in this research. This research accounts for the literature that was published in the 1970s and 1980s, most of which predicted that rapprochement between the two camps (systems) would continue until they had merged into one system. All predictions prophesized that the unified socio-economic system would be realized through an extended, gradual process. However, the hoped-for outcome was realized in an astounding, single leap! The question that remains is: What next?

3   Independent theoretical practice reflects the genuine cultural development in any region and era (i.e., it expresses this general concept at a high level of abstraction). However, at a lower level of abstraction, and particularly in the Arab and Muslim world, the term indicating this process is ijtihad, or "interpretive induction/deduction".

4   Reference here can be made to the writings of such contemporaries as Ahmed Hussein, Sayyid Qutb, Abdul Qadir Odah, Yusuf al-Qaradawi – and from outside of Egypt, Malik Bennabi and Muhammad Baqir al-Sadr. They all agree on the basic idea of the predominance of the social side over the economic. Reference can also be made to an important author who presents a general view of the development of modern Islamic Arab thought in the entire Arab region, namely, Fahmy Jadʿaan, in *The Foundations of Progress as Viewed by the Islamic Thinkers in the Modern Arab World* (Beirut: The Arab Institute for Studies and Publication, 1979).

CHAPTER THREE

1   Ismail Sabri Abdallah, "Independent Development: An Endeavor to Define a Neglected Concept," in *Independent Development in the Arab World* (in Arabic) 1st Edition (Beirut: Center for Arab Unity Studies, 1987), p. 31.

2   Anwar Abdul-Malik, *al-Fikr al-ʿArabī fī Maʿrakat al-Nahḍah* (Arab Thought in the Battle for Revival) (Beirut: Dār al-'Adāb, 1981), pp.120–121.

3   Hisham Djait, *Europe and Islam*, translated by Peter Heinegy (Berkeley, CA: University of California Press, 1985), p. 73.

4   For more on the beginnings and development of Orientalism, see Nasr M. Arif, *Contemporary Theories on Political Development: A Comparative Critical Study in Light of Islamic Civilizational Perspectives* (in Arabic), MA Thesis, Faculty of Economics and Political Sciences, Cairo University, 1988, p. 56.

5   Jules Henery, "The Term 'Primitive' in Kierkegaard and Heidegger," in Ashley Montagu, ed., *The Concept of the Primi-tive* (New York: Free Press, 1968), pp. 227–228.

6   Gerard Leclerke, *Anthropologie et Colonialisme*, translated into Arabic by George Katura (Beirut: Maʿhad al-'Inmā' al-ʿArabī, 1982), pp. 78–85.

7   Pierre Clastres, *La Societe Contre L'Etat: Recherches d'Anthropologie Politique* (Paris: Edition de minuit, 1974), translated into Arabic by Muhammad Hussein Dakroob (Beirut: al-Mu'assasah al-Jamiʿiyyah lil-Dirāsāt, 1982), pp. 17–19.

8   Katherine George, "The Civilized West Looks at Primitive Africa: 1400–1800" in A. Montagu, ed., *op. cit.*, p.182.

9   Edward W. Said, *Orientalism* (New York: Vintage Books, 1979), pp. 206–207.

10 Ali Hassan al-Kharbutly, *al-Mustashriqūn wa al-Tārikh al-Islāmī* (Orientalists and Islamic History) (Cairo: al-Hay'ah al- Miṣriyyah al-ʿĀmmah lil Kitāb), 1988, pp. 11–21.

11 Nasr M. Arif, *op. cit.*, pp. 42–44.

12 Oswald Spengler, *The Decline of the West*, translated into Arabic by Ahmad al-Sheebani (Beirut: Dār Maktabat al-Ḥayāt, 1964), pp. 60–61.

13 Muhammad Asad, *Islam at the Crossroads*, translated into Arabic by

Omar Farrukh (Beirut: Dār al-Iʿtiṣām, n.d.), p. 76.
14. Muneer Shafeeq, *al-Islām fī Maʿrakat al-Ḥaḍārah* (Islam in the Battle of Civilization) (Beirut: Dār al-Kalimah, 1983), pp.54–55.
15. Ibid., p. 55.
16. Muta Safadi, "Authority under its Lost Names" (Arabic), *al-Fikr al-ʿArabī al-Muʿāṣir*, No. 23, Beirut, December 1984-January 1985, p. 4.; George Balandier, *Political Anthropology*, translated from the French by A. M. Sheridan Smith (New York: Pantheon Books, 1970), pp. 123–157.
17. Fuad I. Khoori, "The Rise of Anthropology and its Development" (in Arabic,) *al-Fikr al-ʿArabī*, Beirut, Nos. 37 & 38, March and June 1983, p. 16; Stanley Diamond, "The Search for Primitive" in A. Montagu, ed., *op. cit.*, pp. 99–104.
18. Szymon Chodak, *Societal Development: Five Approaches with Conclusions from Comparative Analysis* (New York: Oxford University Press, 1973), pp. 18–41.
19. Al-Sayyid al-Hussayni, *Development and Backwardness* (in Arabic) (Cairo: Maṭābiʿ Sijill al-ʿArab, 1980), 1st Edition.
20. W. W. Rosto, *The Stages of Growth: A Non-Communist Manifesto* (London: Cambridge University Press, 1961), pp.5–11.
21. Mahmoud al-Kurdi, *Backwardness and the Problems of the Egyptian Society*, in Arabic (Cairo: Dār al-Maʿārif, 1979), 1st Edition, pp. 43-49.
22. Ronald H. Chilcote, *Theories of Development and Underdevelopment* (Boulder, CO: Westview Press, 1984), pp. 279–280.
23. Adil Abdul-Mahdi, "The State of Eastern Despotism: The Western State in the East," *al-Fikr al-ʿArabī al-Muʿāṣir*, Beirut, Nos. 14–15, August-September, 1981, p. 100.
24. Ahmad Ismailovich, *The Philosophy of Orientalism and Its Effect on Contemporary Arab Literature* (in Arabic) (Cairo: Dār al-Maʿārif, 1980), p. 209; Said, *op. cit.*, pp. 91–92.
25. Djait, *op.cit.*, p. 16.
26. Ibid, p. 48.
27. Atif Wasfi, *Cultural Anthropology* (in Arabic) (Beirut: Dār al-Nahḍah al-ʿArabiyyah, 1971), p. 42; Muhammad Abduh Mahgoub, *Political Anthropology* (in Arabic) (Cairo: al-Hay'ah al-Miṣriyyah al-ʿĀmmah lil Kitāb, 1981), p. 81; Salman Khalaf, "A Critical Review of Models and its Utilization in Middle East Anthropology" (in Arabic), *al-ʿUlūm al-Ijtimāʿiyyah* (Social Sciences Journal), Kuwait, No.4. Vol.13, Winter, 1985, p. 373.
28. Mahgoub. *op. cit.*, p. 76; Khalaf, *op. cit.*, p. 37.
29. Muhammad al-Gawhari, *Anthropology: Theoretical Foundations and Practical Applications* (in Arabic) (Cairo: Series of Contemporary Sociology, 1980), No. 33, 1st Edition, pp. 273–274.
30. Khalaf, *op. cit.*, p. 373.
31. Ibid, p. 394.
32. Hagen, *Experiments in Civilization: The Effects of European Culture on a Native Community of Solomon Islands* (London: 1934), pp. 153–154.
33. Muhammad al-Gawhari, *Sociology and the Issues of Development* (in Arabic) (Cairo: Dār al-Maʿārif, 1982), 3rd Edition, pp. 165–173; Muhammad Ali Muhammad, *The Foundations of Political Sociology, Change and Political Development* (in Arabic) (Alexandria: Dār al-Maʿrifah al-Jāmiʿiyyah, 1986), p. 146.
34. Maʿan Ziyadah, *Maʿālim ʿalā Ṭarīq Taḥdīth al-Fikr al-ʿArabī* (in Arabic) (Kuwait: ʿAlam al-Maʿrifah Series, No. 115, July, 1987), pp. 46-47.
35. Tariq al-Bishri, "Al-Mas'alah al-Qānūniyyah bayna al-Shariʿah al-Islāmiyyah wa al-Qānūn al-Waḍʿī" (The Issue of Law between Islamic Jurisdiction and Positive Law), (Beirut:

Center for Arab Unity Studies, 1985), 1st Edition. presented at a conference entitled "Heritage and the Contemporary Challenges in the Arab World," (Beirut: Center for Arab Unity Studies, 1985), 1st Edition.

36 For more on the notion of social equation, see Malik Bennabi, *The Muslim in the World of Economics* (in Arabic) (Beirut: Dār al-Shurūq), p. 109.

37 Howard J. Warda, "Toward a Non-Ethnocentric Theory of Development: Alternative Conceptions from the Third World" in Howard J. Warda, ed., *New Directions in Comparative Politics* (Boulder, CO: Westview Press, 1985), pp.30–35.

38 Edward G. Stockwell and Karen A. Laidloe, *Third World Development: Problems and Prospects* (Chicago: Nelson-Hall, 1981), pp. 30–35.

39 Ibid., pp. 41–43.

40 Lewis Mumford, *The Myth of the Machine: The Pentagon of Power* (New York: Columbia University Press, 1970), Vol. 2, pp. 86, 349.

41 Malik Bennabi, *op. cit.*, pp. 127–236.

42 Ali Shariʿati, *Returning to the Identity*, translated into Arabic by Ibrahim al-Dusuqi Shita (Cairo: al-Zahrāʾ for Arab Media, 1986), 1st Edition, pp. 260–272. The author elaborates on the notion of "geography of the word," as a central tool to understand ideas and theories within their own frameworks without overlooking their overall connotations.

43 Arif, *op. cit.*, pp. 19–46.

44 Sayyid Dusouqi Hassan, *Premises for Civilizational Revival*, (in Arabic) (Kuwait: Dār al-Qalam, 1987), 1st Edition, pp. 26–33.

45 Consult the literature sources known as "The Education and Discipline of Teacher and Disciple."

CHAPTER FOUR

1 Mahmoud al-Dhaoudi, "Cultural Psychological Backwardness as an Analytical Concept in the Arab and Third World Societies," in M. Ezzat Hegazy, et al., *Towards an Arab Sociology: Sociology and Current Arab Problems* (Beirut: Center for Arab Unity Studies, 1986), p.164.

2 Abdelwahab Elmessiri, *Palestinian Intifada and the Crisis of Zionism: A Study in Perception and Dignity* (Cairo: Published by the author, 1998), p.10.

3 Burhan Ghalyoun, *The Assassination of the Mind: The Crisis of the Arab Culture Between Literalist Fundamentalism and Dependency* (Cairo: Madbuly, 1990), p.436.

4 Heidar Ibrahim Ali, "Sociology and Ideological Conflict in Arab Society," in Mohammed Ezat Hegazy, et al., *Towards an Arab Sociology: Sociology and Current Arab Problems* (Beirut: Center for Arab Unity Studies, 1986), p.111.

5 Adel Hussein, *Towards a New Arab Thought: Nasserism, Development and Democracy* (Cairo: Al-Mustaqbal al-ʿArabī, 1985) p.22.

6 D.A. Hjelle, & D.J. Ziegler, *Personality Theories: Basic Assumptions, Research and Applications* (Aukland: McGraw-Hill, 1981).

7 J. Brozek, "Soviet Psychology," in M.H. Marx & W.A. Hillix, *Systems and Theories in Psychology* (New Delhi: Tata McGraw-Hill, 1973).

8 W. Mischel, *Personality and Assessment* (New York: Wiley, 1968); B. F. Skinner, *Beyond Freedom and Dignity* (Toronto: Banton, 1971); B. F. Skinner, *Walden Two* (New York: Macmillan, 1976).

9 B. Evans, & B. Waites, *IQ and Mental Testing: An Unnatural Science and its Social History* (London: Macmillan, 1981).

10 Mohammad Shakroun, "A Crisis of Sociology or a Crisis of Society," in Hegazy, et al.

11 M. Ezzat Hegazy, "The Present Crisis of Sociology in the Arab World," in Hegazy, et al., p.20-21.

12 M. Ezzat Hegazy, "The Present Crisis

of Sociology in the Arab World," in Hegazy, et al., p.26.
13 Salem Sary, "Sociology and Arab Social Problems: Concerns and Interests," in Hegazy, et al.
14 M. Abid al-Jabiri, *Problematics of Modern Arab Thought* (Beirut, Center for Arab Unity Studies, 1998), p.173.
15 Ghaly Shoukry, "Some Methodological Problematics on the Arab Path to the Sociology of Knowledge," in Hegazy, et. al., p.88.
16 Ali al-Kinz, "The Theoretical and Political Question of Arab Sociology," in Hegazy, et al., p.8.

CHAPTER FIVE

1 The 1972 books represent the ideological views of the 1960s, namely, Nasserism or Arab Socialism. It was not until 1972 that the Egyptian reading textbooks were revised so as to match the views of the era of market economy and private enterprise.
2 Robert A. Nisbet, *The Sociological Tradition* (New York: Basic Books, 1966), p. 257.
3 Throughout this article I have relied heavily on the following works: Reinhard Bendix, *Max Weber: An Intellectual Portrait* (New York: Doubleday, 1962); Lewis A. Coser, *Masters of Sociological Thought: Ideas in Historical and Social Context* (New York: Brace Jovanovich, 1971); Max Weber, *The Sociology of Religion*, translated by Ephraim Fischoff and introduction by Talcott Parsons (Boston: Beacon, 1994).
4 See in particular Bendix, *Max Weber*, Chapter 12.
5 Ibid.
6 Lloyd I. Rudolph and Suzanne Hoeber Rudolph, *The Modernity of Tradition: Political Development in India* (Chicago: University of Chicago Press, 1967), p. 7.
7 *International Journal of Middle East Studies*, 1974, 3, pp. 260–73.
8 Ibid., p.271.
9 Maxime Rodinson, *Islam and Capitalism* (New York: Pantheon, 1973), pp.99, 103.
10 Ibid., p.56.
11 Ibid., p.107.
12 Ibid., p. 35.
13 Bryan Turner, *Weber and Islam* (London: Routledge and Kegan Paul, 1974). See especially the last chapter, "Marx, Weber and Islam," pp.171–84.
14 Gustave von Grunebaum, *Medieval Islam: A Study in Cultural Orientation* (Chicago: University of Chicago Press, 1971), p.233.
15 Ibid., p. 346.
16 *Review of Middle East Studies*, 2, 1976.
17 Peter L. Berger and Brigitte Berger, *Sociology: A Biographical Approach* (New York: Basic Books, 1972), p. 339.

CHAPTER SIX

1 W. Buckle, *Sociology and Modern Systems Theory* (Englewood Cliffs, NJ: Prentice-Hall, 1967).
2 E. Feigenbaum and P. Cohen, *The Handbook of Artificial Intelligence* (Reading, MA: Addison Wesley, 1982), Vol. 3.
3 G. Pessis-Pasternak, *Faut-Il Brûler Descartes?* (Paris: Découverte, 1991), pp.213–226.
4 J. Searle, "Minds, Brains and Programs," *The Behavioral and Brain Sciences* 3 (1980), pp.417–457.
5 J. Searle, "Is the Brain's Mind a Computer Program?," *Scientific American* (January 1990), p.26.
6 Ibid., p.32.
7 Ibid., pp.31–33.
8 Pessis-Pasternak, *op.cit.*, pp.213–226.
9 R. Penrose, *The Emperor's New Mind: Concerning Computers, Minds, and the Laws of Physics* (Oxford, UK: Oxford University Press, 1987).
10 G. Johnson, "New Mind, No Clothes: Book Review of *The Emperor's New Mind*," *New Encounter* (April 1988), p.48.
11 L. White, "The Evolution of Culture,"

in *Theories and Paradigms in Contemporary Sociology*, eds., S. Denisoff, O. Callahan, and M. Levine (Itasca, IL: F.E. Peacock Publishers, Inc., 1975), pp.224–225.
12. O.D. Duncan, ed., *William Ogburn on Culture and Social Change* (Chicago: The University of Chicago Press, 1964), p.3.
13. E. B. Tylor, *Primitive Culture* (London: Murray, 1871).
14. J. G. Manis and B. N. Meltzer, eds., *Symbolic Interaction: A Reader in Social Psychology* (Boston: Allyn and Bacon, 1968).
15. L. White, "The Evolution of Culture," p.220.
16. Ibid.
17. G. Johnson, "New Mind, No Clothes," p.49.
18. E. Morin, *La Methode IV: Idées* (Paris: Le Seuil, 1991).
19. E. Morin, *Introduction à la Pensée Complex* (Paris: ESF editeur, 1990).
20. Taken from a Canadian Broadcasting Corporation ideas program (18–19 January 1988) on artificial intelligence.
21. M. Hunt, *The Universe Within: A New Science Explores the Human Mind* (New York: Simon and Schuster, 1986), p.54.
22. Ibid., 74.
23. Ibid., 81.
24. Ibid., 93.
25. Ibid., 127.
26. Ibid., 227.
27. "Artificial Intelligence: A Debate," in *Scientific American* (January 1990), p.31.
28. M. Hunt, *The Universe Within*, p.322.
29. Ibid., 319.
30. "Artificial Intelligence," p.31.
31. R. Shweder and R. Levine, *Culture Theory* (London: Cambridge University Press, 1989), p.27.
32. Ibid., 28.
33. Ibid., 38.
34. Ibid., 40.
35. R. Penrose, *The Emperor's New Mind*.
36. Pessis-Pasternak, *Faut-Il Brûler Descartes?*, pp.215–216.
37. M. Dhaouadi, "An Operational Analysis of the Other Underdevelopment in the Arab World and the Third World," in *International Sociology* 3, No. 3 (September 1988), pp.219–234.
38. *The Globe Mail* (Toronto, Canada), 15 September 1990, p.4.
39. Pessis-Pasternak, *Faut-Il Brûler Descartes?*, pp.213–219, pp.229–237.
40. M. Gardner, *Frames of Mind: The Theory of Multiple Intelligences* (New York: Basic Books, 1985).
41. H. B. English and A. C. English, *Encyclopedia of Psychology* (Guilford, CT: The Dushkin Publishing Group, Inc., 1973), p.129.
42. J. White, *Anthropology* (London: The English Universities Press, 1967), p.23.
43. "L 'Autre Sociologie," *Cahiers de Recherche Sociologique* 5, No. 2 (Automne 1987).
44. H. B. English and A. C. English, *Encyclopedia of Psychology*, p.129.

CHAPTER SEVEN

1. Chinua Achebe, *Things Fall Apart* (London: Heinemann, 1958).
2. Tayeb Salih, *Season of Migration to the North*, trans. Denys Johnson-Davies (London: Heinemann, 1969).
3. Tahar Ben Jelloun, "I am an Arab, I am Suspect," trans. George Black, *The Nation* (April 15, 1991).
4. Achebe, p.162.
5. K.V. Tirumalesh, "Writing-English versus Writing-in-English," *Economic and Political Weekly* (November 23, 1991), XXVI: 47.
6. Samia Mehrez, "The Poetics of a Tattooed Memory: Decolonization and Bilingualism in North African Literature," *Emergence* 2 (Spring 1990).
7. Barbara Harlow, "Sentimental Orientalism: *Season of Migration to the North* and *Othello*," in Tayeb Salih's *'Season of Migration to the North': A Casebook*, ed. Mona Takieddine Amyuni (Beirut: American University of Beirut, 1985), pp.75–79.

8. Eldred Jones, *Othello's Countrymen* (London: Oxford University Press, 1965).
9. William Shakespeare, *Othello the Moor of Venice* (New York: Penguin, 1958), (I, I, II, pp.86–92).
10. *Othello the Moor of Venice* (I, I, II, pp.108-113).
11. Ibn Khaldūn, *The Muqaddimah: An Introduction to History*, trans. Franz Rosenthal (Princeton, NJ: Princeton University Press, 1967), I, pp.175–176.
12. M.M. Badawi, "Shakespeare and the Arabs," *Cairo Studies in English*, ed. Magdi Wahba (Cairo: The Anglo-Egyptian Bookshop, 1963/1966).
13. Ferial J. Ghazoul, "The Arabization of Othello," *Comparative Literature* 50:1 (Winter, 1998), pp.1–31).
14. Nadia Hijab, "Meet the Maker of Modern Arab Mythology," *The Middle East* (June 1979), pp. 67–68.
15. Tayeb Salih, *Season of Migration to the North*, p.95.
16. Ibid., p.25.
17. Ibid., pp.145–146.
18. Tahar Ben Jelloun, "I am an Arab, I am Suspect," p.482.
19. Ibid.
20. Ibid., p.483.
21. Ibid.
22. Ibid.
23. Ibid.
24. Ibid.
25. Ibid., p.484.
26. Ibid.
27. Ibid.
28. Ibid.

CHAPTER EIGHT

1. Ḥāzim al-Qarṭājannī, *Minhāj al-Bulaghā' wa Sirāj al-ʿUdabā'*, ed., Muhammad al-Habib bin al-Khawajah (Beirut: Dār al-Gharb al-Islāmī, 1981), p.68.
2. Muhammad Mandour, *Fī al-Mīzān al-Jadīd* (Cairo: Dar Nahḍat Miṣr, 1973), p.178.
3. Abdallah Laroui, "al-Manhajiyyah Bayna al-Ibdāʿ wa al-Ittibāʿ," *al-Manhajiyyah fī al-Adab wa al-ʿUlūm al-Insāniyyah*, ed. Abdallah Laroui et al. (Casablanca: Dār Tubqāl, 1986), pp. 9–10.
4. Abu Deeb adds, "Structuralism does not change language or society ... but ... it changes the thought examining language and society," Introduction to *Jadaliyat al-Khafā' wa al-Tajallī*. Kamal Abu Deeb, *Jadaliyat al-Khafā' wa al-Tajallī: Dirāsāt Bunyawiyyah fī al-Shiʿr* (The Dialectics of Covertness and Overtness), (Beirut: Dār al-ʿIlm Lil-Malāyīn, 1981), p.7. The only problem with this is that it does not explain how structuralism can change thought without having some philosophical foundation. For a well-informed discussion of the philosophical foundation of structuralism, see Fuad Zakaria's "al-Judhūr al-Falsafiyyah lil-Binā'iyyah" in his book *Āfāq al-Falsafah*.
5. Muhammad Ghunaimi Hilal, *Dirāsāt fī Madhāhib al-Shiʿr wa Naqdihi* (Cairo: Dār Nahḍat Miṣr, n.d.), p.57.
6. See, for example, Matthew Arnold, *Culture and Anarchy*, ed. J. Dover Wilson (Cambridge: Cambridge University Press, 1971), p.184, as well as *A Matthew Arnold Prose Selection*, ed. John D. Jump (New York: Macmillan, 1965), pp. 1–29, and T. S. Eliot, *After Strange Gods* (N.Y.: Harcourt, Brace and Co., 1934), pp. 15–44.
7. Salah Fadhl, "Ishkāliyat al-Manhaj fī al-Naqd al-Ḥadīth," *al-Muḥāḍarāt* (Jiddah: Al-Nādī al-ʿAdabī al-Thaqāfī, 1988), Vol. 5. p.393. For a more detailed analysis of this subject see M. A. al-ʿAlim, "al-Judhūr al-Maʿrifiyyah wa al-Falsafiyyah li al-Naqd al-Adabī al-Ḥadīth wa al-Muʿāṣir," *al-Falsafah al-ʿArabiyyah al-Muʿāṣirah* (Beirut: Markaz Dirāsāt al-Waḥdah al-ʿArabiyyah, 1988), pp.71-123.
8. M. A. al-Jabiri, *Takwīn al-ʿAql al-ʿArabī* (Beirut: Dār al-Ṭalīʿah, 1985);

also *Bunyat al-ʿAql al-ʿArabī* (Markaz Dirāsāt al-Wahdah al-ʿArabiyyah, 1985); Ali Umlil, "Mulāḥaẓāt Ḥawla Mafhūm al-Mujtamaʿ fī al-Fikr al-ʿArabī al-Ḥadīth," *Dirāsāt Maghribiyyah fī al-Falsafah wa al-Turāth wa al-Fikr al-ʿArabī al-Ḥadīth*, Ahmad Shahlan, et al. (Casablanca: Al-Markaz al-Thaqāfī al-ʿArabī, 1985). Assaeed Binsaeed, "al-Mafāhīm al-Siyāsiyyah fī al-Tadāwul al-ʿArabī al-Muʿaṣir: Mulāḥaẓāt Manhajiyyah," *Ishakāliyyāt al-Minhāj fī al-Fikr al-ʿArabī wa al-ʿUlūm al-Insāniyyah*, A. Bin Abd al-Ali, et al. (Casablanca: Dār Tubqāl, 1987).

9   Abū ʿAli al-Ḥussain ibn Sīna, *Manṭiq al-Mashriqiyyīn wa al-Qaṣīdah al-Muzdawijah fī al-Manṭiq* (Cairo: Al-Maktabah al-Salafiyyah, 1910), p.9. For a discussion of the relationship between methodology and logic in Ibn Sīna's thought see Muhammad Aziz Nadhmi Salim, *Tārīkh al-Manṭiq ʿInd al-ʿArab* (Alexandria: Muʾassasat Shihāb al-Jāmiʿah, 1983), p.119.

10 Abū ʿAli al-Ḥussain ibn Sīna, *Manṭiq al-Mashriqiyyīn wa al-Qaṣīdah al-Muzdawijah fī al-Manṭiq* (Cairo: Al-Maktabah al-Salafiyyah, 1910), p.3.

11 Ḥāzim al-Qarṭājannī, *Minhāj al-Bulaghāʾ wa Sirāj al-ʿUdabāʾ*, ed. Muhammad al-Habib bin al-Khawajah, (Beirut: Dār al-Gharb al-Islāmī, 1982), p.20.

12 Ḥāzim, 1981, pp.68-69.

13 Yāqūt al-Ḥamawī, *Muʿjam al-Udabāʾ* (Cairo: Dār al-Maʾmūn, n.d.), Vol. 8, pp.190-227.

14 Abū al-Walīd Muḥammad ibn Aḥmad ibn Rushd, *Faṣl al-Maqāl fī Mā Bayna al-Ḥikmah wa al-Sharīʿah min al-Ittiṣāl*, ed. Muhammad Imara (Beirut: Al-Muʾassasah al-Aʿrabiyyah lil-Dirāsāt wa al-Nashr, 1986), p.26.

15 Zaki N. Mahmoud, *al-Manṭiq: Naẓariyyat al-Bahth* (A translation of John Dewey's *Logic: The Theory of Inquiry*), (Cairo: Dār al-Maʿārif, 1969), p.56.

16 Northrop Frye, *The Anatomy of Criticism: Four Essays* (Princeton, N.J.: Princeton UP, 1957), p.7.

17 Northrop Frye, *The Anatomy of Criticism: Four Essays* (Princeton, N.J.: Princeton UP, 1957), p.99.

18 Northrop Frye, *The Anatomy of Criticism: Four Essays* (Princeton, N.J.: Princeton UP, 1957), p.19.

19 T. S. Eliot, "The Function of Criticism," *Selected Essays* (N.Y.: Harcourt, Brace and Co., 1950), pp.12-22.

20 M. H. Abrams, *Natural Supernaturalism: Tradition and Revolution in Romantic Literature* (New York: W. W. Norton, 1971), p.13.

21 Michel Foucault, *The Order of Things: Archaeology of the Human Sciences*. World of Man Series, ed. R. D. Laing (N.Y.: Vintage Books, 1973), p.xx.

22 Harold Bloom, in an interview with Robert Moynihan, in R. Moynihan, *A Recent Imagining* (Hamden, Conn.: Archon Books, 1986), p.18.

23 Northrop Frye, *The Anatomy of Criticism: Four Essays* (Princeton, N.J.: Princeton UP, 1957), p.315.

24 Robert Lowth, *Lectures on the Sacred Poetry of the Hebrews*, ed. Calvin E. Stowe (Andover: Crocker and Brewster, 1829), p.17.

25 Robert Lowth, *Lectures on the Sacred Poetry of the Hebrews*, ed. Calvin E. Stowe (Andover: Crocker and Brewster, 1829), p.xv.

26 E. S. Shaffer, *Khubla Khan and The Fall of Jerusalem: The Mythological School in Biblical Criticism and Secular Literature: 1770-1880* (Cambridge: Cambridge University Press, 1975), p.10.

27 E. S. Shaffer, *Khubla Khan and The Fall of Jerusalem*, p.20.

28 Benedict de Spinoza, *A Theological Political Treatise*, tr. R. H. Elwes (N.Y.: Dover Publication, 1951), p.99.

29 Benedict de Spinoza, *A Theological Political Treatise*, tr. R. H. Elwes (N.Y.:

Dover Publication, 1951), p.15.
30 R. W. Emerson, *The Collected Works of Ralph Waldo Emerson* (Cambridge, Mass.: The Belknap Press of Harvard University, 1971), p.56.
31 Geoffrey Hartman, *Beyond Formalism* (N.Y.: Yale UP, 1970), p.361.
32 Northrop Frye, *The Secular Scripture: A Study of the Structure of Romance* (Cambridge, MA: Harvard UP, 1976).
33 Terry Eagleton, *Literary Theory: An Introduction* (Oxford: Basil Blackwell, 1983), p.93.
34 Martin Heidegger, *On Time and Being*, tr. Joan Stambaugh (N.Y.: Harper and Row, 1972), p.24.
35 Robert D. Denham, *Northrop Frye and Critical Method* (University Park: The Pennsylvania State UP, 1978), pp.229-32.
36 Northrop Frye, *The Secular Scripture: A Study of the Structure of Romance* (Cambridge, MA: Harvard UP, 1976), p.60.
37 Tzvetan Todorov, *Literature and Its Theorists: A Personal View of Twentieth Century Criticism*, tr. Catherine Porter (Ithaca: Cornell UP, 1987), p.2.
38 Ibid., p.7-8.
39 Tzvetan Todorov, *The Poetics of Prose*, translated from the French by Richard Howard (Oxford: Blackwell, 1977; Ithaca, N.Y.: Cornell University Press, 1977).
40 Tzvetan Todorov, *Literature and Its Theorists: A Personal View of Twentieth Century Criticism*, tr. Catherine Porter (Ithaca: Cornell UP, 1987), p.190.
41 Roland Barthes, "Introduction to the Structural Analysis of Narratives," in *A. Barthes Reader*, ed., Susan Sontag (New York: Hill and Wang, 1982), pp.252-54.
42 Roland Barthes, *The Grain of the Voice: Interviews 1962-1980*, tr. Linda Coverdale (New York: Hill and Wang, 1985), pp.48-49.
43 Northrop Frye, *The Anatomy of Criticism: Four Essays* (Princeton, N.J.: Princeton UP, 1957), p.7.
44 Claude Levi-Strauss, "A Confrontation" in *New Left Review* 62 (July-August, 1970), p.64.
45 Ibid.
46 Jean-Paul Sartre, "Jean-Paul Sartre Repond" in *L'Arc* 30, 1986.
47 Claude Levi-Strauss, "A Confrontation" in *New Left Review* 62 (July-August, 1970), p.74.
48 Fredric Jameson, *The Prison-House of Language: A Critical Reading of Structuralism and Russian Formalism* (Princeton, N.J.: Princeton UP, 1972), p.v.
49 Ibid., pp.viii–ix.
50 Fredric Jameson, "Beyond the Cave: Modernism and Modes of Production" in *The Horizon of Literature*, ed. Paul Hernadi (Lincoln: Nebraska UP, 1982), pp.159–160.
51 Ibid., p.181.
52 Frederich Nietzsche, *The Works of Friedrich Nietzsche*, ed. Oscar Levy (London: T. N. Foulis, 1910), pp.x, 8.
53 Roland Barthes, *The Grain of the Voice: Interviews 1962-1980*, tr. Linda Coverdale (New York: Hill and Wang, 1985), p.155.
54 Roland Barthes, *The Grain of the Voice: Interviews 1962–1980*, tr. Linda Coverdale (New York: Hill and Wang, 1985), p.133.
55 Fredric Jameson, *The Political Unconscious: Narrative as a Symbolic Act* (Ithaca: Cornell UP, 1981), p.9.
56 The concept of "écriture" is discussed in *The Political Unconscious*, p.20; Paul de Man's *Blindness and Insight: The Rhetoric of Contemporary Criticism* (New York: Oxford UP, 1971), p.20; and Barthes's *The Grain of the Voice*, p.162.
57 Jonathan Culler, The Pursuit of Signs: Semiotics, Literature, Deconstruction (New York: Cornell UP, 1981), p.31.
58 Fredric Jameson, *The Political Unconscious: Narrative as a Symbolic Act* (Ithaca: Cornell UP, 1981), p.20.

59 Ibid., p.23.
60 Ibid., p.10.
61 Fredric Jameson, *The Political Unconscious: Narrative as a Symbolic Act* (Ithaca: Cornell UP, 1981), p.10.
62 Pierre Macherey, "Literary Analysis: The Tomb of Structures" in *A Theory of Literary Production*, tr. Geoffrey Wall (London: Routledge and Kegan Paul, 1978), p.154. Elsewhere Macherey compares structuralist analysis to Leibniz's "God" who wants to move from one structure to the other but has no means of doing so (p.145). In *Writing and Difference*, p.291, Derrida makes a similar remark, but with no reference to Macherey.
63 Frederich Nietzsche, *The Works of Friedrich Nietzsche*, ed. Oscar Levy (London: T. N. Foulis, 1910), pp.x, 8.
64 J. Hillis Miller, "The Critic as Host" in *Deconstruction and Criticism* (New York: Continuum, 1979), pp.228-29.
65 Robert Scholes, "Some Problems in Current Graduate Programs in English" in *Profession 87* (N.Y.: The Modern Language Association, 1987), pp.41-2.
66 In his work Nietzsche criticizes Kant's metaphysics. See *The Philosophy of Nietzsche* (New York: the Modern Library, 1927) p.785. Later on, Heidegger came to criticize Nietzsche himself for the same laps into the metaphysical. See Heidegger, *Nietzsche*, tr. Frank A. Capuzzi (San Francisco: Harper & Row, 1982), pp. 203–205.
67 Jacques Derrida, *Writing and Difference* (Chicago: The University of Chicago Press, 1978), p.281.
68 Paul de Man, *Blindness and Insight: The Rhetoric of Contemporary Criticism* (New York: Oxford UP, 1971), p.18.
69 Edward Said, "Reflections on Recent American Left Literary Criticism" in *The Question of Textuality: Strategies of Reading in Contemporary American Criticism*, ed. W. V. Spanos, et al. (Bloomington: University of Indiana Press, 1982), p.17. Said also makes the important remark that methods are always part of a network of power relations, a remark reinforced by Evan Watkins: *The Question of Textuality*, pp. 13, 32. From a slightly different viewpoint, Terry Eagleton points out that one can find entire social ideologies in what appears to be a neutral critical method (*Literary Theory: An Introduction*), p. 93.
70 George Steiner, *Real Presence,* The Leslie Stephen Memorial Lecture at the University of Cambridge (Cambridge: The University of Cambridge Press, November, 1985), pp.12, 18.
71 M. H. Abrams, "The Deconstructive Angel" in *Critical Inquiry* 3.3, Spring 1977, p.431.
72 Robert Moynihan, *A Recent Imagining* (Hamden, Conn.: Archon Books, 1986), pp.104-105.
73 Jacques Derrida, *Writing and Difference* (Chicago: The University of Chicago Press, 1978), p.320.
74 Susan Handelman, "Torments of an Ancient World: Edmund Jabés and the Rabbinic Tradition" in *The Sin and the Book: Edmund Jabés*, ed. Eric Gould (Lincoln: University of Nebraska Press, 1985), p.70. In her translation of Derrida's *Of Grammatology* Gayatri Spivak remarks that Derrida used to sign some of his articles with the pen-name "rabbi," which is exactly what happens in his articles on Jabés in *Writing and Difference*, p. 317. (Gayatri C. Spivak, "Preface" in J. Derrida *Of Grammatology* [Baltimore: The Johns Hopkins University Press, 1976]).
75 Paul Auster, "Introduction," *If There Were Anywhere But Desert: The Selected Poems of Edmund Jabés*, tr. Keith Waldrop (Barrytown, N. Y.: Susan Hill Press, 1988), p.x.
76 Susan Handelman, "Torments of an Ancient World: Edmund Jabés and the Rabbinic Tradition" in *The Sin and the*

Book: Edmund Jabés, ed. Eric Gould (Lincoln: University of Nebraska Press, 1985), p.70.
77 Edmund Jabés, *The Book of Questions*, tr. Rosemarie Waldrop (Middletown, Conn.: Wesleyan UP, 1984), p.143.
78 Derrida, "Living On," in *Deconstruction and Criticism*, p.84.
79 Edmund Jabés, *The Book of Questions*, tr. Rosemarie Waldrop (Middletown, Conn.: Wesleyan UP, 1984), p.146.

CHAPTER NINE

1 A symposium held by the Aga Khan Program for Islamic Architecture at Harvard University and the Massachusetts Institute of Technology, Cambridge, Massachusetts, November 6–8, 1987.

CHAPTER TEN

1 H.I. El-Mously, "The Valorization of Traditional Technology and Functional Adaptation of Modern Technology for the Realization of Endogenous Development." Division for the Study of Development, UNESCO, 1984.
2 H.I. El-Mously, "The Valorization of Traditional Technology and Functional Adaptation of Modern Technology for the Realization of Endogenous Development." Division for the Study of Development, UNESCO, 1984.
3 Ralph Linton, *The Study of Man: An Introduction* (New York: Appleton-Century, 1936).
4 Ralph Linton, *The Study of Man: An Introduction*.
5 J. Galtung, "Development, Environment and Technology: Towards a Technology for Self-Reliance." United Nations Conference on Trade and Development, 1978.
6 J. Galtung, "Development, Environment and Technology."
7 The same feelings were voiced by other researchers: "I always feel uneasy when I use the term 'technology'" (A. Sabet, "The Role of Science and Technology Policy in Technological Change in Developing Countries," in *The Proceedings of a Seminar of the United Nations Economic Commission for Western Asia*, Beirut, 9–14 Oct., 1977, p.93). "...the main concern of scientific bodies nowadays is 'technology transfer.' The word has become hackneyed and has been used to denote various, and sometimes contradictory, meanings" (Usama Amin al-Khuli, "al-Siyasah al ʿIlmiyyah wa Takhṭīṭ Baʿīd al-Madā," *al-Nadwah al-ʿArabiyyah li al-Taḥḍīr li Muʾtamar al-ʿUmam al-Muttaḥidah li al-ʿIlm wa al-Technūlūjīa* (Baghdad: 1978), pp.7–8.
8 "That large black box which we all fear" (A. Sabet, "The Role of Science and Technology Policy in Technological Change in Developing Countries," p.93).
9 *New Encyclopedia Brittanica* (Chicago: Encyclopedia Brittanica, 1986), p.451.
10 C.L. Barnhar, *The American College Dictionary* (N.Y.: Random House, 1957), p.1243.
11 This in no way means overlooking the role of heredity as one of the mechanisms affecting human beings. What it means is that the effect of heredity is not realized directly through human behavior. Rather, heredity prepares what can be called the "infrastructure" of the individual, both physically and mentally. The mechanism of natural selection, which mainly operates through heredity, represents a technological pattern acting to spread a number of genetic features that qualify different species or peoples to coexist with their natural environment (their geophysical and climatic conditions). "Each human group has developed its distinctive features to cope with a given set of environmental conditions... The price that the West African man, for instance, had to pay in order to have a strong build that is immune to local malaria and capable of working actively in

severely hot and humid environment was hundreds of thousands of deaths over hundreds of generations. Any West African carries in his blood malaria parasites which could kill a white man within one week" (Ralph Linton, *The Study of Man*, p.473).

12 The use of the plural form with the former and the singular with the latter implies the following: First, the situation that was dominant in human history suggests the presence of different technologies in different cultures. Did the nature of technological activity differ from one culture to another? Were there different patterns of rationality that governed the technological activity in each culture? It is assumed here that there are, despite the differences, features shared by traditional technologies, stemming from the relative isolation of local societies, limitation of trade, and the low level of production potentials and dynamism of technological development. Thus, there was no surplus for exchange between different cultures. Considerations of balance with the environment and survival (in the biological sense) were dominant.

Second, some modern technological activities are based on different models of rationality and represent different cultural "attitudes." It is assumed here that, in spite of the dominance of the Western model with its distinctive rationality, there can still be other patterns governing technological activity in different cultures. The Chinese model of industrialization and agricultural development till the end of the Cultural Revolution may cast more light on this assumption.

13 E.E. Schumacher, *Small is Beautiful* (N.Y.: Perennial Library, 1975), p.7.

14 We can conceive of the difference between technique and technology by comparing the former to an idea and the latter to thinking (as an activity or ability). Ideas are the products of thinking just as techniques are the products of technology. Ideas are also transferable, just as techniques are more or less accurately transferable. The question is: Can the ability to think be transferred? The answer is assumedly negative. In the same way, the transfer of techniques does not automatically lead to technology transfer.

15 "Moral obsolescence" may be the result of changing fashion, as in consumer goods, or of necessity to obtain the latest products, as in weapons (Ismail Sabri Abdu Allah, "*Strātijiyāt al-Technūlūjīa*," *al-Muʾtamar al-ʿIlmī al-Sanawī al-Thānī li al-Iqtiṣādiyyīn al-Maṣriyyīn* (Cairo: Al-Hayʾah al-Maṣriyyah al-ʿĀmmah lil-Kitāb, n.d.), p.533.

16 According to one study, the engineering products and equipment imported by Arab countries every year is estimated at US $70 billion. Most of these are repeated projects which could have been carried out through mutual cooperation at a much lower cost while making progress in building endogenous technological abilities (ʿUthmān Abū Yazīd, "Naql al-Technūlūjīa Wa bʿaḍ Subul Taṭwīʿihā? Wa tawṭīnihā fī al-Duwal al-ʿArabiyyah," Nadwat al-Taʿlīm al-Handasī wa al-Technūlūjīa al-Mulāʾimah [Amman, 1985], p.2).

17 "International Symposium on the Conditions for Interaction between the Processes of Modernization and the Traditional Cultural Values of Different Societies" (Paris: Working Paper by Secretariat UNESCO, 19–23 June, 1989), p1.

18 It is interesting to observe that the term *tanmiyah* (the Arabic term for "development") carries the same connotation of 'quantitative increase.' In *Mukhtār al-Ṣiḥāḥ*, the verb *namā* is used with reference to money to mean "grow" or "increase". See Muḥammad ibn Abū Bakr ibn ʿAbd al-Qādir al-

Rāzī, *Mukhtār al-Ṣiḥāḥ* (Cairo: Dār Nahḍat Miṣr, n.d.), p.68. Similarly, Ibn Khaldūn uses the term *tanmiyah* with reference to trade in the sense of "growth of money." See Ali Nassar, *Mahazeer amam Tawaguh Misr a-Technuluji*, Durus Mu'asirah wa Tarikhiyyah.

19 See, for example, the writings of UN organizations such as UNESCO since the 1970's, and particularly in the 1980's.

20 One of the reactions to the failure of the Western pattern of development in many Third World countries was UNESCO's declaration of the decade 1988–1998 as "the decade of cultural development." The declared targets of that decade were: to attend to the cultural character and elements of different societies and to consider them in the process of development.

21 H.I. El-Mously, *Ma Warā' al-Baḥth: Mulāḥaẓāt Maydāniyyah* (Beyond Research: Field Observations) in *Nadwat Mushkilat al-Manhaj fī Buḥūth al-ᶜUlūm al-Ijtimāᶜiyyah* (*The Problem with Methodology in Social Sciences Research*), (Cairo: Al-Markaz al-Qawmī li al-Buḥūth al-Ijtimāᶜiyyah wa al-Jinā'iyyah, 1983), p.23.

22 Linton, *The Study of Man*, p.452.

23 H.I. El-Mously, *al-Technūlūjīa wa al-Namaṭ al-Ḥaḍārī: Dirāsat Ḥālah min al-ᶜArīsh* (Cairo: Markaz Buḥūth al-Sharq al-Awṣaṭ, 1982), p.157.

24 Newer tools and methods of production are not always necessary or suitable. One of the most interesting examples in this respect was encountered by an Egyptian expert while he was buying electronic calculators in Japan. The salesmen were using a simple wooden counting device (the abacus). When he asked them why they did not use the commonly used calculators, they replied that the simple wooden ones were more than adequate.

25 The European furniture style started to spread in Egypt as early as the 19th Century thanks to: First, the adoption of that style by the pashas and nobles of Cairo and Alexandria (the furniture industry first appeared in Alexandria and Cairo at the hands of Greek and Italian craftsmen); second, its adoption by the pashas and nobles of the countryside and the top official employees in Cairo and the provinces (the European furniture industry appeared in Damietta in the 1920s and flourished until the early 1950s); third, its adoption by the middle and lower classes from the 1960's and 1970's till now (low quality furniture, called '*bazārī*', i.e., basically commercial, appeared in Damietta and then spread to all the provinces of Egypt).

26 See the author's study of the socio-economic, psycho-social, and environmental characteristics of the large house/extended family pattern which had been dominant in Arish, North Sinai, before the Israeli occupation in June, 1967.

27 Early in human history (and perhaps up to the Industrial Revolution), many societies observed 'sumptuary rules;' see J. Goody, *Technology, Tradition and the State in Africa* (London: Hutchinson University Library for Africa, n.d.), p.32, according to which society did not allow sumptuary distinctions among certain social categories (clan chiefs, priests, nobles, etc.). Sumptuary distinctions were then associated with the social roles of such categories. There are many examples from Egyptian history. In ancient Egypt, the pisus (light linen) fabric was used to make priests' clothes and mummy covers. See Abdul Rahman Amar, *Tārīkh Fann al-Nasīj al-Maṣrī* (Cairo: Dār Nahḍat Miṣr, 1974), p.43. Similarly, the royal cloth, of which Egypt produced the finest varieties, was used by kings for religious and secular purposes and as trophies for princes and noblemen (*Tārīkh Fann al-Nasīj al-Maṣrī*, p.68). In the Islamic period,

caliphs had special centers for weaving the fabric they needed, which were called embroidery houses (*Tārīkh Fann al-Nasīj al-Maṣrī*, p.54).

28 The main weakness of the 23rd July Revolution is that it lacked a cultural content. Its leaders did not note any differences with the West except with respect to colonialism and economic exploitation. The question of cultural differences per se was not posed at all.

29 I owe my understanding of such rules and their influence on the environment to the late Omar Darraz. Laws of protection, which go back to the pre-Islamic period but were preserved by Islam, stipulate that every tribe has the right to breed in a certain area that is forbidden to other tribes. If a tribe encroaches upon another tribe's area, it is severely punished. Darraz observed that the lands that still follow the law of protection in Saudi Arabia and Iraq are rich in plant and animal life compared with the lands in which the law is no longer applied.

30 It would have been possible to think of alternative communication patterns in which the same scientific principle (the transmission of electromagnetic waves) achieves a horizontal type of communication between individuals or groups (an example is the videophone). Such devices could effectively contribute to social integration and expression of cultural identity. However, they are associated with a sender-recipient relationship that differs in quality from the one currently represented by TV.

31 In Western industrial societies, the percentage of direct communication among people compared with total human communication has dropped from 90% to 10% in 50 years (Nady Ashis, "Dialogue on the Traditions of Technology," in *Journal of the Society for International Development*, 3/4, Rome, 1981).

32 "International Symposium on the Conditions for Interaction between the Processes of Modernization and the Traditional Cultural Values of Different Societies," p.4.

33 For instance, what Britain looted from India from 1750 to 1800 equals more than one billion sterling pounds, which exceeds the total capital of the industrial projects run with steam power and dominant in the whole of Europe up to 1800.

34 H.I. El-Mously, "The Valorization of Traditional Technology and Functional Adaptation of Modern Technology for the Realization of Endogenous Development," p.9. The USA, which represents no more than 5.6% of the world's population, is responsible for 40% of the world's total consumption of primary resources (K. Seethram, et. al., "Science and Technology in India, An Alternate Perspective," IFDA Dossier, No.20, Nov-Dec, 1980, p.119), including non-renewable resources such as natural gas (63%), coal (44%), aluminium (42%), oil (33%), copper (33%), platinum (31%), cobalt (36%), gold, silver and zinc (26%), and lead (25%) (K. Seethram, et. al., "Science and Technology in India, An Alternate Perspective," p.121).

35 Such as artificial dyes, which, unlike vegetable dyes are not biodegradable.

36 An example is the danger represented by the combustion exhaust resulting from industrialization and the consumption of petroleum products by means of transportation. The increase of carbon dioxide in the atmosphere leads to the absorption of infrared rays at a rate higher than the normal. At a certain point, the balance between earth and sea may be disturbed as a result of the melting of ice at the two poles. See H.I. El-Mously, "The Valorization of Traditional Technology and Functional Adaptation of Modern Technology for the Realization of Endogenous Development."

37 In dealing with nature, man has in fact only two options. First, he may follow a balanced approach out of awareness of the features of his biosphere and his various material and spiritual needs, in which case balance is achieved through his belonging to the whole biosphere and his recognition of his responsibility towards it. This is the true application of the principle of ecodevelopment. Second, he may adopt a one-dimensional, self-centered approach that is indifferent to the laws of nature. In this case, when the accumulation of destructive effects reaches a certain level, the earth is subjected to enormous catastrophes and the biosphere returns to balance, this time by the force of nature, not by virtue of human awareness. Man here returns and belongs to nature, as matter, not through his awareness. Unfortunately, this second option is the one that is being adopted.

38 E. Baark and Andrew Jamison, "The Technology and Cultural Problematique." Report of the Afro-Nordic Seminar on the Cultural Dimension of Development. Organized by the Finnish Commission of UNESCO, 22–26 April, 1985, p.158.

39 These are embodied, for example, in various forms of plastic art, folklore, language, and worship.

40 A view embodied in the Western proverb, "Time is money: Use it or lose it."

41 The watch, checkbook, private car or plane may embody the concept of individualism in Western culture, i.e., the absolute freedom of the individual to move along the axes of time and place.

42 Many oversimplified views on the universality of science are mere embodiments of Western chauvinism, which calls for rendering different societies and nations soulless, disfigured imitations of Western society. The achievement of true universality for science lies in faith in the right of the various cultures to existence, mutual interaction, participation and creativity. The whole world is in need of such ongoing participation on the part of various cultures and nations.

43 T.M.A. Shariffadeen, "Integrating Science and Technology in National Development: The Malaysian Experience." Conference on Technological Integration of Islamic Countries, Cairo, 27–29 May, 1989, p.4.

44 Science can never be considered a national phenomenon in any society as long as it is regarded as the product of another culture to which the society has contributed nothing either in the past or the present; see Rushdi Rashid, *Tārīkh al-ʿIlm wa al-ʿaṭāʾ al-ʿIlmī fī al-Waṭan al-ʿArabī* (Beirut: Markaz Dirāsāt al-Waḥdah al-ʿArabiyyah, 1985), p.163.

45 According to George Sarton, *A Guide to the History of Science* (Waltham, MA: Chronica Bottanica, 1952), some Medieval scholars belonged to Arab culture. Among mathematicians and astronomers we have, for example, al-Khawārizmī, al-Ferjānī, al-Batānī, Abū al-Wafā, ʿUmar al-Khayyām, al-Bayrūnī; among philosophers there appeared al-Fārābī, al-Ghazālī, Averroes, and Ibn Khaldūn, and finally, among scientists there were al-Rāzī, al-ʿIsrāʾīlī, ʿAlī ibn ʿAbbās, Abū Alqāsim, Avicenna, and the Maymounis. Few of these great men were Arabs, and not all of them were Muslims, yet they all belonged to the same culture, the Islamic culture, and were speakers of Arabic. This clearly shows the absurdity of claiming that learning during the Middle Ages was the product of Latin writings only. Over many centuries, the very few scientific books which appeared in Latin were outdated and full of superstitions. Moreover, Arabic, next to Greek only, was acknowledged as the universal language of science, for it was the language of different nations and

peoples with different religions.

The best Arab scientists were not satisfied with the Indian and Greek learning which they inherited, for they aspired to keep pace with the latest developments in learning and science and their thirst for knowledge drove them to seek more knowledge. This is why they criticised the views and the ideas of Iklides, Apollonius and Archimedes, discussed Ptolemy's views and tried to introduce improvements to astronomical tables as well as rid contemporary theories of pitfalls and wrong views. They also contributed to the development of algebra and trigonometry and thus paved the way for the European Algebraists during the 16th Century to make their own contributions to this scientific discipline. Moreover, they were able to contribute their own new ideas to the various disciplines and raise new issues and problems as well as to fill in some of the gaps in the scientific heritage known then to them.

46 In his excellent essay on this subject, Rushdy Rashed criticizes many Arab intellectuals for their willingness to accept Orientalists' views on the supposed Western origin of science, the emergence of the empiricist approach for the first time during the scientific revolution in the Renaissance and the role of Arab scholars as mere translators of Greek writings without making any of their own contributions. Rashed holds that ideologically based attempts at disregarding the role of Islamic Arabic scientists is detrimental to the formation of an accurate understanding of the history of science. According to him, there have been many findings by recent researchers concerning the role of Muslim scientists such as Muw'ayid al-Dīn al-Aaraḍī, Naṣīr al-Dīn al-Ṭūsī, Qoṭb al-Dīn al-Shīrāzī, Ibn al-Shāṭir al-Demishqī, Ibn al-Haytham, al-Khwārizmī, Banū Mūssā, al-Bayrūnī as well as non-Muslim scientists such as Thābit Ibn Qurrah and other scientists of al-Saaba, the Bagtishiuas, Qesṭā Ibn Lūqā and other Christians, as well as Sand Ibn ʿAlī the Jew, and the skeptic Mohamed Ibn Zakariyya. Such findings stress the fact that science belongs in its origin to Islamic culture, under whose banner it flourished and achieved progress. This Islamic science, as we may call it, was part of the social life of all classes of Islamic society. Such scientific activity was not the privilege of the Caliph or the court, neither was it confined to centers of learning, observatories, hospitals or schools; on the contrary, it was to be found in both the diwan and the mosque.This national and religious multiplicity was unprecedented in the history of science. (Rushdi Rashid, *Tārīkh al-ʿUlūm*, p.156).

47 And hopefully a short-lived one.

48 In the history of ancient Egypt we find many examples of the borrowing of technological components from other cultures and civilizations. Egyptian farmers during the pre-dynasty era adopted methods of growing maize from the Greeks and, at the beginning of the historical era in Egypt, technology for growing grapes and olives from the Mediterranean countries. Egypt likewise borrowed methods of cultivating clover from India via Iran, rice and sugarcane from India during the Islamic era, as well as a brand of maize, tomatoes, potatoes and long-stock cotton from the American continent (Ali Nasar, "Maḥādhīr Amām Tawajjuh Miṣr al-Technūlūjī: Durūs Muʿāṣirah wa Tārīkhiyyah," al-Muʾtamar al-ʿIlmī al-Sanawī al-Sābiʿ li al-Iqtiṣādiyyīn al-Miṣriyyīn, Cairo: 1982, Rushdi Rashid, *Tārīkh al-ʿUlūm*, Abdul Rahman Amar, *Tārīkh Fann al-Nasīj al-Maṣrī*) at the turn of the 19th Century. The ancient Egyptians borrowed *al-ṭanbūr* (a primitive tool for irrigation) from the Greeks, and the waterwheel and watermill from the

ancient Romans. They borrowed the military chariot from the Hittites but stopped using it after the end of the war. During the French expedition in Egypt, French scientists expressed their admiration for many Egyptian industries such as gypsum, textiles, nitrates and the hatching of eggs. As for the manufacturing of nitrates from the soot resulting from the burning of cattle droppings, it was not known in Europe, and this industrial product was exported mainly to Europe (16 : 334). Since the hatching industry was unknown in Europe, French expedition scientists recorded detailed descriptions of the processes involved. As for the Egyptian gypsum industry, it was much more developed in its technique than the gypsum industry in France (16 : 2411). Hence, upon noticing the Egyptians' lack of machines run by natural sources of energy (steam - wind - water), they did not attribute it to inherent industrial backwardness on the Egyptians' part; rather, they could see that there was no economic need for the use of such machines when the available human and animal sources of energy were so cheap.

49 Linton, *The Study of Man*, p.426.
50 J. Galtung, "Development, Environment and Technology," p.100.
51 Only the minority who live in luxury in some poor societies or the majority in some rich countries enjoy these basic needs.
52 In describing Third World countries, the West identifies the concept of "intermediate technology" as being identical with the concept of "developing countries." However, this concept of technology entails no solution to the problem of technological subordination to the West or the possibility of surpassing it. Rather, it implies that it is only a matter of time which makes Third World countries lag behind, and hence their need for less advanced Western technology.
53 Bernal asserts that science was not a definitive factor in the revolutionary substitution of mechanical production for manual production, which took place during the last quarter of the 18th Century. On the contrary, he asserts that the production process during this period proved that it was capable of motivating progress in scientific knowledge. In this respect Bernal says, "The basic achievements in textile industry were made in fact without any radical applications of scientific principles. The real importance of these achievements lies in the emergence of a new social variant, namely, the worker with the small amount of money he invested in this industry, which helped to change the production process and take it in a new direction. Success was possible because economic conditions were favorable." J. Bernal, *Science in History* (London: C.A. Watts & Co. Ltd, 1969).
54 In this respect, individuals are considered a very important source of technological knowledge, which is not to be ignored in conducting a study of such societies with a view to developing them. For instance, when I was conducting a study of endogenous technologies in the northern coast of the Mediterranean Sea in Egypt (northwest and southwest of Mersa Matrouh) I asked one of the most experienced farmers in the area about certain wells and who had dug them. He replied: "It's we who dug them, for the benefit of wayfarers. We take everything into account ... I mean ... whoever has a piece of land digs a well on it, since we know where water is to be found, whether at great depths or near the surface. When I say at great depths ... I mean that one may dig 50–60 meters without finding water. Water may be found at 2 or 3 meters deep under the ground. In fact, we know exactly the different depths at

which water is located."
55 "We depend on the clouds for our living rather than on logic and calculations. We haven't had good rain for almost ten or twelve years. Rain doesn't fall at the appropriate time. For fourteen years, rain has failed to come when needed; it has come either too early or too late. Last year we had some good rain but it didn't fall on our lands, it fell somewhere else ... we carried the water over here ... but it came late ... we cultivate our land as you know during March, but rain fell a month after March, which we used in cultivating small amounts of watermelon, melon, figs and olives." This quote is from a bedouin farmer who lives in the Western desert, 20–30 kilometers south of the northern coast of the Mediterranean sea near Mersa Matrouh. It reflects the difficult living conditions in this area compared with life in the rural areas in the Nile valley. Such conditions would be quite intolerable but for the relevant sets of values and personality traits they have developed in adaptation to them.
56 H.I. El-Mously, "A Study in Traditional Technologies and their Role in the Evolution of Infrastructure for the Application of Science and Technology." Engineering Education Section, UNESCO, 1983, p.10.
57 It's a pity that in a field like that of medicine in Egypt, which has provided and still provides the best opportunities for "Egyptianising" science and technology, we have not benefited from the rich traditional technologies which are now declining gradually with the ascendancy of Western technological methods of treatment. In the field of obstetrics, for instance, obstetricians do not recognise the practice of midwives as being legitimate, though they, for cultural and social reasons, render their services to the vast majority of individuals (80% of all births are performed by them). Given this illegitimacy, midwives perform their job in secret and obstetricians know this. They don't interfere except when people resort to them, as, for example, in the case of some fatal mistake committed by a midwife in a difficult childbirth. Such a failure on the part of a midwife is considered an additional excuse for attacking them as a group and calling upon the medical authorities to prevent them from practising in this field. Moreover, obstetricians have taken to performing Caesarean operations which typically reflect the influence of Western technology. The propagation of such a technology is motivated by: (1) The realization of greater profit, as obstetricians charge at least double the amount of money they get for natural deliveries (notice the time factor also, as natural delivery takes from 12–24 hours of close supervision and care depending on the case, while a Caesarean takes about half an hour). (2) The propagation of birth-control through undergoing a Caesarean, since it would be quite impossible to undergo the same operation repeatedly (only 2–4 times). Thus obstetricians favor this Western method of delivery for their own benefit at the expense of the interests of the mother or the family. The main excuse they give for preferring a Caesarean is to reduce the risks to which the baby might be exposed, a mere excuse which does not really reflect a concern about the preservation of a human life; rather, it reflects their concern for their professional reputation, which determines the number of their clients. It wouldn't have been difficult to achieve progress in the field of mother-care and obstetrics by devising methods and equipment for better supervision of cases during the last stage of pregnancy, and for facilitating natural delivery. In addition, there should be a division of labor among midwives (who should be

provided with relevant medical information and the equipment necessary for their job) as well as among obstetricians (through the building of specialised hospitals according to delivery cases). What stands in the way of achieving such progress is the competitive stance revealed in high-tech medical procedures, with their characteristic bias against traditional methods.

58 Which develops economic, scientific and technological interdependence among the different parties involved.

59 The best definition of the concept of self-reliance and which shows the relations underlying the different levels of application is given by Neirary in the "Arosha" Declaration. He says that in order to be able to preserve the freedom and independence of our people, we have to rely on ourselves in every possible way and avoid relying on the assistance coming from other countries. If each individual in a family is self-reliant, then a family unit consisting of ten individuals will be self-reliant. If all family units were self-reliant, the whole area consisting of those units would enjoy self-reliance, and if all areas/provinces are self-reliant, the whole nation will be self-reliant. This is our ultimate aim. To apply this policy of self-reliance we must teach people the meaning of self-reliance and how to attain it. We must achieve self-sufficiency in the fields of food production, services, housing and clothes.

60 When we consider samples of these traditional techniques (see, for example, the volume of illustrations appended to the Description of Egypt written by the French Expedition scientists),we shall discover that these techniques, bearing in mind the limited sources of energy and raw materials available during that period of time, reached a degree close to perfection as testified by those scientists themselves.

61 We can give many examples from Egypt in such fields as smithery, the textile industry and carpentry.

62 Ismail Sabri Abdu Allah, *Naḥwa Niẓām Iqtiṣādī ʿĀlamī Jadīd* (Cairo: al-Hayʿah al-Maṣriyyah al-ʿĀmmah li al-Kitāb, 1976), p.205.

63 Each nation or culture has its own mechanism for securing a sense of belonging and reintegrating its socio-cultural structure. By virtue of these processes, each cultural unit or structure is revitalized by restoring its relation with the source of its being which might have been weakened by temporary causes. Thus socio-cultural structures come to transcend themselves and effect a fusion with a larger structure. The individual melts into the family pot and the family melts into the local community, which, in its turn, melts into the nation. In this way socio-cultural structures regain their vitality and are actually reborn through such processes. We may view many rituals, celebrations and forms of worship as cultural processes through which the cultural structure is resurrected, restoring its distinctive features and characteristics.

64 In his essay "al-Mawqif min Ghayr al-Muslimīn' wa min al-ʿIlmāniyyah" (Attitudes towards Non-Muslims and Secularists), in *al-Shaʿb*, Cairo: 27 May 1986, Tarek al Beshry illustrates the attitude of Islam towards socio-cultural structures during a period which witnessed the profoundest and most drastic socio-cultural changes in history, by highlighting its attitude towards the tribal system at the dawn of Islam. When the Islamic nation was established on the basis of unity in the worship of God Almighty, it decided to put an end to the pre-Islamic tribal fanaticism which would politically hamper the achievement of a more comprehensive sense of belonging to one religious creed. However, the tribal system represented a collective entity

based on relations of marriage and kinship, an entity consisting of hundreds, and sometimes thousands, of individuals. Islam, therefore, did not destroy this system; rather, it benefited from its socio-cultural potentiality in building a social hierarchical structure which begins with the private and moves to the more general until we reach the greater Islamic nation. This concept of hierarchy underlay the plan used in the construction of the city of "Fustat" which was divided into sections or quarters; the soldiers in each tribe were to live in a certain section, isolated from the soldiers belonging to other tribes, yet all were united by a common feeling of fighting for the cause of Islam and its call to the worship of God.

65 M.W. Jackson, "Science and Depoliticization" in *Impact of Science on Society*, Vol.28, No.4, 1978, p.359.

66 George Sarton (G. Sarton, *A Guide to the History of Science*) was the first to warn against the supremacy of the technocratic view after it gained wide publicity following the Second World War. In the early 1950's Sarton wrote, "The technocrat may be so deeply engrossed in his own problems that the whole world loses its credibility for him and his public interests fade away. Thus he develops his own pattern of cold, calm, but frightening radicalism. Plato had wanted the philosophers to rule the world, but we wish it had been ruled by those rational scientists. As for the technocrats, may God protect us from them."

67 Jalal Amin, *al-Khaṭar al-Technūlūjī ʿAlā al- Mustaqbal al-Iqtiṣādī al-Maṣrī; al-Muʾtamar al-ʿIlmī al-Sanawī al-Sābiʿ li al-Iqtiṣādiyyīn al-Miṣriyyīn* (Cairo: 1982), p.6.

68 J.E. Clayson, "Local Innovation: A Neglected Source of Economic Self-Sufficiency," in *Impact of Science on Society*, Vol.28, No. 4, 1978, p.353.

69 J.E. Clayson, "Local Innovation: A Neglected Source of Economic Self-Sufficiency," p.354.

70 In his description of the scientific revolution in Europe (1440–1560) Bernal (J. Bernal, *Science in History*) expresses the same view, saying, "Apart from previous experiences in this field, where there was a scientific reconstruction on the ruins of the past such as that witnessed during the decline and fall of the Roman Empire, or the transfer of scientific achievements from one culture into another such as what happened at the beginning of the Middle Ages, the modern scientific revolution in Europe did not witness any act of discontinuity or foreign interference. Rather, a wholly new system of thought was being constructed in the bosom of the new society, from elements derived directly from the old traditions. However, those elements were not used as such, but were transformed by virtue of the new ideas and achievements of those who contributed to that revolution."

71 During the Renaissance and until the Industrial Revolution (1760), Western science was directed mainly to the unraveling of the mysteries of the world (which was expanding in a hitherto unprecedented way with the making of new discoveries in the old as well as the new world). Description and observation were the two main tools used by science. That is why, during the Renaissance, science came to be associated with art in general, and the realistic movement in art in particular. During this period, the role of science in the Industrial Revolution was marginal. However, production activities motivated progress in the field of scientific knowledge and research after the Industrial Revolution (1760 until 1870), when science took a leading role. Many industries owed their existence to scientific discoveries, such as the chemical and electrical

industries. Ever since 1870, science has widened the scope of its applications as evidenced by the technological applications in the fields of electronics, nuclear energy and space; indeed, it would be impossible now to find a field of human activity which has not benefited from modern science. This gradual change which science has undergone from theory to practice has not been haphazard or undisciplined; rather, it has been consonant with the logic of the development of Western society itself in response to its needs. It would be quite impossible to understand the changes which Western science has undergone without reference to the political, economic and social circumstances which occasioned these changes.

72 In a field study I conducted along the northern coast of Egypt West of Mersa Matrouh, I was accompanied by a young local. Despite the fact that he was a mere seventeen years of age, he displayed astoundingly vast knowledge about the environment of the area, for he could identify the names of all desert plants, some of which could not be identified by my companion-colleague (assistant professor of agricultural sciences). The young man also knew their different medicinal uses, the different animals living in the area and ways of capturing them. But what really astounded me was his profound knowledge of the geology of the area. He displayed wide knowledge of the characteristics of the various geological formations in the area (igneous rocks, limestone, sand rocks, etc), the relative depths at which water is to be found, and local methods for digging wells and construction of dams.

That young man embodied the importance of affiliation, the sense of belonging to the local community, and its relation to knowledge and technological capabilities – a sense quite unknown to any university graduate specializing in corresponding subjects. He also embodied the importance of linking education to the environment.

CHAPTER ELEVEN

1 There exist two different popular theories on gravity: general relativity which presents the gravitational field as a second rank tensor, and a competing theory which adds a new function in the form of a particle which has not yet been discovered. Both theories agree on the conservation law for gravity and all observed phenomena, but disagree in realms exterior to experiment and observation. This example illustrates how conservation laws fall short of defining a unique theory for natural phenomena.

2 Parity conservation requires that the fundamental laws of nature not distinguish between left and right. This is an expression of the belief that under the same conditions, the mirror image of a physical event and the physical event itself can occur with equal likelihood. For example, watching a movie on television through a mirror reflection does not arouse in us any curiosity. If it were not for televised texts (written words distinguish left from right), we would not be able to tell whether we were watching the screen or a mirror image of the screen. In 1957, it was discovered that weak nuclear force (the force responsible for the decay of subatomic particles) violates parity conservation. This means that by carefully observing certain nuclear phenomena, it is possible to determine whether we are watching "reality" or its mirror image. All nuclear phenomena, which violated the law of parity conservation, abided by the law of parity-charge conjugation conservation until 1964 when a violating physical process was discovered. This law states that the mirror image of a physical process is

also a physical process provided that every particle is replaced by its antiparticle. An antiparticle and a particle have identical mass but carry opposite charge. This new conservation law was proposed in 1957 to justify the parity violating processes by means of a simple redefinition: The "mirror of physics" replaces right with left and particle with antiparticle like a negative image in a photographic machine. The demise of the modified parity conservation law was soon to follow, which had far-reaching implications for theory and experiment and which remains one of the active topics in current research.

3 Baryons are a group of subatomic particles that share a common feature. The well-known proton and neutron belong to this group. The baryon number conservation law states that the number of baryons before a given nuclear reaction is equal to that after the reaction. In particular, this means that the number of baryons in the universe is constant over time. Since protons are the least massive members of the baryon group, and since decay involves a reduction in mass, this law requires that protons be stable against radioactive decay. Moreover, the so-called grand unification theories – which are attempts at unifying the known fundamental forces of nature and returning them to a single origin – predicts the downfall of the conservation law for protons and suggests the evolution of observed matter in the universe from a non-material origin. In particular, these theories predict a finite proton lifetime (which is obviously a very long lifetime), and experiments for detecting proton decay are currently being carried out.

4 For a simultaneous measurement of a particle's momentum and position, the uncertainty principle states that the product of the uncertainty in momentum with the uncertainty in position must be greater than or equal to a very small finite value that is greater than zero. This implies that our simultaneous knowledge of momentum and position cannot be precise: an accurate determination of a particle's location must be at the expense of our knowledge of its momentum and vice-versa. This principle also applies to energy and time variables. The physical interpretation in this case, however, was a subject of dispute because of the implications it has for the law of conservation of energy. One of the interpretations was that if the duration of a given process is well defined, then our knowledge of the energy associated with this process cannot be precise. The limitations on our knowledge of the energy of a process allows for the appearance or disappearance of an amount of energy for a given time interval as long as this time interval does not violate the energy-time uncertainty principle. It appears to me that much of the confusion about this point occurred because of the reference to simultaneity in the momentum-position uncertainty principle. That is, it relates to the accuracy in measuring the location and momentum at the same instant. The truth of the matter is that it pertains to specifying the state of a physical system by using the values of certain observables such as position and momentum. The underlying principles of quantum mechanics require that one use either the position variable or the momentum variable for specifying the state of the system, but not both. A pair of such variables (like position and momentum) are said to be non-commuting or incompatible observables of the system. From this perspective, the situation with the energy and time pair is no different from the position and momentum pair, and the law of conservation of energy has nothing to do with the interpretation of the uncertainty principle.